How to
rescue
a tiger

and other
animals

ABOUT THE AUTHOR

Roger Allen has been a photographer for fifty years, winning the British Photographer of the Year Award twice, as well as News Photographer of Year and Arts and Entertainment Photographer of the Year.

He began his career in a darkroom at a national news agency in Guildford, Surrey before taking up photography full time. He went on to join *Today* newspaper, the first colour paper in the UK.

After being invited to join the *Daily Mirror*, he spent twenty-five years travelling the world, covering major events including wars and armed conflicts during the 1980s and 1990s and the Romanian uprising of 1989. He was also sent on three tours of duty to Afghanistan.

After the *Mirror* he became involved in animal welfare, helping to save animals from distressing and cruel situations by bringing their plight to public attention in the print media.

He is married with three daughters and two granddaughters.

How to rescue a tiger

and other animals

by

Roger Allen

EnvelopeBooks 27

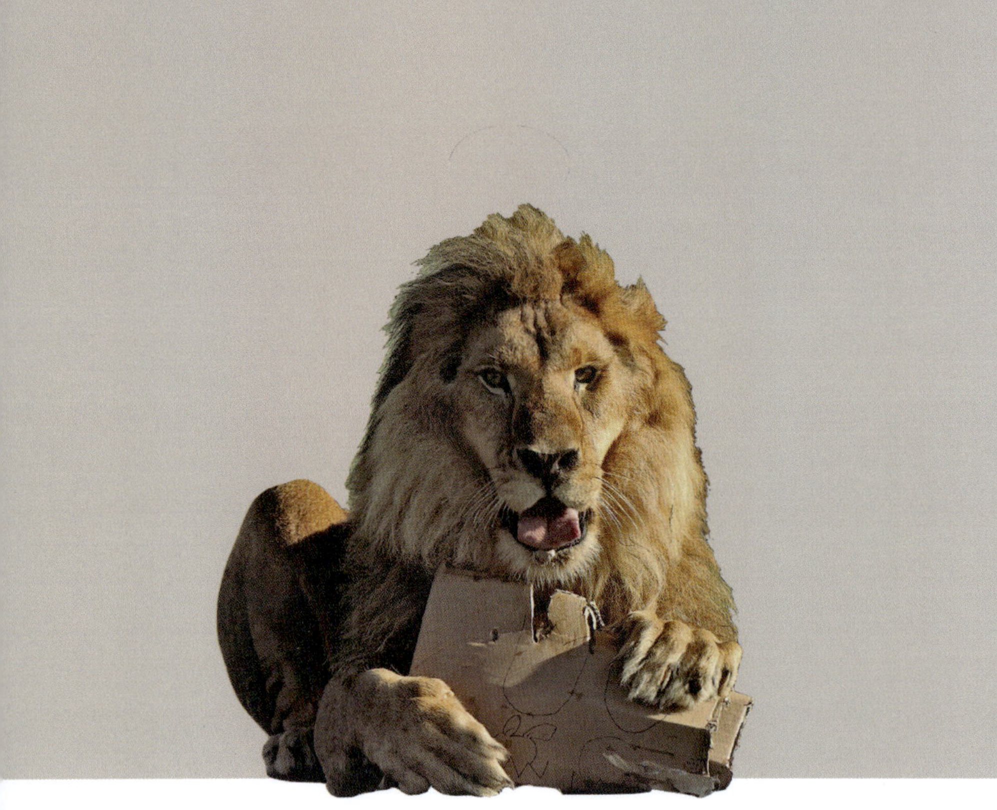

Published in the UK and USA in 2025 by EnvelopeBooks

12 Wellfield Avenue, London N10 2EA, England
116 West 73rd Street, New York, NY 10023

www.envelopebooks.co.uk

Cover design by Stephen Games | Booklaunch
Main text set in Plantin 9/10.25

A CIP catalogue record for this title is available from
the British Library and the Library of Congress Cata-
loging-in Publication Data

EnvelopeBooks 27
ISBN 9781915023575

Picture credits

Contents

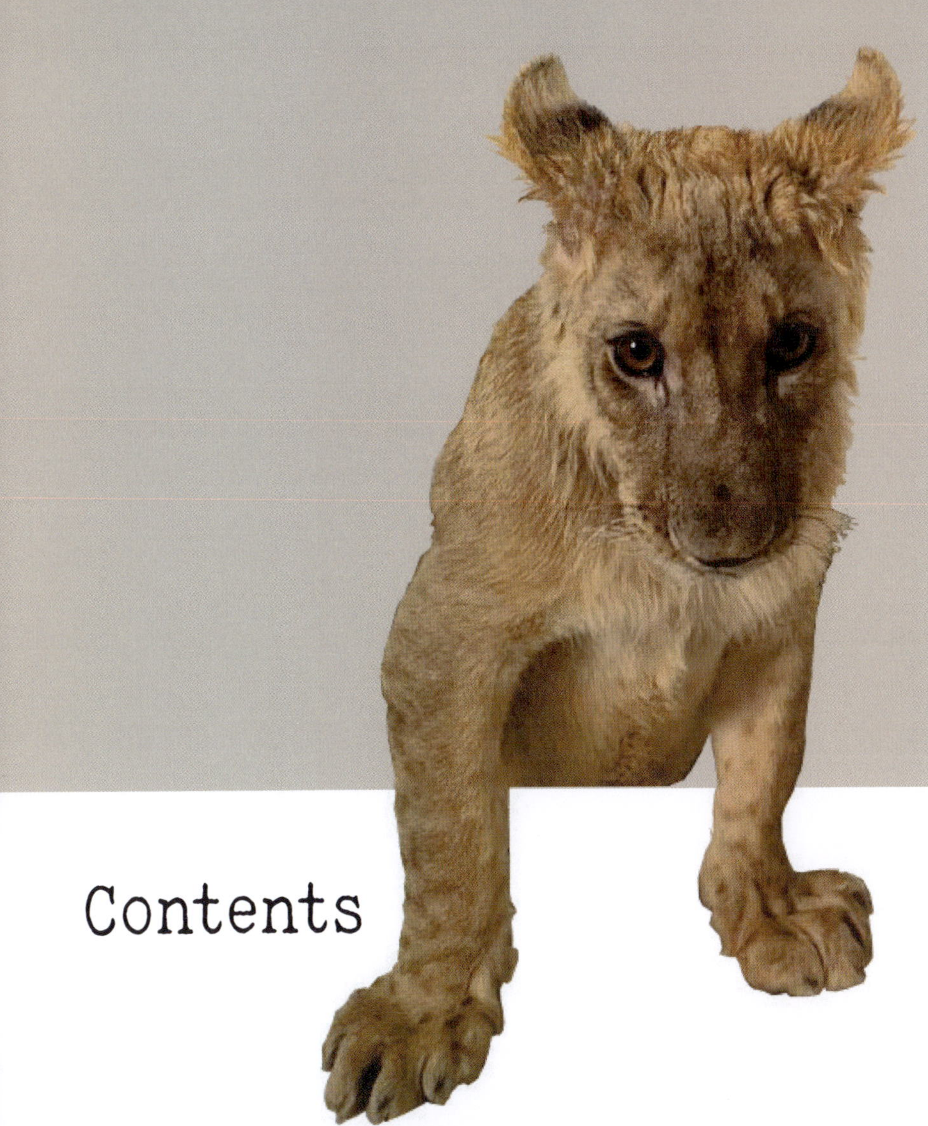

To my wife Ro
and daughters Rachel, Natalie and Alice

Preface

One of the problems with trying to help exotic animals, whether by rescuing them or by reporting on them and highlighting the challenges they face, is that they tend to live in tricky places that are awkward to get to, or are owned by tricky people who are awkward to deal with.

As a photographer, I don't mind travelling to awkward places or sticking my nose into the affairs of awkward animal owners. That's why, over the last ten years, I have become involved with exposing nasty governments, rapacious companies and loathsome individuals who have all made animals' lives a Hell on Earth.

So this is partly the story of how, through pictures and words, I have worked with reporters to highlight the plight of tigers, lions, bears, dogs, slow lorises, elephants, rhinos and many other creatures.

I have been present at many rescues, some of which I describe in this book. Sometimes the experience has been dangerous, sometimes scary, but always it has been satisfying to know that, working together, we have made things better for some of the most innocent and magnificent animals we share this planet with.

But there is another problem with photographing abused animals. However barbaric the treatment meted out on them, animals are also regarded as cute and can be exploited by the media because they make us say *ooh* and *aah*. I know very well that however important it has been to cover the stories illustrated on the pages that follow, there have been times when those stories were given space because animal stories are feel-good journalism: manipulative click-bait, if you like.

I know this, because I had very little emotional investment in the first animal stories I covered. They were largely entertainment pieces: newsworthy but not to such an extent that I felt there was any need to dig deeper or follow through on their consequences.

That all changed when I was sent to cover the story of Mely, an orangutan that had been kept in chains for several years on a balcony beside a river in a remote part of Borneo, as I explain.

But I have included five of my earlier stories to highlight just how different my later work became and how passionate I now am about the cause of animal rescue.

Roger Allen

Introduction

The first time I saw a lion close up, it was sitting on the back seat of a double-decker bus. It was 1976, I was nineteen years old and I was working at the Southern News Service, a press agency in Guildford, in the South of London.

I was a photographers' gofer—the lad in the darkroom who was told to go for coffee, go for equipment, develop film, make prints, and dash on the train to the old Fleet Street newspapers, where I would run like a whippet up the grand staircases of the *Daily Express, Mail, Times, Telegraph* and *Mirror,* and hand over pictures to the picture desks in time for them to be printed in the next morning's edition.

One autumn morning all the photographers were out on jobs and I was the only staff member left in the office. One of the agency's partners, Peter Cassidy, called over to me to grab my camera and get into his car, quickly. I had no idea why. It was the first time I had never been sent on an assignment as a photographer before.

Whatever story we were going off to cover had started to unfold about thirty minutes earlier. One of the agency's reporters had been doing his usual round of phone calls to the emergency services, to find out if there was anything horrible or dangerous or funny to report.

He got all the usual comments back in reply: 'If we did have any news, you'd be the last to know' and 'You're the reporter; you should be telling us.' It was always a lot of effort for very little return . . . until he rang the Surrey Fire Brigade, which gave him the unlikely story that there was a lion loose in Woking town centre.

Thinking they were toying with him, Peter nonetheless sped down the narrow staircase to try the news out on the agency boss. The editor was also suspicious but told him to check the story out with the police. To his surprise, the police confirmed that a large animal had been sighted in Woking and that people were said to be hiding in shop doorways but wouldn't confirm it was a lion.

That was when Peter told me to get in the car.

As we drove into Woking we saw two policemen, apparently armed with guns, running down a road leading to the main shopping area. Peter swung the car up a one-way street the wrong way to try and head them off, but we found nothing. It looked as if the animal had disappeared, which I thought was rather sensible of it under the circumstances.

A quick drive round the town yielded no sight of our quarry so Peter leaped into a phone box—this was long before the days of mobile phones—and called the agency for an update. They told him to go to the offices of an insurance company on the Chertsey Road.

When we got there, we found a small group of people, all clearly captivated by something.

A man in a grey suit turned to us with a regretful expression and told us, 'The man took him back on the bus. The big blue bus.' He said no more and a woman came over and patted him on the shoulder, reassuringly.

'It's OK, Tony,' she said, 'the ambulance is on its way.'

I quickly put two and two together. The poor chap had obviously had a breakdown, imagined he'd seen a lion and had rung the police. That was until a policeman emerged from the building and said that a woman had just woken up from unconsciousness and had asked for a cup of tea.

It was undramatic but we all wanted to know more. A hush fell over us as we all craned forward to hear what had happened.

The policeman said that the woman in question, a Mrs Poppy Hull, had been walking to work with a friend, along the Chertsey Road, wearing a new fake leopard-skin coat. As she approached the insurance company building, a lion had jumped on her.

The officer paused and looked up; he seemed embarrassed by the story's implausibility, but everybody willed him to go on.

He said that the lion had been travelling on a double-decker bus. The bus had stopped at traffic lights, the lion had spotted Mrs Hull in her leopard-skin, had walked to the footplate at the rear of the bus, leapt through the air, landed on her back and pinned her to the ground.'

The policeman stopped again, coughed and looked awkward. It seems that the lion hadn't realised that Mrs Hull was human. He saw the coat she was wearing and thought she was a leopard. A very attractive leopard. A very attractive female leopard … and …

He paused while trying to find a suitable form of words.

'… he wanted to be … her friend.'

What happened next, he explained, was that the bus driver had jumped out of his driver's cockpit, run to Mrs Parker's rescue and pulled the lion off the poor woman's back. Then, even more improbably, he had dragged it across the pavement and hauled it back onto the bus, before driving away.

The officer had no idea where the bus or the lion were now but said that Mrs Hull, having fainted with shock, or perhaps hit her head when brought to the ground, had at last come round.

The group stood grinning as they tried to take it all in.

Peter, wanting to interview the woman, tried to get into the office building but was barred by a security guard, so instead we sprinted back to the car and went looking for the bus. It didn't take long to find.

Heading towards Chertsey and crossing a bridge, I pointed out a big blue bus parked in a children's playground. It said 'Leo's Safari Bus' on its destination sign. Peter spun the car round in the middle of the road and pulled up alongside it. It looked as if it had been abandoned.

We got out and peered through the windows. There, inside the front of the bus, was a rather large lion.

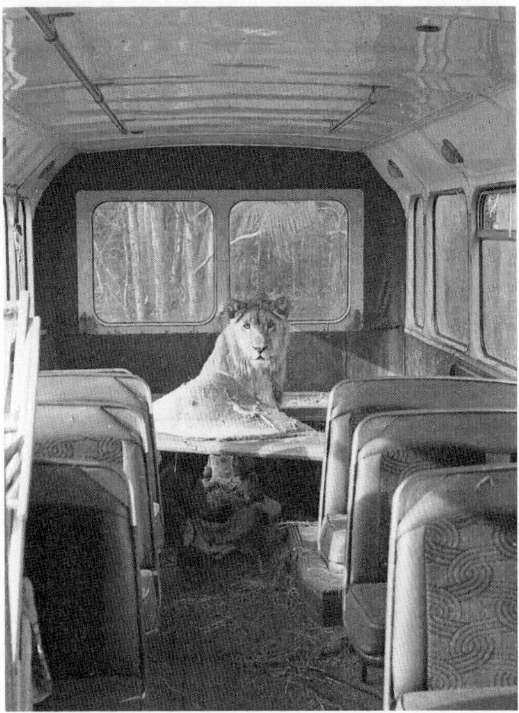

Peter took his Bolex cine camera and I got my Nikon. The huge animal took no notice of us. He was more interested in removing bits of fake leopard skin that were trapped between his claws. Keeping at what I hoped was a safe distance, I took some pictures through the bus window. The click of the shutter must have caught the lion's attention because the beautiful beast turned and looked straight into my lens.

Peter meanwhile was busy filming, trying to get shots from different angles around the bus. Again, the lion looked up at him with indifference and went back to the job of cleaning its claws.

Encouraged by its quiet nature, Peter told me to get onto the bus. 'Just stand in the doorway, let your flash off and see what he does,' he insisted. 'If he makes a move, jump off and we'll try and slam the doors closed from the outside.'

I looked at the lion still sitting there, facing me. He hadn't moved from the long seat he was on, but was now sitting in an upright position. He looked bigger, but still took no notice of us.

I stepped up onto the footplate, held the flashgun above my head, levelled the camera to my eye and pressed the shutter. The flash let off an explosion of light. I glanced up to see the beast's reaction.

Nothing. He hadn't moved. The flashgun had made him blink but otherwise he was totally unconcerned.

Peter joined me at the rear of the bus and started to film from there. At this point the lion loped down from the seat and started to stretch his long front legs. I was sure he was going to spring and attack, but no: he just turned round, hopped back up on the seat and continued to observe us.

It soon became apparent that the lion was tame. He had never seen the great hunting grounds of the Serengeti, had never run at full speed, and had never leapt onto the back of a fleeing antelope to provide dinner for his pride of cubs. The closest he had come to being King of the Jungle was to terrify the whole of Woking town centre . . .

. . . and Poppy Hull who, by the end of the day, had been photographed holding what was left of her fake leopard-skin coat. The next morning images of her adorned the front pages of every paper in the country and many more around the world.

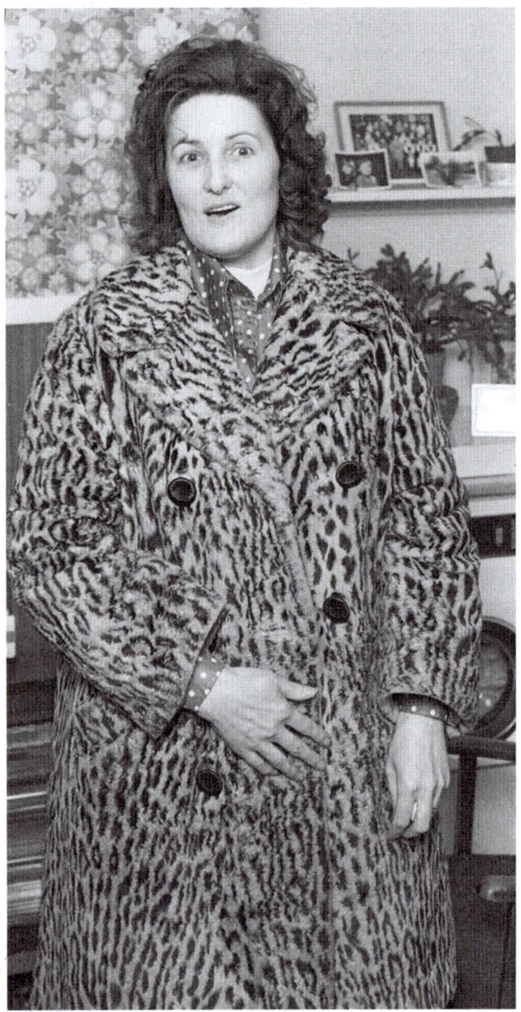

'All I saw were two huge paws around my neck and I fell to the ground,' she told the press. 'I was very frightened. It's not the sort of thing you expect to happen on the way to work.'

Shane—for that was the lion's name—also became famous because all the front pages carried a picture of him looking regal and aloof. The police and the RSPCA had managed to coax him from the bus without the use of a tranquilliser dart. He walked out with great dignity.

As for the bus's owner, he was charged with endangering the public by transporting a wild and dangerous animal without taking due care—presumably something he had been doing for years.

The end of the story was sad for the bus driver. The oddly named Ron Voice had bought Shane as a three-week-old cub from a Birmingham pet shop. The two were inseparable and spent their nights together curled up in bed, the lion sucking his master's finger. During the day, Shane would sit in a van parked in Chertsey Road. In the evenings, Ron would show him off in his local pub, the Albion.

By the time Shane was a year old, on Christmas Day, 1975, he already weighed fourteen stone—196 lbs—and some local people started to be concerned that he might become a danger, but parents would also lift their curious children to peer through the windows of the van where Shane spent much of his day.

To give Shane more space as he got larger, Ron eventually bought the blue double-decker bus, with the intention of converting it into a home for the two of them and starting a new life in the West Country.

After the incident with Mrs Hull, Woking councillors claimed the lion had given the town a bad name, and its member of parliament, Cranley Onslow, had tried to introduce new legislation outlawing the keeping of unlicensed wild animals as pets.

In response, the court decided that Shane must be parted from his owner, and ordered him to be sent to the rolling hills of a wildlife park near St Albans. It was there that he lived out the rest of his days without being called on to entertain the public any more.

THE SURREY PUMA

One of the stories that came round frequently at the photo agency was that of the Surrey Puma, a mythical beast said to stalk the hills and back gardens of London's commuter belt.

When two builders on a roof in Dorking raised the alarm one day, I was dispatched to meet the builders and try to photograph the animal. They told me it had been seen walking up a hill towards some woods.

That is how I came to be standing in a Dorking meadow the following morning, feeling very fed up. Even if the animal had put in appearance for my benefit, I wouldn't have been able to photograph it; we were hemmed in by thick fog. At 10:00 am the sun started to break through, slanting across the green slope, but by that time I had been there for two hours and was getting hungry.

I had just decided to go off to the café round the corner for a bacon sandwich when, out of the corner of my eye, I caught the shape of something large moving along the tree line above the meadow.

I briskly attached my longest lens onto the front of my camera, focused it as well as I could and saw in the viewfinder a very big black animal with a long tail slinking slowly across my field of vision from left to right. Like any big cat, it hugged the ground. I managed to fire off four frames before it disappeared into the undergrowth. After another half hour's wait, it hadn't re-emerged so I went back to the office to develop the film—and there it was in black and white: the Surrey Puma. The elusive beast had at last been caught on camera for all to see.

And all saw it, because the next day the *Evening Standard* used the grainy picture across its front page.

The Surrey constabulary took the story very seriously and sent an armed police officer to investigate. I was invited to join him, with my editor. Once again it was foggy and, once again, with no puma in sight, we eventually lost patience. I suggested we all walk to the far end of the meadow and take a look in the woods. At first, the officer agreed, and then the two of them decided that we could cover more ground if they went one way and I went another. And off we all went.

After a couple of minutes I came across a wooden house with a large veranda. On the steps leading up to the front door sat a group of very large domesticated cats, together with the owner of the house.

I got chatting with him and he told me that the so-called Surrey Puma was in fact Harold, an Abyssinian Tom, the largest of his group. As the cat wound himself around my legs he purred loudly, no longer a fearsome beast but a much-loved pet. I took a picture of him with his 'dad'.

We later decided that to reveal the real identity of the Surrey Puma would be a mistake. For one thing, it would bring the owner unwanted attention, for another it was more fun to let the burghers of Surrey think that their normally sleepy county was wilder than it really was. But mainly it would be helpful to bring him back to life whenever the news agenda was flat.

Thus it was that the legend of the Surrey Puma lived to fight another day. Sadly, my photos of him did not. Like all my early pictures, they were captured on film, stored in the basement of my house, and later ruined when the basement flooded. All I have are my memories.

THE INSECT ON A TWIG

Back in the 1990s, when my children were still small, birthday parties were very special, and everything had to be sacrificed for them. That's why, when my daughter turned five, I took the day off work and a dozen or so of her very excited friends descended on our house in Aldershot.

The kitchen was warm with the delicious smells of baking and there were plenty of finger foods, fizzy drinks and napkins.

In the middle of the party, my boss from the news agency phoned with an assignment, which I told him I could not take on because I could not leave the house. He was very insistent, though, and offered to deliver the news to me exactly where I was.

An hour later, a trainee photographer arrived, holding a big plastic sweet jar with a large insect in it. He hadn't been able to take a picture of the bug because he didn't have the right lens, so he'd brought it to me.

My wife wasn't pleased about my being distracted, but I assured her it would only take a few minutes. I led the trainee through the throng of children to the kitchen as he clutched the precious jar to his chest.

The insect had come to the agency by a roundabout route. A vicar had been driving to his parish church when he lowered his sun visor and discovered the creature hiding behind it. The insect's sheer size had caused the good reverend to screech with fright and slam on the brakes. Composing himself, he then scooped the bug into the cup of his thermos flask, popped a bag over the top and continued on his way.

Curiosity about what he had found meant that the vicar conducted the church service a little more rapidly than he normally would have done. Then, when the last of his congregation had left and the church was empty, he took a closer look at his captive and tried to identify it from an insect book but couldn't find anything that matched.

His next step was to take the little creature to the local inspector at the RSPCA in Woking who, when he saw it, became very animated and offered to take it to the Natural History Museum. After a lot of speculation, it was decided that the unfamiliar creature was a *Monochamus scutellatus* or the spruce sawyer, from Alberta, Canada, a species not normally seen in the UK.

The RSPCA inspector, knowing our agency, rang to say what he had discovered and asked if we would like to take a picture of it. And that was how this native American longhorn beetle came to be picked up from his house and brought over to mine.

I peered into the jar. There, sitting on a twig, was an inch-long arthropod, with two antennae that were double his body length. It seemed to be aware that I was looking at it and put on a bit of a show by waving its feelers at me.

It wasn't looking particularly lively so I told Geoff, the trainee, to open the lid of the jar and hook out the twig with the insect on it. I would take a quick picture of it and then he could pop it back in the jar.

As he put his hand into the jar and drew out the twig with the bug on it, a bunch of children came running into the kitchen, curious to know what was going on.

With the camera poised, Geoff angled the twig

against a white background. The spruce sawyer looked very spruce indeed. This could have been the perfect shot. Unfortunately, the bug had other ideas. Waving its antennae left to right, it jumped off the twig and began strolling up Geoff's arm.

The army of five-year-olds ducked back, shielding their faces and necks and squealing as Geoff began to yell at it to get back on its twig.

My wife, wary that the beetle might not survive the commotion or that the party might not survive the beetle, quickly shooed the children out into the garden.

Unperturbed, the bug ploughed on up to Geoff's shoulder.

While all this was going on, I was taking pictures of the insect, up to the point when, with a renewed confidence about its place in the world, it extended its wings and took flight, disappearing behind the washing machine.

My wife was exasperated. Her parents had just arrived and it was time to light the candles on the birthday cake. I grabbed the front of the washing machine and yanked it out from under the kitchen counter. In the gloom, hidden among the electric wires and water pipes and clumps of accumulated fluff and stray socks sat the beetle. Seemingly relaxed, his feelers darted this way and that as he checked out his new world.

Geoff was apologetic about shouting at the bug, but I told him to concentrate on getting the insect back in the jar. The children were singing 'Happy Birthday to You' in the dining room and I had to get a picture of the candles being blown out. When I got back, I found that the bug had moved onto the drain hose.

Aiming a torch at the insect, Geoff tried to tempt him onto the twig. The little fellow stood stock-still, showing no interest. Geoff moved the twig to within a hair's breadth of its face. It moved his feelers a bit, then turned and scuttled down the hose into a dark recess at floor level.

It looked like we'd lost it. Geoff shone the torch into the black void. All we could see were the ends of two antennae poking out.

Geoff wondered if we could get another one; he was sure no one would know the difference.

'They don't sell them in pet shops,' I barked. 'That's the whole point of this!'

Geoff slowly drew the drain hose towards him. Luckily, the bug sat tight. I stuck the twig in front of it and, with the professional certainty of a performing flea, it obediently stepped onto it and seemed to relax.

Excruciatingly slowly, Geoff laid the hose on top of the washing machine, I passed him the twig, I lifted my camera, the beetle wiggled its feelers happily, and the light from the kitchen window shone on its wings. At last! The picture couldn't have been better.

'Get him back in the jar,' I begged, sighing with relief as the lid went on.

Now that Geoff and the *Monochamus scutellatus*

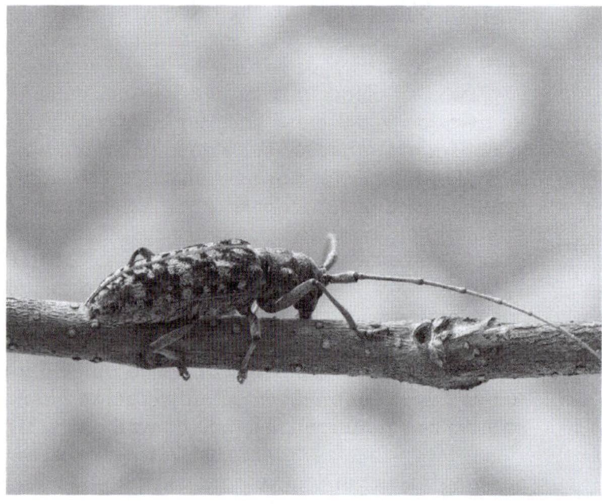

were on their way back to Woking, I could finally join the party. I played games with the children in the garden and at last got a slice of delicious cake.

After an hour of mayhem, all had come right—until I heard my wife in distress in the kitchen.

I trudged in from the garden to find the kitchen floor awash with soapy water. The hose from the washing machine hadn't been returned to its drainpipe. It took ten minutes to mop it up.

It seemed worth it, though. The next day the *Times* and the *Telegraph* featured my picture of the rare spruce sawyer, sitting rather cockily on his twig.

TAFFY, THE REGIMENTAL GOAT

Following the Falklands War in 1982, the Parachute Regiment sailed back from the South Atlantic, marched into Aldershot—where I then lived—and proceeded to drink the town dry. Aldershot had always been a place to avoid if you were looking for a quiet pint, but now it was pretty well off-limits.

The Paras had three pubs in town that they made their own: the Pegasus, the Queen Vic and, most notorious of all, the Globetrotter, which was underground and not a place for the faint-hearted. The only way in and out of its long subterranean bar was via a spiral stairwell.

Aldershot had been the Paras' garrison town since the regiment's formation in 1940. Then, in 1977, the Army decided to post the Royal Regiment of Wales to Aldershot as well, following its service in West Berlin. It wasn't long before the sparks began to fly. It all came to a head one Saturday night when the Welsh arrived at the Globetrotter and the Paras defended their ground.

After the Royal Military Police had separated the two sides and the wounded had been taken away, an air of resentment and menace hung over the town. The Paras were out for revenge, feeling their beloved Globetrotter had been violated.

Two weeks after this incident, a friend who wrote for *Soldier* magazine rang up, asking if we could meet for a drink. He said he had a funny story to tell me, so we met in a pub on the outskirts of Aldershot and settled down to hear it.

Paul asked if I'd read about the punch-up in the town between the Welsh and the Paras. Of course I had. He told me that the Paras had subsequently exacted their revenge.

One dark night, two of their quietest chaps jumped the fence surrounding the Royal Regiment of Wales's barracks on Browning Lines, the military camp housing the various different barracks, training facilities and admin buildings). Their target was a small wooden shelter in a paddock that was part of the Welsh compound. Housed in that shelter was the much-revered regimental mascot, Taffy the Goat.

Taffy accompanied the regiment on all official outings and regimental parades, where he would have his head patted by dignitaries and royals alike. He would march at the head of the band with his chest puffed out and dressed in his full ceremonial outfit.

'Operation Taffy' was highly dangerous. If the two lads had been caught, the boys from the valleys would have kicked them into oblivion. Yet these brave soldiers were armed with only two things: a small plastic bag and a pair of scissors.

As they approached the side of the wooden hut, they checked to see if the coast was clear. All was quiet. One of the lads pulled out his small plastic bag and produced a very tempting parsnip. In a second, the hut door flew open and out stepped their prey, Taffy. He was a fine specimen, a big boy with an evil glint in his eye.

'Hello, son. Have a parsnip,' whispered Para number one.

As Taffy took a bite, Para number two grabbed the beast round the neck and pulled the scissors up to his throat—not to kill him but to snip off his famous, perfectly groomed eighteen-inch beard.

Taffy's beard was the animal's focal point, his pride and his glory. It was thick and strong at the top and swept down to a point, like a Turkish dagger.

Having secured the beard in the empty parsnip bag, the two paratroopers slipped off into the night and back to the Globetrotter. The trophy was displayed, sending the occupants of the pub into ecstasies of triumph.

Paul handed me a ten-by-eight-inch envelope. I reached inside and pulled out a pin-sharp picture of Taffy in full ceremonial dress, his beard blowing in the wind. The picture had been taken when the Welsh had arrived in Aldershot some weeks earlier.

'All we need now is a picture of Taffy minus his marvellous caprine beard,' I said.

'Funny you should say that, because I know where he's staying while it grows back.'

The next day, I parked my Volkswagen Beetle opposite the Royal Military Police barracks in Aldershot, where Taffy was being kept in a stable block.

Every morning the mounted Royal Military Police trotted out on their horses for a saunter around the town. I watched them clip-clop down the road, and when they had turned the corner onto Queen's Road, I hung my Nikon over my shoulder, put my coat on to hide it and crossed the road to the barracks. There was a small guardroom at the entrance to the old Victorian stables that had housed hundreds of horses and troopers at the turn of the twentieth century, but I had a hunch it would be empty, even though Aldershot was the town that had suffered the first IRA bomb attack on mainland Britain in 1972.

My heart was pumping hard and the adrenaline was rushing. I felt like one of the Paras who had clipped Taffy's beard. I walked as quickly as I could past the guardroom and no one stopped me. It was unmanned. After the horses had left for their walk, the barracks were all but empty. My gamble had paid off.

I kept my head down and walked straight ahead. When I looked up, there was a line of about twenty stable doors. Most of the tops were open, but there were no horses poking their heads out.

Suddenly, the door two along from where I was standing flew open and a steaming pile of dung came flying out. The stables were being mucked out. If I didn't find Taffy soon I'd be caught.

I looked around to see if there were any other stables when I heard a kicking noise against the door next to me. I walked the two paces and peered into the stable. Staring back was Taffy, larger than life. He had jumped up to see who was outside.

I undid my coat and tried to get my camera into position before he jumped again. Just as I managed to look through the viewfinder, the goat forgot what he'd been interested in. I had just seconds to focus the lens, get the exposure right and retain his attention before the person in the next stable emerged. It meant I only had time to take two frames before Taffy went back to munching carrots on the stable floor.

I pushed the camera back under my coat just as a burly stable hand kicked open the door to the stable he had been mucking out. I'd manage to get three paces away before he shouted out to me. I didn't look back but ran as fast as I could, sidestepping a young officer who was wondering what all the noise was about, and kept going all the way into town, leaving my car until I thought it was safe to return. I waited an hour before going to pick it up, and then drove to the office to process the film.

One of the two frames was a blur but the other was sharp.

We sold the story as an exclusive to the *Daily Mirror*. They used the picture of Taffy across the whole of page three.

A couple of years later I had to go to the Globetrotter to check out a story. To my delight, there behind the bar was a framed copy of the *Daily Mirror* with a beardless Taffy staring balefully back at me.

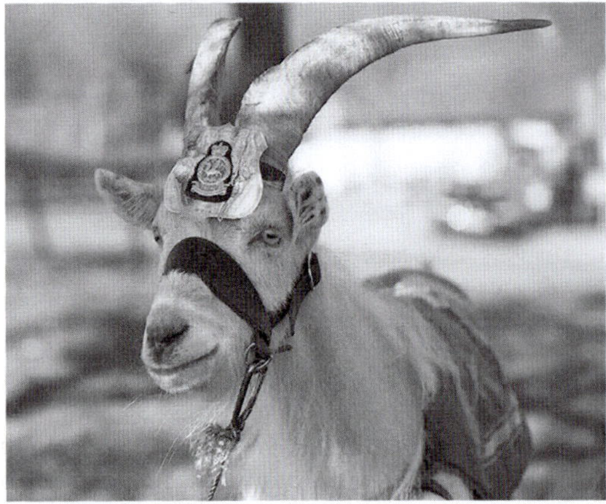

A SHELL-SHOCKED BEAR IN BOSNIA

My early ventures into the world of animals must have lodged in my brain because, in later years, whenever there was a story about an animal, I put my hand up for it.

I got them when, after twelve years at the agency and an eighteen-month stint at *Today*, Britain's first colour newspaper, I was offered a job at the *Daily Mirror*.

The *Mirror* had money to burn in those days: journalists had vast expense accounts, travel was always Club Class, and our accommodation was in top hotels. For all this luxury, though, you needed to be willing to put in long hours and go to dangerous places. In 1993 the most dangerous spot in Europe was Yugoslavia. The country was tearing itself apart in a series of civil wars.

In the new country of Bosnia Herzegovina there was the added element of systematic ethnic cleansing, carried out by the forces of all three of the main ethnic groups: Bosnian Serbs, Croats and also Bosniaks (Bosnian Muslims), though generally on a smaller scale.

The UN decided to intervene and the first UN-flagged force to be sent was the British Army's Cheshire Regiment. I was asked to go and cover the events.

After weeks of reporting on killings, refugees and military campaigns, the *Mirror*'s reporter Ted Oliver and I were desperate for something else to cover, when Mark Laity, the BBC's defence correspondent, bustled into the kitchen of PINFO (Public Information Office), the army house being used for the press bureau.

He told us that a big brown bear had been abandoned and left to die in its cage outside a hotel, and that it would not last if it stays there.

We knew we couldn't investigate without protection, so Ted came up with the idea of persuading the Army to help the animal, which would also provide good publicity for our forces.

An hour later we put the suggestion to the Regimental Sergeant Major, who shook his head. 'We can't go around rescuing bears. We're not even allowed to rescue people. It's not part of our mandate.'

'We're not asking you to rescue him,' Ted said. 'Just get the army to feed him, and take us down with you so we can take a picture of you doing it. The RSM made no promises but asked us to leave it with him.

He found us that evening in the sergeants' mess, and said he'd arranged for us to go out on patrol with some of the troops the next morning. They would swing by the hotel where the bear was but we would have to be quick because it was close to the frontline and dangerous.

We set off just after 8 o'clock the next day in the back of one of three tanks staffed by three male soldiers and one female, Trooper Sarah Collins. She would be the one to feed the poor beast his breakfast, and she had been supplied with burgers, sausages and a big pot of honey.

It took ten minutes to reach the deserted hotel. Its sign was full of bullet holes and two of the front windows had been destroyed by a mortar shell. The car park, which was full of vehicles that had been wrecked by heavy arms fire, looked like a breaker's yard.

At the far end was a cage made of thick steel wire secured to four metal posts, one at each corner. Inside the cage was a collection of boulders forming a shelter just big enough for the bear to crawl into. It would have been a very sad place, even in peacetime.

The soldiers moved the three tanks into a V formation and checked over the whole area before Ted and I were allowed to leave the vehicle and approach the cage. The bear was cowering inside, too frightened to move. The poor thing had been shot and hit by mortar fire, so I didn't blame him for being suspicious of two strange Londoners urging him to smile for the camera.

Trooper Collins soon had his attention. She unwrapped some of the burgers and waved one at him through the bars. As the smell of meat wafted across the cage, his nose twitched and his ears pricked up. Soon he was padding towards us.

As he reached our side of the cage, he stood up on his hind legs. The top of his head touched the roof of the cage. We all took a step back when we saw the size of him. He was all of six feet, six inches tall.

Sarah stepped up and offered him a burger.

With one swish of his paw, the bear grabbed the burger, stuffed it in his mouth and looked back for more. He ate so many, we named him Mac.

The patrol's young captain saw that the bear's water bucket was empty and told a soldier to get a bottle of water from the tank. The bear held the bottle and drank straight from it like a man who'd just emerged from a desert. Then he devoured the contents of the honey pot.

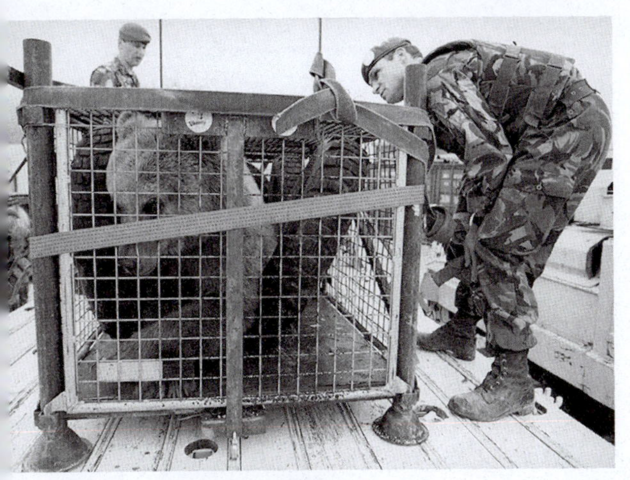

Mac made a half page in the next morning's *Mirror* under the headline 'Bearlift: our boys rescue war victim, Mac.' (Other reports called him Mackenzie.) Later that day, we got a call from Libearty, a charity that rescued bears from conflict situations. They asked if the paper wanted to help Mac further.

Within a week, the sorry-looking animal was sitting on a flatbed army lorry in a wire cage built by the Royal Engineers. We followed him on a fourteen-hour drive from Vitez to Split, where he spent a couple of months in a zoo before being taken to a specialist sanctuary in Hungary.

Animals are frequently ignored as casualties of war. In this case, at least, one innocent victim of the hostilities had a lucky escape.

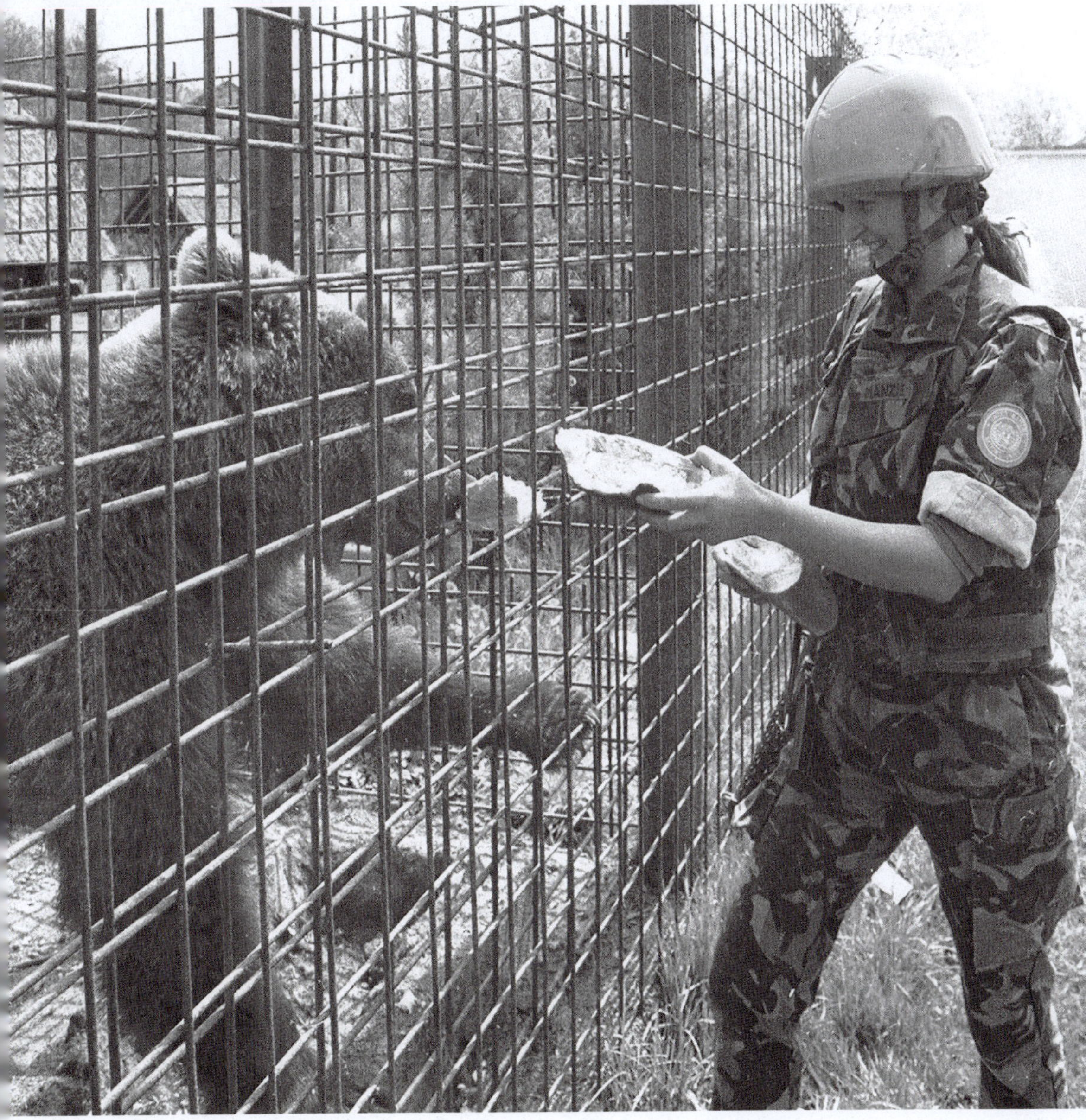

Mely in chains

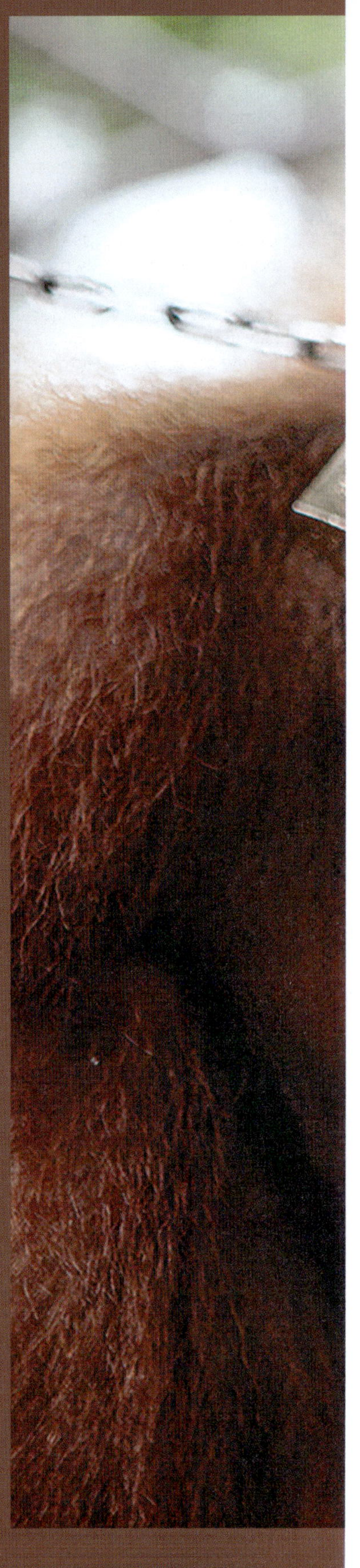

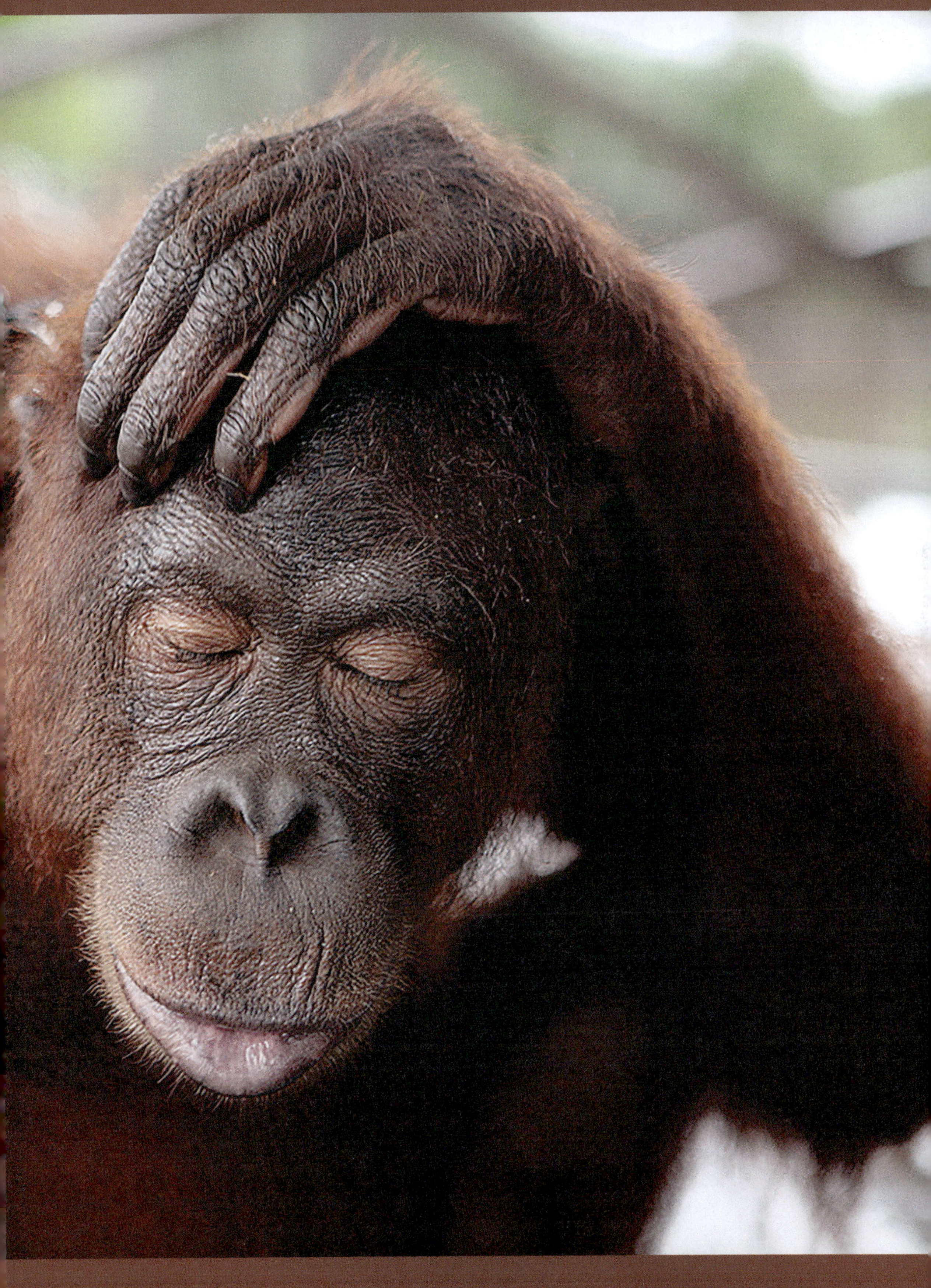

Mely in chains

In the twenty years after Bosnia, I covered everything from local bingo winners to the 9/11 terrorist attacks in 2001 but quickly learned that for a national newspaper, animal stories were an essential part of the territory.

The tabloids were especially good at getting behind campaigns to save unhappy or imprisoned animals, especially if they'd been alerted to them by loyal readers. Knowing that a happy outcome boosted a newspaper's sales and profile, reporters and photographers were often sent on expensive, long-distance missions to gather words and pictures for special reports that were sure to tug at the heartstrings of the British public.

One such trip came my way in 2009, when my picture editor announced—as casually as if he was sending me to Birmingham—that he was packing me off to Borneo.

I wasn't exactly sure where Borneo was but a quick search on Google informed me it was a giant, rugged island in the Malay Archipelago in Southeast Asia, 1,100 kilometres east of Singapore and shared by Malaysia, Indonesia, and Brunei.

The story, which had something to do with baby orangutans that had been orphaned, sounded simple enough: at the British-run International Animal Rescue (IAR) centre in West Kalimantan, local women had become surrogate mums to the young apes. The combination of photogenic volunteers and baby primates would secure a nice spread in the paper—as indeed it did. But that, I thought, was as far as it went. A touching story, some local colour, and another page filled. It didn't occur to me that there was anything else to say.

Later, as I worked on the story, the scales fell away from my eyes and, really for the first time, I became emotionally involved, to such an extent that my life changed ever after. Animal stories, up until then, had largely been distractions from human news: a mix of sensationalism and sentimentality that often exploited the very values we were criticising. My only question, at the time, was how to get to Borneo and whether they'd have mosquito nets for me there or whether I'd need to take my own. What I ended up working on made me question much that I'd previously taken for granted.

Reporter Mike Swain and I flew from London to Abu Dubai to Jakarta, where we had just five hours in a hotel before a dawn flight to the town of Pontianak, home to one and a half million people. From there, we travelled by small twin-propeller plane to Ketapang, in West Kalimantan on the south-west coast of Borneo. The whole journey lasted thirty-three hours. The only hotel of note in Ketapang was a modern four-storey block on the main street, running parallel to the Pawan River, a wide brown torrent that I could look out on from my shabby balcony.

By the time I had dropped my bag in the room, I was already drenched in sweat. The weather was oppressive, a constant twenty-eight degrees with a waterfall of rain every other hour. All I wanted on my arrival at the modern four-storey accommodation block was a cold beer, but even that took time and patience, as Ketapang was a largely Muslim community where alcohol was almost impossible to come by.

The reason for the IAR being in this part of Borneo was palm oil. This cheapest and most productive of vegetable oils has a lot to answer for. Palm oil, a versatile source of food and energy, is harvested from vast tracts of land often brutally denuded from the rainforests by giant machines. It is used in everyday items such as ice cream, pizzas, biscuits, margarine, chocolate and bread. It's also used in

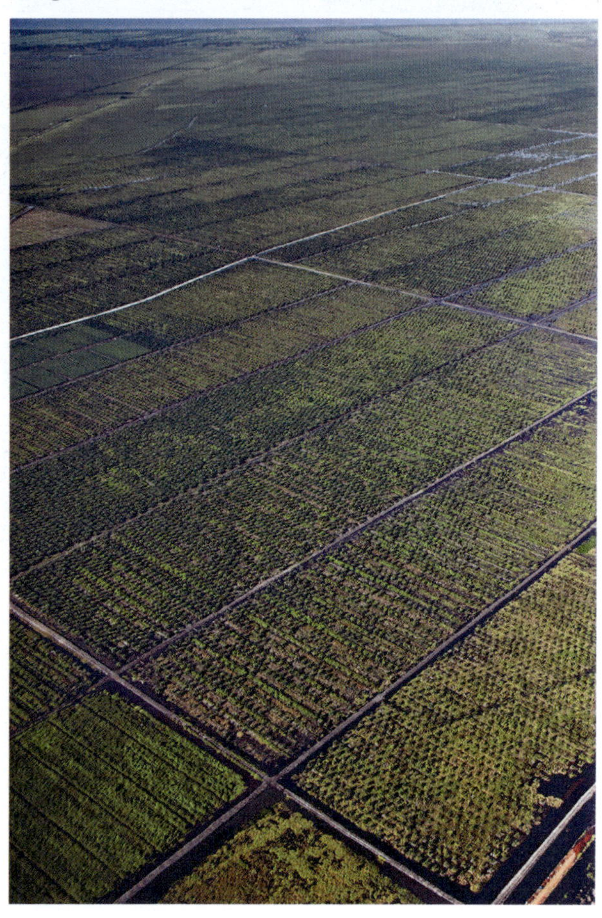

products where animal fats are unacceptable on religious grounds, and as a biofuel for transport, power and heat, and in consumer products such as cosmetics, soaps, and cleaning agents.

Malaysia and Indonesia alone account for over eighty per cent of the world's total palm oil acreage, producing more than 41 million tonnes of the stuff annually. Within Indonesia alone, production ballooned from 600,000 hectares in the mid-1980s to 6 million hectares twenty years later. (The illustration below shows an intensive oil palm plantation at Ketapang.)

The problem with the product is that the wholescale deforestation that often accompanies its production is endangering hundreds of species to the point of extinction. Elephants and orangutans are especially vulnerable because of the huge areas of land they need to roam around in.

In the past few decades, the orangutan population in the area has halved to less than 40,000 as the logging increases. Fleets of bulldozers the size of small houses cut swathes through the forest by dragging webs of thick metal chains behind them. These massive links snag and drag out every bit of vegetation from the finely balanced ecosystem that many creatures rely on. Terrified animals flee as best they can, with mothers often carrying their young.

The animals often find shelter in the trees around a village. If they are lucky, the village head-man encourages his people not to taunt or kill the poor beasts. Less fortunate animals run into labourers working in the forests. Then, they are often put through unimaginable horrors.

If a mother finds a tree left standing in the devastated forest, she often instinctively runs up the spindly trunk, clutching her offspring, expecting that it will provide safety. It's usually the worst thing she can do.

While she is up the tree with her young, laughing crowds of workers will pour petrol around its base and set it alight. As the flames climb higher the mother has two options: stay and be burned alive, or jump.

If she jumps, the baby will probably be fatally injured. If she tries to escape from the fire, she will most likely be caught and subjected to cruel and humiliating treatment. Often, she will be beaten to death by the workers or hogtied to a pole and paraded around, before enduring a slow, painful death in captivity. I heard of a mother and her baby being bound with ropes and hurled into a village pond to drown. By the time the IAR officials had arrived to try and save her, the mother was in her death throes, the baby still clinging to her chest.

Thankfully, scores of babies are rescued by those who still possess a shred of humanity and these are collected by the IAR to be taken to a sanctuary and nursed back to health. It is a heart-warming sight to behold. The orphan apes swing in hammocks, sit in buckets of straw or are fed by those who work at the centre. Coaxed onto climbing ropes, tyres and swings suspended from trees, they hang upside down like little acrobats, often dropping to the floor when they lose their grip.

It all seems like a lovely game but there's a more important lesson to be learned at this jungle survival school. Just as their mothers would have done, their human helpers scoop up the fallen infants and lift them back into the tree so that they can learn how branches can provide safety.

The straw is used to help them build nests and interact with the other orphans, which is vital if they are to develop the complex socialisation networks that apes are accustomed to. The centre's veterinary director, Karmele Ilano Sanchez, explained to me that orphans are often traumatised from having watched their mothers die or from having been kept in small cages as pets, leaving them depressed and with no idea how to interact with their own species.

Sindy, a two-year-old orphan, had been kept in a cage just 40 x 50 cm and was now unable to move or climb. Bunga, the same age, had been fed on a diet of sugary human food and didn't know how to forage. Sigit was afraid of heights. Monti, the smallest and cutest baby, still needed to be bottle-fed. At nighttime, the orphans were given giant teddy bears to sleep with for comfort. Human interaction was kept to the minimum, as far as possible, so that the babies could develop a natural fear of man, ready for the day when they were finally released back into the wild. But it wasn't always easy . . .

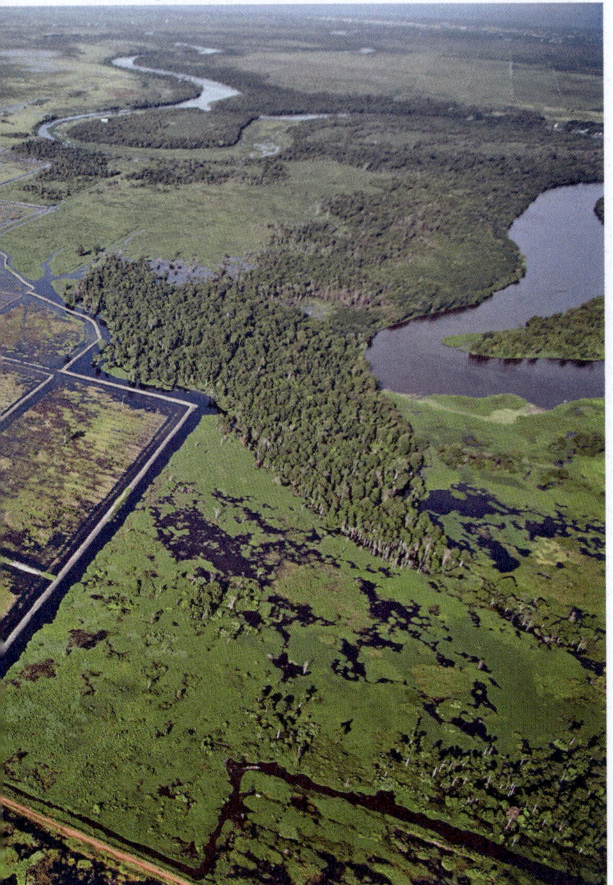

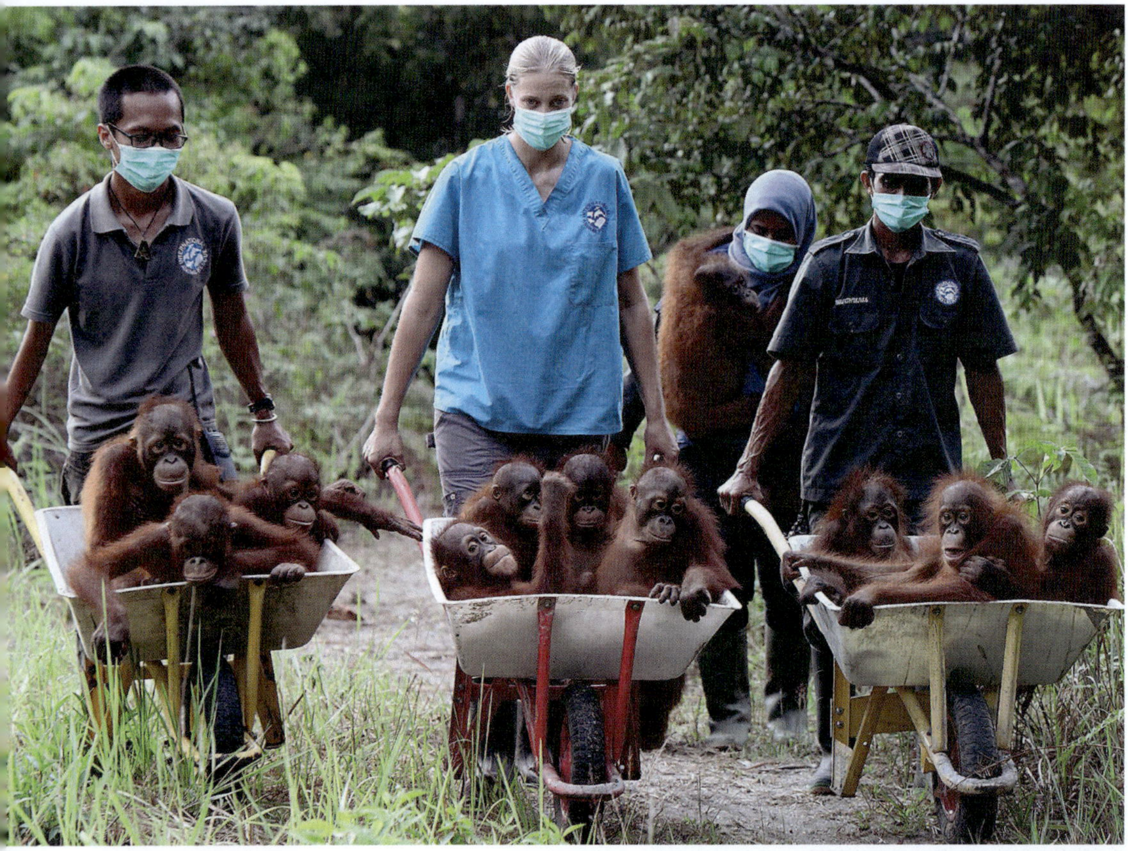

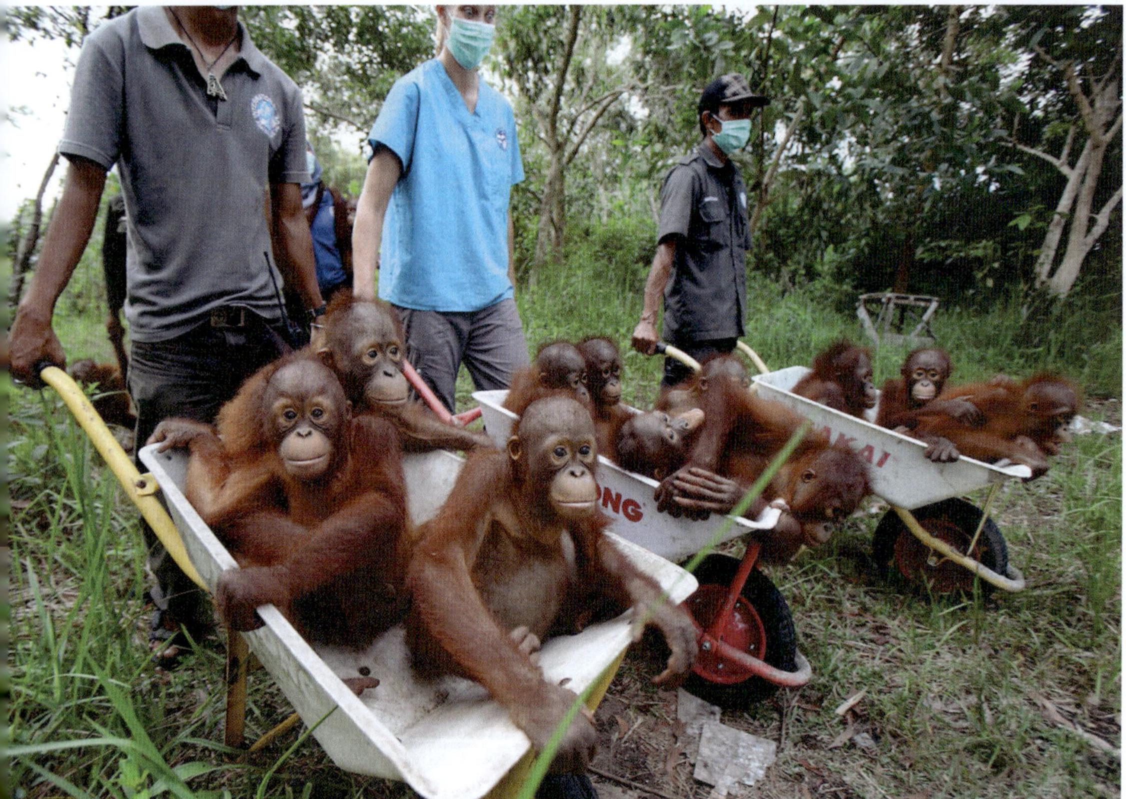

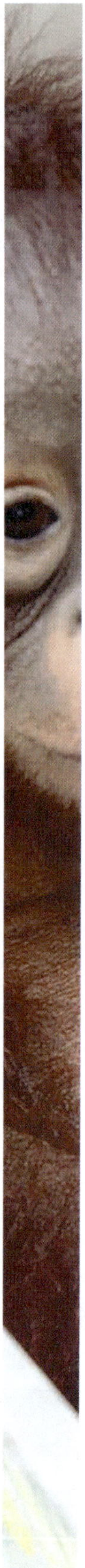

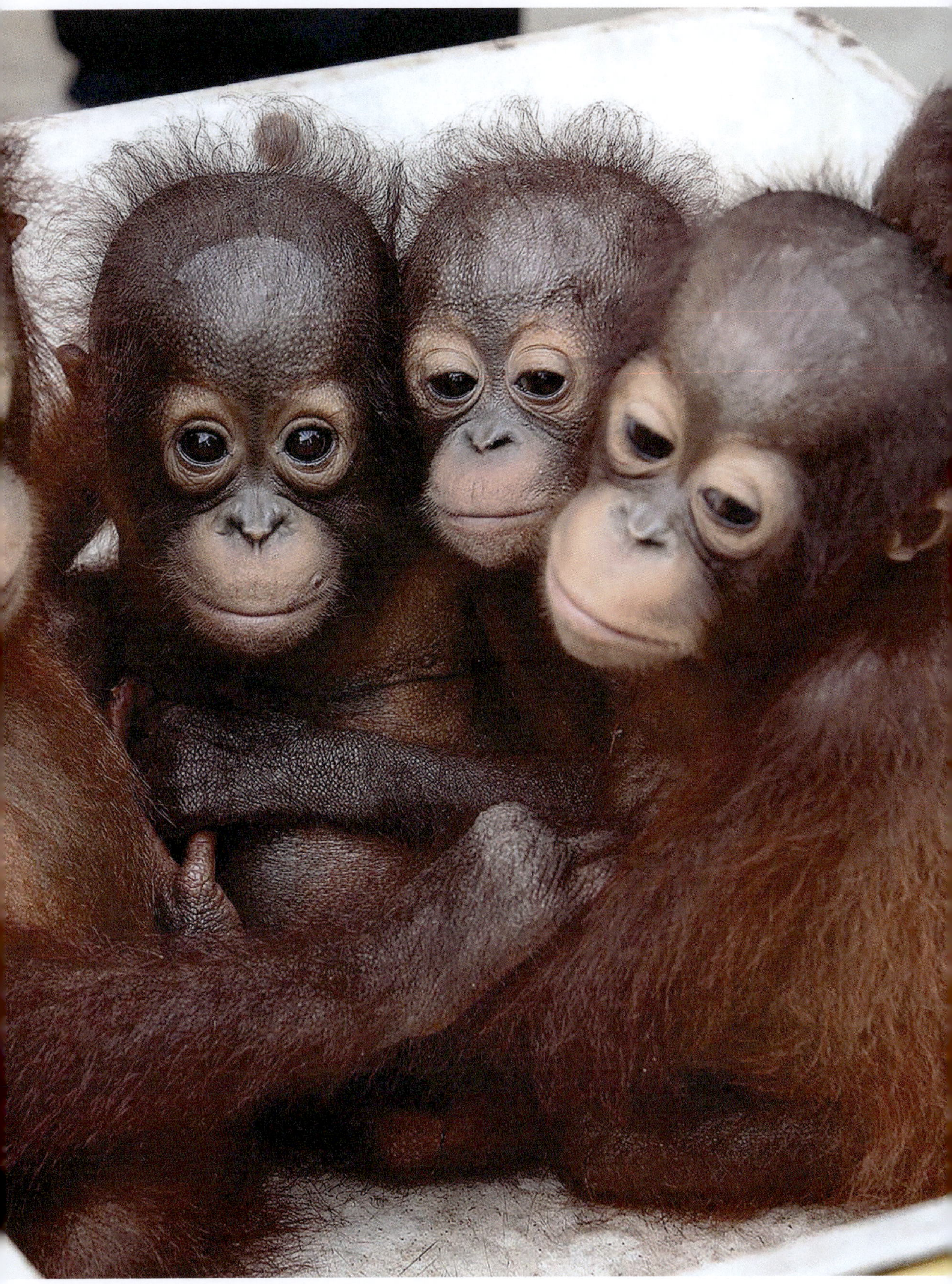

spent a long and very rewarding day, furtively photographing orangutans at the Ketapang ape sanctuary. That night I went for a drink with the vets of IAR, a dedicated band of people without whom the orangutans wouldn't stand a chance. The conversation drifted to the worst cases they'd seen, the most difficult rescues and the best outcomes.

As the evening was drawing to a close, one of the vets, Dr Adi, told us we should go and find Mely, a fourteen-year-old female orangutan that he believed had been chained by the neck for almost all its life to the wooden veranda of a house next to a river. According to his story, a fisherman wanted her as a pet for his children, so he shot her mother and took her home with him when she was very small. Now fully grown, she was still kept there.

Dr Adi was unsure exactly where the house was but said we could ask at the nearest big town, a river port called Sambas.

Two days later he accompanied us on the flight back to Pontianak, and we set out on the five-hour drive in a sedan. For much of our journey we hugged the river and, as we approached the docks, saw huge ships tugging at their anchor ropes as the waters ebbed and flowed. Men in high-vis jackets busily unloaded timber, bales of cotton and drums of God knows what, with forklift trucks loading goods onto waiting lorries.

Our attention was diverted by our driver's excitement as we neared a roundabout. As we got closer, I spotted a space-age shiny obelisk with an eighty-foot tower complete with viewing platforms and what looked like the insides of a broken watch; two large cogs intertwined in the style of an armillary.

Dr Adi explained that it marked the spot where the equator cuts through the city, the cogs representing the northern and southern hemispheres. It wasn't the most attractive landmark I'd ever seen but it certainly made a point.

The road north to Sambas involved four hours of hard driving up through mountainous countryside. An hour into the drive, we stopped for fuel. As we stepped out of the car, a wall of ferocious heat hit us, as if someone had opened an oven door. The rest of the journey was made up of long stretches of boring dual carriageway. We passed through small towns that all looked the same, with lines of wooden shacks selling takeaway food in plastic bags, lotto tickets, phone cards, condoms and fizzy drinks in lurid colours.

On a steep hill, we passed Singka Zoo, a sprawling collection of neglected buildings. Dr Adi told us he had worked there for a while but had left because a combination of bad hygiene and rotten food meant the animals struggled to survive.

Having been on the road since dawn, we finally arrived in Sambas mid-afternoon. The driver knew the best place to ask about an orangutan and nosed the car through the crowds heading down to the dock. He parked outside a shop selling a bizarre collection of electrical goods, jumbo fans, flash-

lights the size of a small car, fridge freezers, washing machines piled five high on the pavement, fuses, a Santa Claus set of fairy lights, and the smallest plugs in the world.

Running down the side of this electrical emporium was a rutted lane cramped with hawkers selling cooked food and fruit, at the far end of which was the wide brown river, flanked by planked wooden boardwalks. Dozens of wooden boats with slanted roofs were huddled together, and the minute one pulled away in a plume of black smoke, another immediately took its place. At first glance there didn't seem to be any order to the comings and goings but, like many things in the Far East, it was all controlled by a system of shouting and pointing.

Mike and I watched in awe as our driver plunged into the throng of people, working the crowd and chatting to women with wicker baskets on their heads and babies slung on their backs. They in turn shouted to other women on the boats. From this noisy interaction came the answer: the oran-

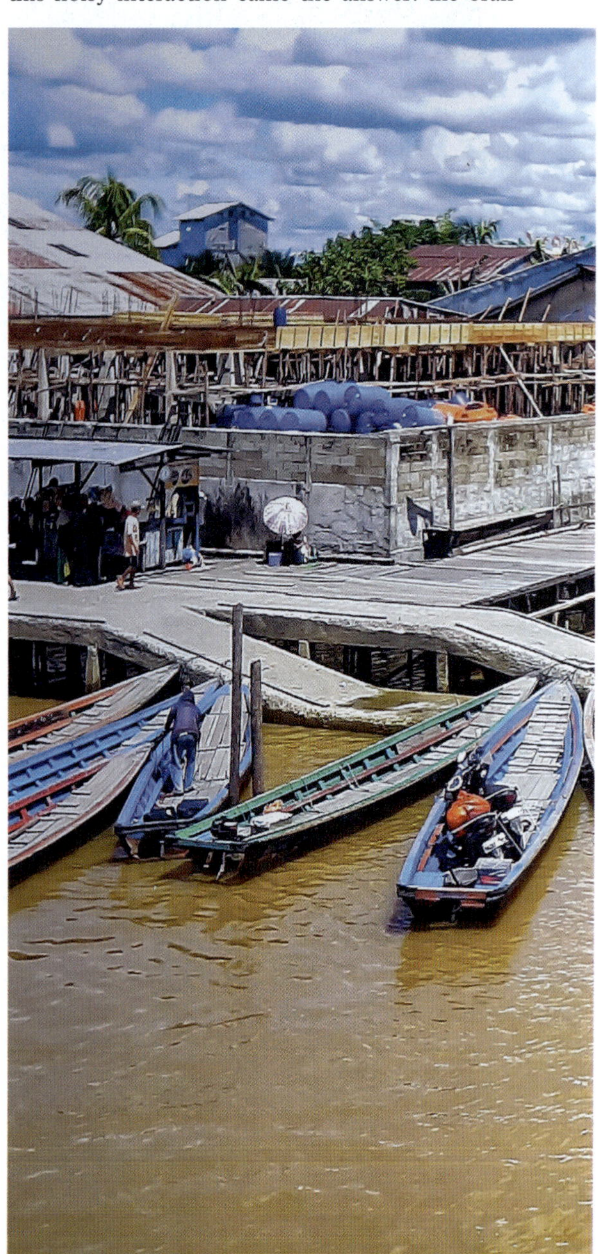

gutan was about an hour up-river. Like a couple of Western missionaries, we handed the equivalent of about fifty pence to each of the women, one of whom bowed low and offered us bottles of ice-cold water in return.

The next challenge was to find a boat going the right way. Dr Adi courageously stepped onto the first boat, its hull crafted out of what looked like bits of packing crates, and spoke to the skipper. The enquiry was passed to the captain of the next boat out and, after a lot of hand waving and gesticulating, Mike and I were summoned on board. Clambering onto the nearest vessel, we picked our way through the crowds of passengers waiting on wooden bench seats, climbed over the side onto the second boat and then onto a third.

In the middle of the river, we reached a vessel that Dr Adi said would take us in the right direction. We sat on plastic chairs at the back of the boat and the skipper cast off, just as another boat glided up alongside, which our vessel nudged slowly out of the way. There was no fuss and no conflict, just the smooth running of commercial life.

The town of Sambas thinned out as we cruised along the slow-flowing river, the last of the houses and small shops giving way to rampant foliage tumbling right down to the muddy banks, punctuated by spindly wooden jetties that looked like they'd blow over in the wind. Tiny wooden boats were tethered to the thin poles holding up the piers, and on one I saw skinny men fishing.

After a few stops the other passengers had disembarked, leaving just the three of us and the captain at the wheel. The banks of the river drew closer, the jungle got denser. Dark clouds loomed up ahead of us as a breeze picked up. Troops of monkeys chattered noisily in the branches of large trees as they swayed in the wind.

Dr Adi went forward to talk to the skipper as he stood at the wheel of his vessel, a cigarette clamped between his lips. He thought the house we were looking for was twenty minutes further upstream.

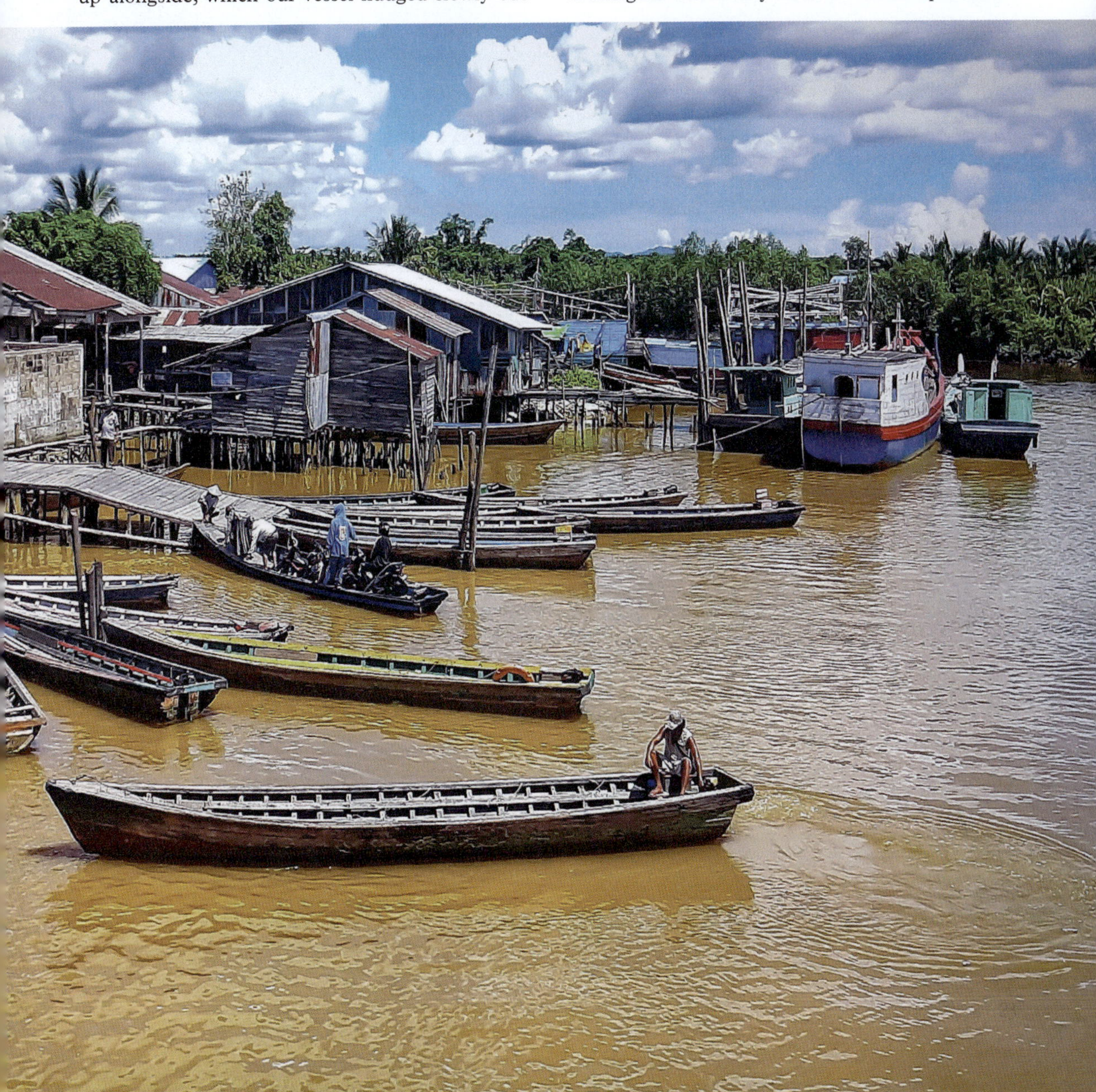

Suddenly the sky darkened over, a crack of thunder took Mike and me by surprise, and the hot humid air disappeared as a cold chill swept along the boat. Rain was suddenly falling so hard and fast, one struggled to understand how Nature could be so fickle.

The downpour made it impossible to see the river's edge yet, out of the gloom, the sound of an outboard motor crept nearer until a small boat arrived alongside us. It was a floating shop. I found it hard to believe that anybody would be on the water in a small homemade boat in rain like this, but there stood a short man smiling at us, offering packets of potato crisps. Perhaps out of sympathy, Dr Adi bought three. The man laughed and steered off into the torrent.

The captain brought the boat alongside a flimsy pontoon leading up the riverbank to a wooden shack and shouted over the noise of the downpour that this was where Mely was. Soaked to the skin, the three of us clambered onto the wooden walkway and ran for the cover of the house. A large veranda encircled the house, approached by three uneven steps. Chickens trapped in wicker domes clucked and ruffled their feathers as two happy ducks padded around them in the wet mud.

Dr Adi knocked on the door as I wondered what we would do if the owners were out and whether we might have travelled all this way for nothing.

Then, at last, the door swung open and we found ourselves face-to-face with a frail, barefoot woman aged about fifty, dressed in a bright orange and black wrap. She stared at us, bemused as to why three uninvited strangers had paid her a visit in the rain.

Mike and I could not get the gist of the conversation between the woman and Dr Adi until we heard him mention the word 'London', which she echoed in surprise. There was another bit of chatter before Dr Adi told us she'd take us to her orangutan when the rain stopped.

She invited us to wait on a chair that hammered together out of bits of wood. As we sat down, I noticed our boat had floated away downstream. Dr Adi made a pained expression before saying that he'd find another one to take us back.

After thirty minutes or so, patches of blue sky drifted into sight as the rain-laden clouds drifted on their way and the sun began to shine again. The blistering heat returned, insects began chirping and birds flew from the trees.

The barefooted woman emerged onto the veranda and without a word walked down the steps towards the river. We followed her. Just before we reached the pontoon where we'd disembarked, she stepped onto a wooden platform jutting out into the river.

As we stepped off the path, I noticed an orange ball huddled on the planks. It was Mely, the chain that held her hanging limply from a wooden post.

Two young boys joined our little group and settled on the rail close to the water to watch. Mely stirred. She moved on her haunches, to make herself look bigger, as we slowly walked towards her. Dr Adi approached first, a look of concern on his face.

He squatted to the same level as Mely. I started taking pictures but was sorry to see that her whole demeanour seemed to communicate that she didn't care who was in front of her or what happened to

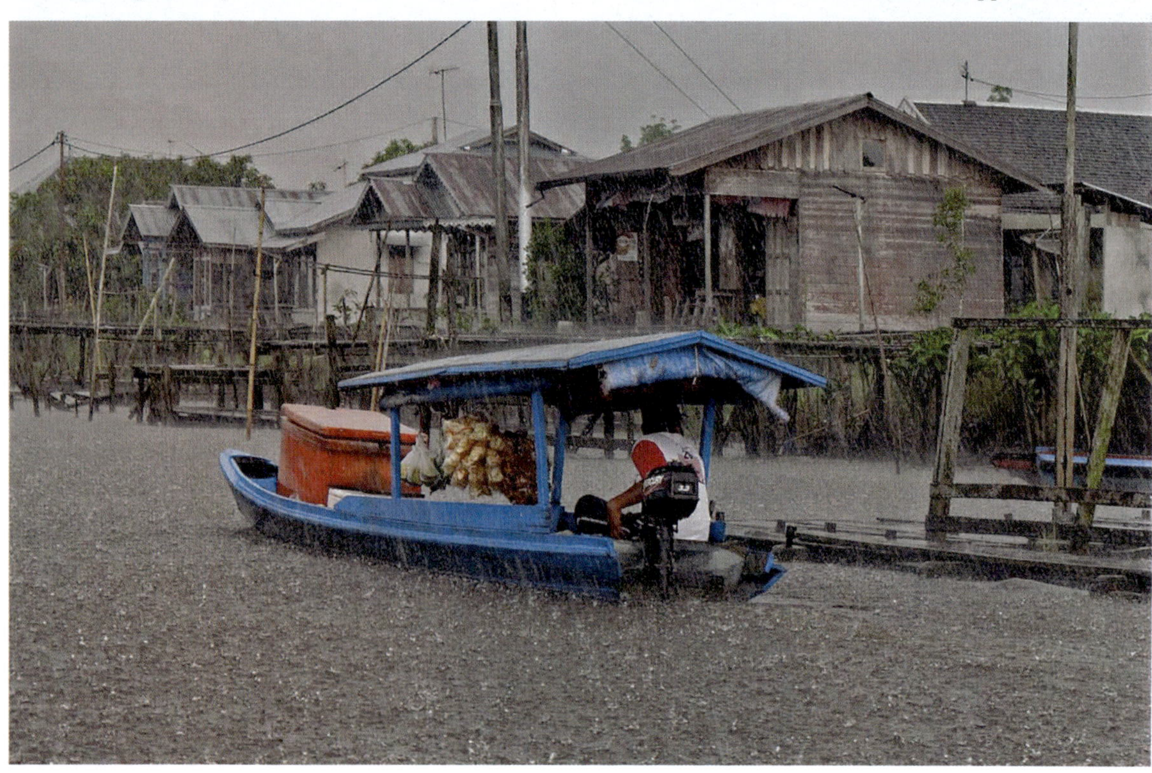

her. When the vet moved away, I crouched down too, just two feet away from her, as she sat in her own filth. What happened next will stay with me forever.

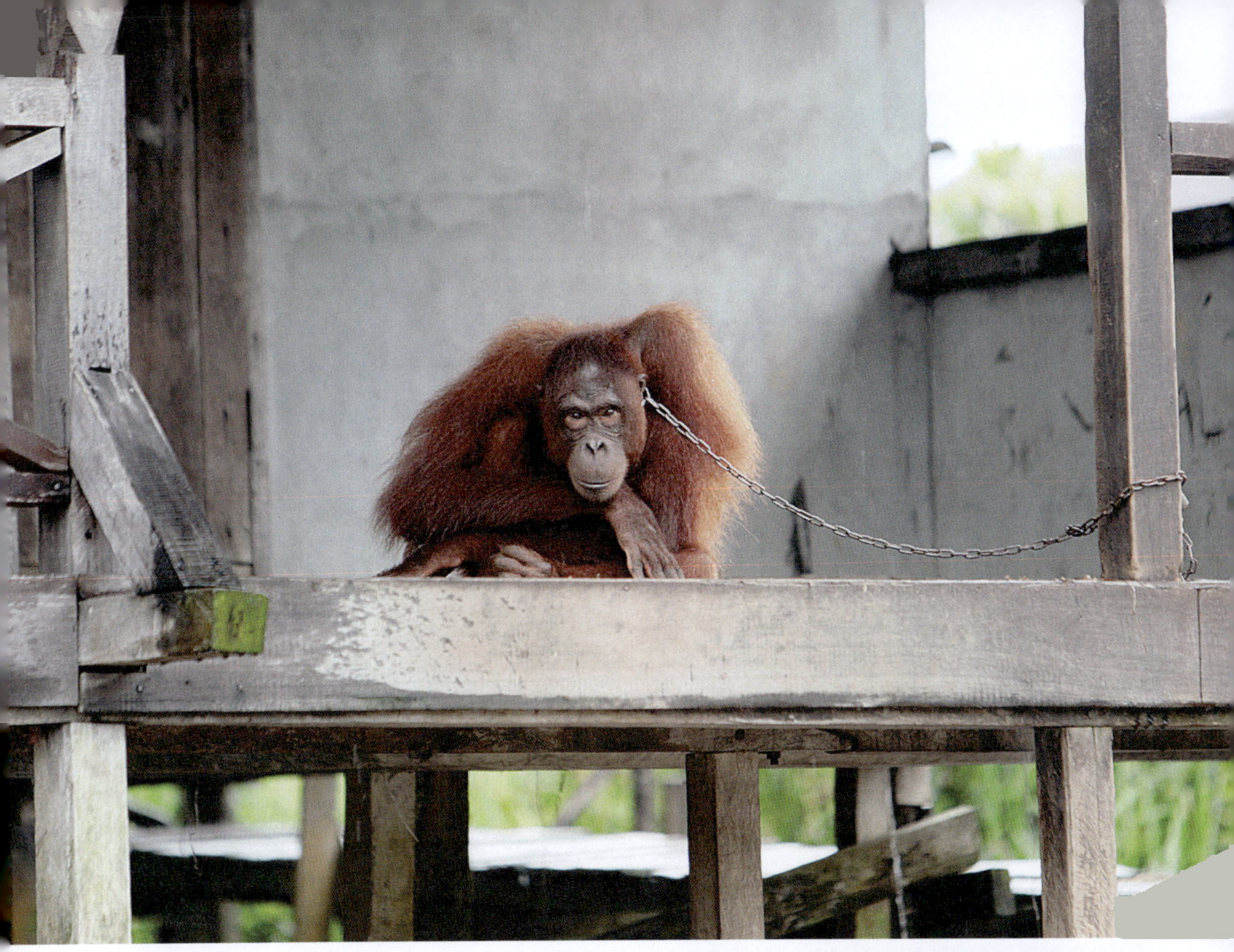

She looked at me as if asking for help, then slowly put her arm out with her palm extended. I did the same, and our hands touched. Her palm was hard and rough. She didn't squeeze my hand but held it gently, all the while looking me straight in the eye.

Speechless, I could only look back in wonder that this poor animal, who had spent her short life chained up and mistreated by humans, still had the capacity to express need and tenderness.

I thought of my youngest daughter, who was the same age as this forlorn creature. I couldn't help but think what an unhappy fourteen years Mely had had by comparison. Having seen her mother killed, she'd been kept as an amusement until she'd got too big and unruly, and then had been chained up. She had never been loved as any youngster should be, had never been taught how to swing through the upper branches of the forest canopy or build a fresh nest to sleep in each night. The muscles in her arms and legs had become so wasted that they were barely able to support her, never mind propel her through a rainforest.

My daughter had spent her life being cared for and taught how the world works; Mely deserved no less.

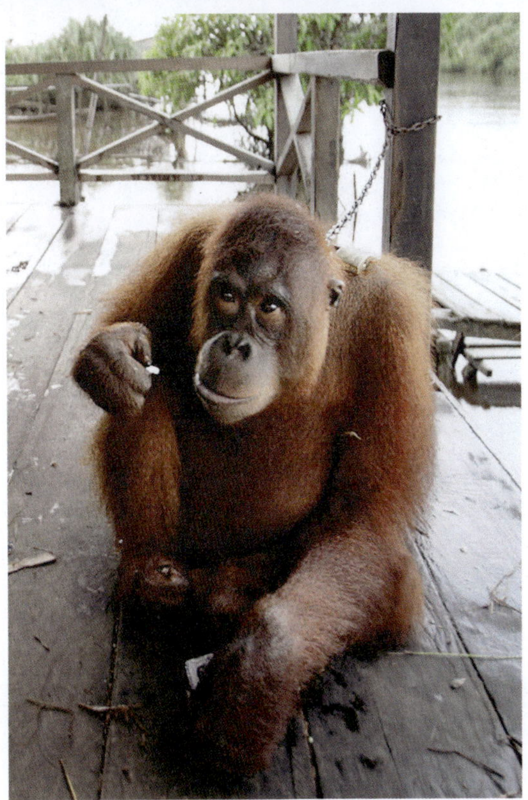

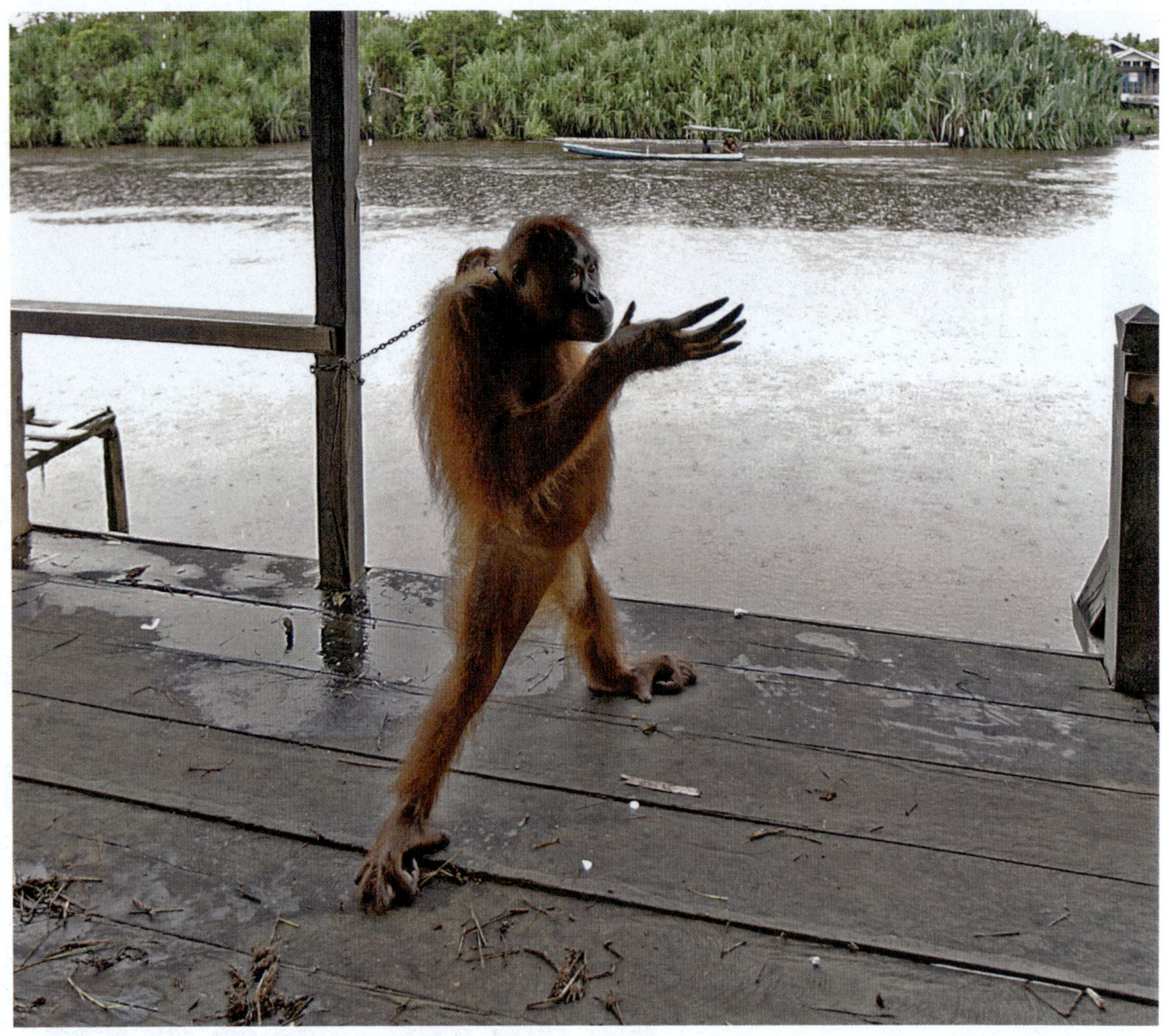

Dr Adi asked the woman what Mely's diet was. The woman shrugged and threw a packet of dried noodles at her and a sachet of chilli powder. Mely fell on the food, ripping open the packet and crunching on its hard contents. Hunched over, she made a pitiful sight.

The IAR vet watched with growing anger. He moved close to Mely again and magically produced from his pocket some soft balls of rice, into which he pushed two large tablets. As I carried on taking pictures, he handed them to Mely and she devoured them hungrily. Just where he'd got them from, I'll never know.

The woman was becoming impatient with all the attention her captive was getting. Her expression was easy to read: 'They must be mad. It's just an animal.'

Dr Adi picked up the uncomfortable atmosphere and said, 'Let's get back to Sambas before dark. I've got a phone number for the boatman. He'll pick us up.'

With no more food on offer, Mely had reverted to her hunched position. As we walked away, I turned and saw her sitting with one hand on the chain and the other on her head. Her eyes were closed. The image burned itself on my mind more clearly than all the pictures I had taken.

After another downpour and with daylight now fading, we boarded a little ferry. Mely had turned to watch us go, her body crumpled, dripping with rain. As we drifted downstream and away from her platform, she got smaller and smaller in my lens, I couldn't help wondering what would happen to her.

Back home, the *Mirror* gave half a page to the story about teaching rescued baby orangutans how to climb, but gave Mely only a few paragraphs. I was distraught, and had to remind myself that, as news gatherers, we're nothing more than delivery boys; it's up to the people on the editorial desk to decide how to use what we bring them.

At the same time, it was a tough time for newspapers. Things were changing, especially at the *Daily Mirror*. 2009 was the year of the Great Cull. The axe was falling and 280 staff had to go, including nine photographers, leaving just two: one in Manchester and one in London.

I didn't wait to be pushed. I had done twenty-five

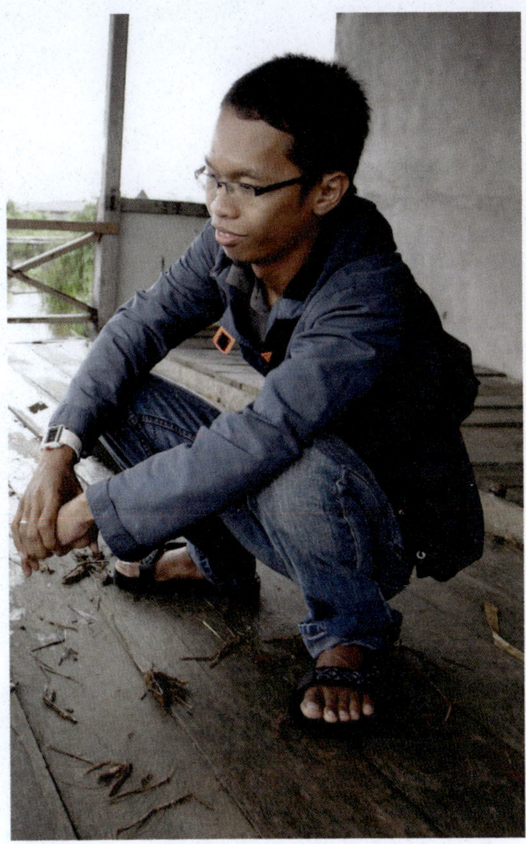

became such a sensitive political issue for the Indonesian government that everything happened very quickly and I couldn't get there in time, but Dr Adi went back to oversee the release and the IAR sent back a report of its own, with pictures.

I passed these on to the *Mail* which gave another double-page spread to Mely and the story of her release from her filthy balcony. The news touched the heart of one of the IAR's wealthiest donors, who sent a gift of half a million pounds. This allowed the organisation to buy twenty-seven hectares of rainforest and build a new centre complete with sleeping quarters, hospital, isolation building and plenty of room for the apes to swing through the trees.

Mely's rescue had not been simple, however, and there had been several pitfalls on the way, Dr Adi told me. The sanctuary staff heard that, following our visit, the barefooted woman had tried to sell the orangutan privately, perhaps out of fear that she would be made liable for its poor condition. Worried that Mely might then disappear into another life of captivity somewhere unknown, the team swung into action. Armed with an official licence to confiscate the orangutan, they asked the local police and some forest rangers to accompany them, but then got lost on the long journey.

When they finally arrived at the house, Mely's owner was nowhere to be seen and, when eventually located, claimed not to have the key to unlock the poor beast. Rather than stress her by trying to break the link in the chain that was closest to Mely's head, they cut the end of the chain that was furthest away, As a result, Mely had to make the entire journey with the length of chain still attached to her.

The poor creature was bewildered and frightened by the upheaval and only with difficulty let herself be coaxed into the travel crate that had been made for her.

After the river journey to Sambas, and then a road trip to Pontianak, she was flown to Ketapang where Head Vet Karmele supervised her rehabilitation and initial quarantine.

In a report dated 30 October 2010, the IAR said, 'On arrival at the centre, Mely was lightly sedated so that Karmele could remove the cruel padlock and chain from her neck and carry out a swift medical examination without upsetting her. In due course blood tests and xrays will establish whether she is suffering from any serious ailments or diseases. In the meantime she will be kept quiet and comfy and allowed time to adjust to her new surroundings. She is showing a healthy interest in food and eagerly trying all kinds of fruits for the first time. … Mely has never seen another orangutan since she lost her mother, so it will take time and patience to help her through this stage of her rehabilitation.'

Hearing this made me feel that the connection that Mely and I had made as we held hands on that rain-sodden platform was even more significant. It really felt as if, this time, a photo-journalist had made a difference.

years on the paper and been awarded *Photographer of the Year* on two occasions. In that year alone I'd been to Afghanistan twice and visited Mount Everest. It was time to move on. I didn't know where to, but I did know that Mely's face had captivated me.

As the *Mirror* hadn't done much with Mely's story, I made a set of large prints of her and called the *Daily Mail*'s picture editor, whom I'd known for thirty years.

Two nights later Paul Silva and I met in a pub opposite the *Mail* offices. I told him Mely's tale of woe and he took the prints and the outline of the story. Two Saturdays later the *Mail* printed a double-page spread of Mely, featuring my story and pictures, under the stark headline, 'Shackled'. Donations flooded in from generous readers keen to help rescue her. I couldn't have been happier

The power of the *Daily Mail* should never be underestimated. Its editor, Paul Dacre, had taken Mely's story to heart, knowing that Middle England would never stand for such cruelty. The article kick-started a sequence of events that resulted in the orangutan's being released from her personal Hell.

The IAR swung into action, pressure was put on Indonesia, and just three weeks after the *Mail*'s story, Mely was crated down the river to a new life of love and care at the Ketapang sanctuary.

I was asked by the *Mail* to go back to cover her being cut free from her chain—something I longed to see more than anything else I had ever been assigned to. Unfortunately, though, the operation

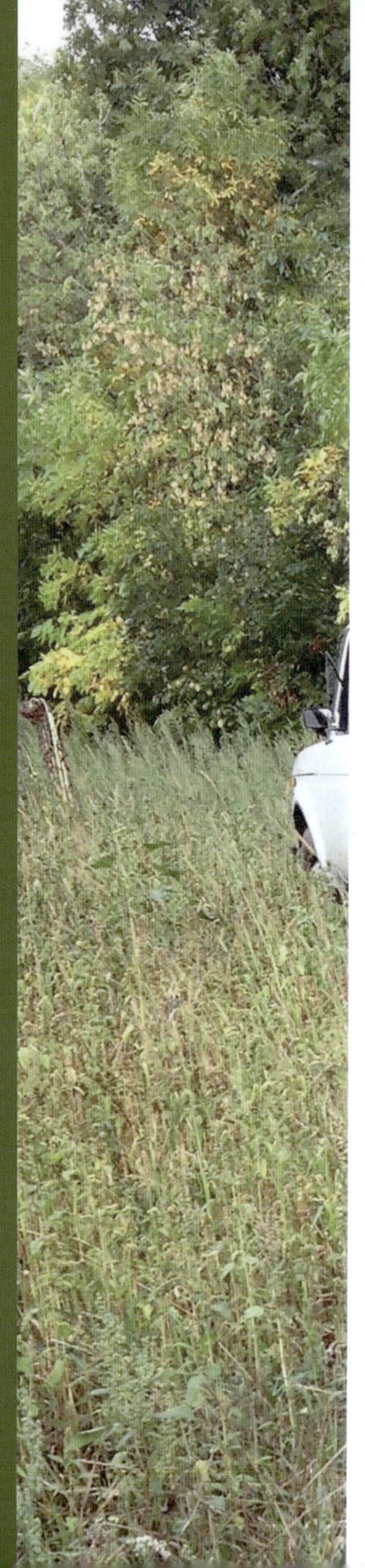

Masha and her escape from the mafia

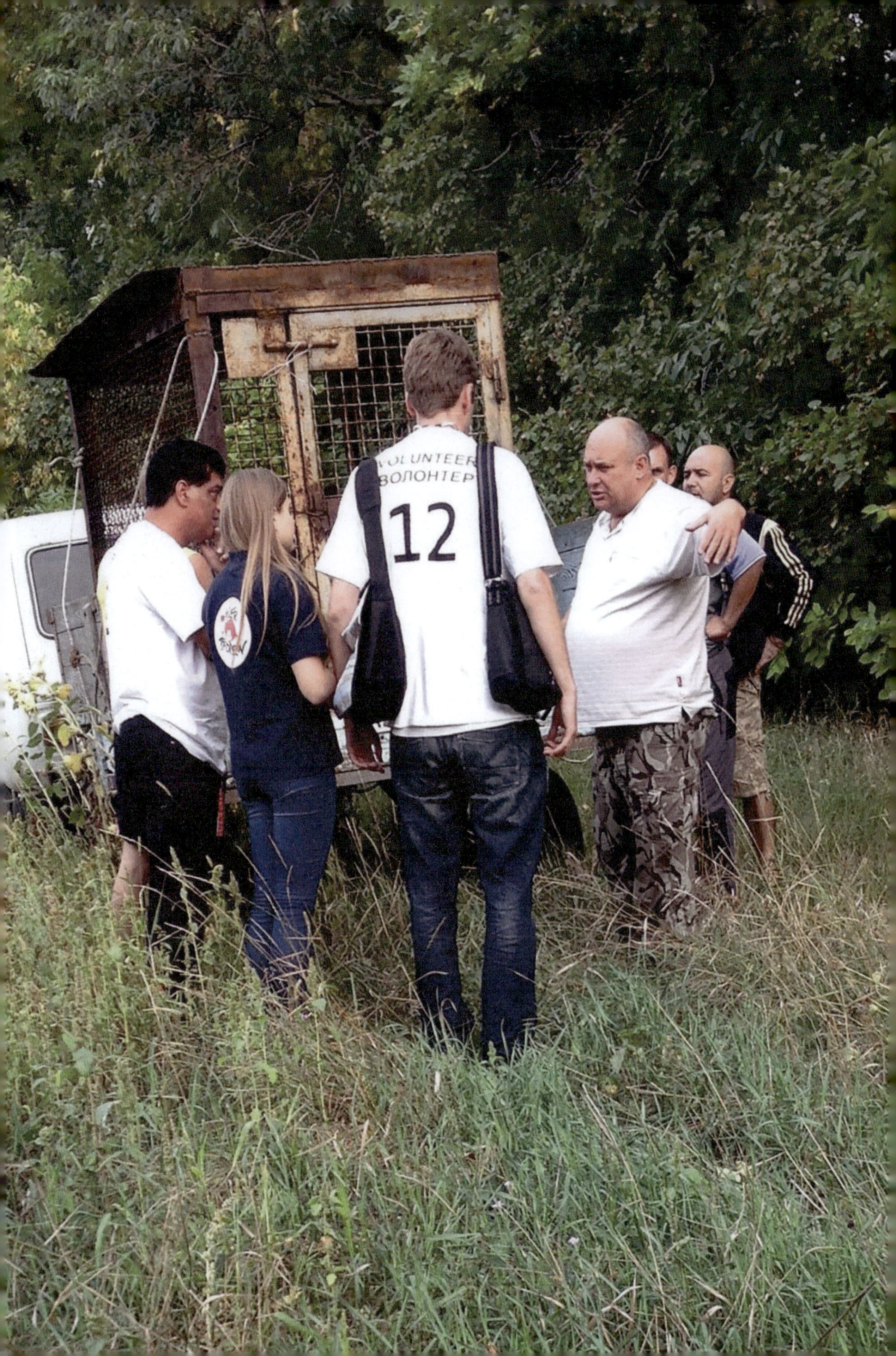
VOLUNTEER
ВОЛОНТЕР
12

Masha and her escape from the mafia

Having left the comfort of my job at a newspaper with vast resources, I found adapting to freelance work a little unsettling. The phone didn't ring as much, the regular pay cheque was gone, and I found myself mowing the grass a lot more often.

So when the *Daily Mail* asked me to go to Ukraine to photograph a bear being rescued from the Russian mafia, I jumped at the opportunity. This was long before the Russian invasions of 2014 and 2022.

The Fours Paws animal charity had learned that the dog-food manufacturer Royal Canin had been sponsoring bear-baiting in eastern Ukraine, which involved dogs attacking a bear tethered to a post. The company had paid for cups to be presented to the owners of the winning dogs. Pictures had emerged of the presentation ceremonies surrounded by banners emblazoned with the Royal Canin logo. Four Paws had challenged the company, which had come up with all manner of excuses to explain away how this had happened.

The charity then found out that behind the animal cruelty was organised crime. One of the poor bears was owned by a Russian gang, but they wanted to get rid of it because it had become more trouble than it was worth to them. The police had warned the gang that they had to turn the animal over or face prosecution. Someone from the gang had contacted Four Paws and arranged to hand over the bear. It had to be done in secret, though: the mafia didn't want to be seen doing something nice.

A team from the *Sun* had also been invited on the trip: photographer Louis Wood and reporter Ruth Harrison. I had not met either of them before, although I had visited Ukraine on two occasions: once during the Orange Revolution of 2004–2005, and long before that to visit the still-glowing Chernobyl nuclear power plant, which had exploded in 1986.

A meeting with Four Paws was set up in a bar near our hotel in Kyiv. The charity's director had assembled his rescue team, an eclectic mix of women with green hair, men in their forties wearing leather jackets, an Egyptian vet and the charity's boss, Dr Amir Khalil.

Dr Amir, a permanent smile on his face, welcomed everybody to the cramped bar as the vet set out the plan of operation for the next day. In my experience, animal rescues always seem to be timed for dawn and, true to form, a convoy of cars was to leave our hotel at 5:30 am for the long drive to Kharkiv, where we'd meet a second team with the animal ambulance. From there we'd drive to the Russian border and wait to hear from the men with the bear.

It all sounded very simple in the comfort of a smoke-filled bar.

We had been given the choice of going to Kharkiv by car or by train: the train option meant getting to the station at 3:30 am, so of course the British press contingent chose the car.

A dull rainy dawn was breaking as we set off. The three of us squeezed ourselves and our equipment into a small Soviet-era car that had smoke coughing from the exhaust. We wondered if it would last the journey.

We shouldn't have doubted the old machine. Six hours later, the five Four Paws cars pulled up at the new glass-and-chrome Kharkiv airport. In the large car park another meeting was convened by Dr Amir.

He told us that the animal ambulance would meet us there and travel in convoy with us right up to the Russian border, where we would wait again

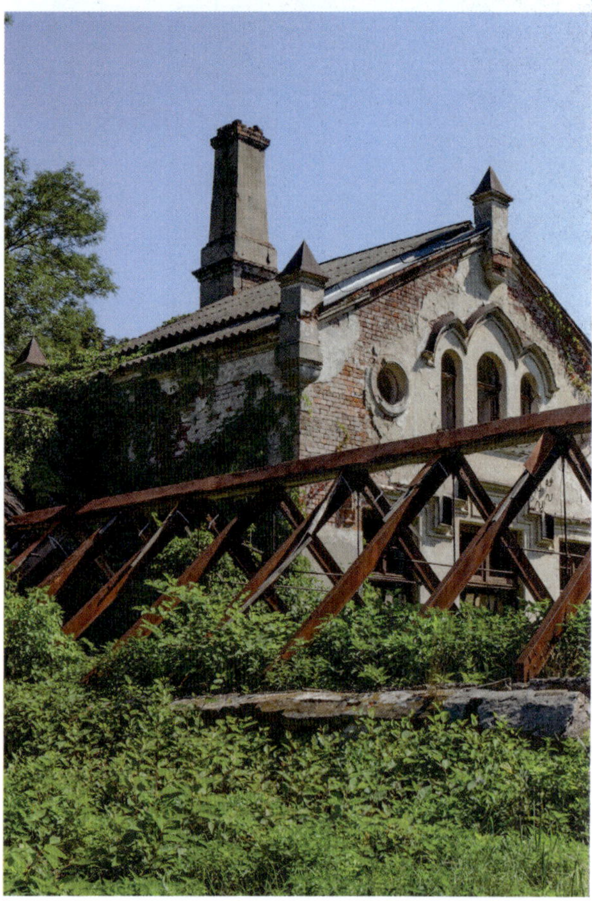

"

to make contact with the bear's owners. It was now only 2:00 pm, but it promised to be a long night.

The hinterland between Kharkiv and the border was a place that time had forgot. Buildings, collapsed in on themselves, were overgrown with trees and brambles. Whole villages seemed to be abandoned—until we noticed people moving among the dereliction.

A man with a cow on a piece of string came into view. Women wandered along the dirt roads. Flashes of activity could be seen in the front yards of houses that we had assumed were deserted. It was not a countryside of working farms and livestock but of abject and soul-destroying rural poverty.

In a scruffy town near the border, lots of heavy-set men sat outside bars, smoking and glaring at cars they didn't recognise. This was where we were to meet the mafia through one of their agents. They did not want to lose status by meeting us face to face.

Dr Amir, Louis, Ruth and I would be part of the team that went to collect the bear, assisted by two more vets to check the animal over. Dr Amir told the *Sun* journalists to pretend to be doctors.

I was given the role of an odd-job man, which suited me well, as I would be the one taking the undercover pictures. Dr Amir produced three white T-shirts with the Four Paws logos on them, and we soon blended in.

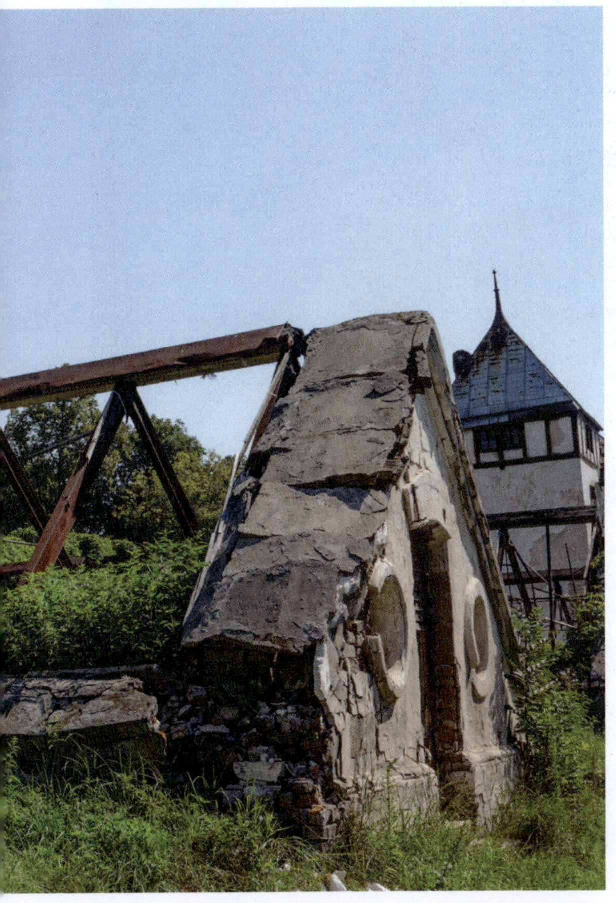

Two men wandered up to our group. A phone was handed to one of the Ukrainians, who spoke on it for a few minutes. The phone was handed back and the two men left.

'We have to go much closer to the border, park in a lay-by and wait for another call,' explained Dr Amir.

The three of us climbed into a battered purple Lada Niva, driven by a man with a wild beard. We soon learned his driving would be even wilder.

The bear ambulance led the convoy; by the time we reached the lay-by it was 5:00 pm, and it would be dark in two hours. We felt a rising tension, wondering if we were being played or whether we would actually see the bear.

One of the men got a call to say the bear was on its way. (We hoped it wasn't doing the driving.) We were to drive for one more mile and wait for another Lada Niva, this time a white one, to flash its headlights. We would then have to follow the mafia car to wherever the handover would take place.

Sure enough a white Lada flashed its lights, coming straight for us. We swerved off the road to get out of the way. The Lada passed us at high speed. Attached to its back was a homemade wooden and wire cage containing a huge brown bear—a female.

Our wild-bearded driver swung the car round and accelerated away, a crucifix swinging wildly from the rear-view mirror. The bear ambulance, now behind us, was struggling to turn on the narrow road, so it was up to us to catch up with the Russians.

Just as we moved to overtake it, the white Lada veered off the road into a field of sunflowers, the trailer with the bear bouncing off the ground. We were just seconds behind it and saw it come to a halt. Nobody moved until the ambulance arrived.

Dr Amir, no longer smiling but very angry, swung the ambulance round in the sunflowers and backed it up to the trailer holding the bear.

I wandered off into the sunflowers while Louis padded round the other side of the bear cage. We both had an app on our phones that enabled us to take pictures without any images appearing on the screen, so we got to work without being noticed.

One of the three mafia guys started shouting orders at the other two: one was told to get on top of the cage while the other one had to get ready to open it. The Four Paws crew pushed a second cage out of the ambulance, just inches away from the trailer. Freedom for the bear was within sight.

The sight of a crowd of people made the bear fractious, and she started rocking the trailer from side to side, making it difficult to line up the two cages so that she couldn't escape. The mafia boss leaped into action, grabbing the trailer and manhandling it into line. Dr Amir pushed the cage from the other side and the lad on the top of the cage was told to pull up the gate.

The bear didn't move but sat rigid in her own cage. This was the most dangerous time. In a fit of anger, the powerful animal could charge the exit

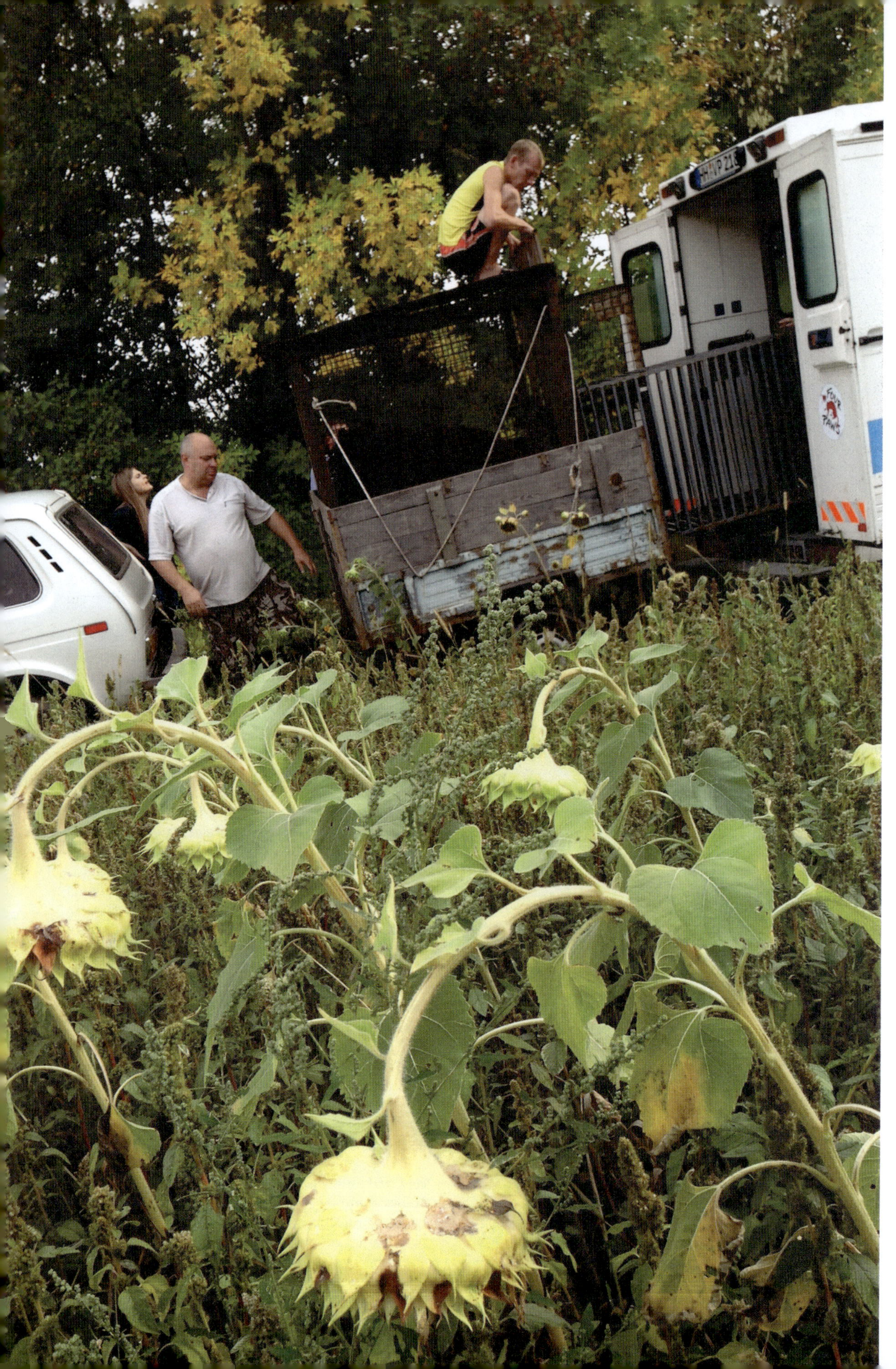

between the gate and the cage, pushing through the gap and running off. I moved closer to the vehicle: if she was going to make a run for it, I didn't want to be in her way.

The situation called for calm. Dr Amir put some large chunks of meat into the Four Paws cage and told everybody to stay quiet. We all stood in silence, watching the bear's nose twitch and head turn as she picked up the smell.

Very slowly she moved towards the cage. She put her head inside, grabbed a piece of meat and nipped back to where it had been before. More meat was placed in the cage but further back; if she went for the second bit, we'd have her, safe and sound.

Being used to the kinds of tricks humans had played on her all her life, the bear knew she was being set up. She sat at the back of the trailer not moving for ten minutes before the head gangster began to lose patience. He strode off to the bushes and snapped a small branch from a tree to use as a prod.

When he pushed the stick through the wire and prodded the bear, she turned and snarled. Dr Amir dropped more meat into the cage, and within seconds the animal leaped forward. The gate was slammed shut and the bear's journey to safety was about to begin.

After a lot of backslapping from the mafia boys and our team, everybody posed for a picture in front of the ambulance. I had expected the gangsters to maintain their hard and cool image, but they seemed genuinely upset to be saying goodbye to their 'pet', whom we learned was called Masha. We were tempted to feel sorry for them until we remembered how they had been abusing the animal.

With Masha safely inside the vehicle, we started the journey back to Kyiv. The thought of an eight-hour night drive with our crazy driver at the wheel filled us all with dread.

Back at the lay-by the team checked that the bear was comfortable and supplied with food and water. It was decided that we should drive back to Kharkiv in convoy and get ourselves something to eat.

On the way, we stopped at a supermarket, the only place we could find that had enough parking space for all the cars and the ambulance. We parked outside the restaurant area and, before long, a crowd had come out of the building and was gathering around the ambulance. Men stood on their

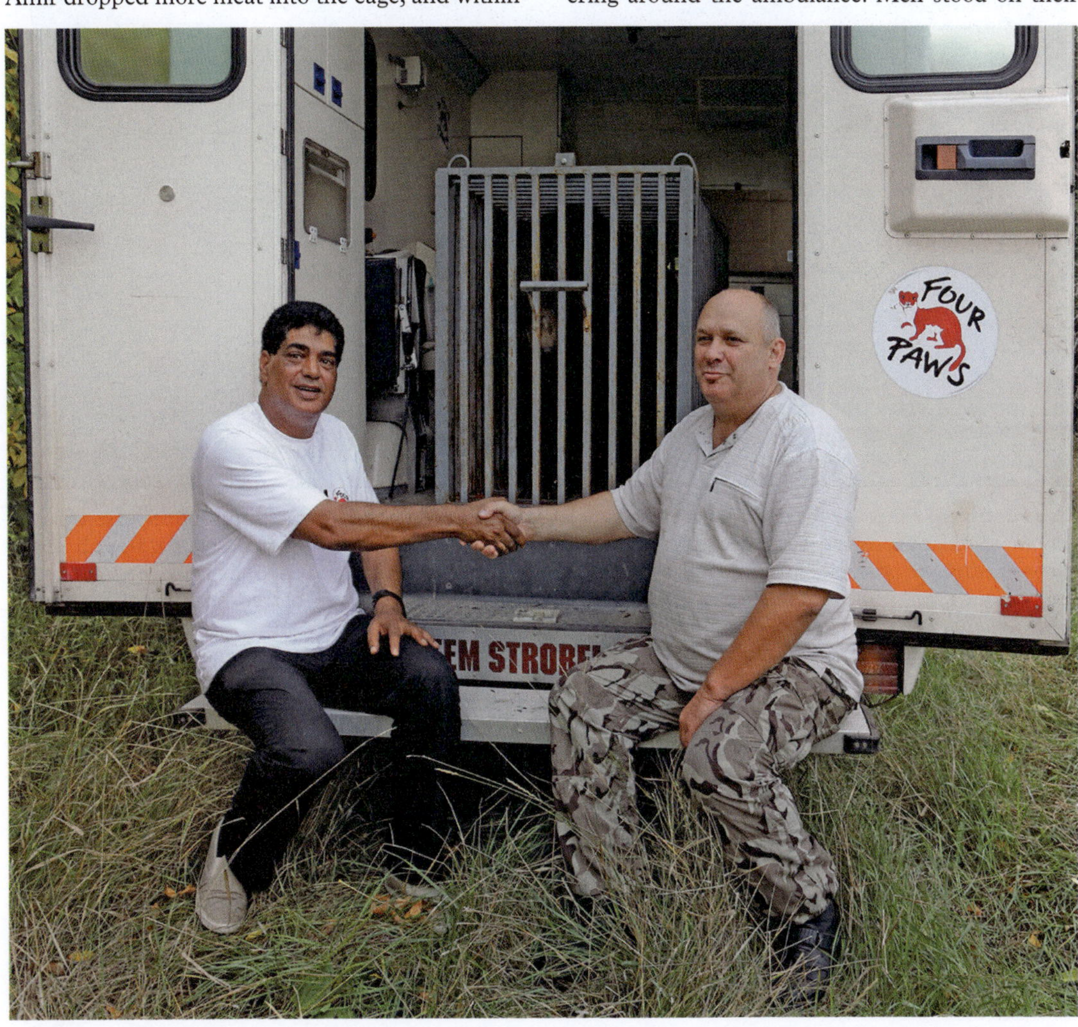

toes, craning to see through the window and lifting children to get a glimpse of what was growling behind the glass.

The vehicle had started moving on its axles as the bear became agitated inside her cage. From inside the café, we could see Dr Amir assuring the crowd that all was well and safe but that it would help if they could move away. The shoppers lost interest and plodded away their shopping trollies.

As we contemplated moving on, a woman dressed in a black leather jacket and black boots with silver studs presented herself to us.

'You have places on the sleeper train to Kyiv,' she said abruptly, adding that her name was Olga. 'Quick, quick: we have to go now."

We thought we had escaped our wild driver, but it was him that drove us at breakneck speed to catch the train we'd been told we had reservations on. He drove along tram lines, cut up lorries and jumped red lights. None of this fazed Olga, who was explaining that the train was already full and that we would have to persuade the guard to give us a bed.

As the car skidded to a halt outside the gothic station, Olga told us to run. We grabbed our kit and did as we were told, tumbling across the tracks. Olga found the guard, a rotund man in a grease-stained uniform standing at the doorway of his cabin.

The three of us stood looking at the guard's expression as Olga gabbled away in Russian. After a minute or so Olga turned to us and told us to hand over a hundred dollars for three beds. We paid the money and boarded the train.

Ruth was given the guard's bed, Louis slept in a compartment with two drunks and Olga and I ended up in a four-berth cabin with a young couple. I pulled a blanket over myself and was soon sent to sleep by the rocking of the train.

As for Masha, she was rumbling towards a new life in the Four Paws sanctuary two hours the other side of Kyiv.

Dr Amir used a cutting tool to work through the chains padlocked around Masha's neck. They had worn away the fur and left a deep scar. In the pouring rain of a thunderstorm, the team carried the sedated animal on a stretcher to a rockery that had been built in the shape of a den and laid her on a bed of straw. Her luxurious new home was set in an enclosure that covered an acre, with climbing frames, a small cabin and a large pond to swim in.

Two hours later, Masha woke up, confused and understandably nervous about leaving the confines of her new home. Her nose popped out, sniffed the air, then disappeared again. We had been told that her former owners used to keep dogs on leads near where she was housed, ready to snap at her when she moved too far. Caution was her watchword.

Finally, she emerged, padded around her vast enclosure and sniffed the air again before flopping down to sleep on her straw bedding. She had performed for the cameras, though, and as far as Louis and I were concerned, our work here was done.

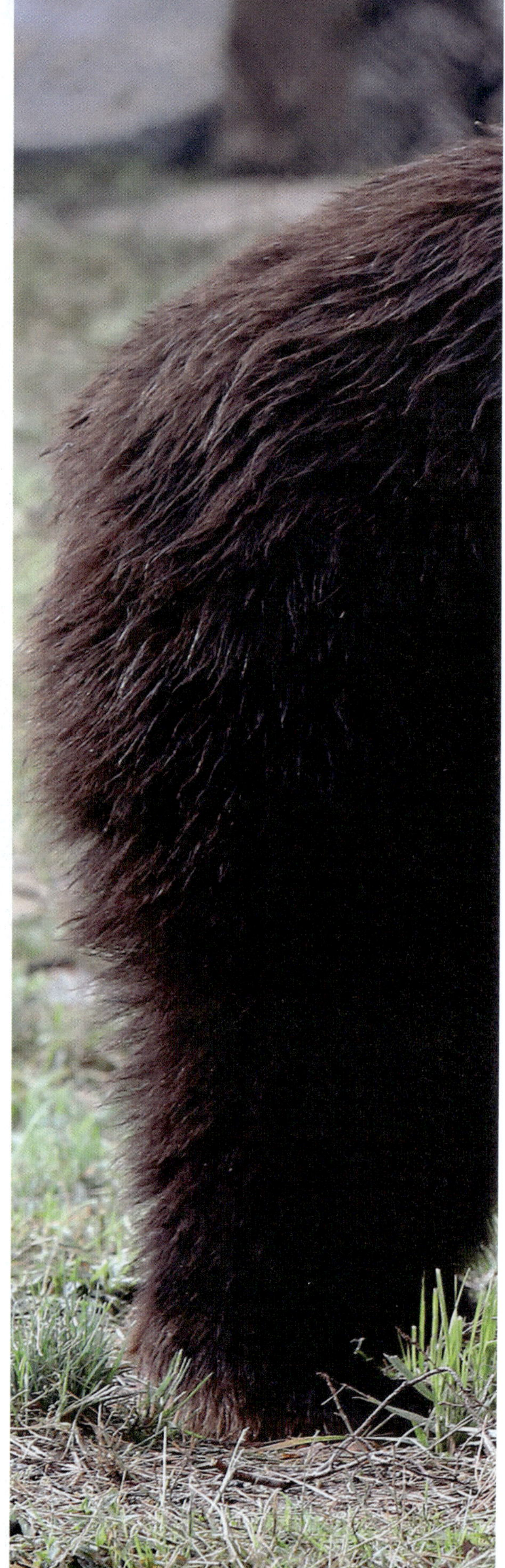

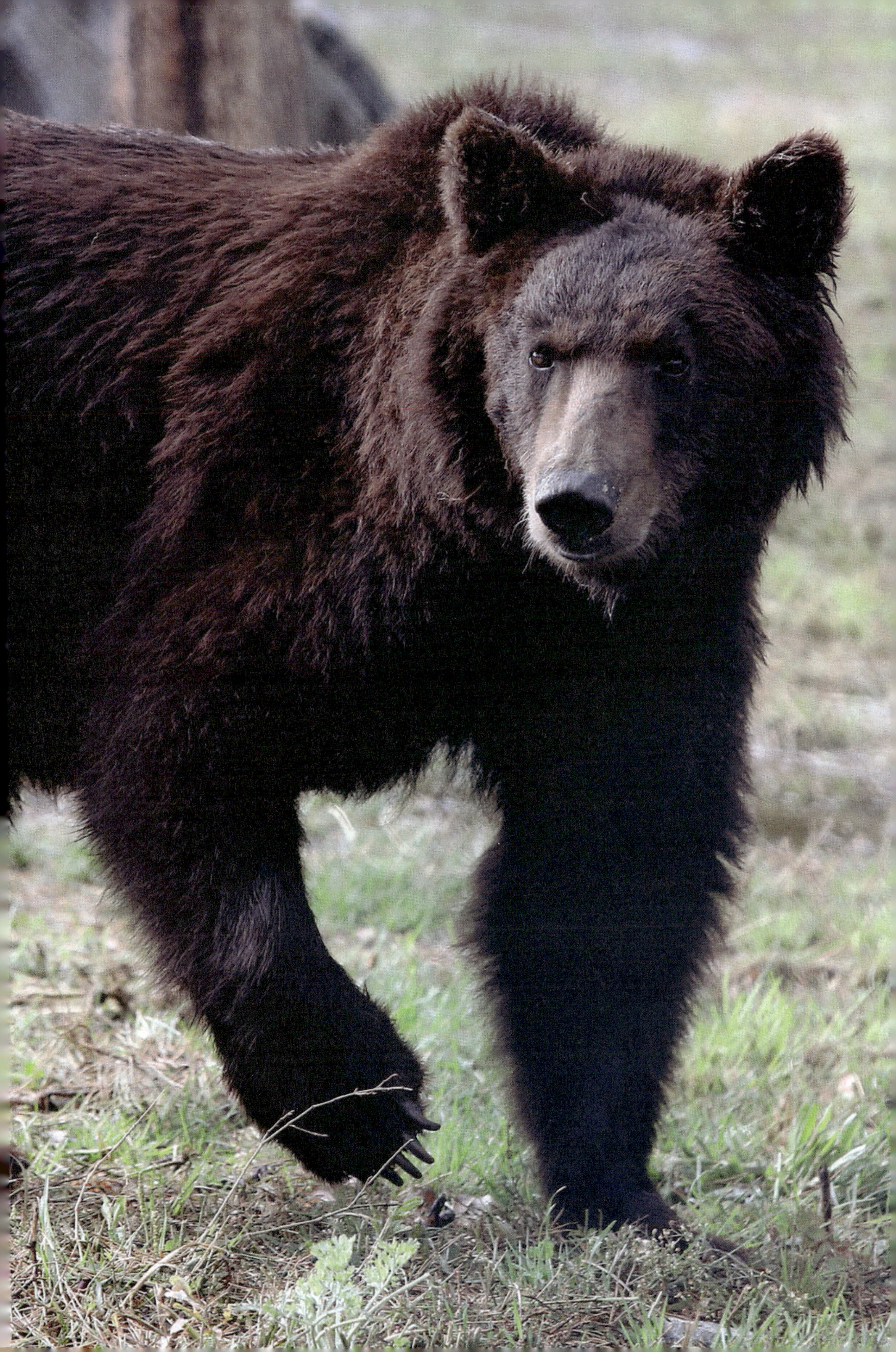

Mely and the lorises of Jakarta

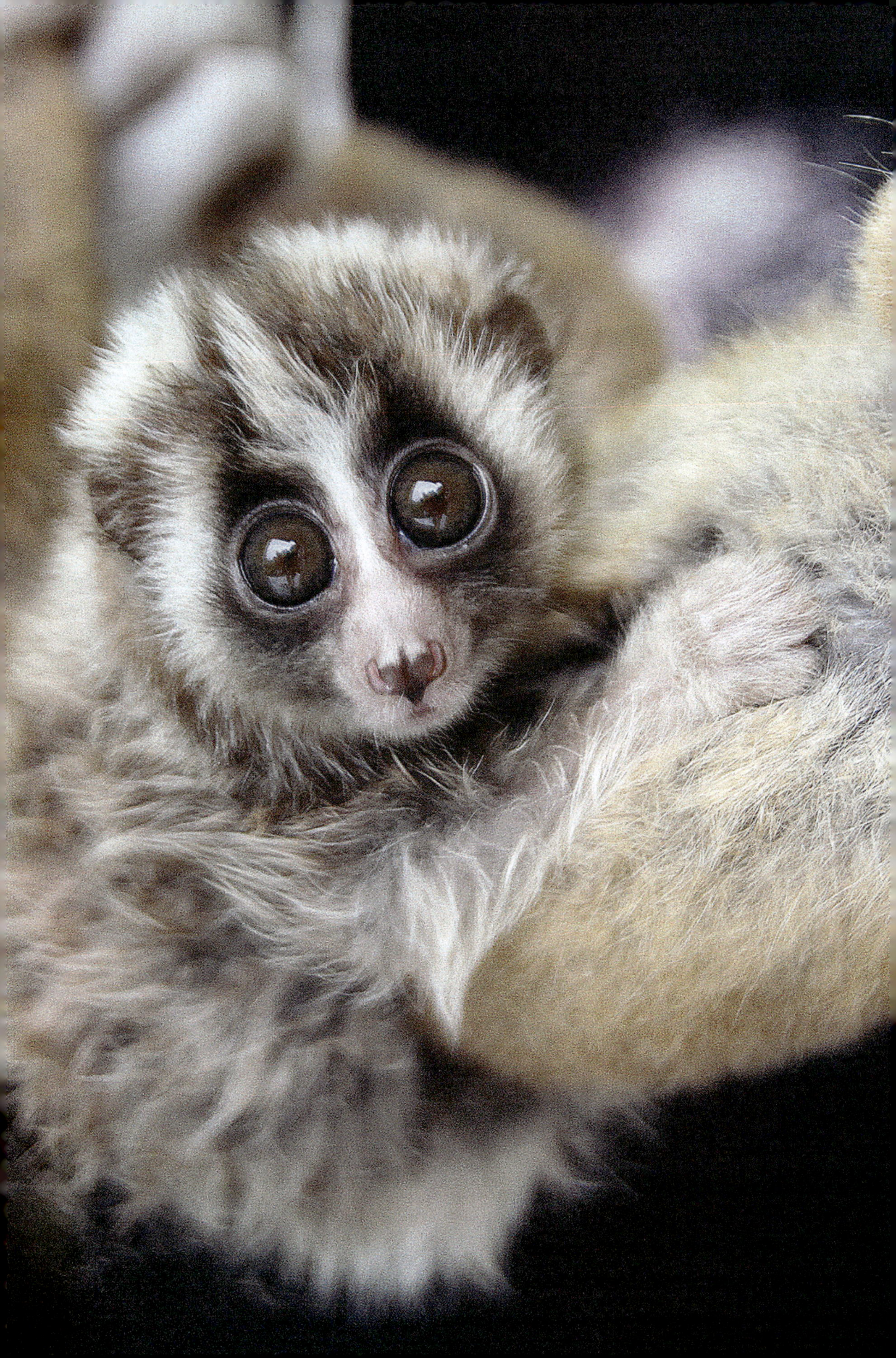

Mely and
the lorises
of Jakarta

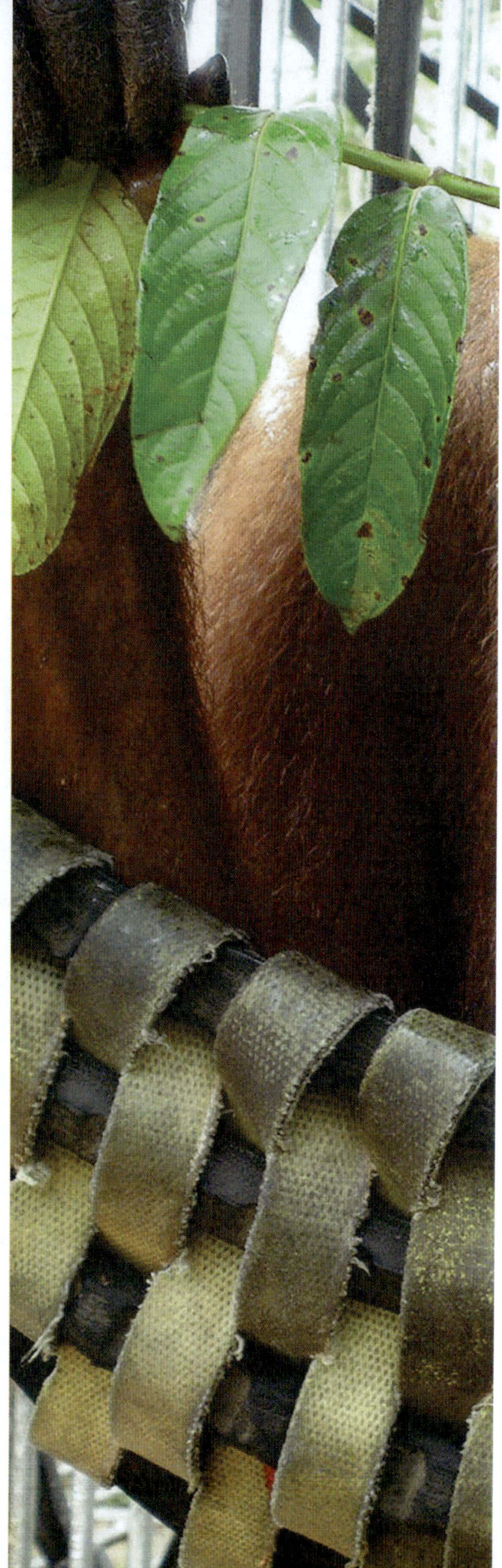

I kept in close contact with my friends at the IAR, and they told me of Mely's progress. She was starting to make herself at home, and when they gave her bundles of branches full of fresh green leaves, she had immediately moulded them into a nest. They regarded this as astonishing. Nest-making was assumed to be a learned behaviour, and Mely had been snatched too early in her life to have seen her mother do it, which suggested that the knowledge of how to make a nest was in fact instinctive.

I nursed the hope that there might be an opportunity to visit her again. Nine months later, when I told the *Mail* of her progress, they agreed to send me back. So off I went on that arduous thirty-three-hour journey, only, this time, the hours flew by. When I got off the plane, the humidity was, as ever, like a wet blanket, with thunder clouds rumbling and sheet lightning flashing, but I was oblivious to it all.

At the sanctuary, Mely was transformed. Aside from the permanent scar around her neck from her chain, she was bigger, stronger and happier. I found her lying on her back on a rubber hammock in her

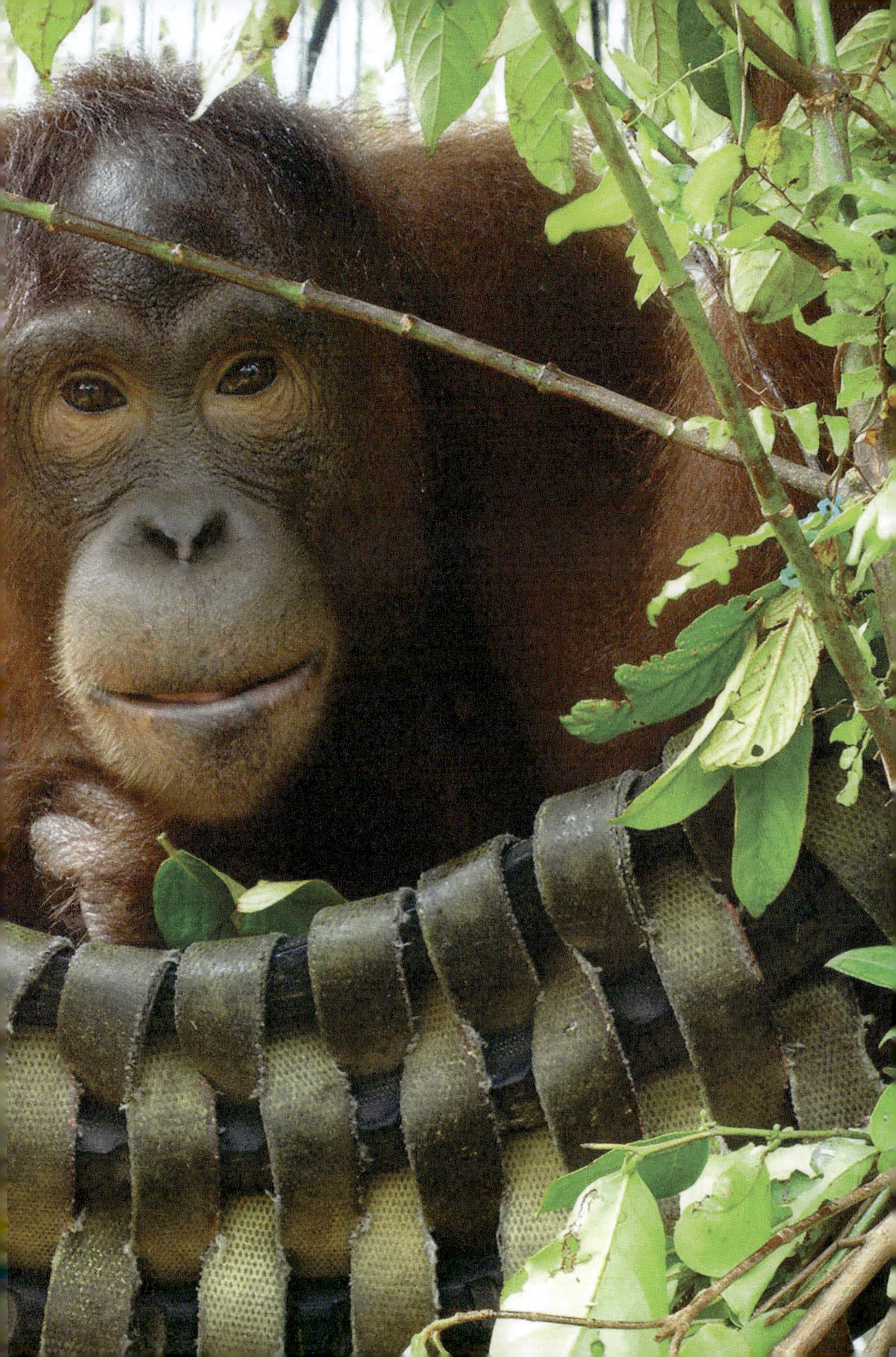

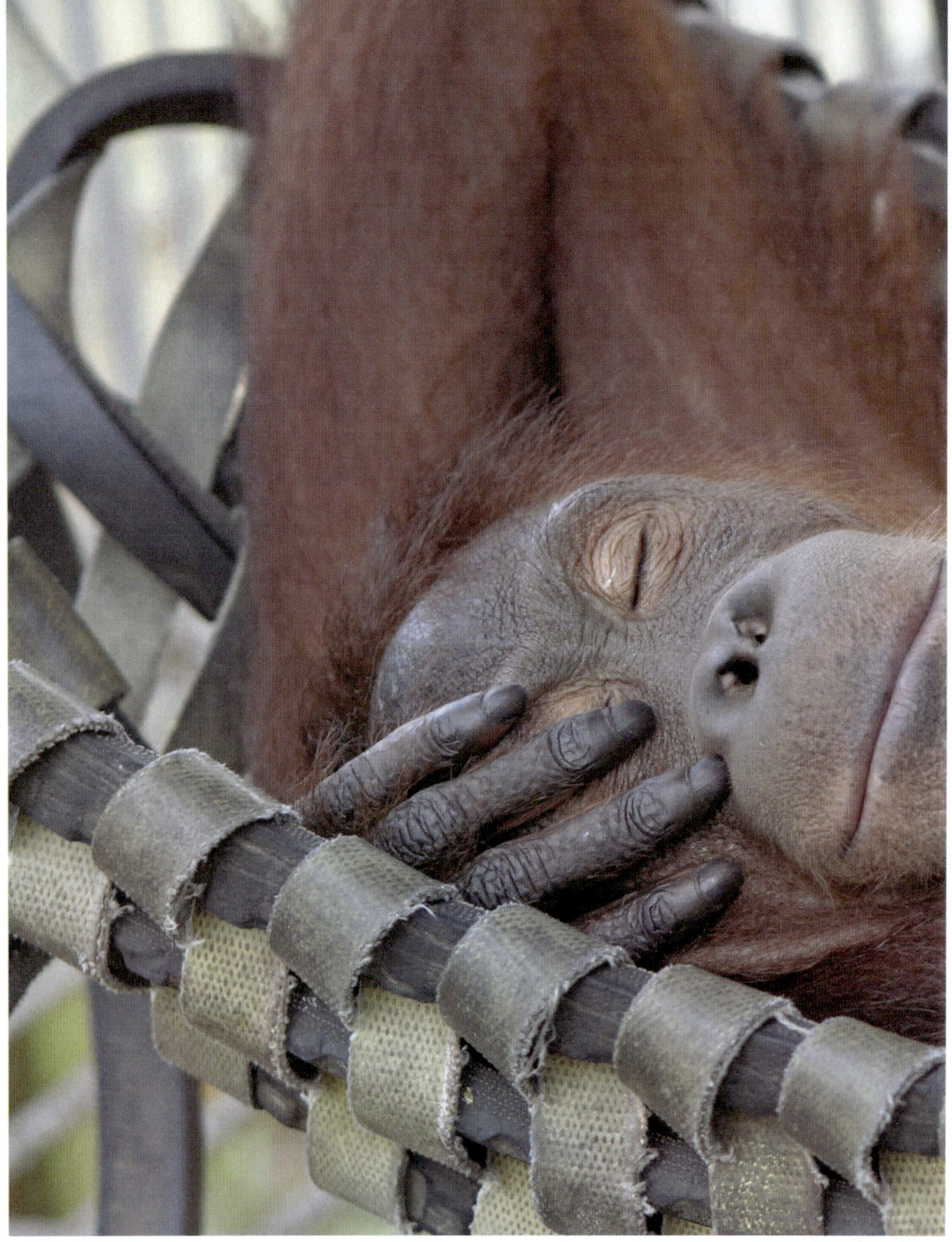

new cage, swinging herself gently from side to side. Later, I took pictures of her looking relaxed and happy, flat on her back, fast asleep with one hand over her face, taking a well-earned rest.

I sat watching her for hours as she slept. When she woke she sauntered around her cage, came to the bars and extended her arm so that one of the keepers could massage it. In a short space of time she had become a different animal from the one I'd seen hunched miserably on the jungle veranda.

Another reason for wanting to return at this time was that Mely was set to meet another adult orangutan for the first time. Her cage, which was thirty-feet high by twenty-feet square, had been divided into two, and another female ape had been moved in next door. The idea was to let them get to know each other through the bars and then lift the

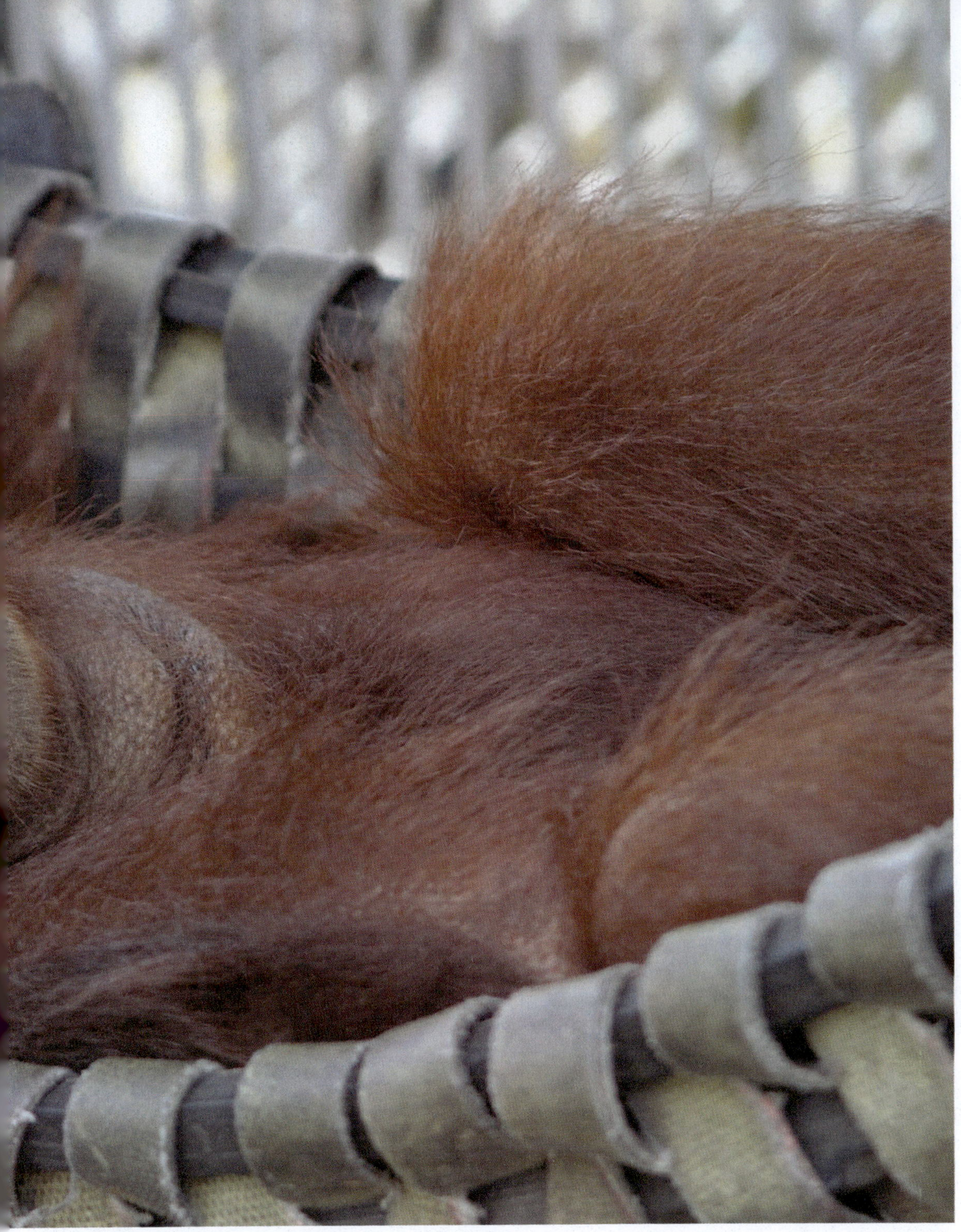

dividing metal gate to see if they socialised. Nicky, who was also an orphan, had been at the centre two months longer than Mely, so it was assumed that she would make the first move.

The gate was due to be opened on the second day of my visit. Following a huge rainstorm, the morning was even hotter than the day before. Mely swung happily in her hammock and Nicky sat picking at her fur, preening herself on the other side of the gate. I sat on a metal chair a few feet away from them, with my camera at the ready.

Half an hour passed before the right key was found and then up went the gate. At the sound of the commotion, Nicky fled to the upper reaches of her cage while Mely remained in her hammock, apparently uninterested in going anywhere.

The keepers seemed unperturbed and told me to give it time. Three hours later I was still roasting on

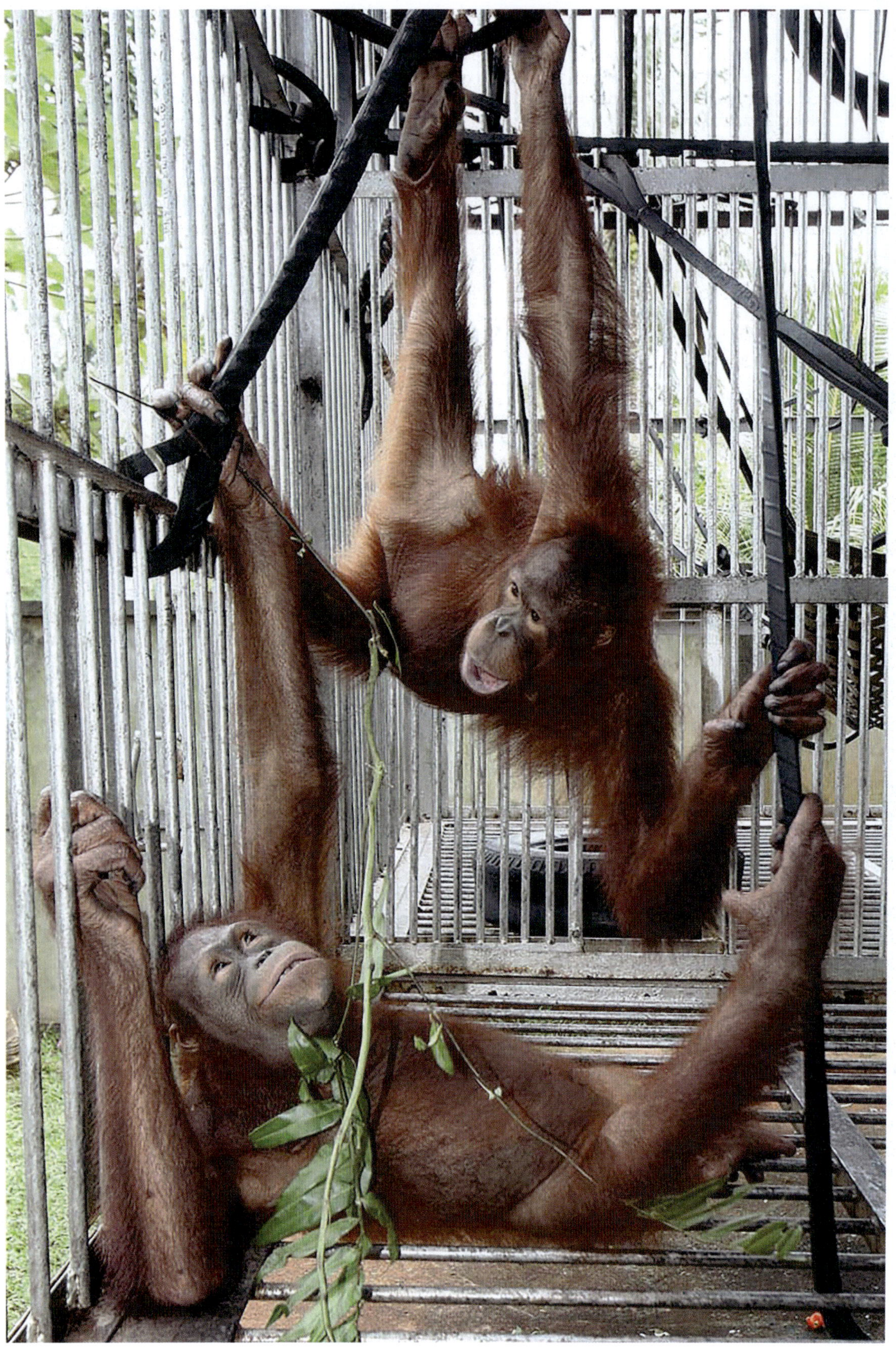

the metal seat. Mely had stepped down and gone to look at the open door but Nicky was still at the top of her cage. Another hour rolled by but nothing happened. I was sweltering.

Then, suddenly, Mely skipped into Nicky's cage. Excited, I jumped up and Nicky swung down from her eerie. To begin with, the two mistreated creatures just stared at each other—shyly, curiously. Then they reached out their long arms and gave each other a hug.

Before long, the pair were playing happily together, swinging from leather straps, chattering, and feeding each other the mangoes and lychees that had been put out for them. It was a brief encounter, but a poignant one and well worth the four-hour wait.

With the previous day's pictures of Mely making her nest and sleeping in her hammock, I now felt I had all the images I needed. I flew back to Jakarta in a light aircraft the next day, happy that we had been reunited and hoping that I would be able to follow Mely's progress in the years to come.

From the tiny window in my plane, I looked down and saw the massive scale of the deforestation that was causing so much suffering to innocent creatures like Mely. Massive tracts of land, home to an untold number of rare and endangered animals, had been entirely scrubbed out. There wasn't a tree left standing. Once pristine rivers, now brown and sludgy from all the dirt that had run off the destroyed land, meandered unhealthily through barren landscape.

Not a single living creature could be seen.

In Jakarta, I was due to meet someone who would show me another species being helped by the IAR. A young researcher from Oxford Brookes University, Dr Richard Moore, was working with the IAR to study and protect the slow loris, a nocturnal animal, with huge eyes, that lives in the rainforests of Java, Indonesia's main island.

Captured lorises were being sold in open-air markets, and my task was to expose the illegal trade in this endangered creature. An American woman, Caroline, was to be my guide to the village of Ciapus, on the slopes of Mount Salak, where the IAR had a slow loris centre.

A long bus journey brought us to the centre, a V-shaped collection of small wooden cabins with a wooden boardwalk connecting them. At the point where the V met was a communal seating area.

I was allocated the cabin nearest this area, only to find it was already occupied by a gecko, which lived on a wooden beam some three feet above my bed. I don't mind geckos, but not when they're in my bedroom, as they make loud, repetitive croaking sounds, and I didn't want to be kept awake. This fellow, though, was not going to be moved.

Richard Moore, the researcher, told me all about the loris and put my mind at ease about the gecko.

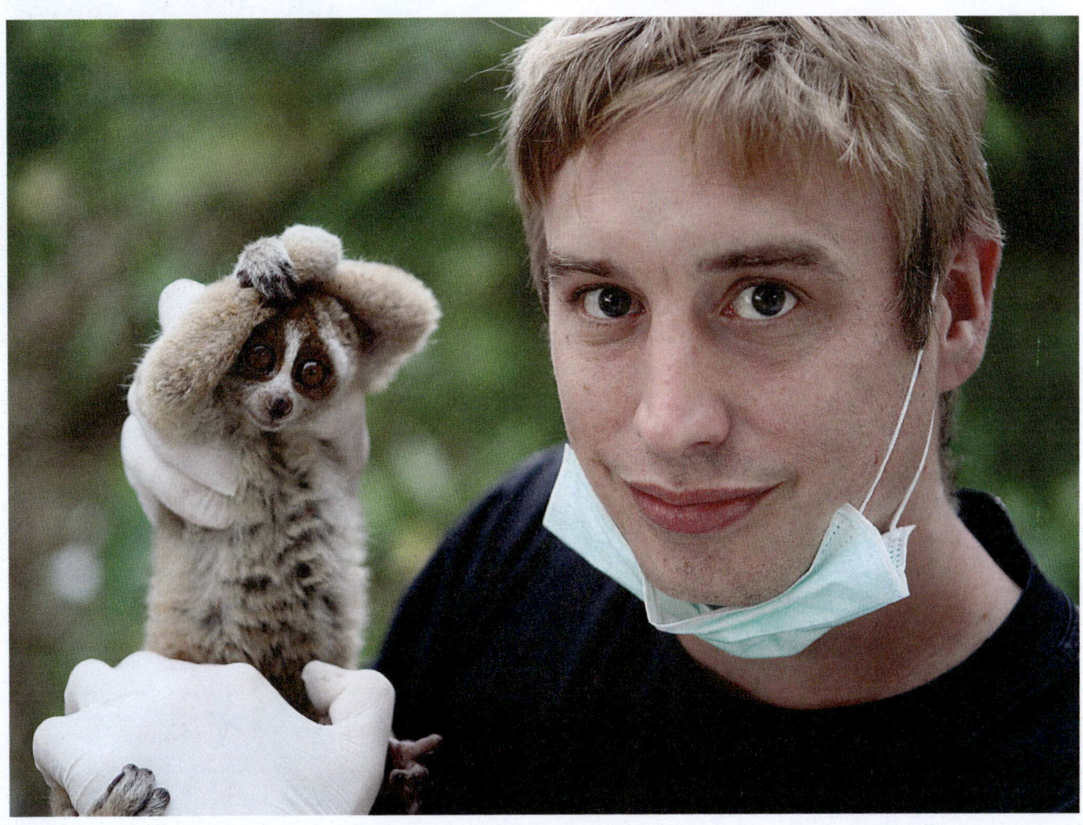

'It won't call all night. Just wait. It will stop at 11:00 pm and start up again at 7:00 am,' he said As if on a timer, the little lizard did exactly what Dr Moore had predicted, and I got a decent night's sleep.

The next morning Caroline and I set off back down to Jakarta to visit the animal market. She had agreed to be my cover so that we could get pictures of the slow loris being displayed in the blinding sunlight.

The day was stifling, with more rain in the air. Over a glass of cold orange juice in an air-conditioned juice bar, we agreed on our angle of attack. She would wander in front of me and I'd snap away with my tourist camera at some other stalls selling kittens, snakes, owls, stoats, bats and parrots until we reached the area where the slow lorises were being sold. Once we were there, I'd ask her to pose in front of the cages.

We sauntered along the line of cages in the owl section of the market. It was heartbreaking to see these magnificent forest night-fliers confined in iron prisons only inches bigger than themselves.

In smaller cages, birds of all kinds were singing the songs that had led them to being trapped in the woods of Indonesia. Now they were doomed to sit on the cramped balconies of houses or flats in the city. We passed lines and lines of suffering.

As we neared the loris cages, we noticed that more men were hanging around. Lorises were the market's big-ticket items and we weren't sure if the men were potential customers or lookouts.

Caroline moved towards the stack of cages. At first glance I counted eleven lorises rammed into three cages, their big round eyes staring out at the crowd.

This was the picture. Laughing casually with Caroline, I lifted my small camera to my eye and managed to shoot two frames before a man sitting on a motorbike to my right leaped up and barged into me, shouting at me to get out of there. These guys had seen it all before: a seemingly innocent tourist snapping away, only to unmask the dirty trade in the media.

The shouts drew the attention of the other sellers around us. The man at the loris stall reached under the loris cages and drew out a large machete. I grabbed Caroline by the arm and pulled her away.

However, the sight of the lorises surrounded by gawping people and breathing in diesel fumes from the trucks and mopeds and taxis in the market made me so angry that I couldn't give up.

I pulled a proper camera from my rucksack. I thought that if I approached the stalls not from the road but from the crowded pavement, I might have a better chance of taking a few strong pictures and escaping without being cut into small chunks.

As luck would have it, a large group of Chinese tourists arrived at the same time, greatly amused at the sight of wildlife shut up in a metal hell. I blended in as well as I could.

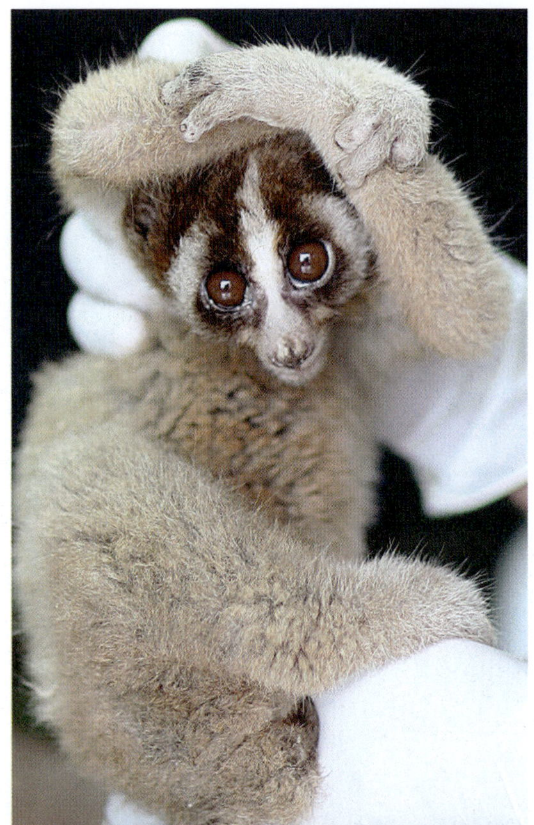

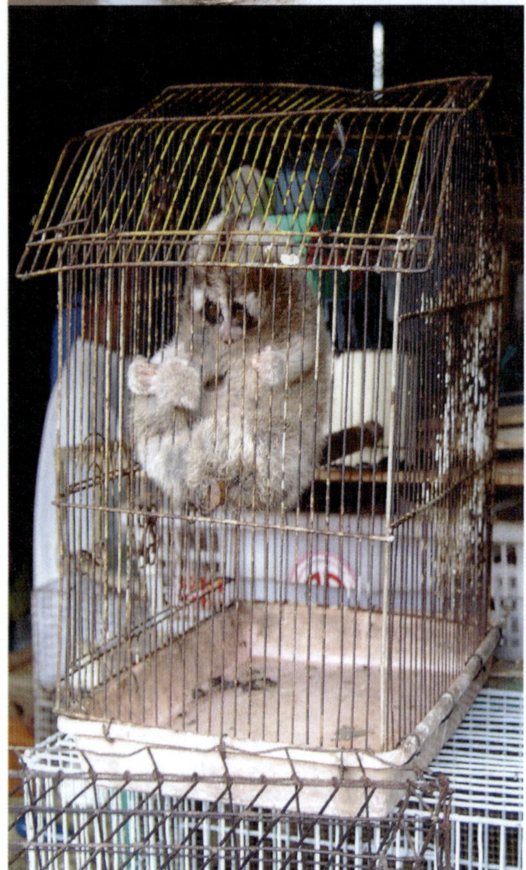

44

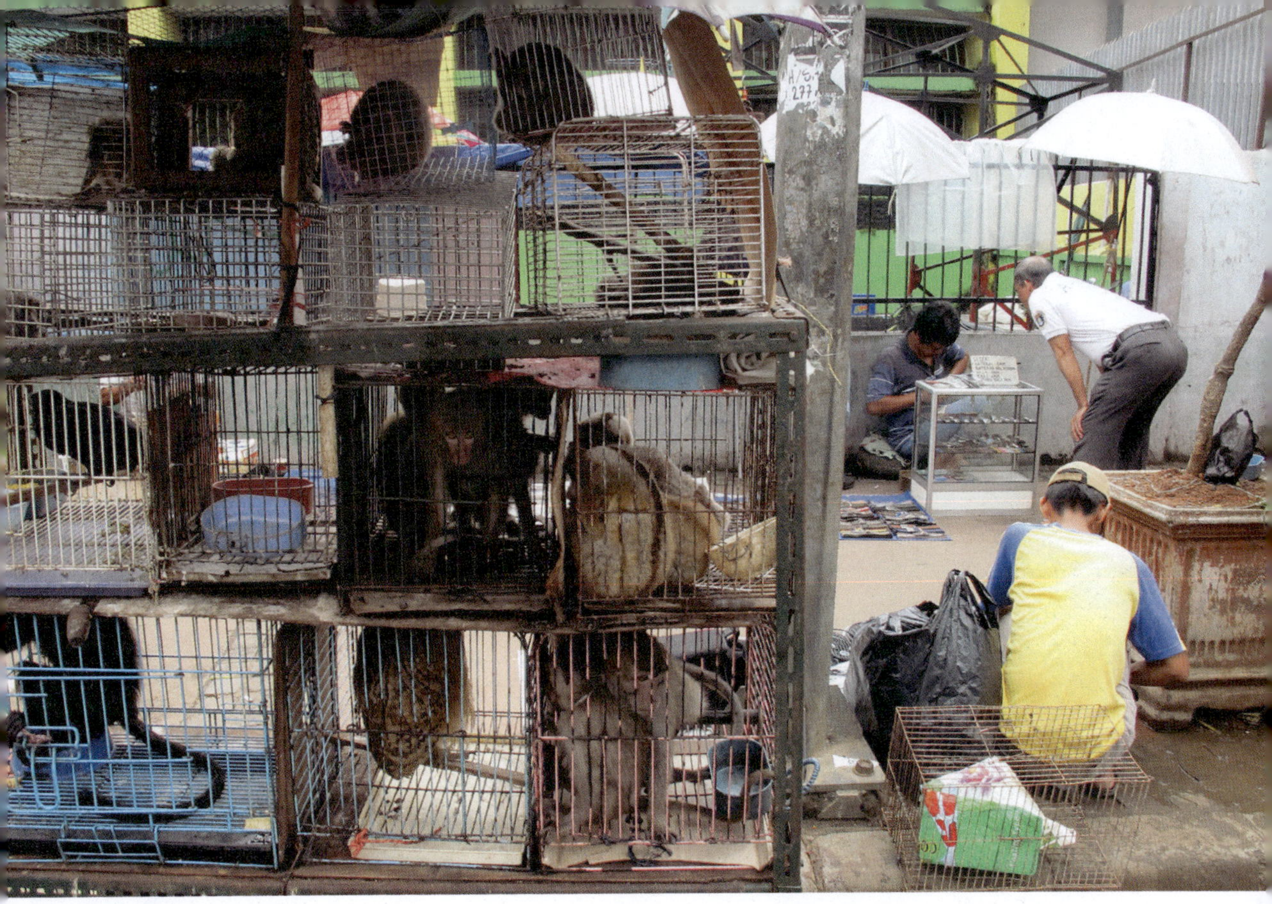

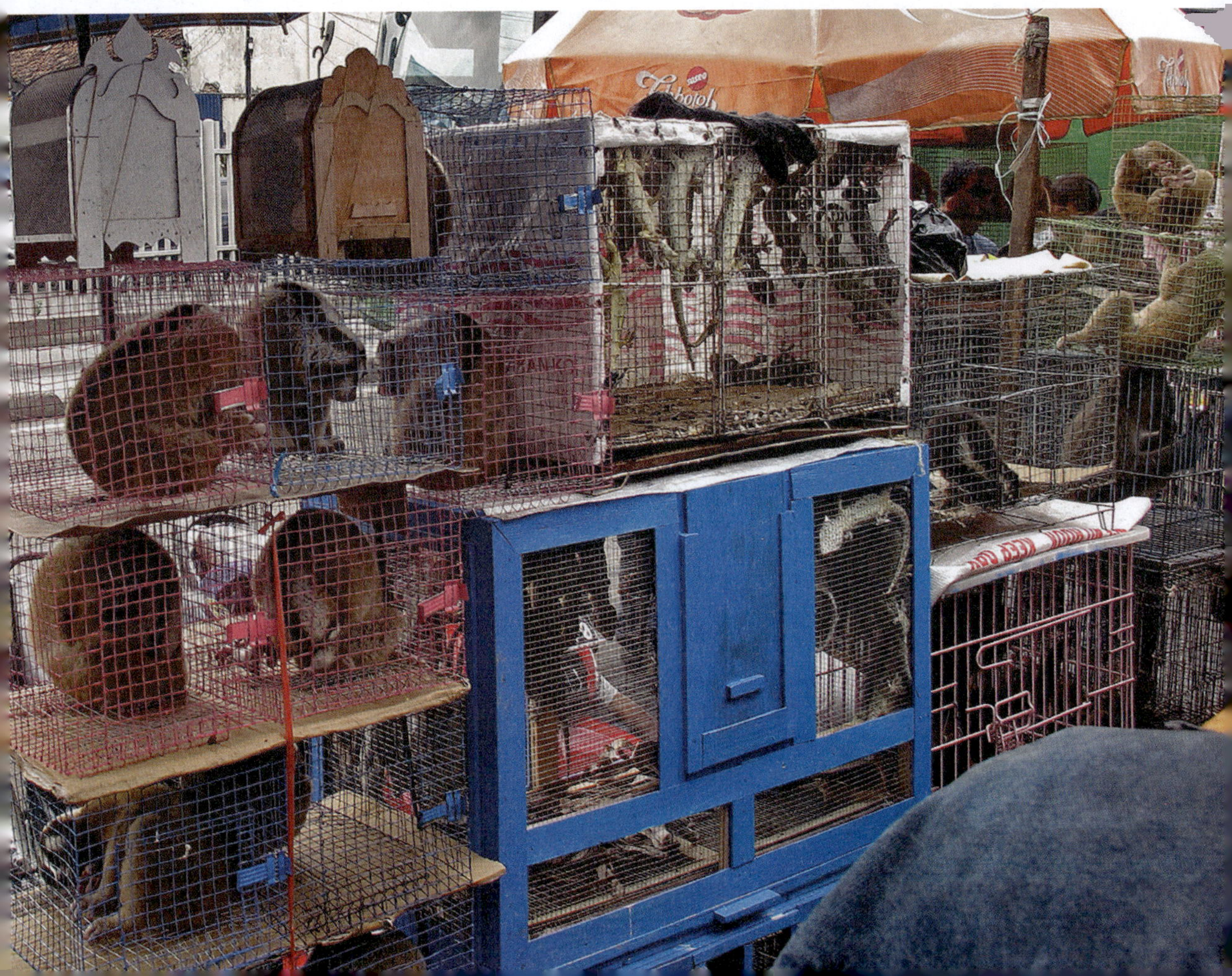

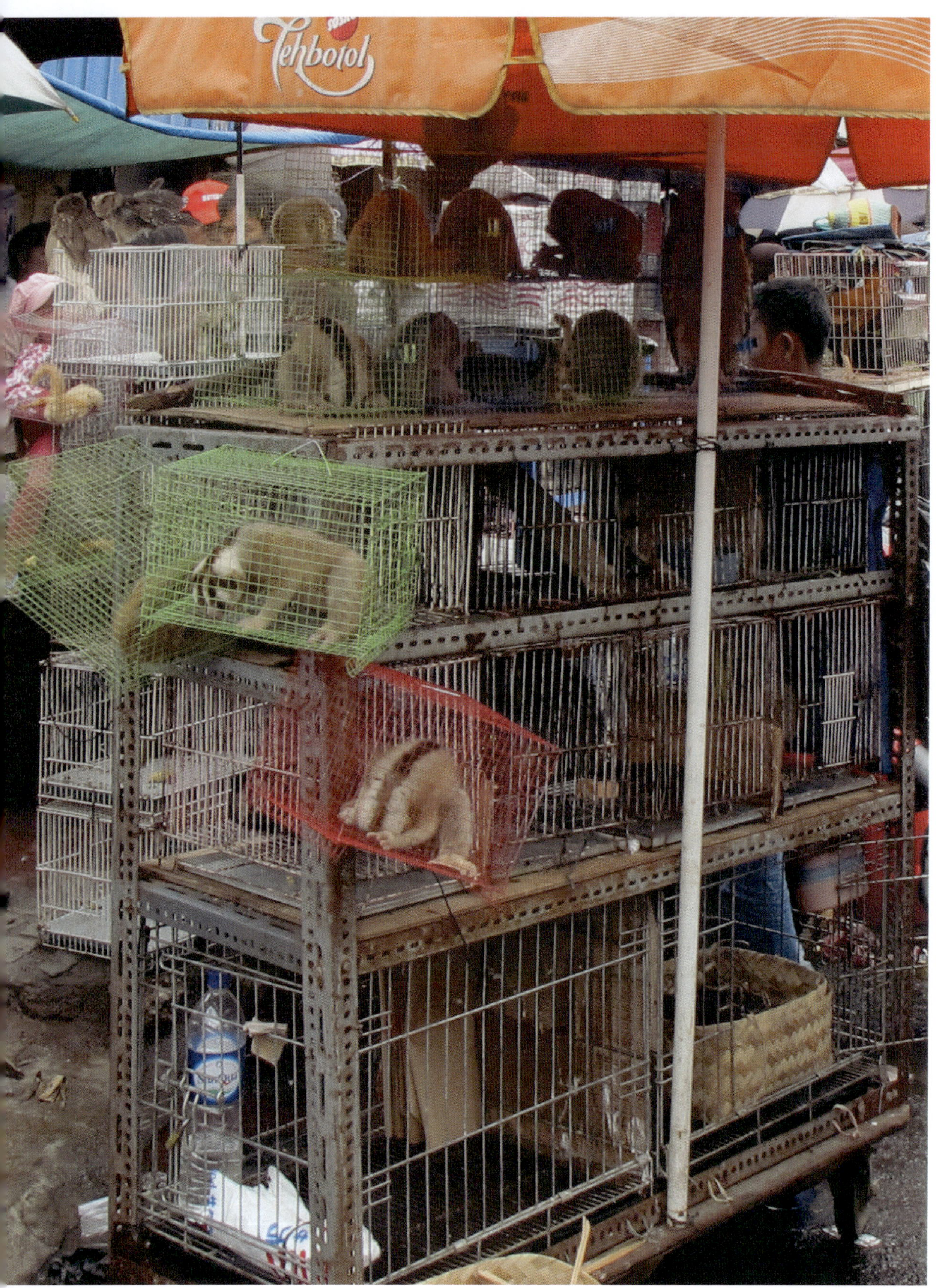

Tehbotol

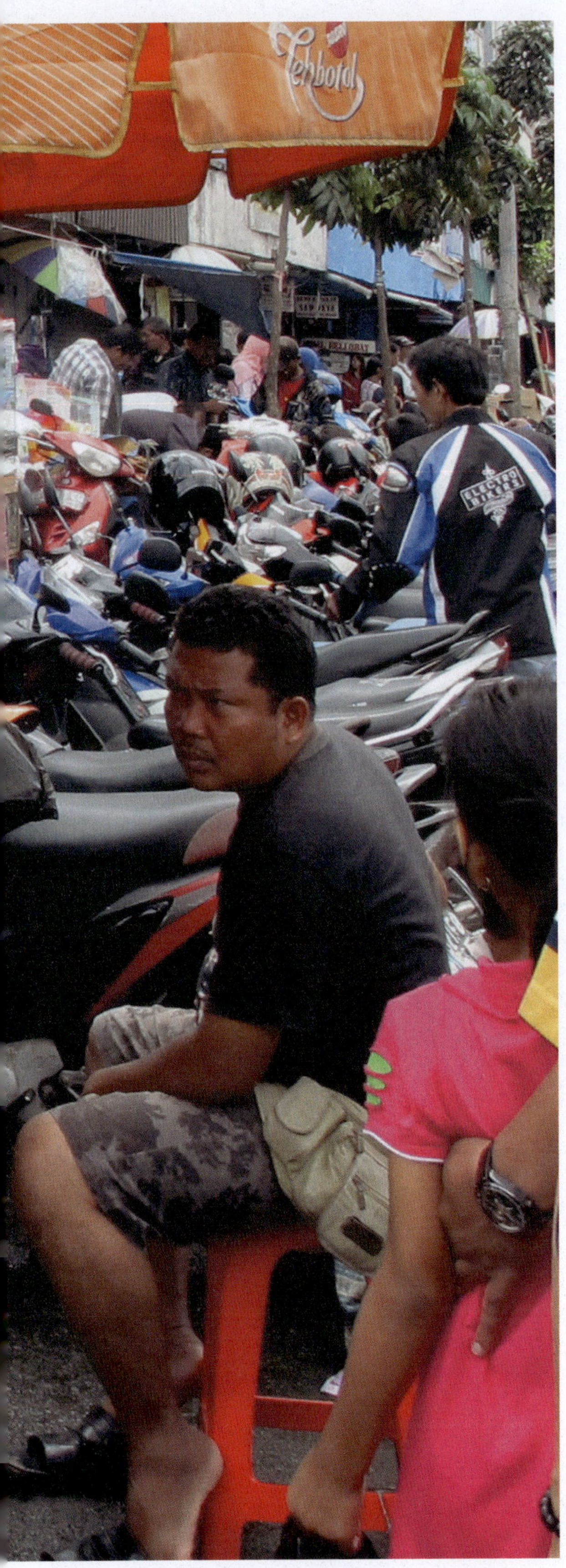

As the group moved forward, we passed a second set of lorises in cages, being sold by another stall-holder. I could see the small creatures hunched up on twigs, their large eyes beaming out at the horror of humans laughing at them.

I managed to take twenty or so frames before I was spotted. This time, the stallholder didn't shout, just calmly drew a black cloth over his illegal merchandise.

I had come round in a circle and the larger collection of lorises was now only a few yards away, at the junction of the main road and a smaller street that led into the market maze of small cabins.

I was sure I hadn't been seen. I checked my camera, took three strides forward and pressed the shutter. Ten seconds went by—ages in the world of digital cameras—before I was seen by motorbike man and the stallholder. Both men made to come at me, but I nipped down the side street. Shouts rang out as I blundered through the crowds. Luckily, none of them tried to stop me but hurled insults at me for running into them and getting in their way.

After a minute or so I stopped and looked back. I couldn't see anyone chasing me but I didn't want to take any chances. The maze of cabins around me was vast and filled with all kinds of creatures, some of which looked deformed. It was a harrowing sight but my main problem was how to get out without going past the loris stall again.

I turned up a lane towards a modern eight-storey building, but instead of leading me back to the main city streets, the lane became darker and narrower until it stopped at a dead end. I was trapped: tat was probably why they weren't chasing me. Then I noticed a door behind the last stall on the lane. Surely it must lead somewhere.

An old woman was sitting at the stall. Desperate to escape, I used hand gestures to communicate that I had to get through. She swung out her arm to usher me in.

What greeted me inside was my idea of Hell—a shop full of spiders, of all shapes, colours and sizes. I love all kinds of animals but I have a real fear of arachnids.

I tried to fix my gaze on the door at the far end of the shop and lunged forward but couldn't help spotting what looked like the biggest tarantula known to man. I howled in fear and pushed the door hard. It sprung open and I burst through it, still screaming.

In contrast to the dark and narrow lane, I found myself in the central aisle of a shopping centre. Passersby stopped to look at this sweaty Western man screaming like a baby. I sheepishly made my way back to find Caroline, but she had gone. I didn't blame her.

Back in London I placed the set of loris photographs with the *Sun*. It used half a page of pictures with a story about a famous singer tickling one of the poor animals. It had been bought for her as a present.

Bears and the Soviet legacy

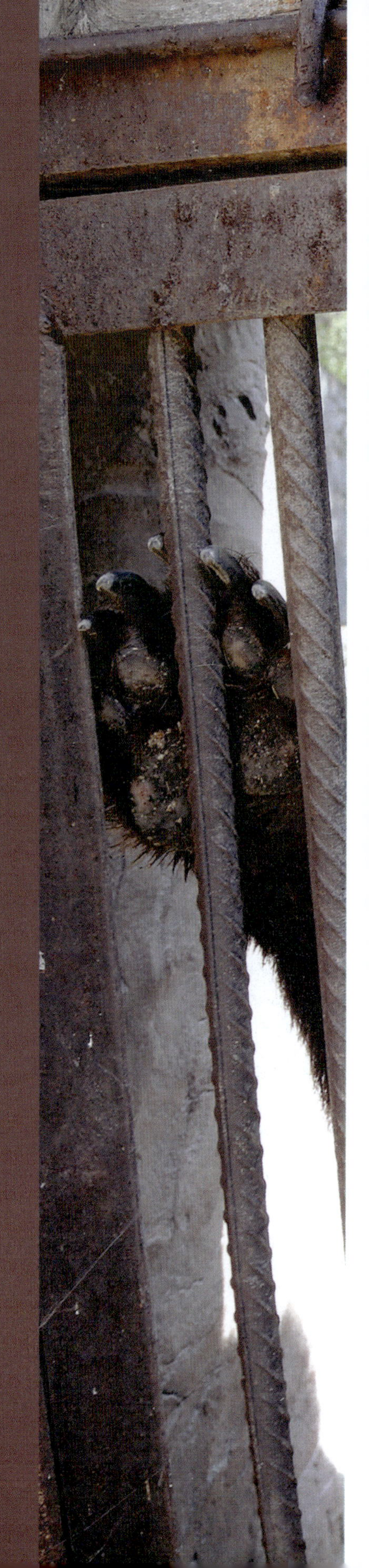

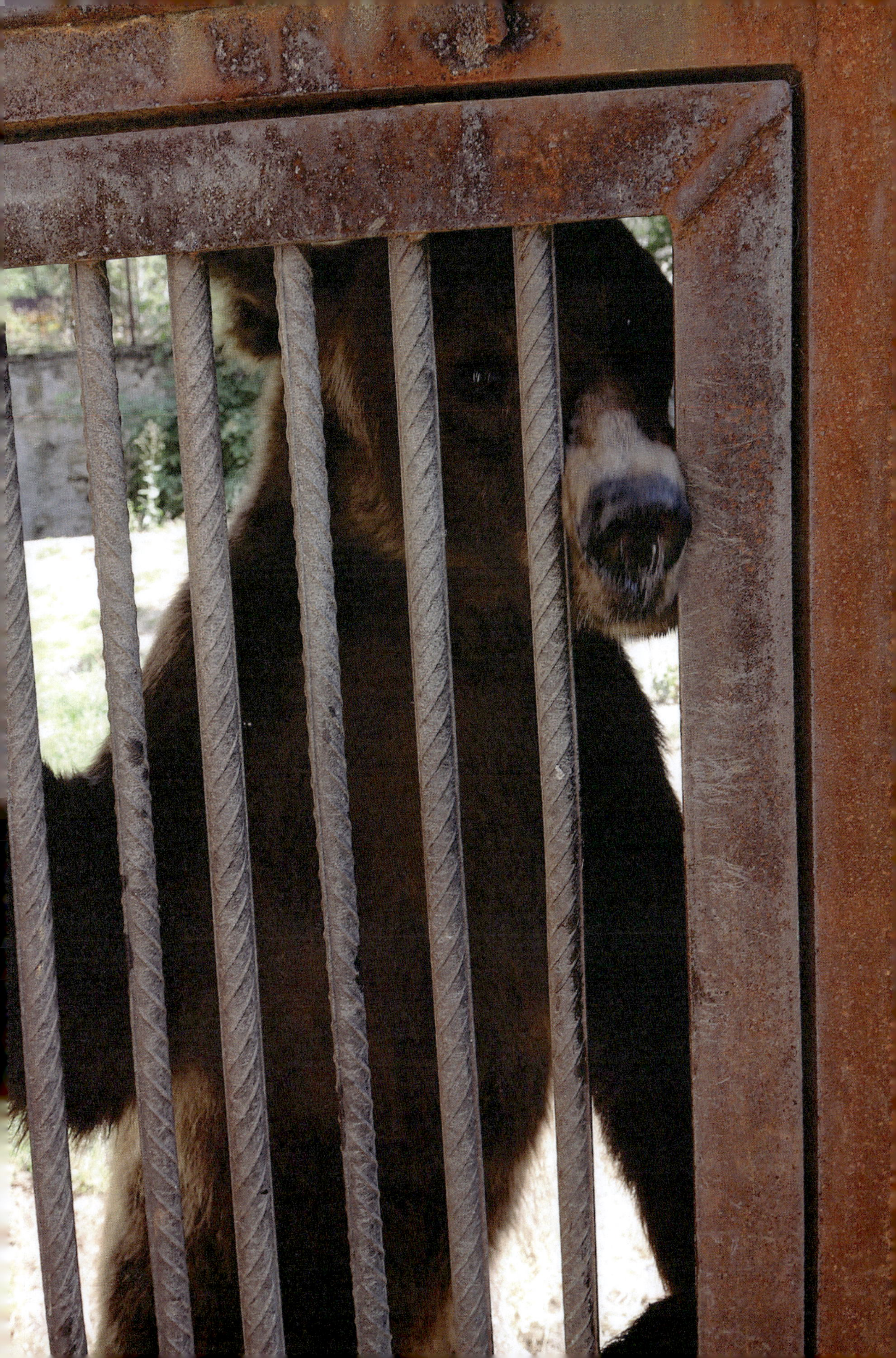

Bears and the Soviet legacy

The former Communist leaders in Eastern Europe loved life's luxuries—as long as it was for themselves—like drinking Armenian brandy or eating Black Sea caviar, while the mass of the population lived lives of impoverishment and drudgery. The top brass also loved hunting and would kill anything that moved in the countryside, especially great big brown bears.

The notorious Romanian dictator Nicolae Ceausescu was said to have an insatiable hunger for shooting bears, and ensured that bears from his own country were airlifted to the dense forests of the Rhodope Mountains in southern Bulgaria, so he could go hunt what he most enjoyed hunting as often as he liked, even when he was abroad.

There could hardly be a more remote spot than the Rhodope Mountains. The nearest town is Devin, a spa resort close to the caves where, according to ancient Greek myth, Orpheus had descended into the underworld to rescue his wife from Hades. It seems like a fitting place for corrupt officials to inflict suffering on wild animals.

When Bulgaria joined the European Union in 2007, one of the conditions was that the government ban the breeding of bears to be shot. This meant that Komishosh, a barbaric breeding facility high in the woods, was abandoned, leaving seven bears to be looked after by one elderly woman, Rositsa Zdravkov.

The plight of the bears at the deserted facility came to my notice through Anthony, a vet working in Bulgaria's capital, Sofia. He had heard about me after I had worked on the story about the bear-baiting in Ukraine, and had tracked me down via the *Daily Mail* offices.

Before long I was standing in the blazing heat of a street in Sofia, waiting for the vet to turn up.

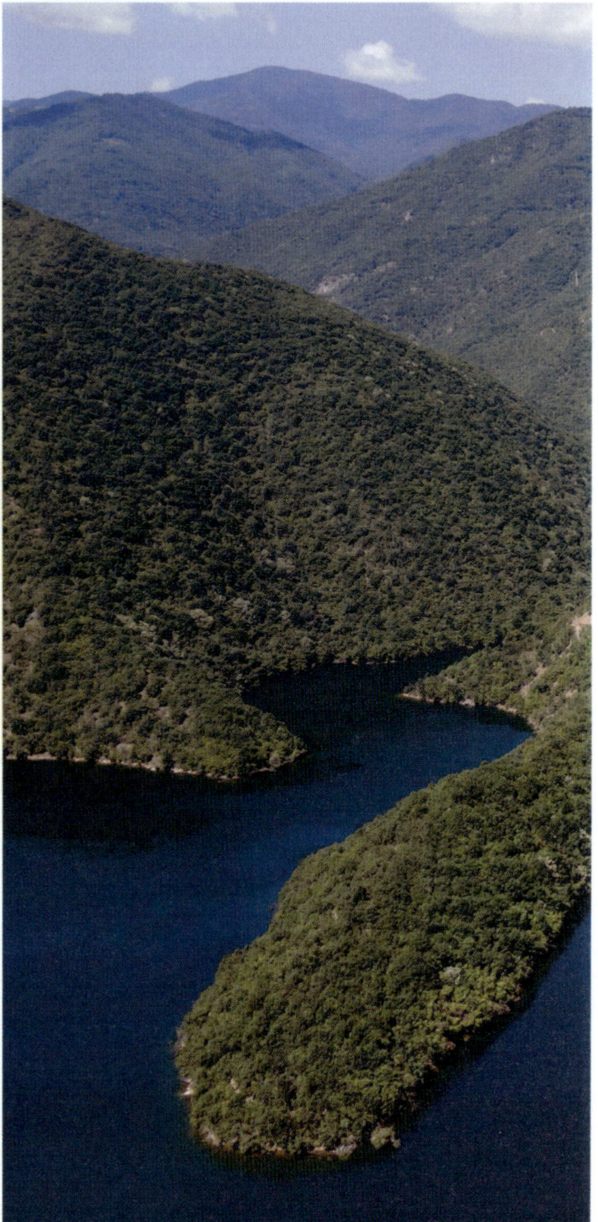

For some reason I had been expecting a man of about forty-five years and wearing a suit. Instead, the person who came skidding to a halt on a mountain bike was dressed in battle fatigues and much younger.

Anthony led me to a battered old Lada Niva and drove for two hours at breakneck speed on the main highway towards Plovdiv, before turning onto a single-lane country road that turned out to be a main route for lorries going to and from the Greek border. From the way he zigzagged between the juggernauts, I guessed his spare-time hobby was playing Russian roulette. I resigned myself to dying on a boiling hot day in the back of beyond.

A narrow road led up through the mountains in a long sequence of hairpin bends, flanked on both

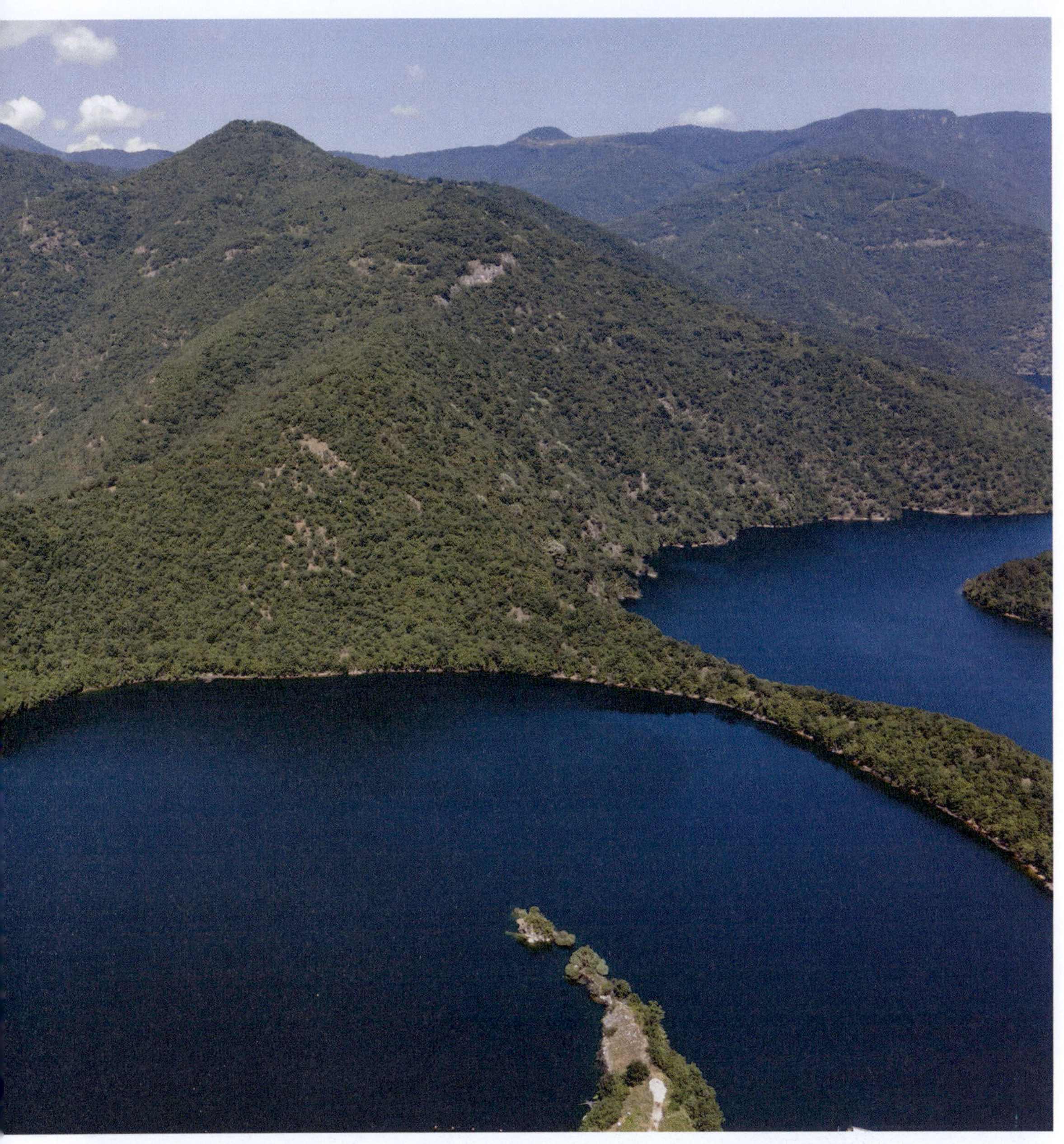

sides by steep, freshly exposed, dynamited rock faces. When the view eventually opened up, we found ourselves facing the spectacular sight of a mountain reservoir held back by a towering concrete dam, the largest of Bulgaria's fifty such structures. The sun played on the water and millions of pine trees formed a curtain around the edges. If this had been anywhere else, it would have boasted a marina with sailing boats, lakeside bars and restaurants, but here, nothing moved on the water. A sense of emptiness made it feel very eerie.

Finally, we bumped our way up a rutted track. Small streams ran through undisturbed woodland, which opened out into meadows beneath a vertical rock face.

'We are here,' announced Anthony.

A run-down house stood in a derelict courtyard, a line of smoke drifting from its chimney. Beside it was a row of low concrete buildings with a series of corroding metal gates. This was where the bears were kept.

A woman, Rositsa, emerged from the house and chatted with Anthony while I sat looking up at the towering cliffs, watching large birds of prey swooping overhead. Every now and then one of them would fold back its wings and dive at a seemingly impossible speed towards an unseen prey. Goats pottered about on rocky ledges. looking as if they would topple to their deaths at any moment. No sound could be heard: no traffic, no aircraft, no everyday babble.

Rositsa served us coffee with a dash of cinnamon,

accompanied by cake with chunks of apple poking out of the top. After the long and unnerving drive, it was the perfect combination.

Then it was time to see the bears.

Instead of going into the concrete buildings, we walked round them into the meadow. There I could see a line of ten huge concrete pits extending out of the buildings. Each one had housed a bear, but now only four were occupied. At the back of each pen was a rusty gate leading to the bear's night quarters.

As we walked up to an occupied pit an enormous bear popped up on his hind legs, and I said hello—in English. This seemed to astonish the bear, and he stepped back with his arms outstretched, like Tommy Cooper about to tell a joke. His name was Milcho and he was fourteen years old.

Rositsa joined us at the fence and spoke calmly to the animal, which relaxed and dropped onto all fours. She took what seemed to be a ball of grass from under her many skirts and threw it to the bear. With incredible dexterity he stood up and caught it, turning away quickly to eat what he'd received.

Anthony explained that the grass had been packed with meat and maize to supplement the bear's diet. It was obvious that these bears would not have survived without Rositsa.

The next two pens were empty, but the last one housed another large bear—Gosho, aged twelve. He didn't seem to notice me as I started taking pictures. He was lost in his own little world.

Anthony explained that these bears were the offspring of the ones that had been bred for hunting.

'They have never walked on grass, climbed a tree or hunted for food,' he said. 'Their whole lives have been spent in these concrete pens. They just sit here, watching the seasons drift by. They watch the birds come and go, the trees bloom and shed their leaves; they watch the snow, the rain and the blazing sun, but nothing ever changes for them. If they don't get moved soon, they will die here.'

It was a heartfelt speech, and it moved me. The animals had been born into a life of passivity and boredom. They enjoyed no interaction with any other animals. They were simply waiting for death.

Anthony then led me through the meadow towards a dilapidated barn. As we approached slowly, he told me to be quiet. A terrible smell emanated from the barn and thousands of flies swarmed round us. Anthony put his finger to his lips to tell me not to speak.

In one wall of the barn was a six-foot metal door topped with a grille of welded metal bars. As Anthony moved towards the door, I raised my camera to my eye. Just as I focused on the opening, a massive paw slammed into the gate, making it shudder. A split second later a bear's face appeared at the grille.

The bear was very agitated: a white foam had formed around his mouth and he kept punching his paw into the metal door. He poked his long snout through the bars at the top, snorting loudly.

Anthony said the bear was suffering from a nasty parasitic infection. The effects sounded horrendou. If he didn't get treatment soon, he'd die in weeks.

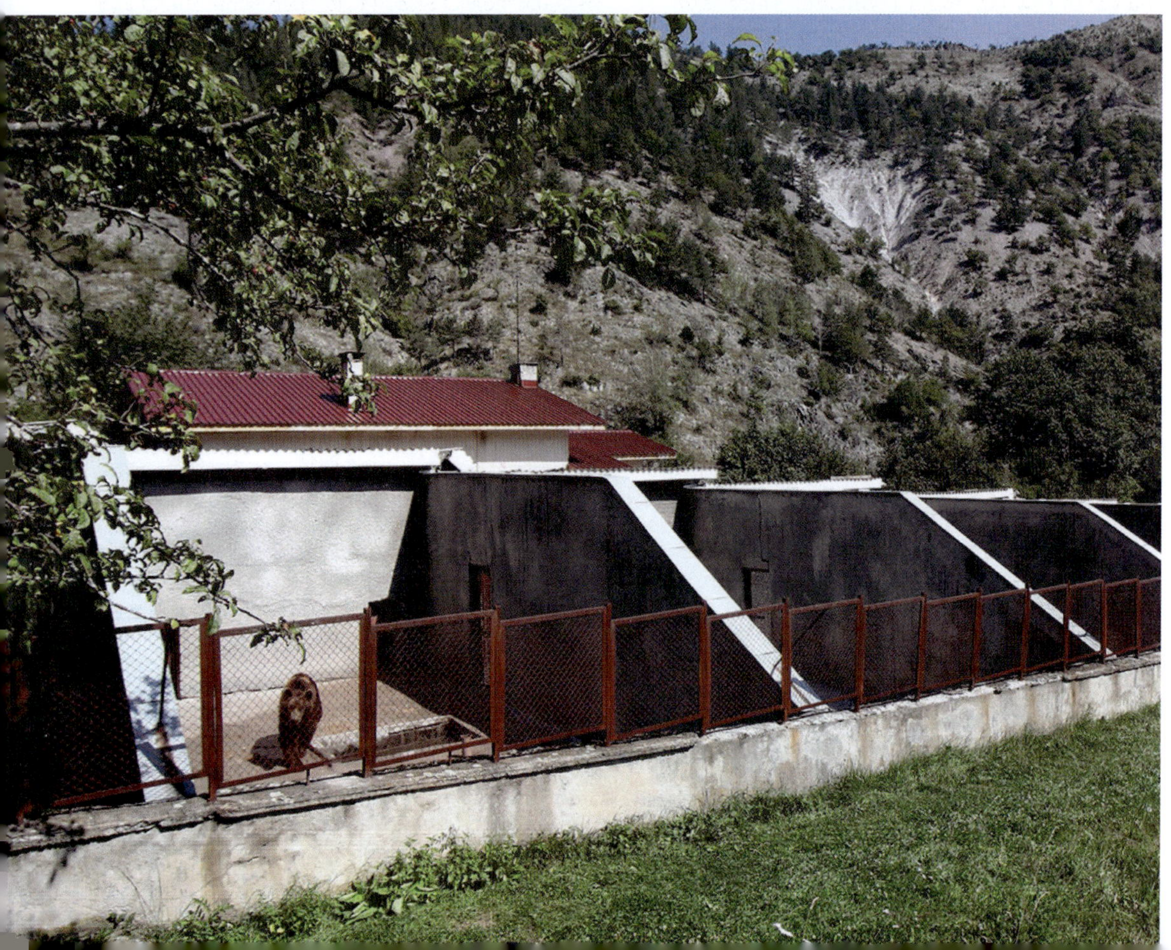

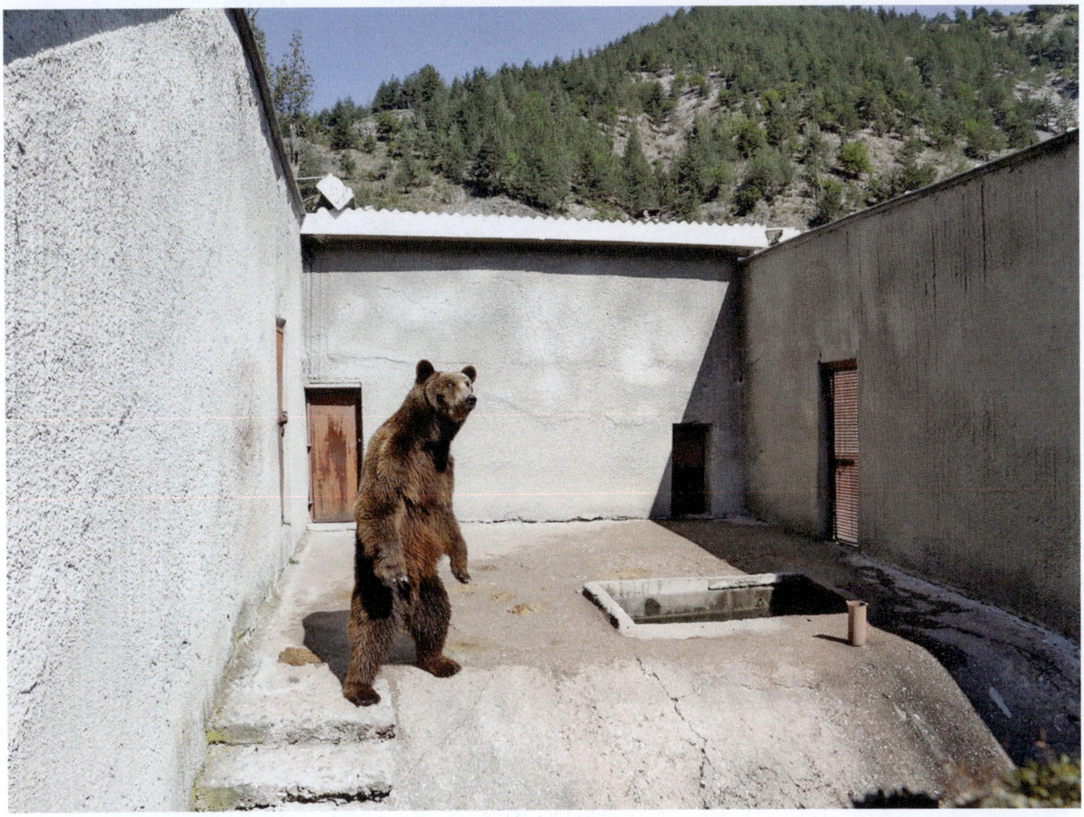

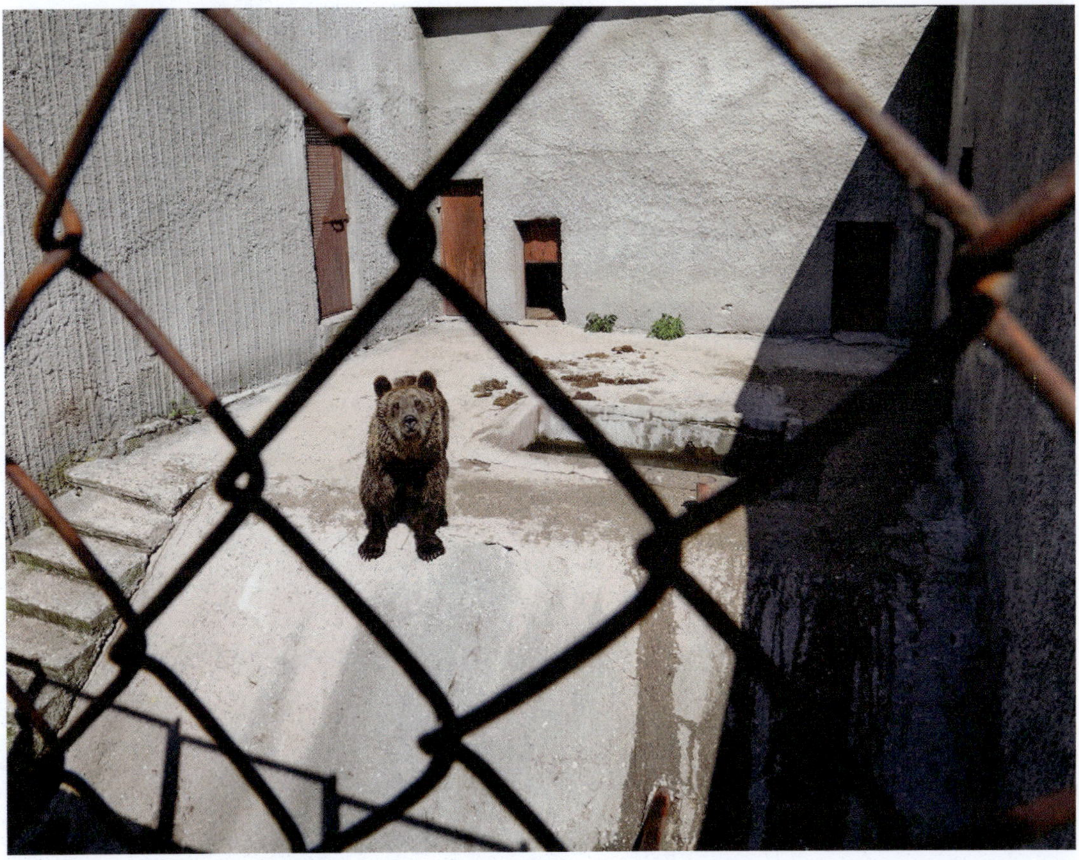

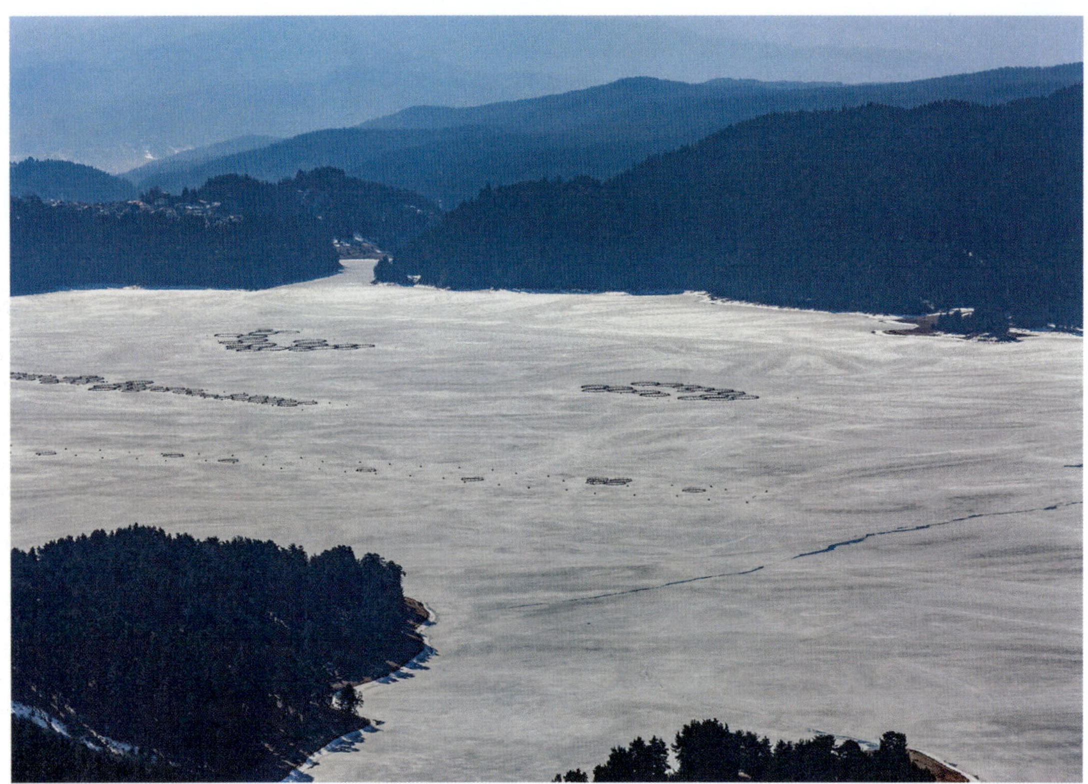

It was time to head back to Sofia, a city I had only visited once before, during the Romanian revolution of Christmas 1989, after the country's Communist dictator, Nicolae Ceauşescu, had been toppled. I now sat drinking coffee on one of the city's wide boulevards as smartly dressed couples strolled arm-in-arm past overflowing restaurants and large neon advertisements. It seemed a modern buzzy city, and a very far cry from the gloomy place I'd seen twenty-five years previously.

The *Daily Mirror* used my pictures to run a rescue appeal for the Kormisosh bears. Within weeks, a wildlife park in Kent agreed to take two of the bears, but it would be a few months before Milcho and Gosho would begin their journey to freedom.

In late October I was back in Bulgaria to cover their rescue. The Rhodope mountains looked very different at that time of year, with thick snow covering everything.

The plan was for Anthony to tranquillise the bears so that they could be loaded onto the back of a pick-up truck and driven down the rutted track to a large lorry that had been driven from the Netherlands. They would then start the long trek to Kent.

I arrived in Sofia and hired a four-wheel-drive to get to Kormisosh, where Rositsa's bears were. The road was just as scary as before, and I had to brake hard to avoid hitting a boulder as it rolled down a slope and landed right in front of me.

The *BBC One Show*, an early-evening programme on television, had taken up the story of the bears and had sent a crew over to film the rescue, accompanied by Peter Smith, the owner of the Kent wildlife park. We had arranged to meet at Peter's hotel, but I hadn't heard from him to finalise the details.

After some difficulty, I found my way to my hotel, one of many that specialised in accommodating tourists who enjoyed hunting and shooting wild animals: wild boar in particular but also red deer, fallow deer, roe deer, chamois, mouflon (wild sheep), capercaillie, wolf, wild cat, fox, marten—and brown bear: in short, a paradise for wildlife killers, all licensed by the state. It was not hard to see why the Ancient Greeks considered this region to be the home of Ares, the god of war.

Somehow, in spite of the atmosphere of officially sanctioned savagery, I got some sleep. At 8:00 the next morning it was still dark; the sun was hidden behind a huge mountain.

I still had not received any word back from Peter Smith. I drove round the empty town looking for signs of a film crew until I spotted a lorry with the picture of a bear on it, outside a shabby guest house. As I walked towards the front door, a group of people emerged laughing. Among them was the BBC film crew. They looked at me oddly.

It turned out that Peter was among them and that he had forgotten to call me. Upset at his lack of courtesy, I headed back to my car. One of the BBC reporters ran after me and asked if I knew where the bears were. They didn't know the way and wanted to follow me.

I drove off without waiting. In the mirror I could see the crew scrambling to get gear and people in their car.

On the way to the track leading up to the bears, I spotted Rositsa talking to a group of hunters and jumped out to greet her. Twenty minutes later we'd bumped up the track to the bear pits. The whole landscape had changed; under an overcast sky a veil of mist hung over the cliffs.

Anthony was already there with a team of assistants. We greeted each other warmly. Trays of tea, coffee and cake were brought out for the assembled team. It was like nectar, a very welcome breakfast after the scares and irritations of the previous twenty-four hours.

The two bears had been kept in their night quarters ready for the rescue. After a lot of toing and froing, the team were ready to dart the first bear, Milcho, and wait for the tranquilliser to take effect. It was so dark inside the bear den that there was no point trying to take pictures until they brought him out into the open.

When the animal was sedated, six burly men slid Milcho onto a thick blanket and hauled him one step closer to freedom. I got pictures of them manhandling the unconscious bear onto the open back of the pick-up. The vets worked on him, monitoring his heart rate and shaving his fur to insert a drip. They gave his paws, feet, teeth and eyes a thorough examination ahead of the two-day drive.

His general health was deemed to be good. His teeth had been worn down where he'd gnawed the bars of his cage in frustration, but all in all he was good to go. With a towel placed over his eyes he was off down the track to be transferred to the air-conditioned lorry.

Back at the concrete enclosure, Gosho had already been darted, and the whole process was repeated. Within an hour of us arriving, the two bears were ready for the off. The group of men who'd carried out the bears were laughing and congratulating themselves on a job well done.

I went in search of Rositsa to say thank you for the coffee and cake and to wish her good luck. I found her standing alone in the darkened alley outside the empty bear cages. She was looking into the distance and seemed to be crying. I backed away, leaving her to her thoughts of better times and caring for her beloved bears. She must have known that they were on their way to a better life, but that made it no easier for her at that moment.

Six weeks later Milcho and Gosho arrived in Kent. When they were let out of their quarantine enclosure, Milcho was the first to run through the metal gate. Initially, he was all caution—looking, sniffing, not trusting anything—but gradually he stepped further and further into his new world, a purpose-built environment with trees to climb, ponds to sit in, bushes to hide in, wooden dens to snooze in and best of all room to roam.

The *Mirror* used five of my pictures from that day, including ones that showed the big bear high up a tree trunk, sitting in one of the ponds and standing on a large rock looking majestic. The headline read 'ROAM FROM HOME: World's saddest bears get new lease of life in UK'. The surprise call I had received from Anthony months earlier had led to a very gratifying outcome for these two descendants of hunting targets.

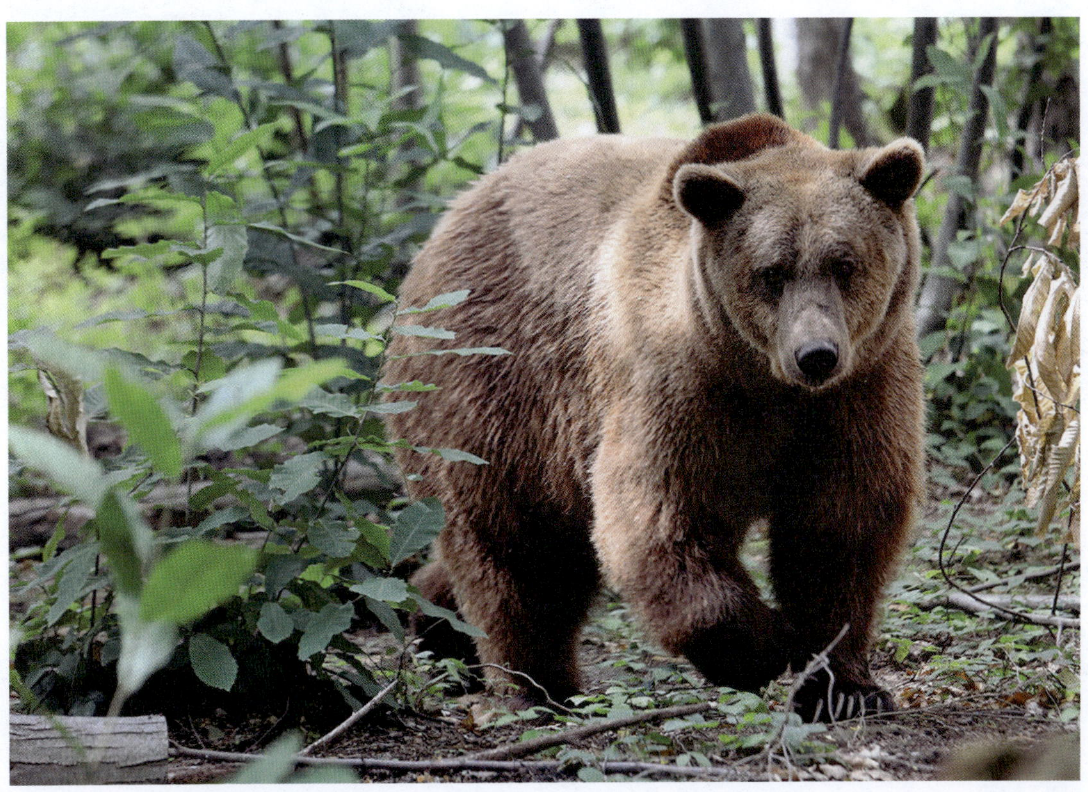

Dog catchers in paradise

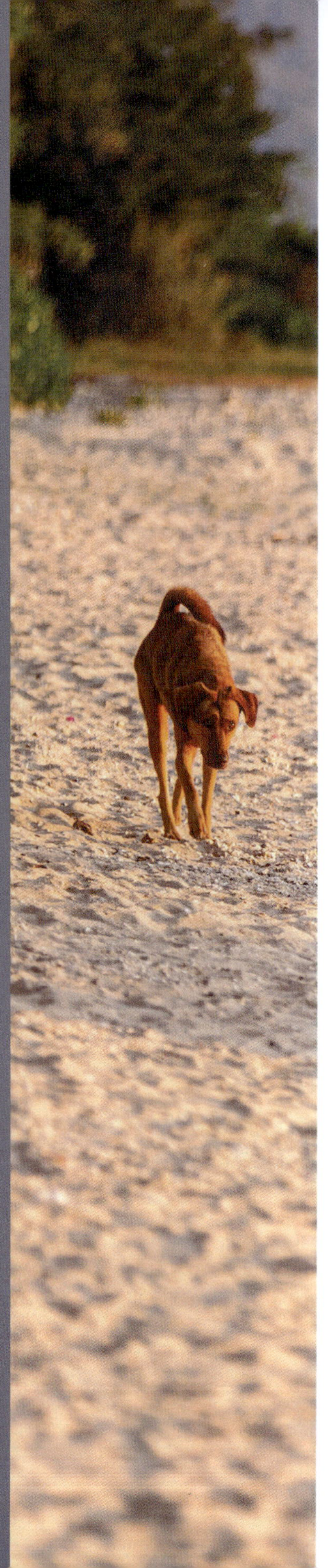

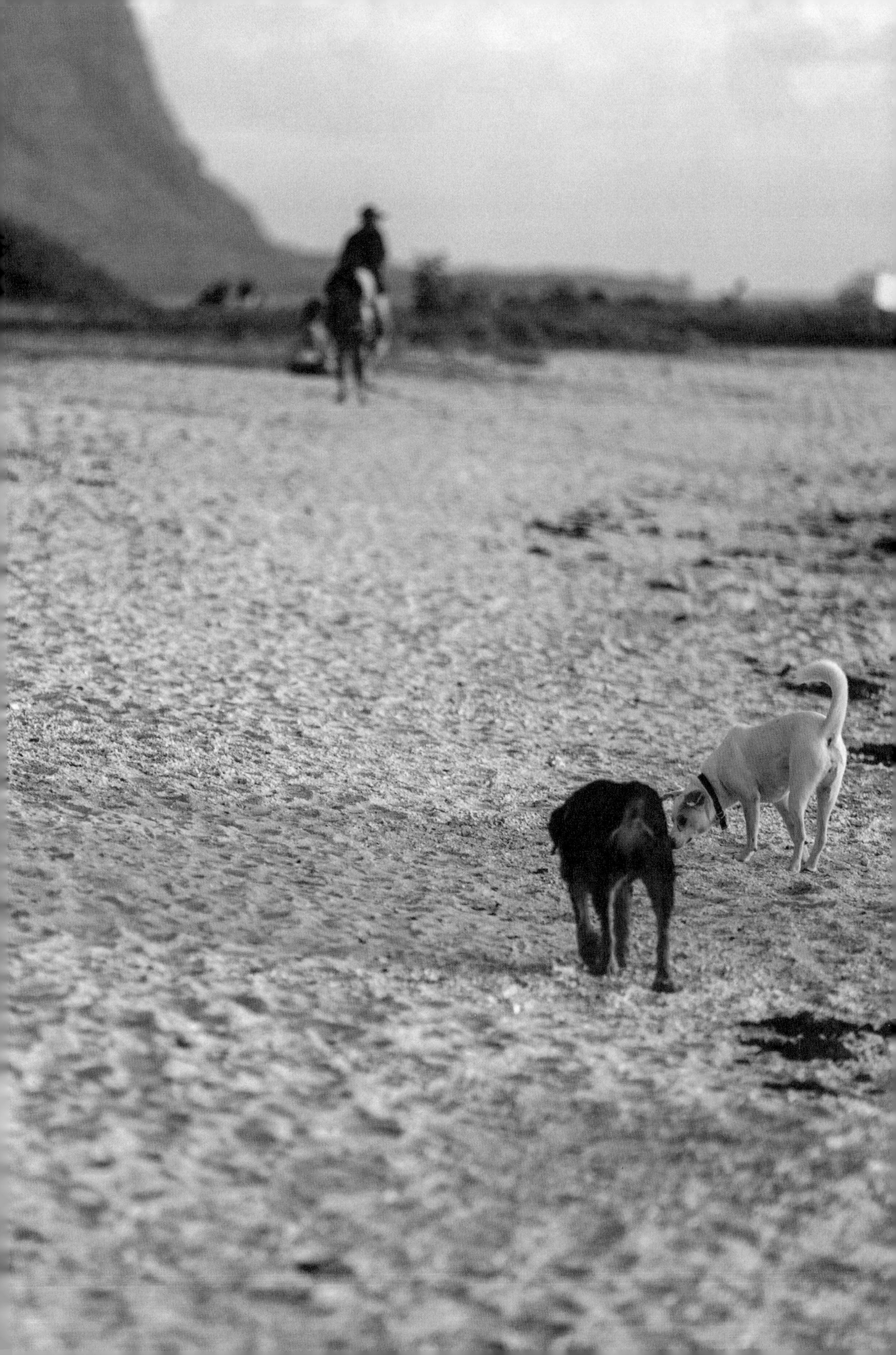

Dog catchers in paradise

The beautiful island of Mauritius is home to year-round sunshine, white sandy beaches, a multicultural population and luxury hotels. It's also a honeymooners' paradise and British Airways flies direct from London. What's not to like?

Government-funded dog snatching, that's what. I received a video from IAR's Alan Knight that shocked me. The twenty-four-second clip shows the catch-and-kill squad doing their work: a van sweeps into view, a man jumps out carrying a large net and, in one movement, a snoozing dog is scooped up and thrown inside the vehicle. The door slams shut and the van moves off.

The whole thing takes less than thirteen seconds.

It was a slick operation and, according to Alan's information, the team was catching as many as forty dogs a day and putting them down, regardless of whether they were strays or pets. The more dogs they caught, the more they got paid.

I did some research and discovered Birgit Wellmann, a German vet who had been highlighting the barbaric practice. She had lived on the island for three years, becoming more and more enraged at the government's catch-and-kill policy. She was now so upset that she was going to be leaving the island for good and returning to Germany in seven weeks' time.

I flew out with reporter Allan Hall and Birgit met

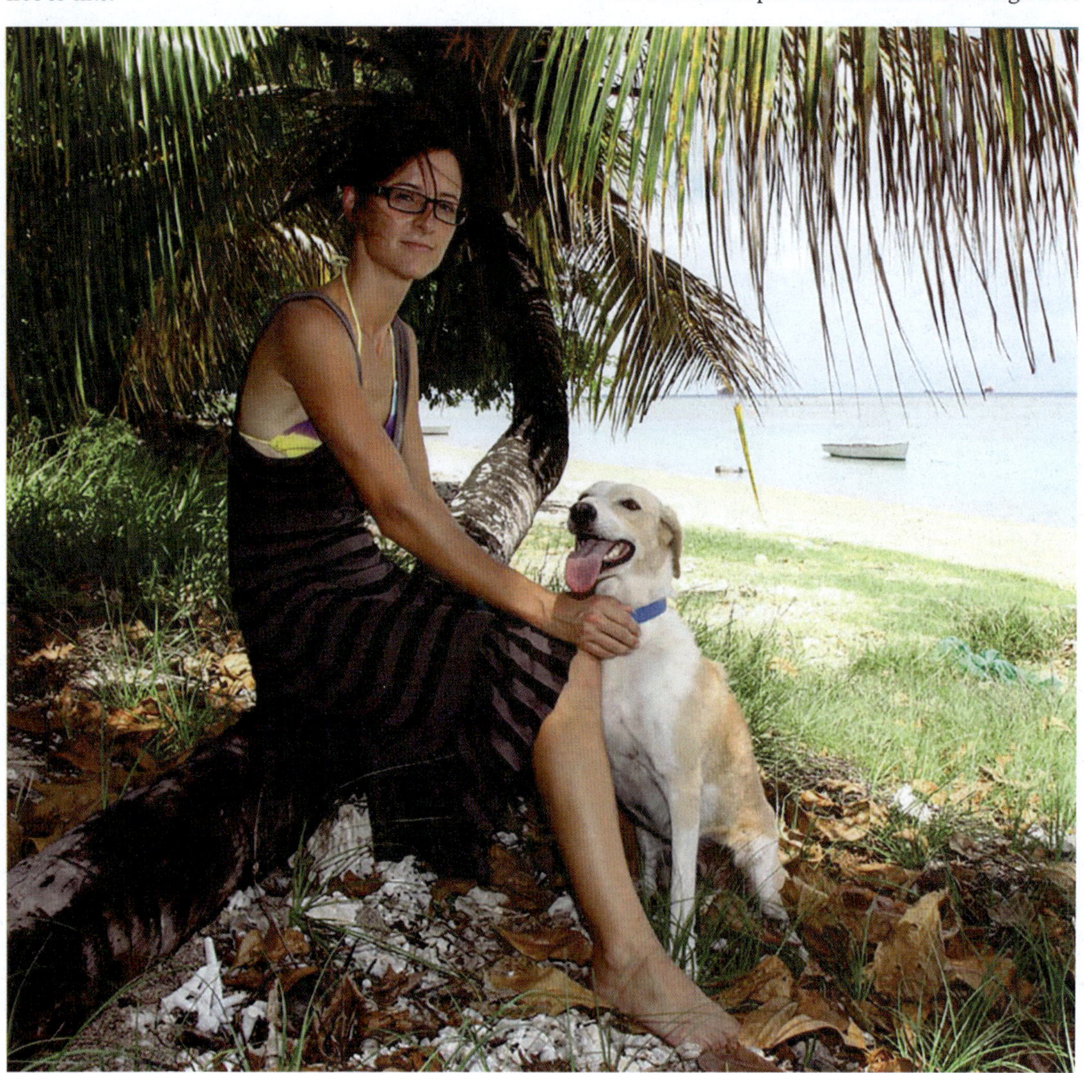

us at the airport. 'The Mauritian Society for the Prevention of Cruelty to Animals (MSPCA) is the official body charged with looking after animals on the island,' she told us, 'but they drive around in an official van stealing dogs from people's gardens and verandas and the grass verges outside their homes.'

She said that the government saw dogs as a problem for the tourist trade, even though tourists generally liked them. Instead of the indiscriminate culling, she had been campaigning for a neutering programme but her pleas had fallen on deaf ears.

If pet owners believed their dog had been taken by the dog catchers, they had only one chance to get them back: they had to go to the pound immediately and pay a £30 ransom. As the average monthly wage on Mauritius was only £60, this option was only open to the better-off. In order to expose this to the world, we decided we had to get into the pound where the dogs ended up after being snatched from the street.

Early the next morning Birgit, Allan and I set off to a shabby neighbourhood three miles from the centre of Port Louis, where the pound was located. Our plan was to watch the place, to get a feel for what went on.

We found an area roughly 400 by 300 yards enclosed by high chain-link fencing. Within it stood a group of shabby one-storey buildings and a maze of holding pens. The barking and howling from the pens could be heard in the nearby streets.

There was no vantage point from which to get a shot of the conditions inside the pound so I walked with Birgit through the patched-up front gates of the MSPCA compound and into the admin building. Our story was that we were a couple looking for our dog, Rex. I had my phone in my top pocket with the lens pointing outwards, set to take a burst of pictures every twenty seconds. It meant that many of the photos I got came out blurred.

We handed our passports to the woman behind the reception desk and were taken through to the pens. The first sight to greet us was a cage containing twenty puppies. Next to that was a crate in which a dog was in the throes of dying. A stream of liquid leaked from its broken body.

A hundred yards further on, we walked into the breeze-block pens holding the dogs that had been rounded up. This was the MSPCA's death row, an extermination camp for dogs. A combined stench of disinfectant, faeces and vomit wafted in the air, making my stomach heave.

We looked into the first pen, shouting for Rex, and a happy-looking dog jumped up to the barred front of the pen. I leaned forward to make sure my phone was pointing at the dog, while in the background twenty others looked on with fear in their eyes. A wide assortment of large friendly dogs and small well-groomed pooches cowered at the back of the concrete area. Many of them had collars on; these were clearly treasured pets, loved by their owners but now awaiting the death sentence. It was truly heartbreaking.

I was desperate to know whether my phone was properly recording the scene of horror, but I couldn't risk taking it out and looking, so we moved on to the next compound, where a large man stood with a pole topped with a wire noose. I stood up straight to aim the phone lens at him.

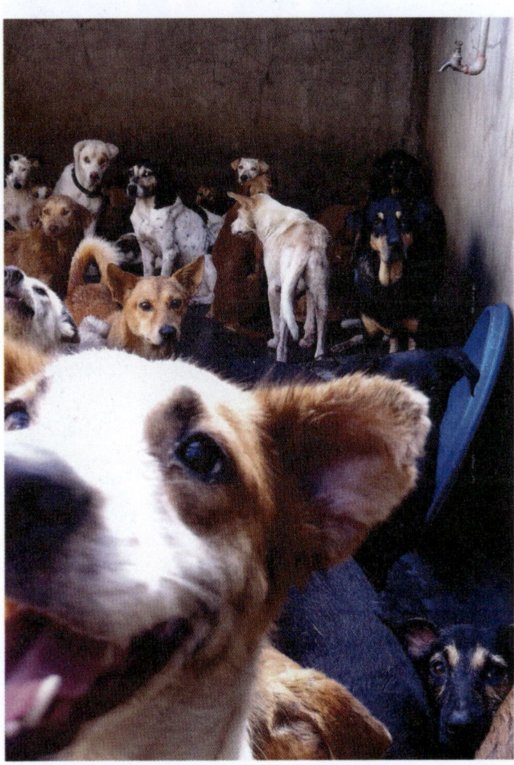

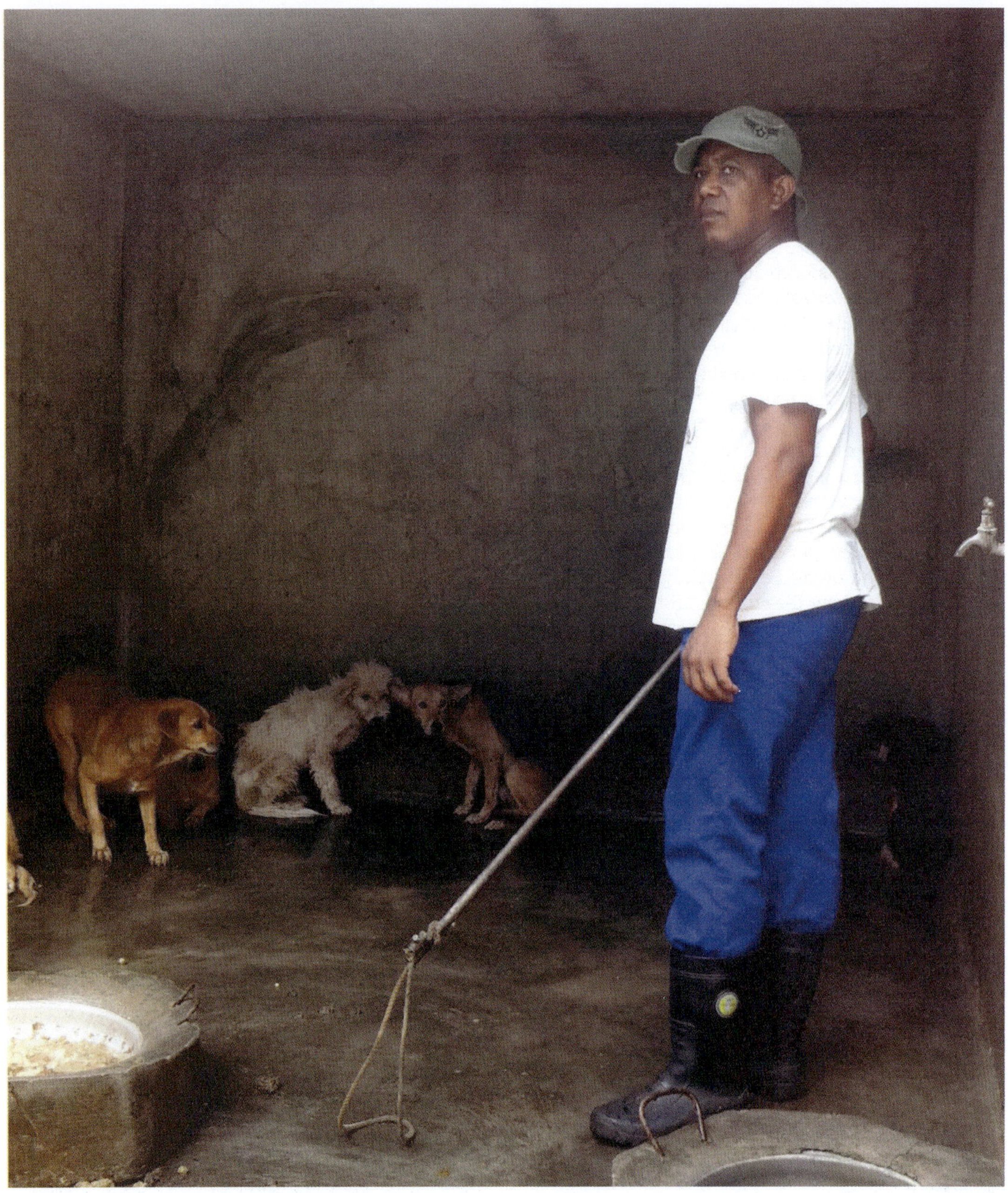

In the dark corner of the sparse pen were five dogs with their ears down and their eyes on the man with the pole. They knew what was coming.

The man shouted at us. Even though we tried to keep up the pretence of looking for Rex, he suspected we were taking pictures and told us to leave. We turned on our heels and walked back to collect our passports. I thought I was going to throw up at the gut-wrenching sights we had witnessed; Birgit was visibly upset.

The phone had done its work and recorded it all. The only thing missing was the dog-catcher vans. Nothing looked remotely like what I'd seen in the video clip but Birgit was determined to find out where they were.

Shortly before six o'clock the next morning, the three of us and two of Birgit's friends drove in two cars to the town of Beau Bassin-Rose Hill in the middle of the island. We saw a mixture of run-down homes, small shops and state-of-the-art office blocks set in open parkland.

Birgit and I drove past the town's MSPCA offices while Allan and the other two waited near the entrance. I looked through the fence and spotted two dog vans, so it looked like we might get the evidence we needed.

We'd been told that the catch-and-kill team started work early, but that wasn't the case this morning. An hour went by with no movement; then Allan called. Two vans had emerged from the yard:

he was tailing them. The game was on, and Birgit and I needed to join the chase.

After thirty minutes getting lost in the labyrinth of streets and rush-hour traffic, we spotted the other car parked outside a large house. A dog van was pulled up a hundred yards further down the road.

A man dressed in a red-and-yellow high-vis jacket jumped out of the van and strode up the driveway of a detached house. Birgit moved the car so I could get a good sight of what was going on.

I took ten frames as the dog catcher pulled his noose tight round a dog's neck. Before he could see us, Birgit drove on with Allan following.

'That dog was somebody's pet. It was on their drive,' Birgit said, shaking her head in despair.

The van carried on up the road. Birgit and her friends had to go, so Allan and I carried on the chase together. I already had pictures of the pound, the van and the dog being taken from the driveway. All I needed now was one of the team using a net to scoop up a dog beside the road, like I had seen in the video clip.

We followed at a distance that wouldn't alert the dog catchers of our presence, which became more difficult as the houses thinned out and we drove along straight roads between open fields. Before long, I think they knew we were watching them.

The man in the high-vis jacket stood on a running board at the back of the van, the big net in his hand. He scanned the pavements, gardens and grass verges for the sight of any dogs.

On a lonely road outside the town of Black River, the van pulled to a halt in a dusty lay-by, turned and faced us. Allan stopped the car. We sat looking at each other for five whole minutes before the van sped towards us with clouds of dust rising from its spinning tyres. Allan and I stood our ground and the van swerved round our car, the dog catchers shouting obscenities at us.

Now that our cover was blown, there was no point trying to hide, so Allan spun the car around and accelerated after the van. Keeping track of it was hard, back inside Rose Hill's maze of streets, as it often veered off without any notice. Allan tailed it until it disappeared.

We were stumped but cruised slowly up and down until we spotted the van hidden behind some tall bushes on a sunken driveway. It shot out onto the road again a hundred yards ahead of us.

After twenty minutes of cat-and-mouse pursuit, we rounded a corner to find the van stopped. The high-vis man was standing on the roadside, wielding his net.

Allan slammed on the brakes and I jumped out of the car just as the man approached a dog dozing on a pile of sand. I focused the camera and fired off a series of fifteen frames, capturing the whole sequence, the raising of the net, the swoop down over the sleeping dog and the animal being thrown into the van.

I had a good set of pictures and assumed we had wrapped the job up.

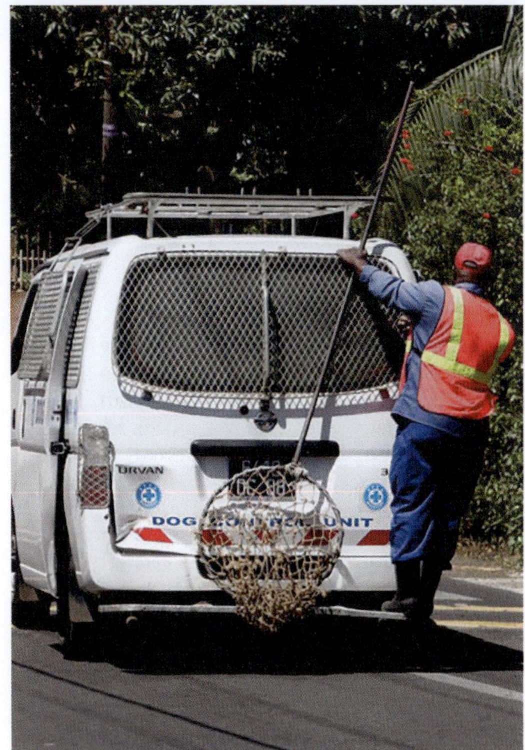

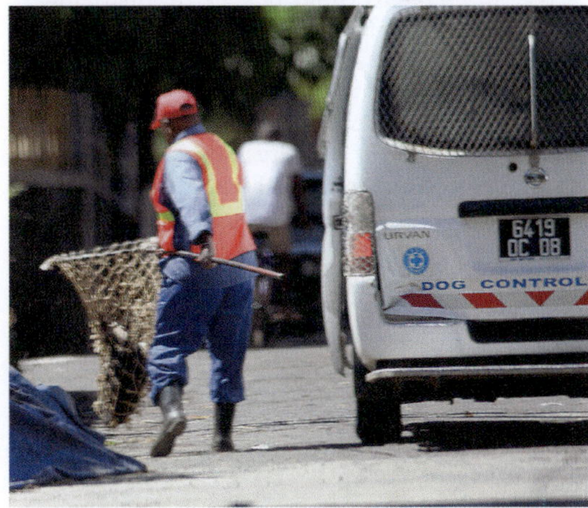

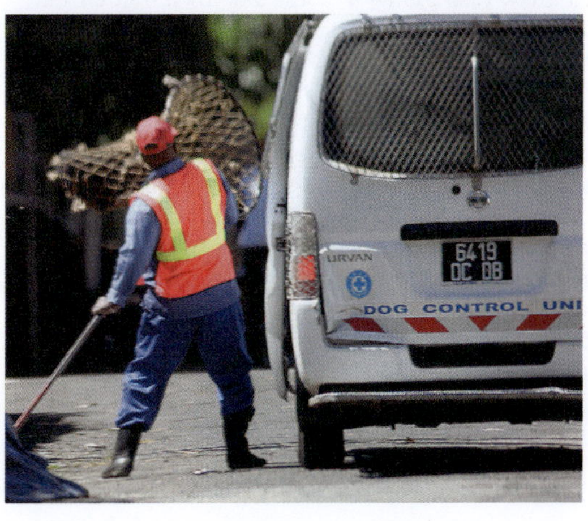

But that evening, Birgit joined us at the hotel and said she had discovered more. 'It seems that the bodies of the dogs killed at the pound are loaded onto a small truck and taken to the Bois Marchand graveyard in Terre Rouge, where they get dumped into open pits,' she said. It sounded not only barbaric but shameless.

For the third morning in a row, the three of us set out to capture evidence of this government-sponsored cruelty. We went direct to the Bois Marchand cemetery on the north-east edge of the capital. Meanwhile, Birgit's husband sat outside the dog pound in his own car, watching the lorry being loaded up with dead dogs. He was to follow it and call us once it had driven into the graveyard.

We walked between the graves of Hindus, Christians and people of other faiths. The graves all looked very orderly, with no open pits to be seen. I wondered if Birgit's informant had got the location wrong. The sun was high in the sky by the time we padded along an overgrown path through a broken gate that led to an open expanse of the rough red earth that gave the area its name, containing Chinese grave plots.

A mix of knotweed and tall grass covered most of the headstones, but we soon noticed piles of soil heaped up beside open pits. Birgit stooped down at one of the mounds and plucked a bone out from the dirt. It was the jawbone of a medium-sized dog. Casting an eye around the area, we could see more bones, fur and legs. It was a horror show.

A message pinged up on Birgit's phone. It was from her husband.

'The lorry is just coming through the front gates,' she breathed. 'We need to hide. If these guys see us, all Hell will break loose.'

Huddled behind some bushes, we watched as the lorry with its shiny blue tarpaulin bobbed its way between the headstones. It stopped in front of the pits and the driver reversed it so the rear was above the graves.

A man hopped out of the cab and pulled on a pair of heavy-duty plastic gloves. I recognised him at once from the dog pound—the man who had shouted at us to get out. A second man flipped open the truck's tailgate, and without further ado the two men leaned into the back of the lorry and started pulling out dead dogs.

The lorry was about a yard from the pit, so each time they pulled a dog out, it dropped onto the ground with a thud. It was like a scene from a horror movie. I bobbed up and took as many pictures as I could without being seen, recording three or four dogs being dispatched. It would all have been pointless—and dangerous—if we had been caught, so I lowered my camera as soon as I'd got what I thought was enough, and we slumped against a tree trunk waiting for the men to finish their macabre task.

When the lorry had driven away, we went to inspect the scene. The MSPCA workers had made only a cursory effort to cover the dogs. A quick

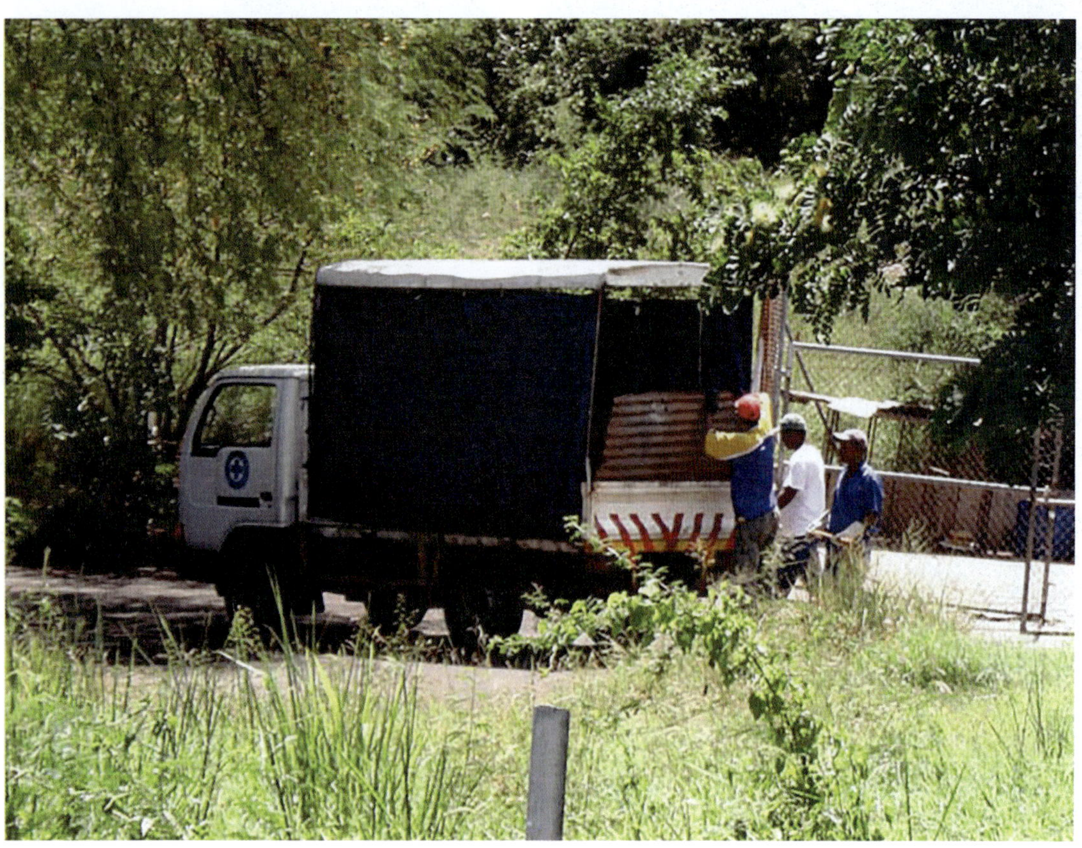

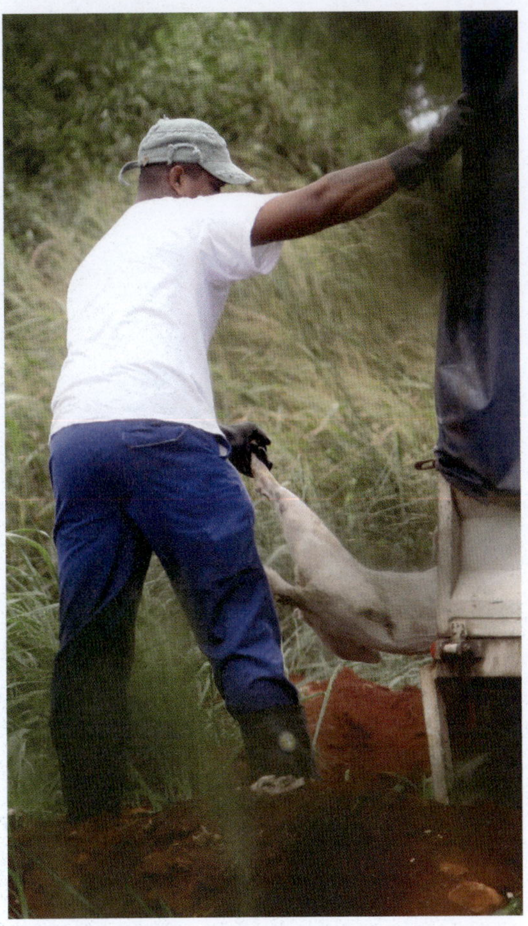

After the long flight home I took my set of pictures to the *Mail*, which quickly accepted them. Allan had done his research: 200,000 British holidaymakers visit Mauritius every year, which prompted the paper to splash the story over two full pages on the Saturday after our return.

The backlash from the dog-loving British public was huge, but the real traction came from the comments people made when the story appeared online. That very day, hundreds of readers pledged to boycott Mauritius, and that number grew and grew in the days that followed.

Enraged by the report, the Mauritius authorities wrote an email threatening Allan and me with the full force of their immigration police, general police and cybercrime unit. The fact that they had got so angry proved that the story had hit the spot.

Months went by without our hearing a word from the people on the island concerned to save its dogs. Then Alan Knight contacted us to say that the Mauritian government had stopped the catch-and-kill policy and was establishing a neutering programme. He was delighted.

The *Mail* asked us to go back to Mauritius to report on the new policy and get some pictures of happy-looking dogs. At the airport, I handed over my passport, expecting to be hauled off to a police cell. Instead, the officer passed it back, smiled and wished me a good holiday. So much for the three police forces being ranged against us.

We visited a rescue centre full of stray dogs that had been brought in from far afield. An on-site vet neutered the females, and many mutts had even been rehomed with families all over the island. It was a good news story . . . for all of three months. Then the government got bored with being nice and rolled out the dog vans again. Catch-and-kill was back on the agenda.

sprinkle of topsoil had barely covered the grave, where we could see the legs, tails and faces of the poor animals. We retired to the hotel and tried to wipe the hellish vision from our minds.

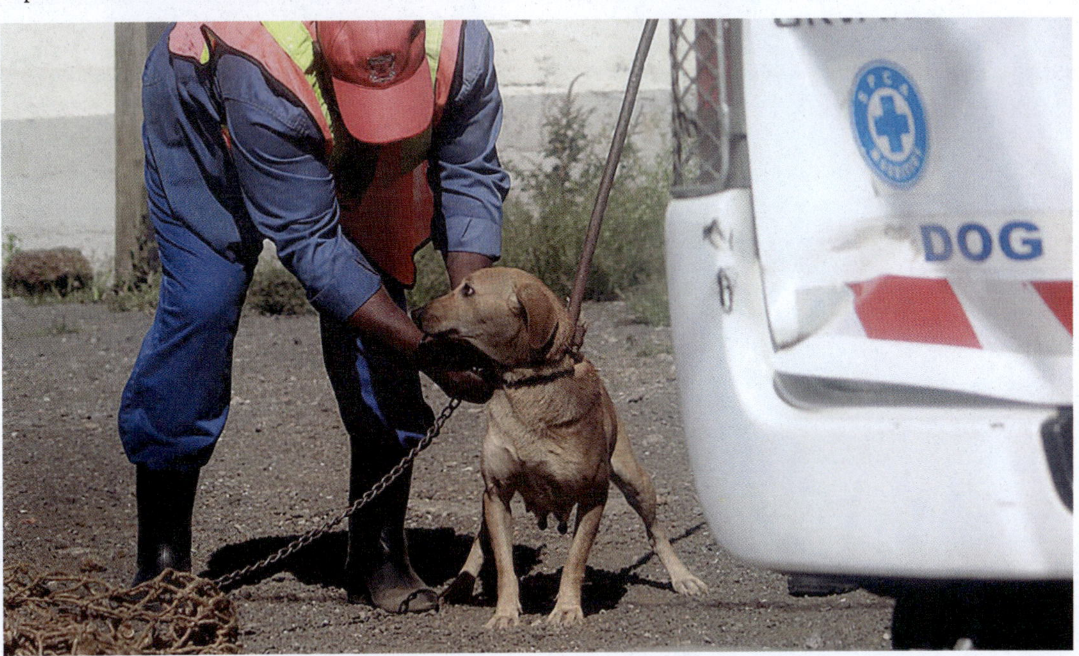

All dogs to the Dream Box

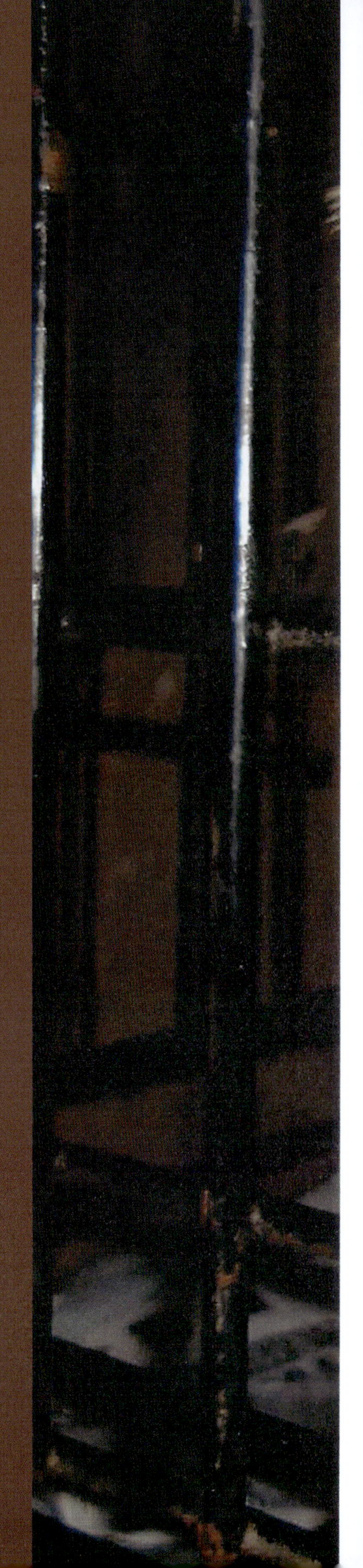

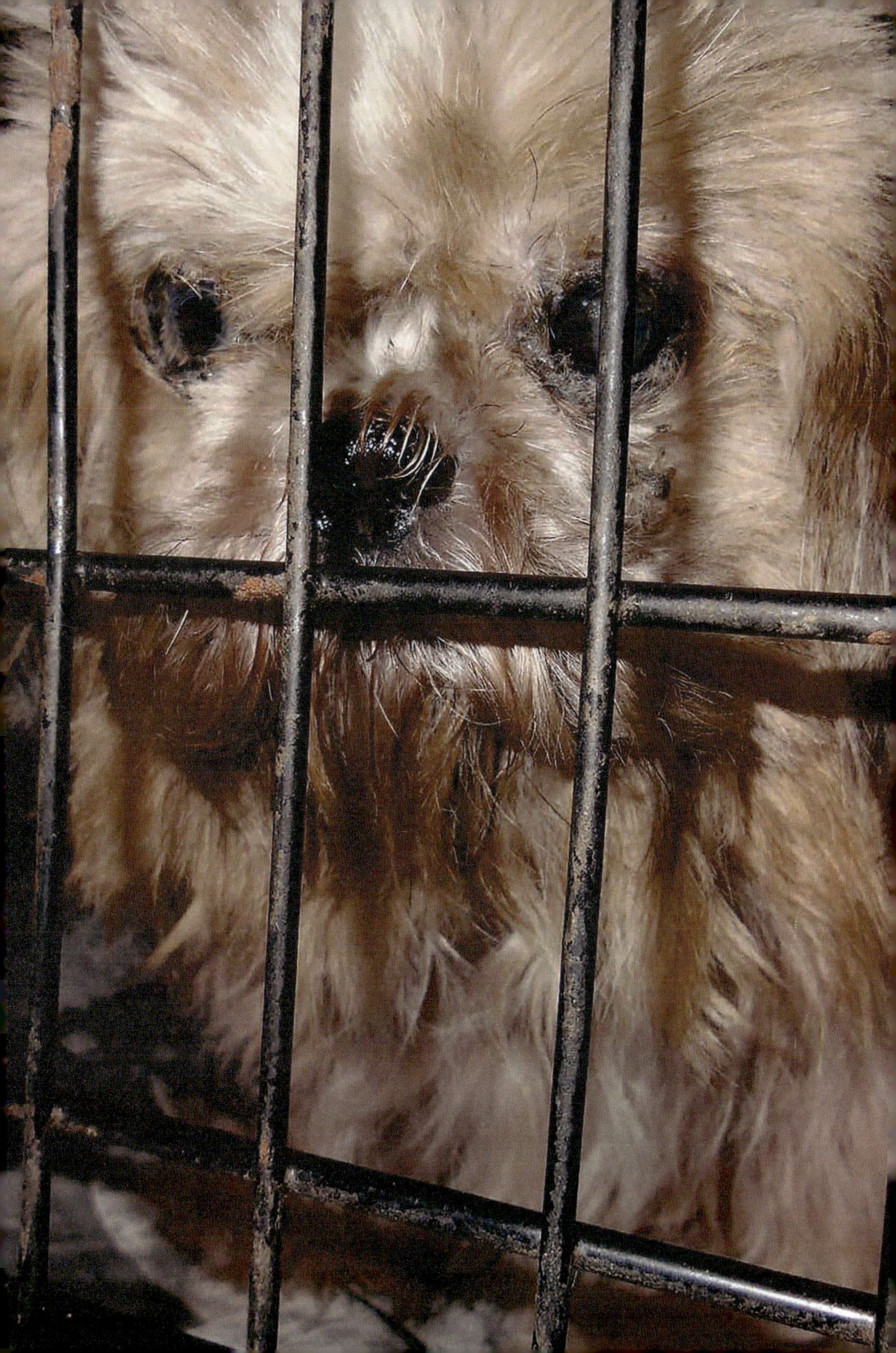

All dogs to the Dream Box

In total contrast to the horrible scenes in the Mauritius graveyard, I found myself, not long after, standing in a spotless, ultra-modern facility in Japan.

I had travelled to Japan to cover a story about North Korean agents abducting people from Japanese beaches in the 1980s. The North Koreans had been sent to snatch people of all ages and all walks of life and take them back to the closed state. There, security forces would study the captives to teach their spies how to blend in when posted to Japan.

The Japanese government had invited reporter Tom Parry and me to report on the practice, and we were treated like royalty. We were put up in a luxury hotel, assigned a chauffeur-driven limousine and given generous expenses. It was a far cry from the usual basic bed-and-breakfast accommodation I was used to.

We had dinner in the hotel restaurant, which slowly rotated to offer diners an all-round view of the dazzling city of Tokyo. We couldn't wait to explore this fascinating place but first we had to make our way to Japan's southernmost city, Kagoshima, which was where most of the kidnappings had taken place.

When we got there the next morning, the local police chief took us to a windswept stretch of beach, pointing out where a North Korean landing craft had come ashore. Later, at the police station, he handed us a folder with pictures of those who had been kidnapped. In some cases, the photos seemed to date from just before they had been shipped off to a dark cellar somewhere in Pyongyang.

In one a loving young couple stood on an iron footbridge, hugging and laughing. Maybe they had asked a passerby to photograph them. Their camera had been found abandoned on the beach, and the time stamp on the photograph showed that they had been abducted just three hours after standing on that bridge. The whole story was bizarre and unsettling.

We spent some time researching it, but by the time we had pretty well wrapped it up, we came across another lead to follow.

We had heard of the work of Elizabeth Oliver, an Englishwoman who had dedicated twenty years of her life to rescuing dogs from breeding farms. She had taken on both the national authorities and the notorious Yakuza mafia and had been awarded an MBE by the Queen for services to animal welfare and civil society.

When we told our handler that we wanted to visit the huge metropolis of Osaka, all our travel and accommodation needs were arranged for us.

We met Mrs Oliver, a spritely woman in her seventies, in the courtyard of a farm in the hills above Osaka. The noise of barking dogs filled the air. A collection of outhouses was home to rescued dogs who were now recovering from neglect and malnourishment.

Oddly, these were not strays but pedigree dogs, bred specially by a multimillion-pound industry but surplus to requirements. This egregious trade was fuelled by a celebrity-driven craze for 'handbag dogs'—cute puppies that could be shown off while their owners were out and about in the city.

What the owners of these trophy pets did not know, or did not care to know, was that the puppies they treated as personal ornaments were taken from their mothers when they were only a week old, to be displayed in glass tanks in upmarket pet shops. They might look content, but the breeding stock was so poor that the puppies would probably die within eighteen months.

Mrs Oliver told us that the criminal gangs in charge of the puppy farms got so overwhelmed by the numbers of small dogs being born that they would abandon the ones they did not need in re-

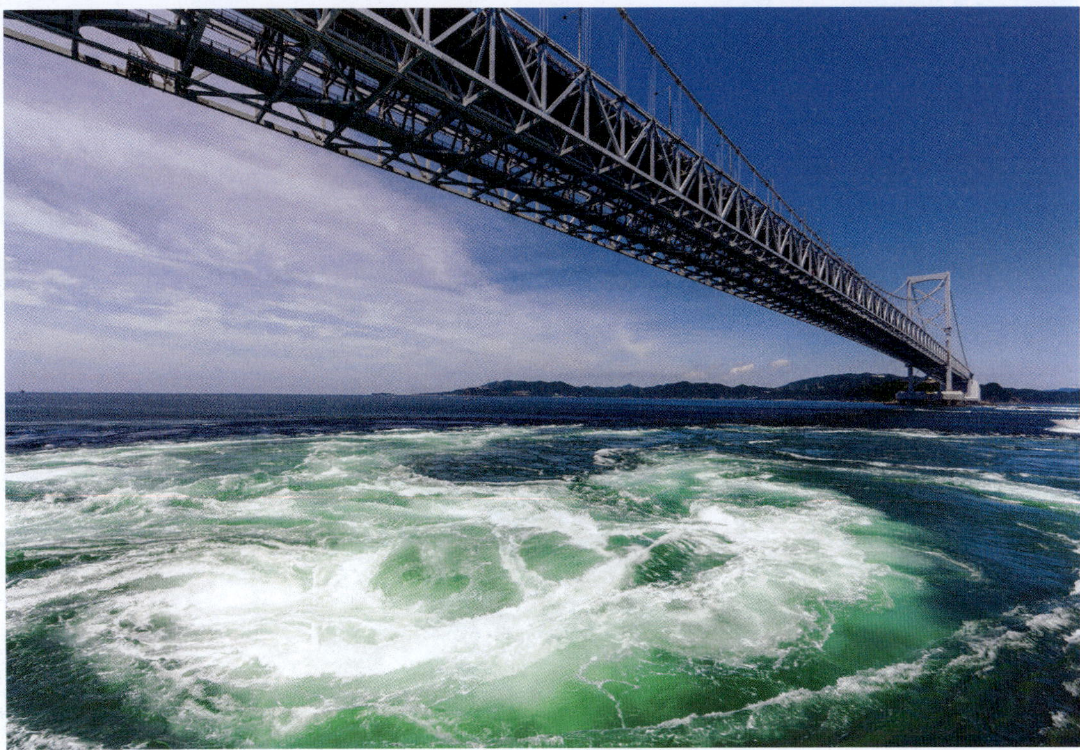

mote farmhouses, leaving them to starve, or die from injuries picked up trying to escape or in fights with other dogs.

After showing us around her farm, she suggested we take a look at the new state-of-the-art 'animal welfare' facility in Tokushima, built at a cost of £16 million. She calmly described it as a 'state-sanctioned extermination centre'.

Abandoned dogs were taken to the centre and given one week to be homed with a family. If they weren't adopted, they were sent to the Dream Box.

We had to see what this was all about.

The department dealing with the Tokushima centre gave us permission to visit, and to take pictures, and two days after meeting Elizabeth we were being driven across one of the world's largest bridges. Below the huge structure were the famous Naruto whirlpools, terrifying eddies of water that rush from the Pacific Ocean to the Inland Sea twice a day.

The drive up to the welfare centre was lined with trees, and with its children's playground and picnic tables, it looked more than anything like a theme park. In the same way, the centre itself looked like a school rather than a government institution, with wide paths leading up to a welcoming front entrance. On a large patio to the side there were open-topped wire cages full of puppies jumping up for attention from the groups of children gathered round them.

I took pictures of the cute dogs, mostly native Japanese Shiba Inu. It struck me at once that the claim that all these puppies could be homed was unrealistic to the point of being misleading: there were too many.

How did the authorities cope with the unwanted animals? The centre's attractive appearance did a good job of hiding the inhumane process that went on inside. So did the name it gave the process: the Dream Box.

A smartly dressed young guide unlocked the door and led us into the plant. The sound of the children's laughter outside faded as we approached the inner workings of the facility. She ushered us into a vast space sixty feet high and gleaming with stainless steel. Inside it stood a row of dog pens faced with unbreakable glass.

Against the sound of constant yapping and yelping and howling, small red lights flashed, harsh electronic noises grated one's eardrums and a smell of disinfectant filled the air.

'These are the next batch of dogs to go into the Dream Box,' said the guide.

I took pictures of the poor creatures with their paws on the glass walls of the pens. Some howled as if they had a premonition of an unpleasant fate while others stood hopefully, wagging their tails. Bowls of food and water had been placed in trays to avoid mess. Everything looked ordered, like a well-run boarding kennel. But these dogs were not going to be picked up by their owners. They had no owners.

The guide proudly explained the system: 'When the gate at the back of the cage opens, the dogs walk to the moving conveyor belt behind the cages. The belt moves along very slowly and has devices that automatically nudge the dogs along it or keep them from going back.'

I found it hard to understand how it was that

I was being allowed to see inside the facility, let alone take photographs. The guide's pride in it all was also beyond my capacity to explain. This must be a society with a very different set of core values, I thought.

The young woman paused and smiled as we reached the end of the moving belt. I thought she expected us to applaud and admire the technology. 'The dogs are then pushed into the Dream Box,' she said proudly.

On the side of the box was written the Japanese word for 'sleep'. It was all so clean and orderly, it was hard to take in that the Dream Box was really a gas chamber.

We were led into a control room behind a glass screen, where a prim-looking woman sat in front of a consul with an array of buttons. In a parking bay beyond the control room, an unmarked white truck waited, its tailgate hanging open. Beside it was a line of tall thin gas canisters.

When the dogs were all sealed inside the box, the woman in the control room pressed a red button, which activated a lift mechanism that lowered the box down onto the tailgate of the truck. It was then pushed inside, the tailgate was then raised and shut, and the vehicle then drove away with its load, unseen by the children and families who had been delighted by the little dogs they had seen at the front of the building.

It was only in the parking bay that I was not allowed to take pictures. This part of the operation was to be kept secret.

After the truck left the premises and was on the road, another red button would release gas into the Dream Box, killing the dogs within two minutes. They would then be taken to a crematorium for their bodies to be disposed of.

The designers of the facility had gone to extraordinary lengths to ensure that no 'bad spirits' were released within the centre by exterminating the dogs on the premises.

Mrs Oliver summed up the whole process: 'Outside it looks like Disneyland; inside it's Auschwitz. They have spent millions coming up with a system so they can press a button to gas the dogs, and nobody knows where the killings take place.'

While what happened at Tokushima was nowhere near as crude as the open graves in Mauritius, the outcome for the dogs was the same. And all because of a desire for a dog so small that it can fit into a tea cup, a perfect little puppy to be paraded around until it grows too big, when it gets abandoned in an alley with the rubbish, or it dies of congenital weakness.

Gangsters make millions from this craze, and the government killing factory goes about its business without any public demur. If I hadn't seen it with my own eyes, I wouldn't have believed it possible.

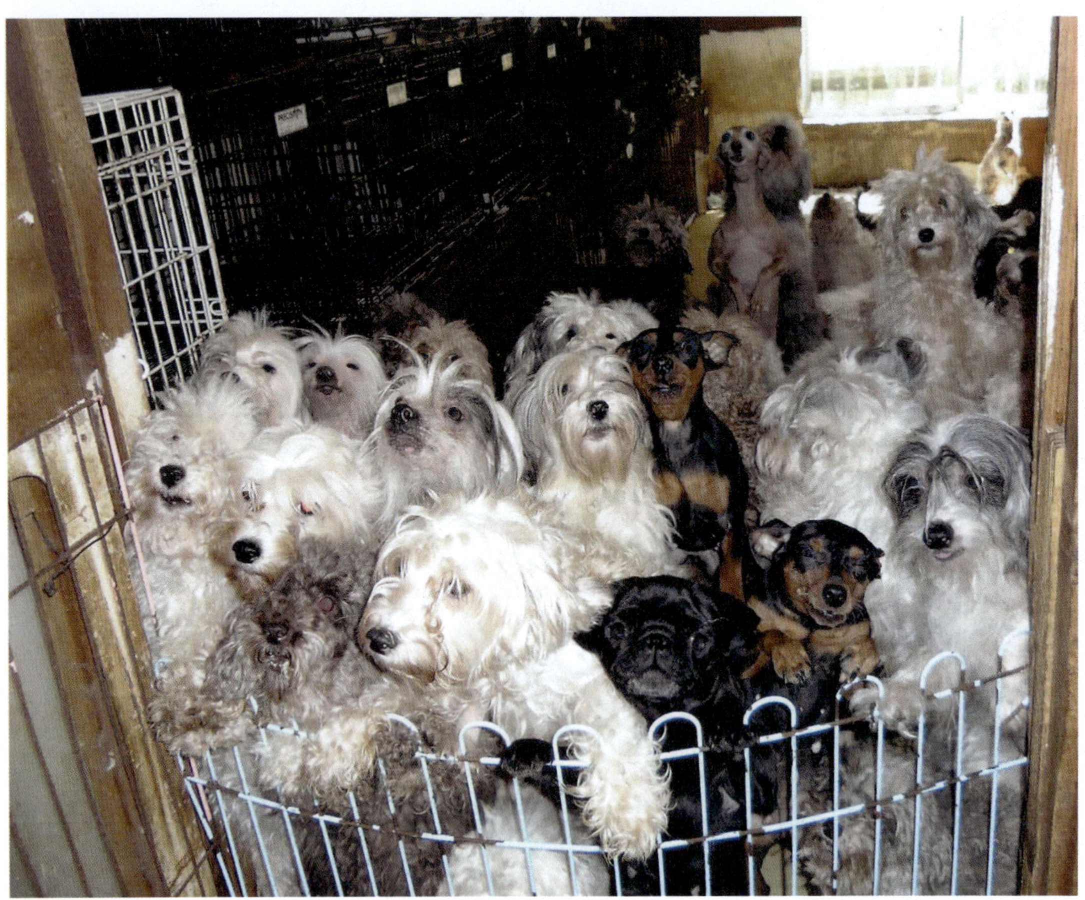

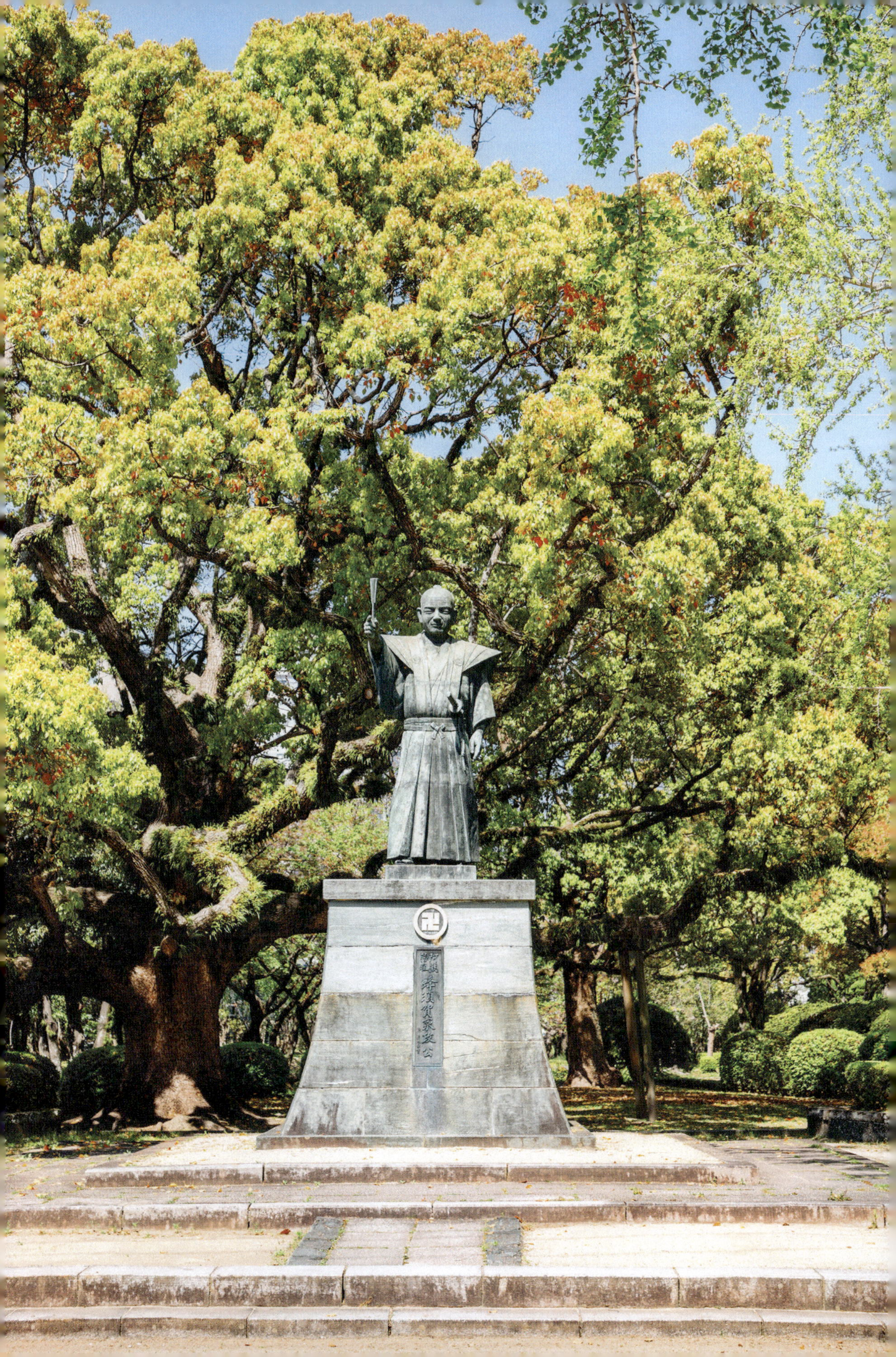
蜂須賀家政公

Vile bile
and the bears of Vietnam

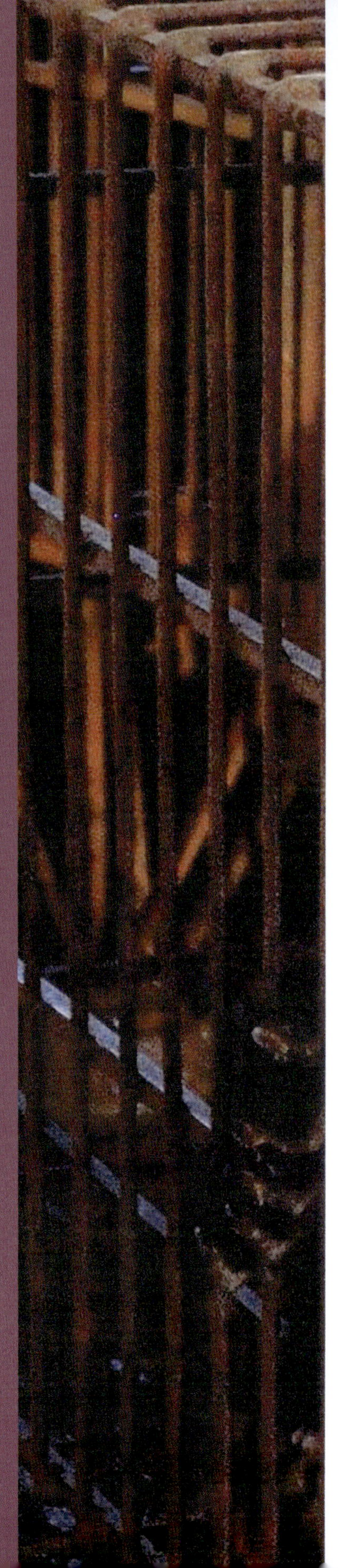

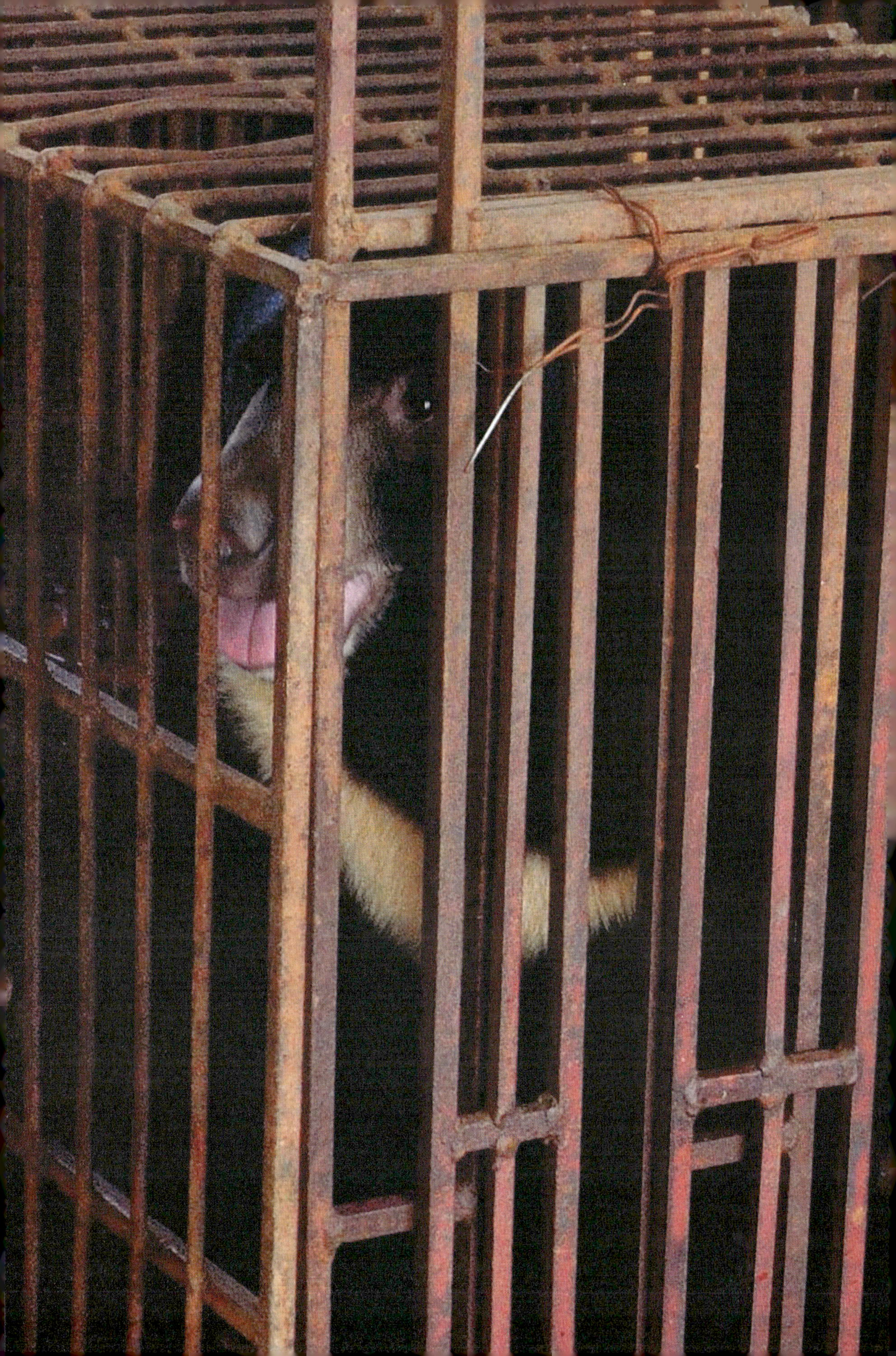

Vile bile
and the bears
of Vietnam

Man's cruelty to animals never ceases to disgust me, and one of the cruellest practices is the milking of bile from bears. This barbaric procedure involves draining the liquid from the gall bladder deep within the animal's digestive system, and is extracted twice a day, all for use in traditional Korean medicine.

To feed this trade, huge moon bears are housed in crush cages only just larger than the animals themselves. Permanent catheters are implanted into the bears' abdominal wall and gall bladder. Sometimes they are embedded just under the skin, right down to the hip, so the farmer can harvest the liquid at a safe distance from the bear's teeth and claws.

Bear bile farming is legal in China, despite laws protecting wild bear species, with an estimated 10,000 bears kept in captivity for this purpose in about 100 farms. It is legal, also, in South Korea, but is set to end by January 2026. In Laos, Myanmar and Cambodia, bear bile farming is illegal but loopholes, such as allowing bears to be kept as pets or displayed to tourists, enable the industry to persist. I had decided to publicise the practice by photographing it in Vietnam, where it is also illegal but tolerated.

Again, I travelled with Allan Hall, but this time we took our wives, Ro and Pamela, to help us access the farms. We had heard that up to thirty bears could be held in one of these places. Our wives' job was to pretend to be tourists wanting to see what moon bears looked like.

Our contact was Jill Robinson, the British founder of Animals Asia, who had set up a rescue centre in Vietnam, but before seeing it in action, we had to track down some illegal bile farms.

It all sounded very cloak-and-dagger. We had pictured ourselves sneaking behind anonymous facto-ries, scaling walls, being chased by angry mobs, or having to snap photos from afar with a long lens. In the end, though, it was far less dramatic than we had imagined.

The trip from the capital of Vietnam to the capital of bile farming started early in the morning when a large people carrier arrived to whisk us away. Jill had put us in the care of two of her local workers, one of whom gave the driver clipped and loud instructions as he carved his way through the morning traffic.

As the dense sprawling high-rises of Hanoi gradually thinned out, the countryside unfolded in a patchwork of vivid green paddy fields, where rows of workers bent low to pull up rice shoots. Beyond them, the hills rose, blanketed in dense, lush jungle.

We drove through small towns where massive neon signs promoted Western consumer goods that were far beyond the reach of most of the locals. Down at ground level, life was more immediate: families on motorbikes, food stalls everywhere, the steady smoke from makeshift barbecues, the air thick with the rich, fatty scent of grilled meat.

It wasn't until we looked more closely that we saw that the animals on the skewers and rotisseries were far too large to be chickens. Were they pigs? No, they were dogs—whole dogs, turning slowly over glowing charcoal: a challenging sight for Westerners but very common in parts of Vietnam, where dog meat is a popular delicacy, especially at the end of each lunar month when men eat dog in the hope of purging bad luck.

Like all things you don't want to see, as soon as we'd noticed them, we began to see them everywhere. The four of us sat in silence trying not to look but morbid fascination kept drawing our gaze back to the street stalls and the shock of seeing animals we took as pets, roasting on a grill.

Before we knew it we were just a mile away from Phuc Tho, the bear bile village. The prospect of encountering an illicit enterprise was intimidating but, instead of anything being carried out in secret, we soon saw three-foot-high signs advertising *Trai Gau*, the name for bear bile. There were slogans like 'Fresh bile: buy here', 'Best bile in town' or 'Freshest bear bile today', all with the graphic of a bear walking along the telephone numbers of the different businesses.

We stopped outside a café selling fresh bile. There was nothing covert about it and no need for skulking around; all we had to do was ask.

Within a couple of minutes a shy-looking man was holding up a plastic bag containing phials of fresh bile, all sealed with a white top and labelled 'Trai Gau' with a little picture of a bear. The containers were sold in batches of ten, held together with an elastic band. I whipped out a camera and snapped away as the man proudly displayed his wares.

Close to the café were large four- and five-storey houses adorned with concrete eagles on plinths, and large metal gates with animals worked into the

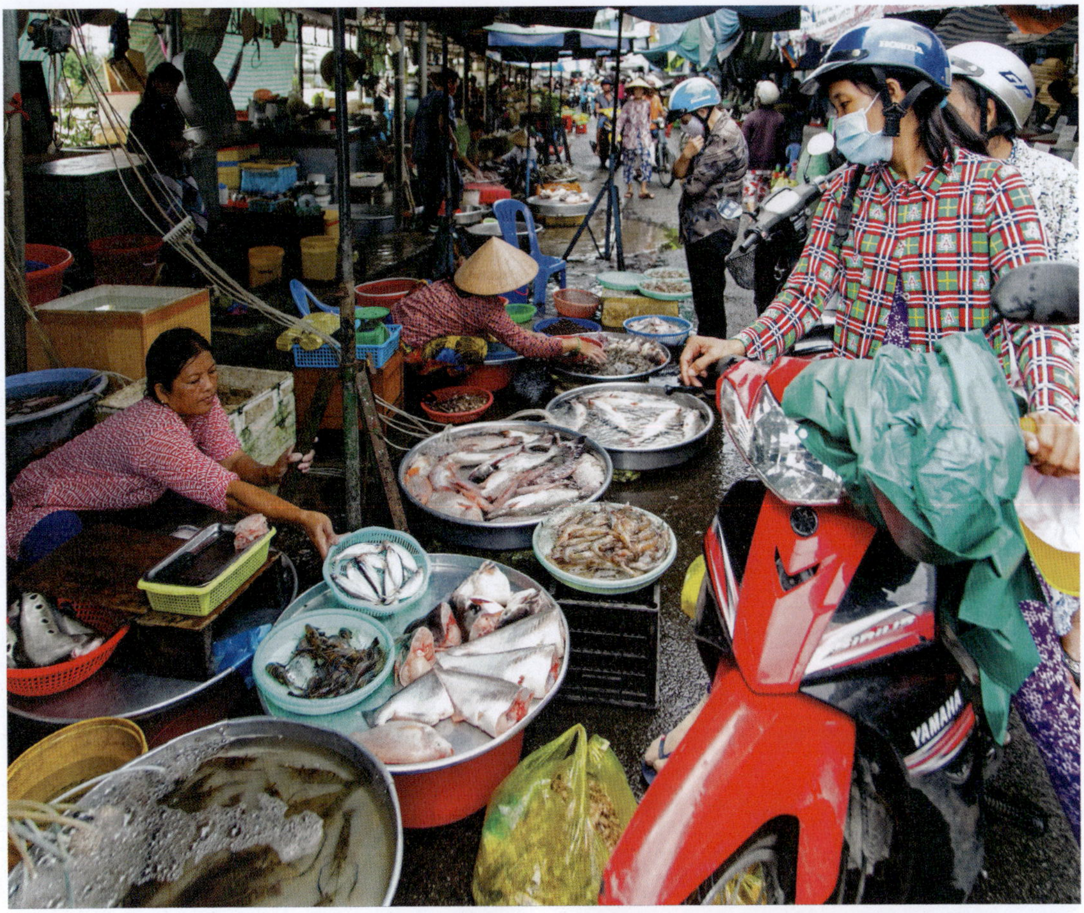

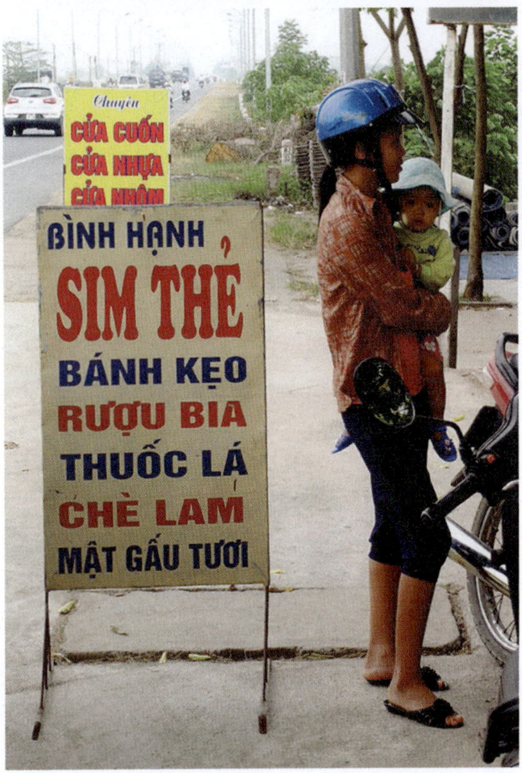
Chuyên
CỬA CUỐN
CỬA NHỰA
CỬA NHÔM
BÌNH HẠNH
SIM THẺ
BÁNH KẸO
RƯỢU BIA
THUỐC LÁ
CHÈ LAM
MẬT GẤU TƯƠI

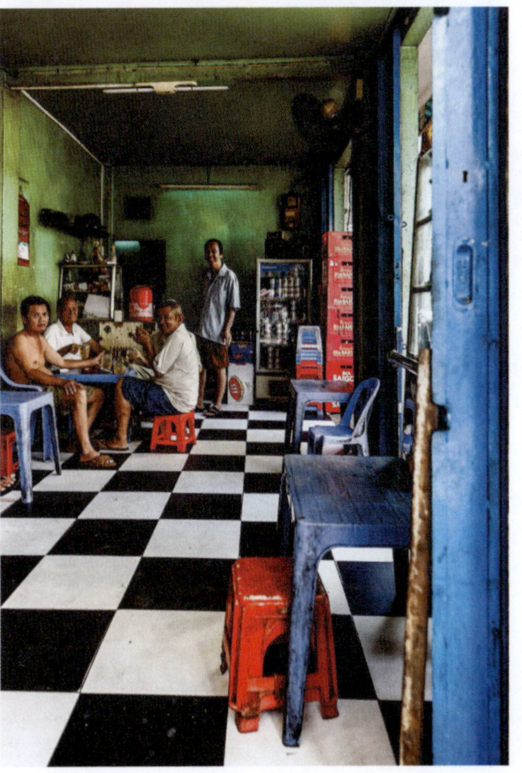

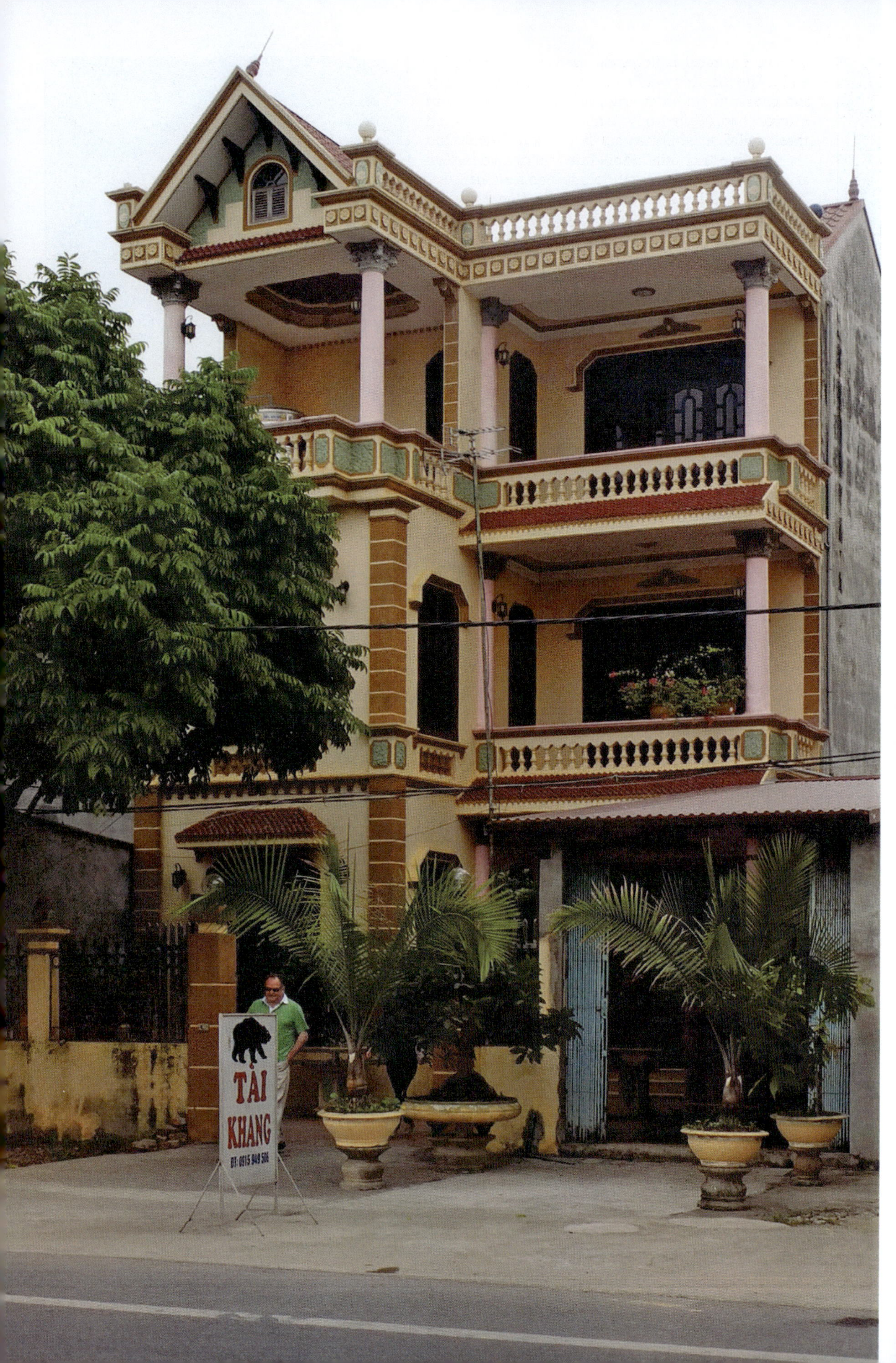
TẢI
KHANG
ĐT: 0915 949 566

ironwork. Four-wheel-drive vehicles and black sa-
loons with dark windows sat outside. They looked
like the homes of wealthy builders until we saw
rows of rusty iron cages in the front yards.

Within each cage lay huge bears and nothing
else: no matting, no straw, no water, no food. The
animals didn't react when we went into one of the
yards to inspect the cages. They just looked at us
with disdain.

Before long a dog on a long lead was barking
at me, a few feet from where I stood. The noise
brought out a woman who waved her arms at me
to stop taking pictures. Ro went to distract her,
launching into a barrage of questions. In the time
it took for the woman to bat her away, I'd got what
I needed.

We moved on to another house across the street.
This one had a row of cages beneath the house, and
a woman was hosing bear waste off the concrete.
There was no talking to the animals, no nice smiles;
the poor animals were just units to be milked.
There was a palpable contrast between the working
woman and the suffering animals that funded her
large lime-green house and three cars.

The last place we saw was truly awful. Under a
vast metal roof set in a factory yard with a large
five-storey house, long lines of metal crush cages
disappeared into the darkness of the building.

What struck me was the silence. None of the animals made any noise; there was none of the usual

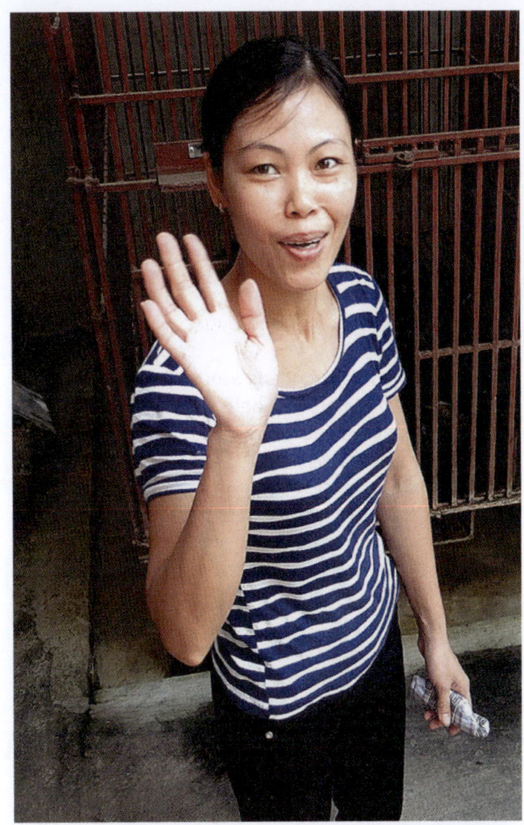

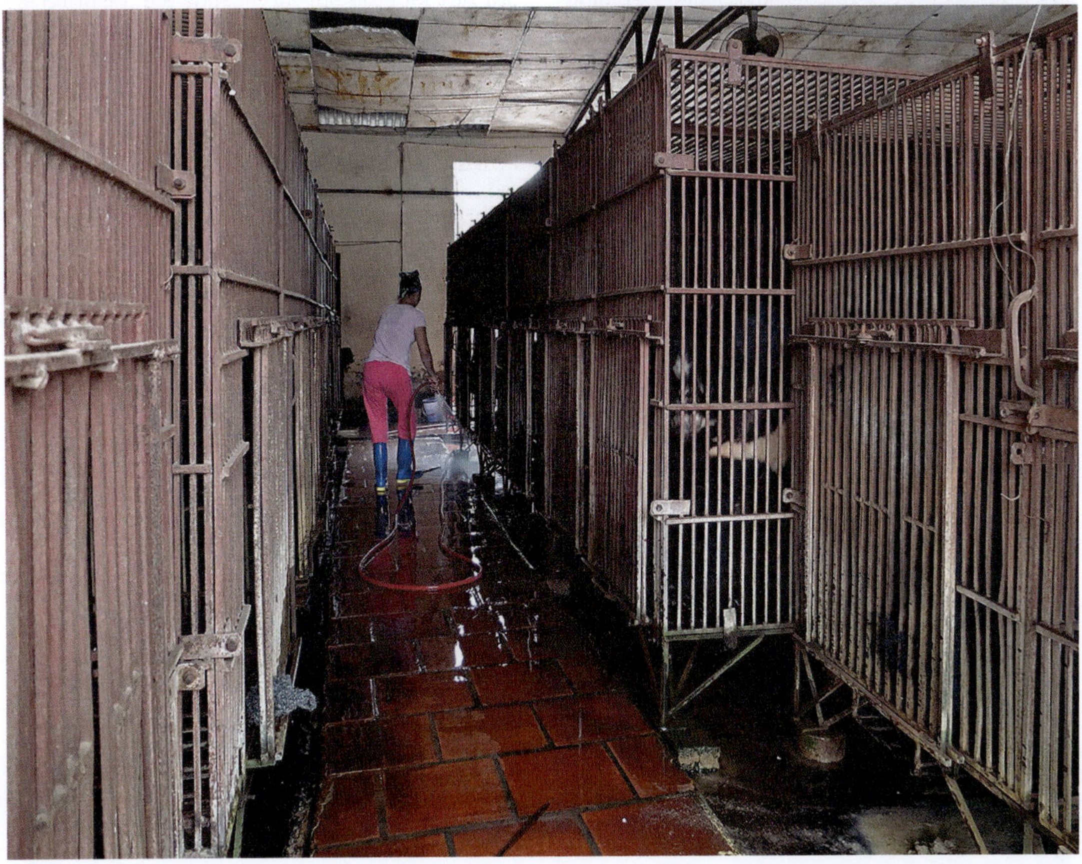

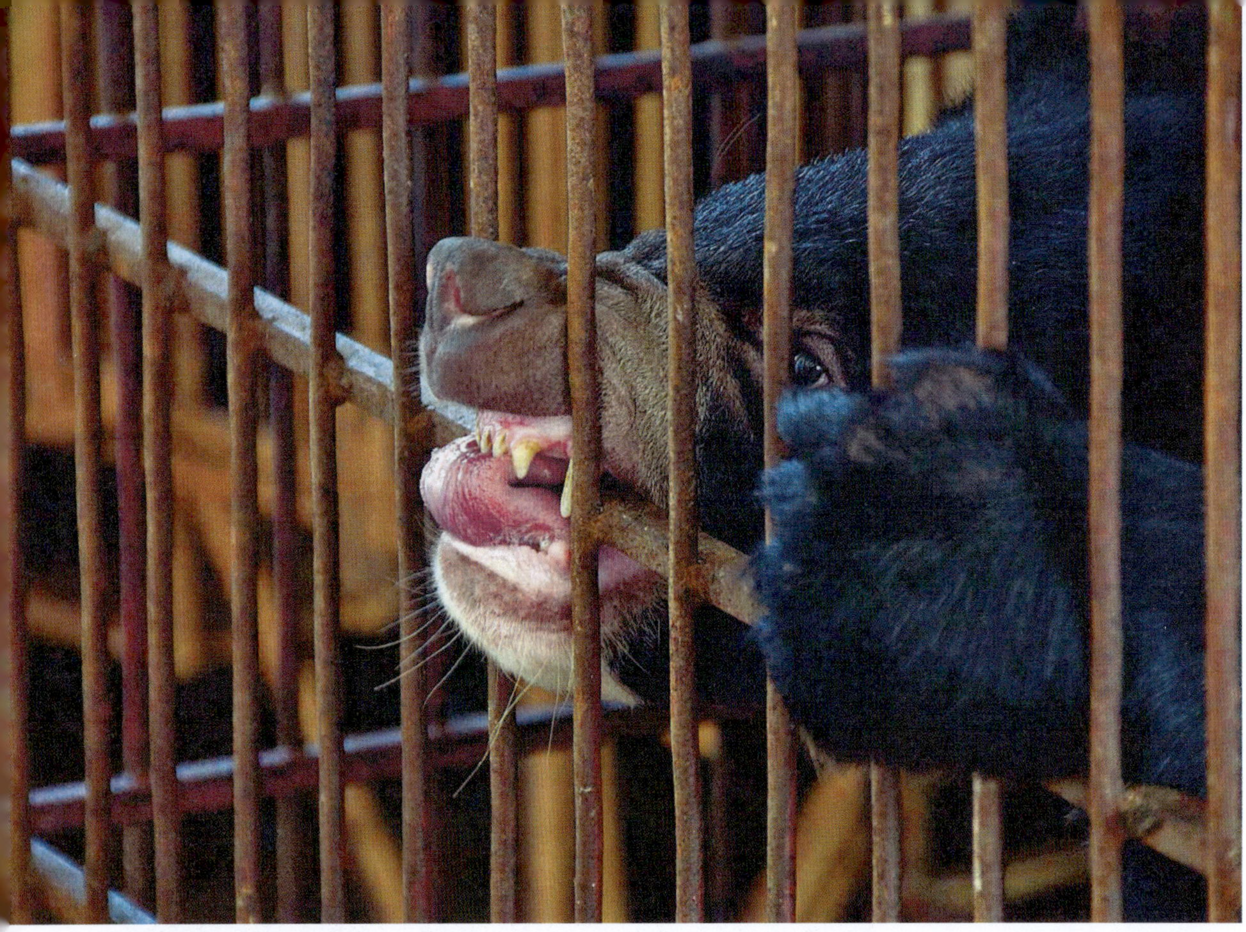

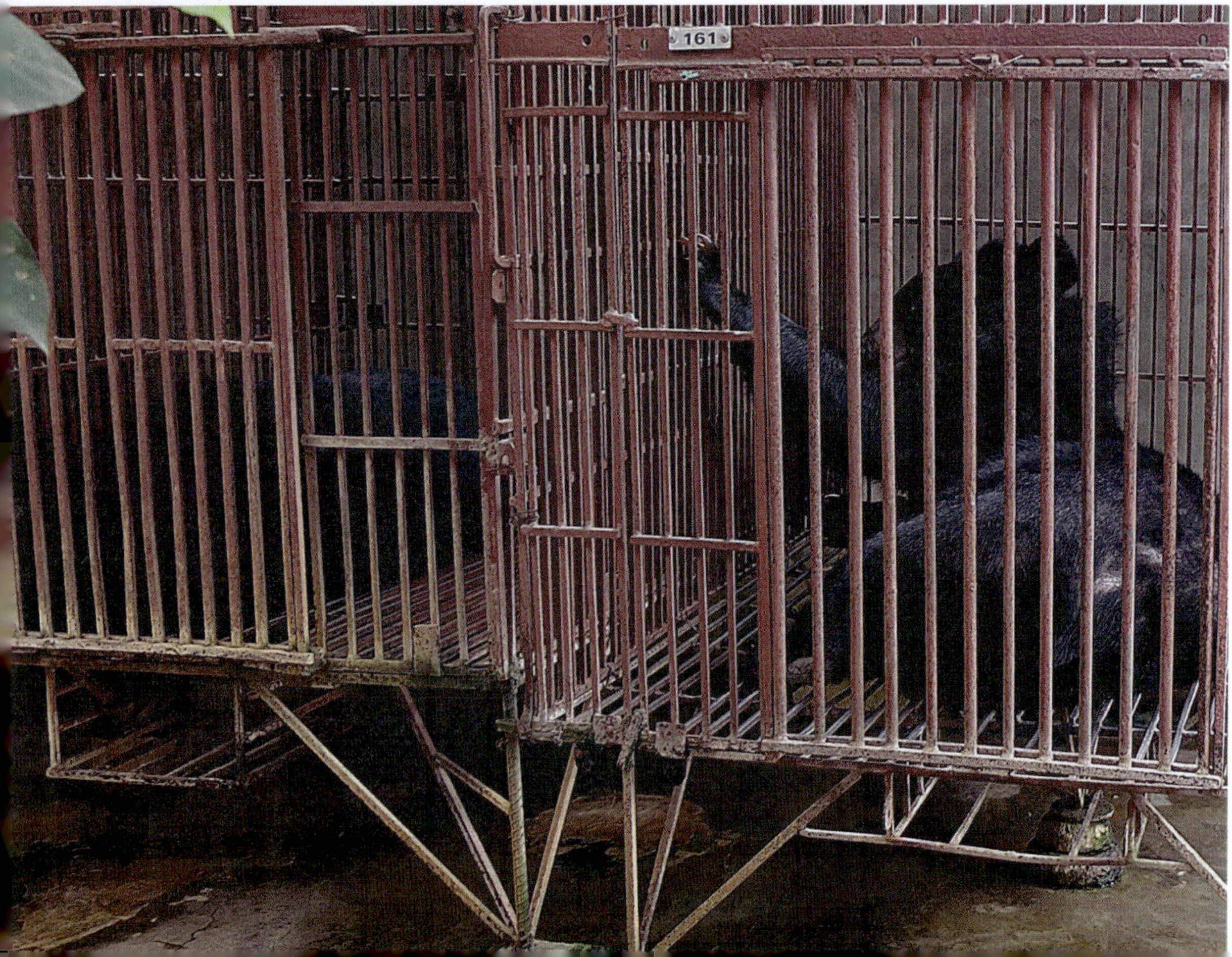

161

grunting or growling. Just broken bears, waiting silently for their next quota of bile to be collected.

What I couldn't understand was why none of the cages had any kind of comfort, anything that would make the animals' lives even a bit better. The conditions were horrific and there was no attempt to mitigate it. Here were ordinary people living ordinary lives who seemed immune to the suffering they were responsible for and complicit with. I saw untreated open wounds from where bears had torn their skin on the ironwork. The bear nearest the road had clamped its jaw onto the bars of its cage, its tongue hanging from the side of its mouth. These were strong images—too strong, I now think, for a book such as this, which might be read by children.

A large man appeared from the gloom of the building holding an iron bar, and it was clear that he was prepared to use it on me if I didn't go away. I returned to the car passing yet more signs for fresh bile and more houses with cages tucked under their frontages.

The bear owners called their animals 'pets' for the benefit of tourists. I thought that anyone getting pleasure from looking at animals in these conditions would have to be very sick. Yet this was the local culture.

I wondered how it was possible for farms such as these to continue operating in Vietnam in the face of official opposition, but seeing the scale of the business, the appetite for the product and the rewards that it brought—big houses, flash cars— it was clear that a few bribes directed to the right people were enough to ensure that officialdom turned a blind eye.

Cruelty paid. Each of the small phials we saw in the café sold for $2.00. Multiplied up, Vietnam's annual turnover was estimated at £2 billion.

No one disputes that bear bile has exceptional properties, nor that those properties are acclaimed in Eastern medicine: the ursodeoxycholic acid it contains is said to aid in the treatment of liver ailments and in the rejuvenation of brain cells, giving hope to sufferers of Parkinson's disease. Mixed with alcohol it is said to reduce bruises and swelling.

But as Jill Robinson had pointed out, the active ingredients have been replicated in the lab with a hundred-per-cent success rate. There is no longer any need for any bear to be kept in captivity or abused.

We were all lost in our thoughts on the way back to Hanoi, pondering the greed that allowed so many animals to spend the whole of their lives being mistreated. After the horrors of Phuc Tho, it would be a relief to visit Jill's sanctuary the following day.

And so it was. Watching the bears roam freely through spacious enclosures, splashing in pools and playing games of hide and seek together, brought tears to my eyes. Climbing frames dotted the landscape, offering places to perch or shelter, and staff tucked honey into tree branches, encouraging the bears to forage and explore.

It was a sanctuary of joy for animals who could never be released into the wild—a second chance at life, even if the freedom to roam free in the nearby jungles was too dangerous for them.

Jill took us on a tour of the sanctuary's hospital wing, operating theatre and isolation building, where rescue animals stayed until they were clear of any infections. It was there that we met Lai Chou and Sin Ho, two young bears who had been brought in as cubs.

Officers had become suspicious of two men on a moped. When they pulled the men over and opened up the large basket mounted on the back, four little eyes stared up at them. These two sibling cubs were being taken to China, where bears are worth even more than in Vietnam and are treated no better.

As they tumbled around in fresh straw, joshing and squabbling as brothers do, the two little bears had no idea what might have become of them. They were learning how to become happy adult bears, not stunned dispensers of alternative medicines but otherwise empty, devoid of spirit, personality or energy. Before long they would be released into the open pens to learn to climb, search for honey and encounter other bears.

Jill showed us a vast open pen containing ten large male bears who had been with her since the sanctuary was established in 1998. Like all bears, they would be active for a while, especially when food was being offered, then go for a nap.

When we arrived they had just been fed, so they were all lolling about, some sleeping in a heap, others lying in hammocks. I got some lovely pictures, but thought the scene would look even better from above. I asked Jill if I could get on top of the cages.

'Yes, but be careful,' she replied.

Ro watched from the ground while I climbed up and walked on top of the cages. The sleeping bears made a nice composition from that angle. As I focused my lens on one bear in his hammock, Ro shouted a warning.

I swung around to see a huge bear just below me, his enormous paws poking through the bars. Just in time I skipped along the walkway and escaped his claws.

The great thing about that little cameo was that it showed the bear using his natural skills. I was a threat, and he needed to see me off, so his instinct kicked in. He had been rescued from a life of passivity in a crush cage and now he was doing what he should be doing, not feeding an illegal and unnecessary trade.

Good for him.

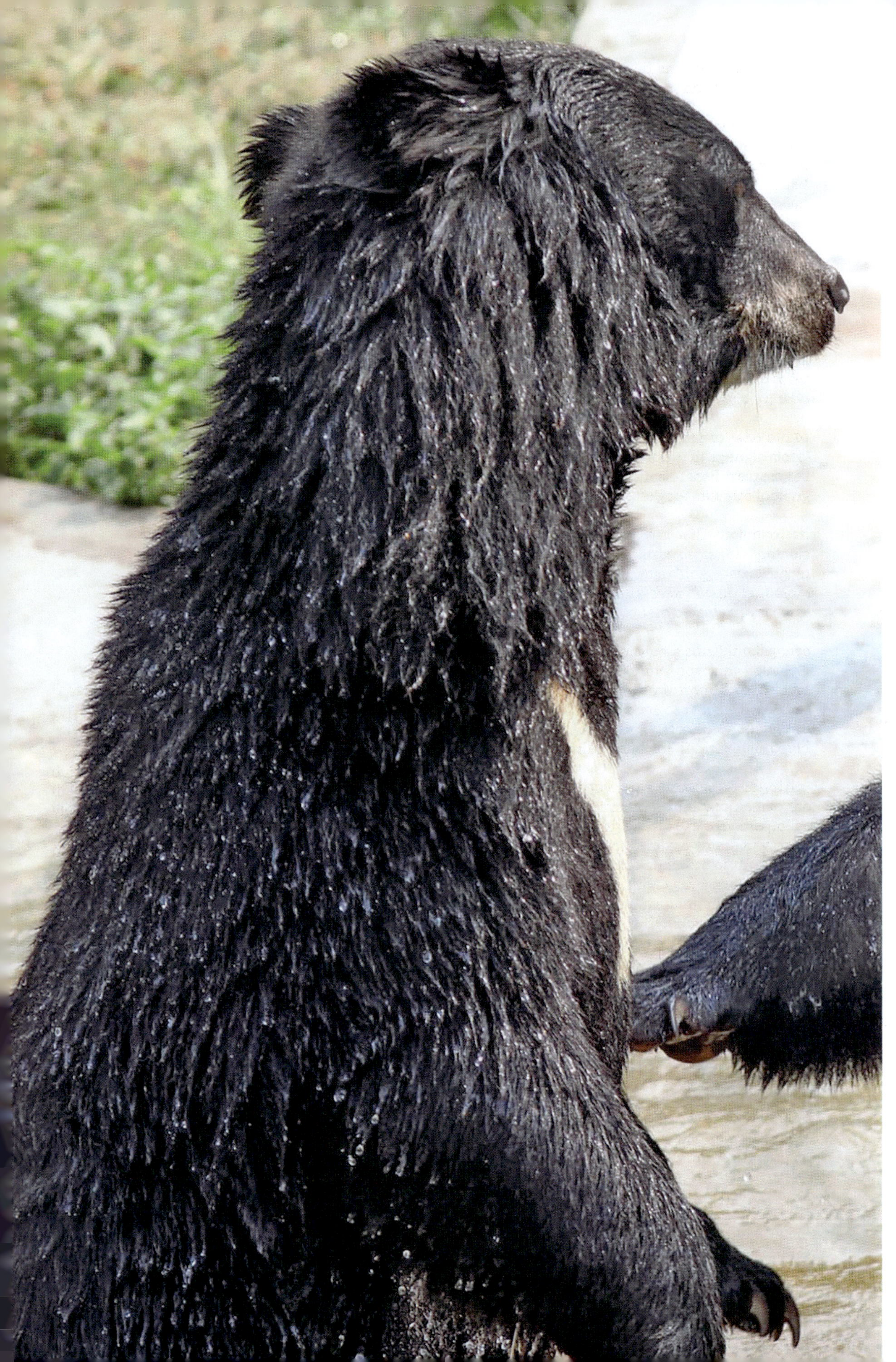

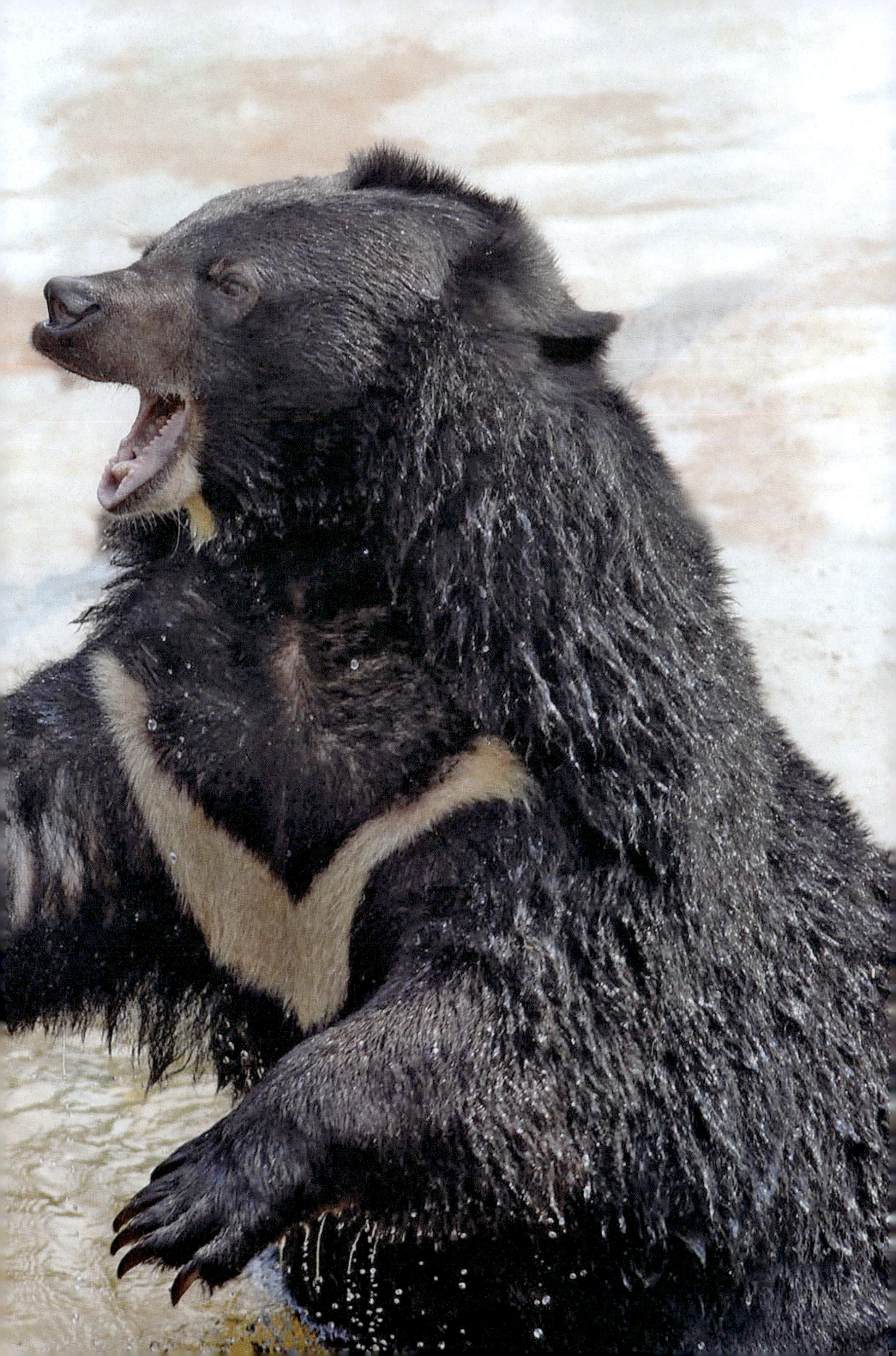

Step
right
up

The
circus
is over

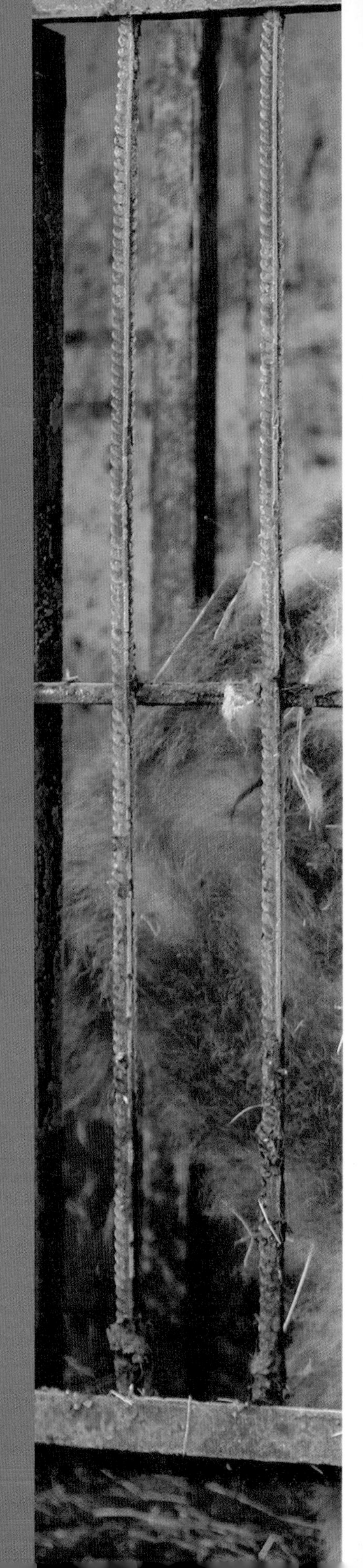

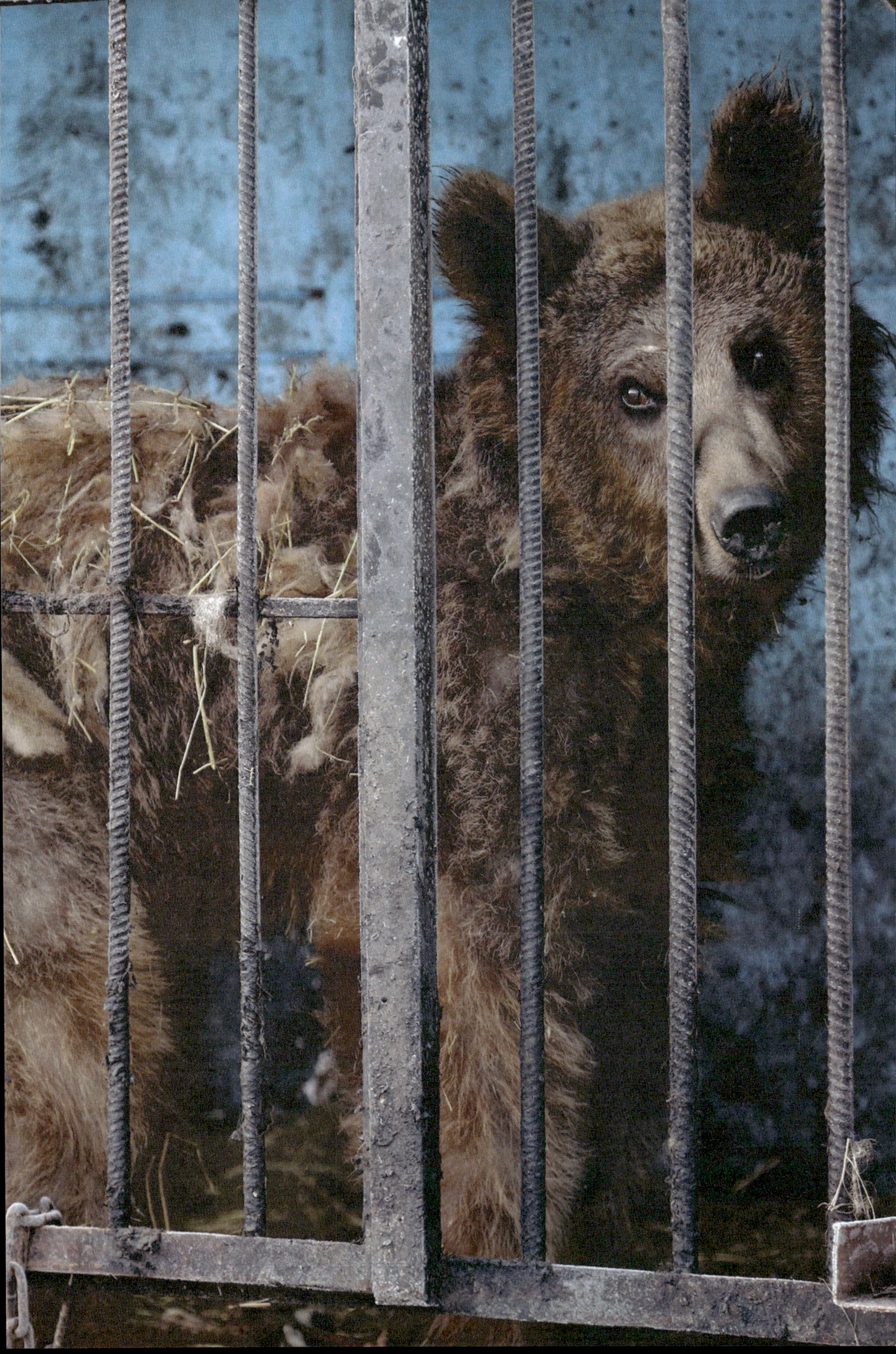

Step right up: The circus is over

Zoos are supposed to be places where animals are cared for, but they sometimes fall short. Sitting hunched over my laptop I watched an extract from an Armenian talk show. I couldn't understand what was being said, but the shaky footage of three bears, two lions and a guinea pig abandoned in a private zoo immediately captured my attention.

The zoo was in the Armenian town of Gyumri. A wildlife activist in the country's capital, Yerevan, had sent the video to Alan Knight of IAR, and he had forwarded it to me. The conditions looked awful.

I have to admit, I didn't know anything about Armenia and had to look it up on the map before carrying out some basic research on this former Soviet republic. But within a week of first contacting the activist, whose name was Maria, I was landing at Yerevan's Zvartnots International Airport.

It was November and a fresh fall of snow had dusted the city's buildings but the clouds had cleared to leave a clear deep-blue sky. Across the valley that runs through Yerevan I saw a large snow-capped mountain: Mount Ararat, which many believe is where Noah's Ark was stranded after the great flood.

The view stirred a memory from the airport: my entry visa stamp had featured a small image of Mount Ararat, Armenia's national symbol, even though the mountain now lies within the borders of Türkiye. Much of historical Armenia had been lost to the Ottoman Empire long ago.

After I had driven into the city, I checked into my hotel and met Maria, who told me the story of the animals I had seen in the video.

As for so often in the field of animal abuse, the private zoo she had alerted IAR about had been the plaything of a wealthy businessman—in this case an oligarch who used to hold jungle-themed parties there. He had fallen on hard times and became ill, fleeing to Russia and leaving the animals to fend for themselves.

Gyumri was three hours' drive north of Yerevan, and Maria and I set off the following morning in a hire car. Perhaps I was too enthusiastic as we travelled across the vast white snowy plain because by the time we reached Gyumri I had picked up three speeding fines.

The town was ramshackle. Rusting railway lines with abandoned rolling stock on them ran parallel with the road into town. The closer we came to the centre, the worse that road became. I had to steer round large potholes filled with water and navigate major road junctions with defunct traffic lights.

Maria had not visited the zoo before, so we stopped in the main square and asked for directions. On a piece of waste ground beside a scruffy roundabout we found a ring of dilapidated circus trucks and converted shipping containers. They were roughly painted in a brown and yellow pattern to represent some kind of animal hide. Tacked over the paintwork were crude paintings of monkeys and vultures.

From the outside we couldn't see the animals; only when we passed through the two half-gates did they and their plight become apparent.

To the left of the gates stood three animal pens. The first was a shipping container with metal bars crudely welded across the front, housing a lone female lion. Next to her, two aging circus trucks housed her cubs, Geeta and Zita. The three enclosures were arranged in a row, which meant that the three lions couldn't even see each other. That was only the first of the many cruelties we were about to encounter.

The mother lion growled half-heartedly as we approached. She was in a bad way, her face pushed against the bars at the front of the container. We could see immediately that the fight had gone out of her.

As we walked to the next animal, an elderly couple came up to us. They were dressed in scruffy clothes. The man was unshaven, the woman looked exhausted.

The woman introduced herself as Alvina Madoyan, the person who had contacted Maria about the animals, and the two of them embraced warmly. Alvina and her husband Hovhammes had since moved into a small metal hut by the front gate, dedicating themselves to the animals' care.

Before I had a chance to take any pictures, Alvina was ushering us towards the hut. Inside was a two-hob cooker, a small sink and a bed just about big enough for two. In the corner, a wood burner pumped out heat. It was in this cramped space that the husband and wife had chosen to live for the sake of the animals.

The pair can only be described as heroes. Without them, the lions, bears and guinea pigs that had been left at the zoo would have perished—and very nastily.

Alvina made us a thick brown coffee, very sweet. I took mine outside to take in the distressing scene and gather up my cameras. Meanwhile, Maria chatted to the couple in the hut.

The two lion cubs walked back and forth, eight paces one way, eight paces the other way, back and forth, back and forth. One of the cubs stopped for a moment and pushed her head against the wooden wall that separated her from her sister. When she

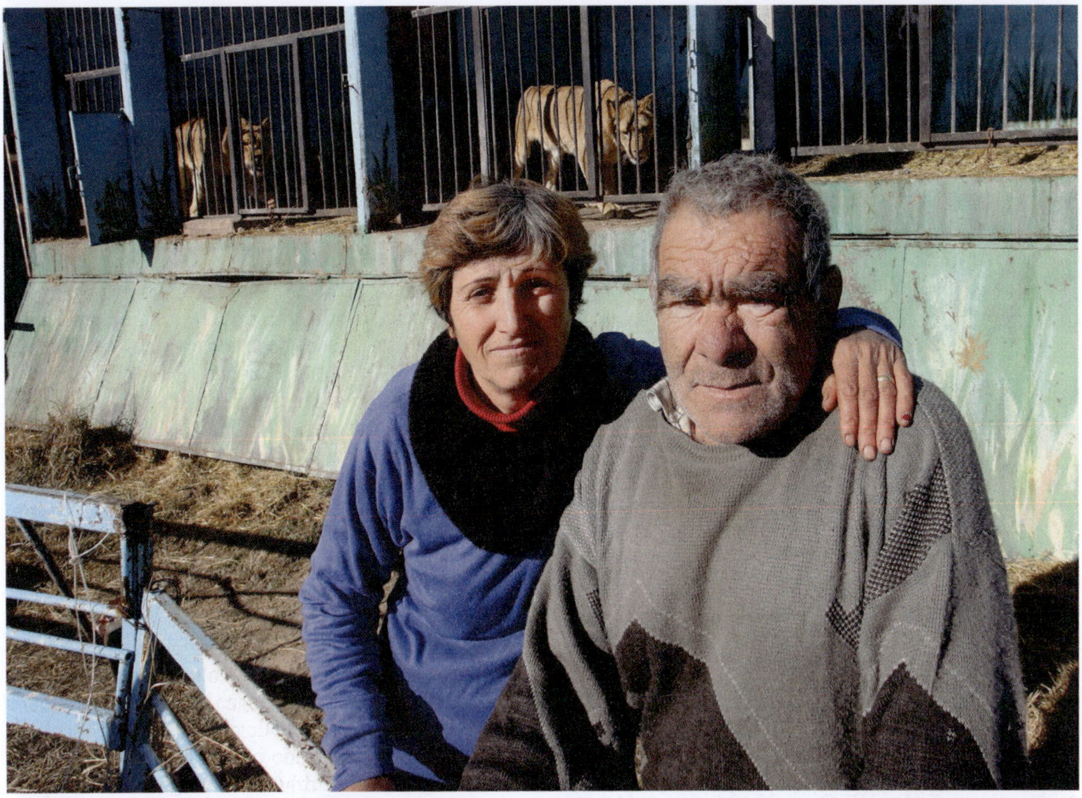

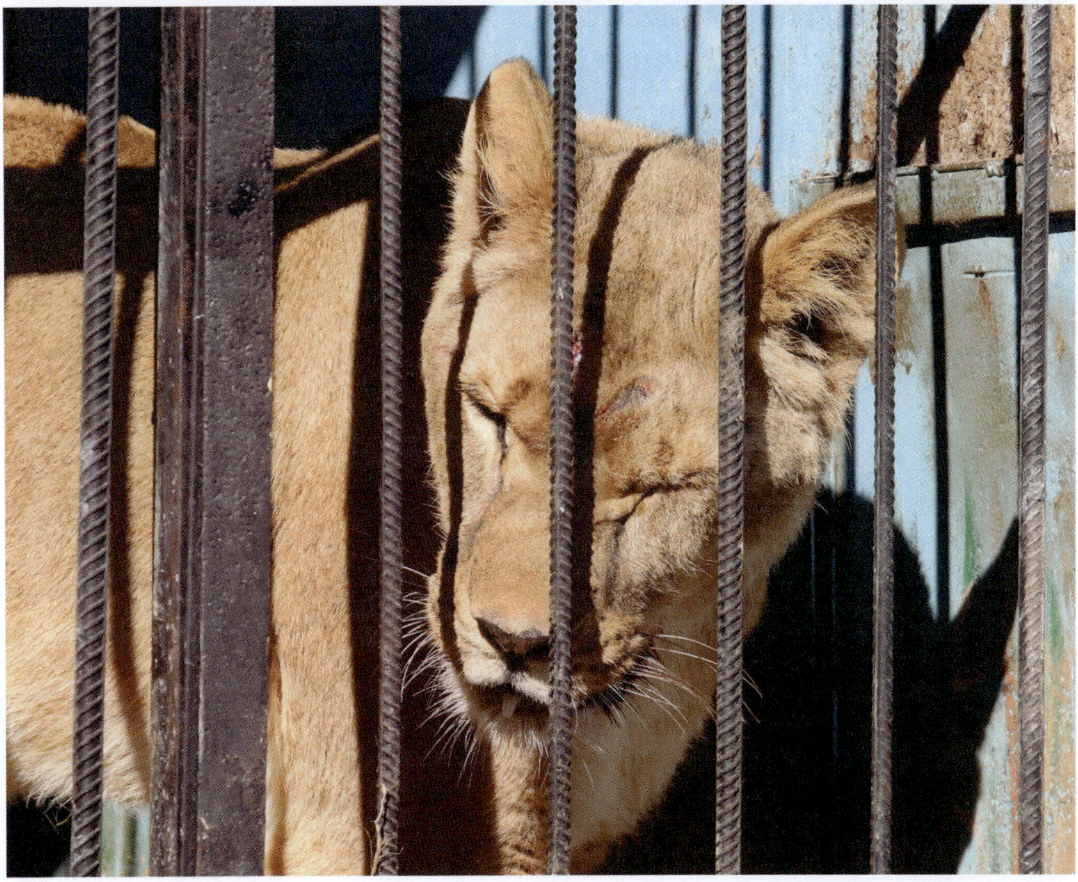

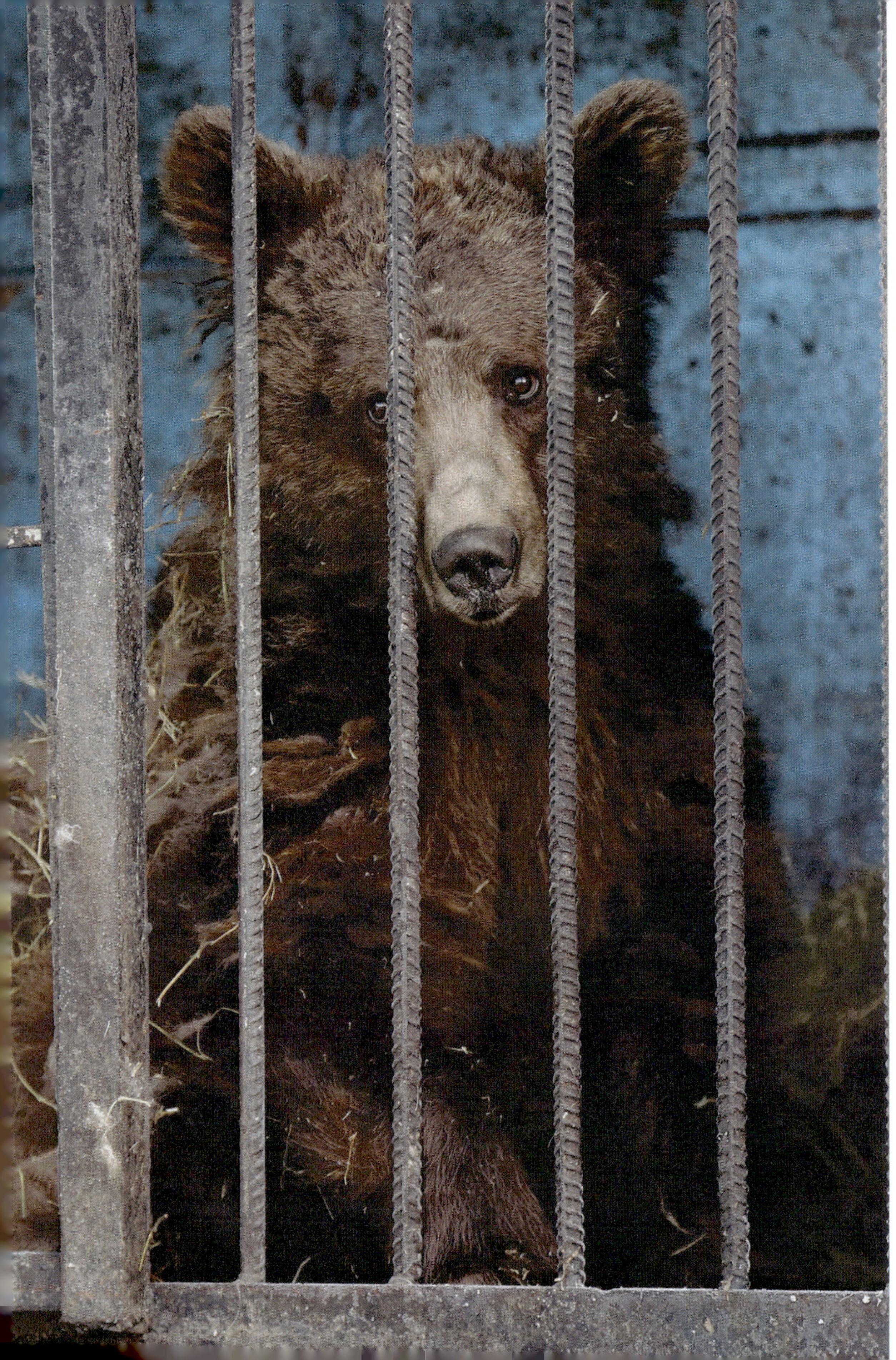

turned I saw large gaping wounds on her forehead.

The two bears in the zoo were also in a bad way. Their fur was matted and both had haunted looks, their long snouts pushing through the bars.

I photographed the lions in their separate cages. Zita sat at the back of her space, looking very sad. A sharp wind gusted past the front of the cages, throwing up a small dust storm that sent grass and litter spiralling up into the air. It was a desolate place.

A barrier had been set up in front of the cages in a half-hearted attempt to stop the oligarch's party-goers from getting too close to the animals. It was a pointless gesture, because the ends of the barrier were open, allowing people simply to walk around it.

In front of the barrier was a small budgerigar cage holding two guinea pigs, one brown and white, the other black and white. The two poor animals looked hopelessly out of place. It seemed somebody had brought them to the circus and left them behind. The juxtaposition of the domestic pets and the great lions and bears emphasised the weirdness of the whole situation.

As I took a picture of the rodents, feeding time for the larger animals began. Alvina began dragging a trolley towards the cages, with her husband pushing from behind. The trolley was loaded with meat chopped into handy-sized chunks for the lions. The couple had an agreement with the manager of the local abattoir to collect scraps of meat. They also got unsold fish from a fishmonger for the bears.

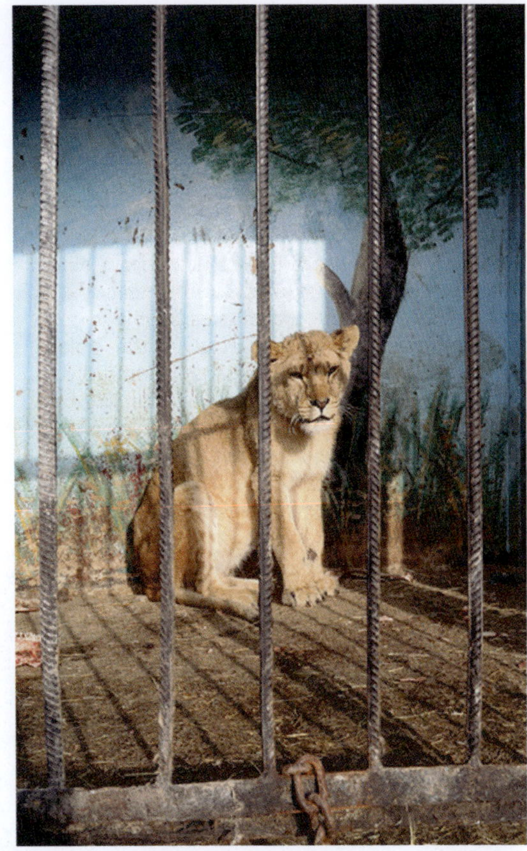

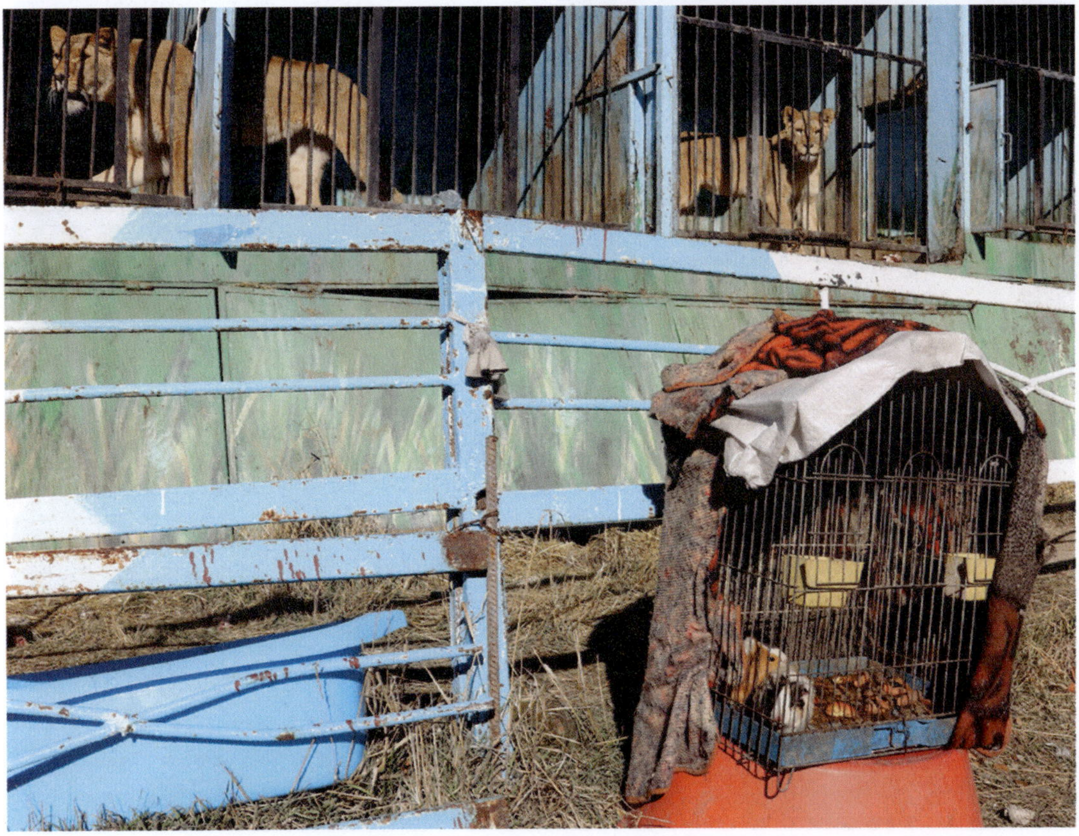

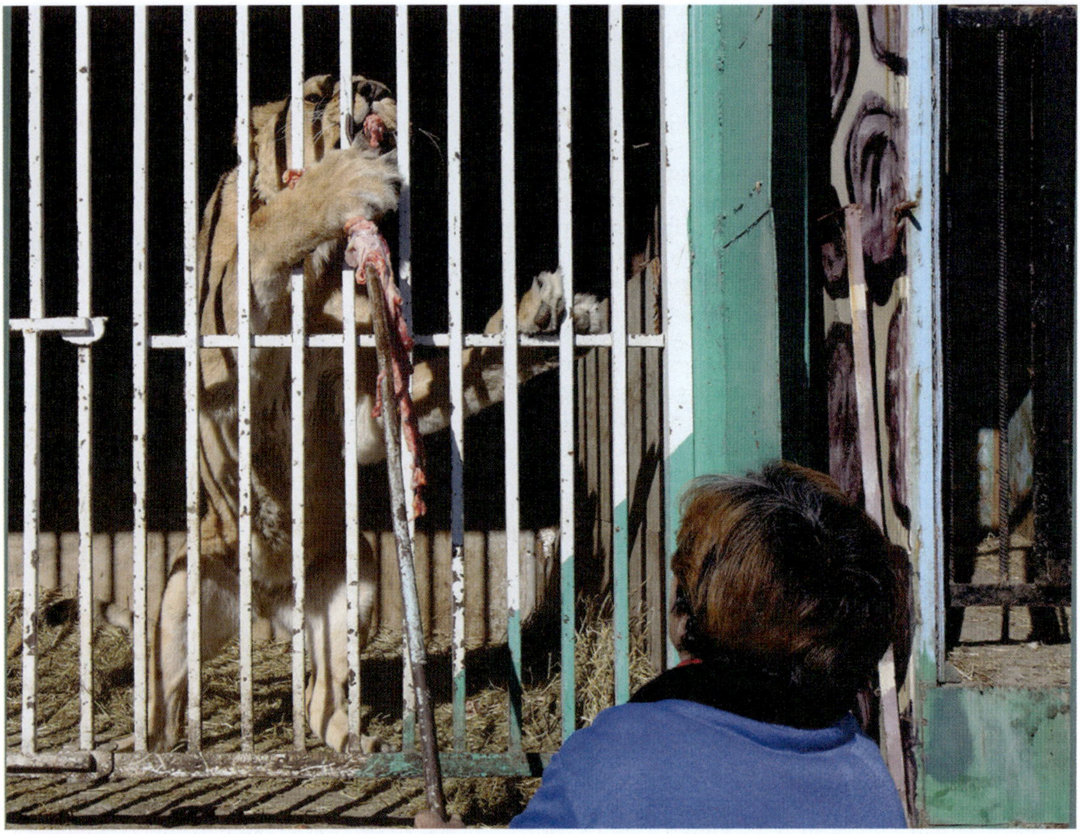

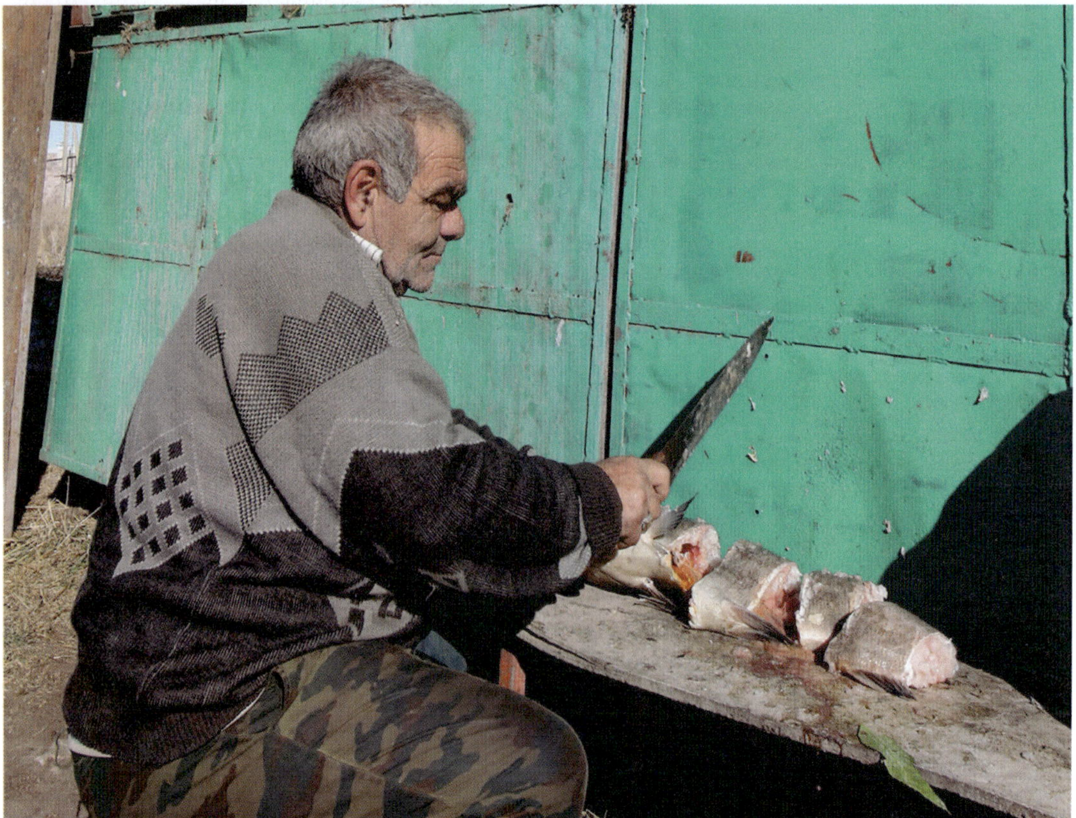

The feeding method was primitive to say the least. Alvina placed a piece of meat on a pole, which she thrust between the bars of the cage. The lion leaped forward and reached through the bars to grab her dinner before dragging it into the back of the cage. The procedure was the same for Mary and the two cubs.

Hovhammes then returned to the hut and brought out a huge fish. The bears started reaching out of their cages as he walked towards them. He lay the fish on the ground and hacked it in two with a large cleaver, giving a piece to each of the bears.

up by the *Daily Mail*, which put fourteen of them on its *Daily Mail Online* website, alongside copy written by Allan Hall. 'Inside the World's Saddest Zoo. Shocking Pictures,' ran the headline.

The story went viral, gaining 25,000 shares and 2,000 comments. Offers of help poured in, along with £46,000 that was raised in one night. One of IAR's millionaire American donors saw the story featured on the wildlife website The Dodo. He was so touched by it that he gave another $20,000 for the lions and a further $2,000 for Mr and Mrs Madoyan.

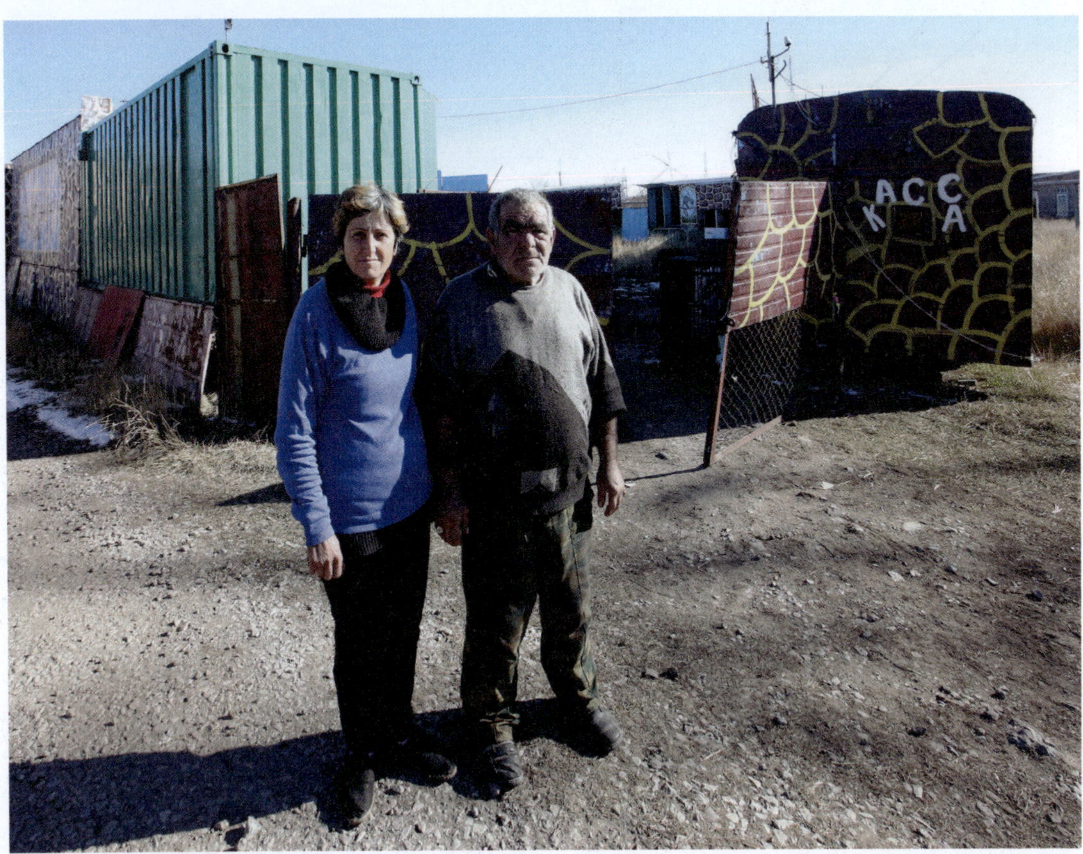

The man then slowly disappeared behind one of the cages. When he came out again, it took me a couple of seconds to register what he was dragging out into the open—a dead foal.

The horse had been rejected at the slaughterhouse as unsavoury, but it was going to feed the lions for another two meals. The couple were really fighting a battle to keep the animals alive.

I had got the photographs I needed, and with dark clouds bubbling up and threatening snow, we decided it was time to head back to Yerevan. Before leaving, though, I ran across the road to a bakery and bought their remaining stock of iced buns.

Back in the hut, Alvina had put the kettle on again, and the four of us sat at the open door eating the buns and watching the animals slowly going mad in their dilapidated prison.

The pictures from the Armenian zoo were picked

The charity Save the Bears was the quickest to move, picking up the two bears within the week and moving them to a sanctuary in Hungary.

It all happened so fast that Maria emailed me, asking for help. She had started the ball rolling and it was now snowballing out of control.

The Bridget Bardot charity offered to get the lions out of Armenia but there was a disagreement about who owned them and, without proper paperwork, the authorities would not let them leave the country. It fell to the Foundation of the Preservation of Wildlife and Cultural assets (FPWC) to use some of the money the story had raised to create a purpose-built holding enclosure for the lioness and her cubs in Armenia.

In the meantime, the Worldwide Veterinary Service sent a team of vets to check over the animals' health.

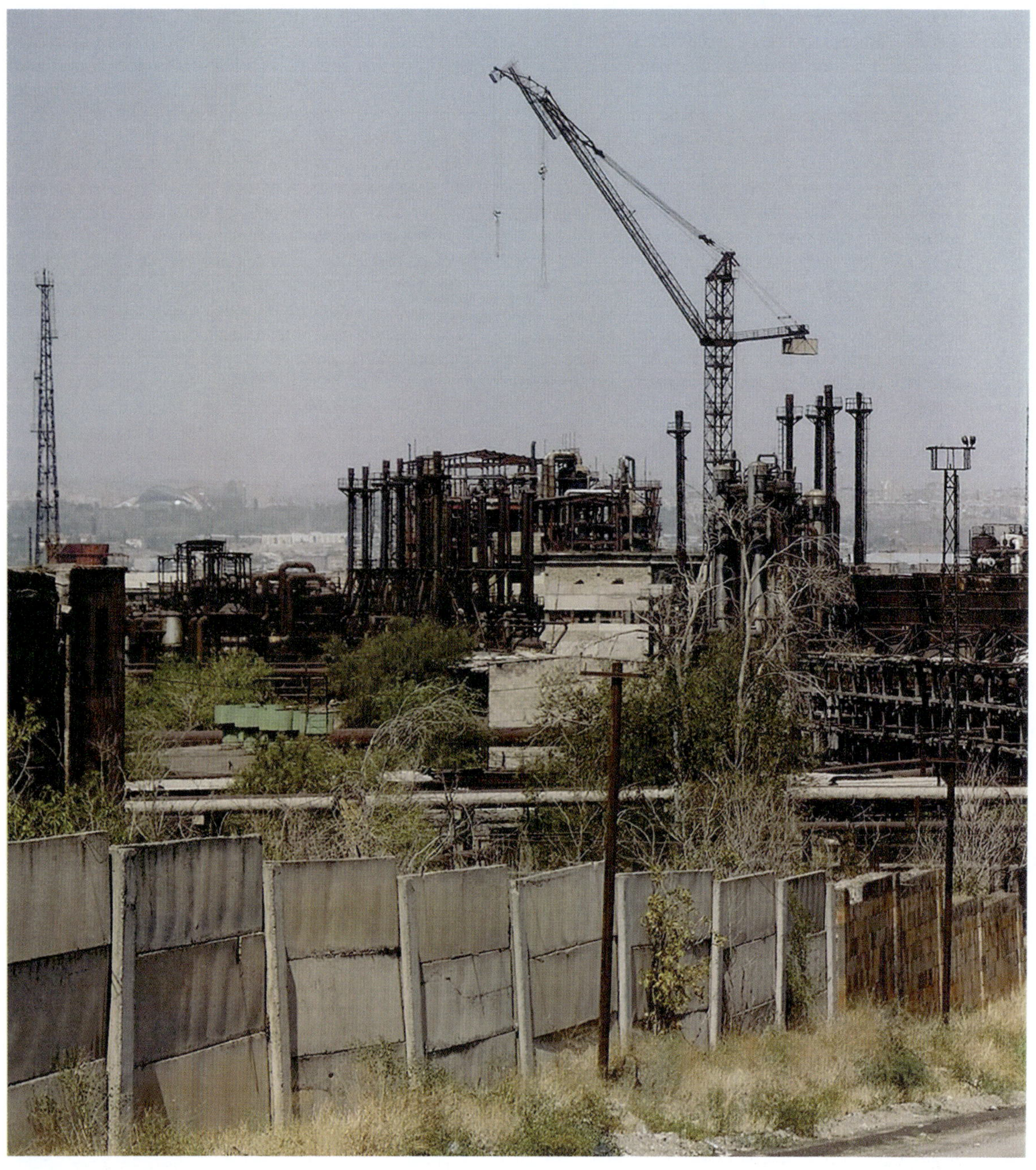

When the time came, Allan Hall, Alan Knight and I travelled to Yerevan to see the lions taken out of their circus cages and moved to a new home, an eco-lodge on the edge of a national park, two hours south of the city. The FPWC lodge had acres of land where horses graze, large birds soar on the thermals thrown up by the mountains and rare mountain goats wander around the lower slopes.

A new building had been constructed with proper safety doors, allowing the lions to be inspected and the cages cleaned. The enclosures, surrounded by double electric fences, had logs for the lions to climb and platforms for them to lounge on.

Before going to see the lions we had to hand over the $2,000 gift to Alvina and Hovhammes. The couple travelled down from Gyumri, and we'd arranged to meet them at a hotel in Yerevan's city centre. They were waiting for us when we arrived with Vicky, an FPWC worker who had come along to translate. The six of us settled down to drinks.

Alan Knight told the couple what had happened to the lions since the story had broken, where they were now and what was planned for them. Vicky relayed the news word for word. Hovhammes sat clutching his beer, obviously ill-at-ease and possibly bored. Unshaven and wearing the same jumper as when we had watched him feeding fish to the

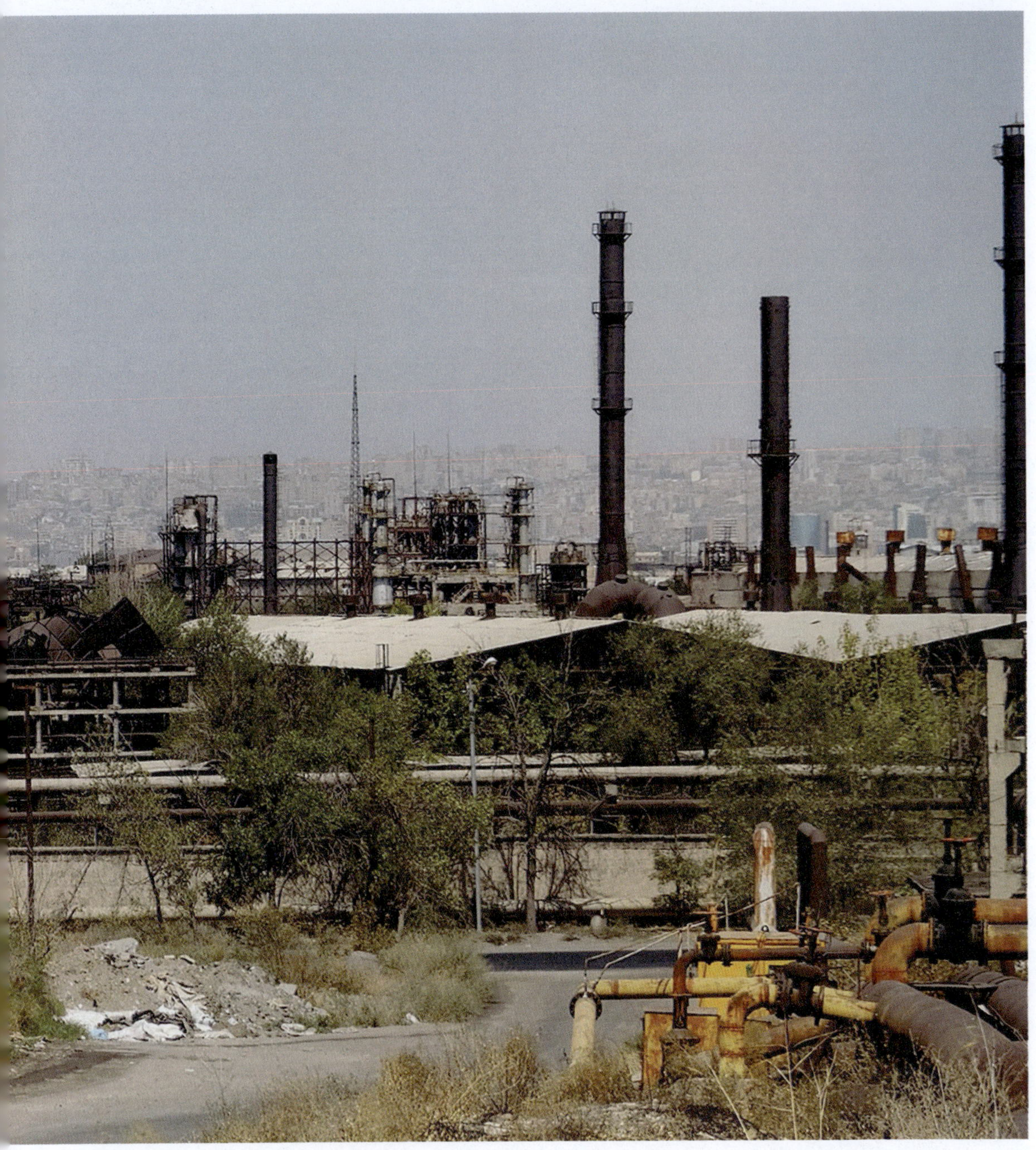

bears, he wasn't skilled at social niceties. Alvina, by contrast, had made an effort and was looking very smart. I can imagine them exchanging words about his appearance before setting out.

Alan produced a thick envelope and laid it on the table. Hovhammes looked at it suspiciously through squinting eyes; his wife stiffened in her chair. Neither of them had any idea about the money that had been sent to them, so Vicky explained. As Alan handed over the envelope, Alvina snatched it away before Mr H could lay a grubby hand on it.

I took a picture of the two of them before they went on their way. Theirs had been a remarkable act of kindness and they deserved every cent they had been given.

Yerevan was a modern, teeming city but as we drove to the eco-lodge, the journey started to feel like a trip back to Soviet times. Broken-down tyre factories flanked the main road out of the city, interspersed with homes that were occupied but looked derelict. Horses and carts mingled with huge lorries trundling southwards towards the border with Iran.

When we arrived at the lodge, I wandered over to look at the lioness, who was still in her crate. This time she growled and leaped up at the bars. Her fight was back. She had put on a good amount of weight and looked much healthier than she had five months before.

The plan was to dart her, then move her into the new block for her first taste of freedom, but the builders had to finish clearing up first. There were piles of rubble, dust and litter in the main area of the cage she was going to be housed in.

I got fed up waiting for the workmen to arrive, so I grabbed a shovel and a dustbin and cleared the cage myself. If I hadn't done, it would have been dark before the move could take place.

Finally, the lioness was darted. She snarled and roared before falling asleep. She was rolled out of her circus cage onto a large blanket and six men carried her over to her new home. She was laid carefully on a fresh bed of straw and left to recover. Her two cubs were moved the same way.

It was dark now, so I returned the next morning to get the pictures I needed of the lions in their new surroundings. Mum was up and about and looking like a proper lioness. Her fur was shiny, she'd put on a hundred pounds and she walked with purpose.

Her two cubs had been put in different sections of the divided pen. They prowled around looking at each other for the first time in years and peering across to their mum in the next section of the cage. My photographs captured the contrast with the horrible conditions back in Gyumri.

But there was even better to come. That afternoon the barrier between the cubs was lifted, and I got great pictures of the two sisters sniffing and prowling around each other before playing together for the first time. That was it; job done. *The Mail Online* ran a follow-up story which got hundreds of thousands of hits.

The bigger follow-up was that the Gyumri lions triggered a set of events that, to date, has seen the rescue of over twenty-five bears, two dolphins and the transfer of a whole other pride of lions to Yerevan Zoo.

In addition, Alan Knight was so appalled by the plight of other bears that had been discovered in captivity in Armenia that he decided to set up a new sanctuary at the eco-lodge and to launch The Great Bear Rescue project.

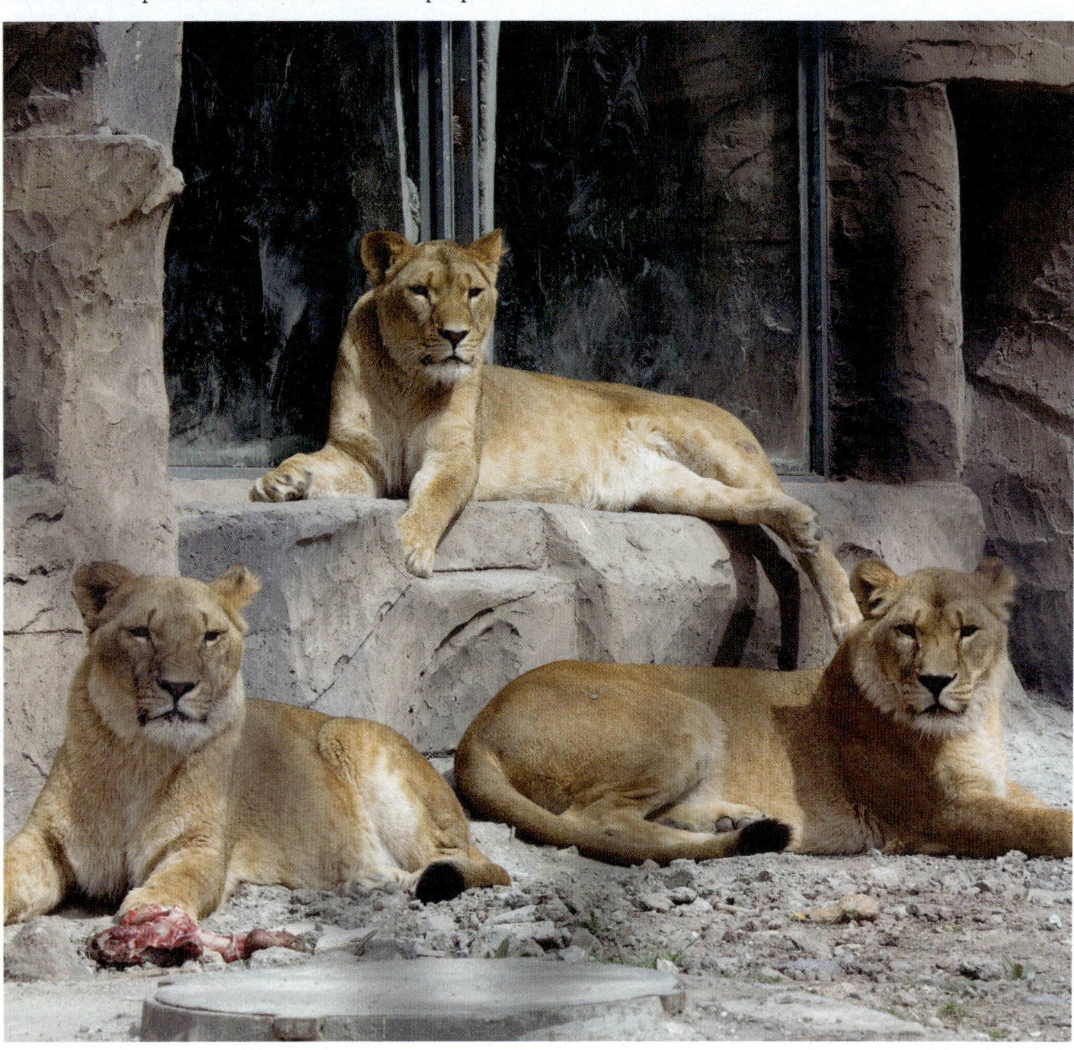

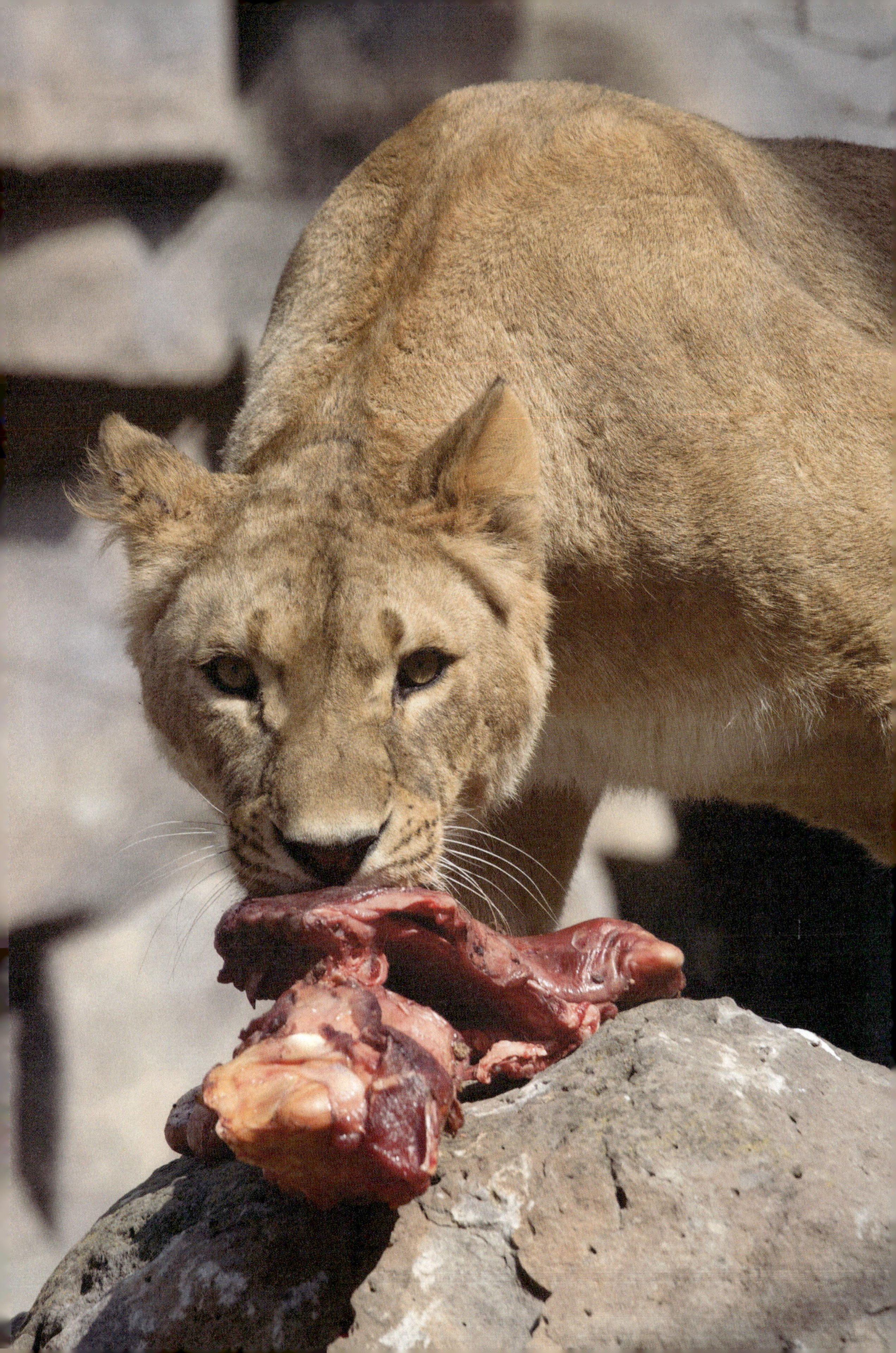

Laziz the Tiger of Gaza

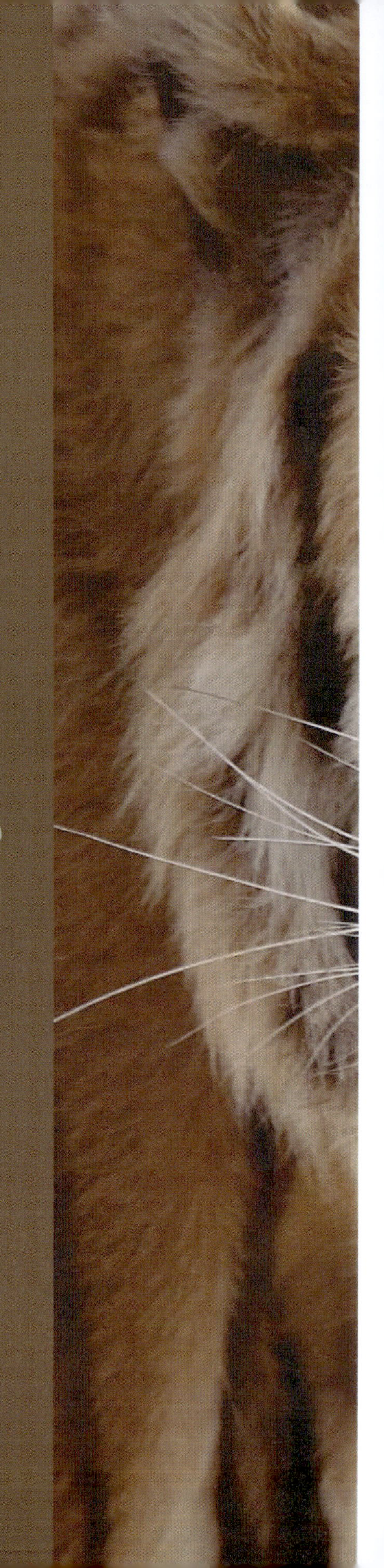

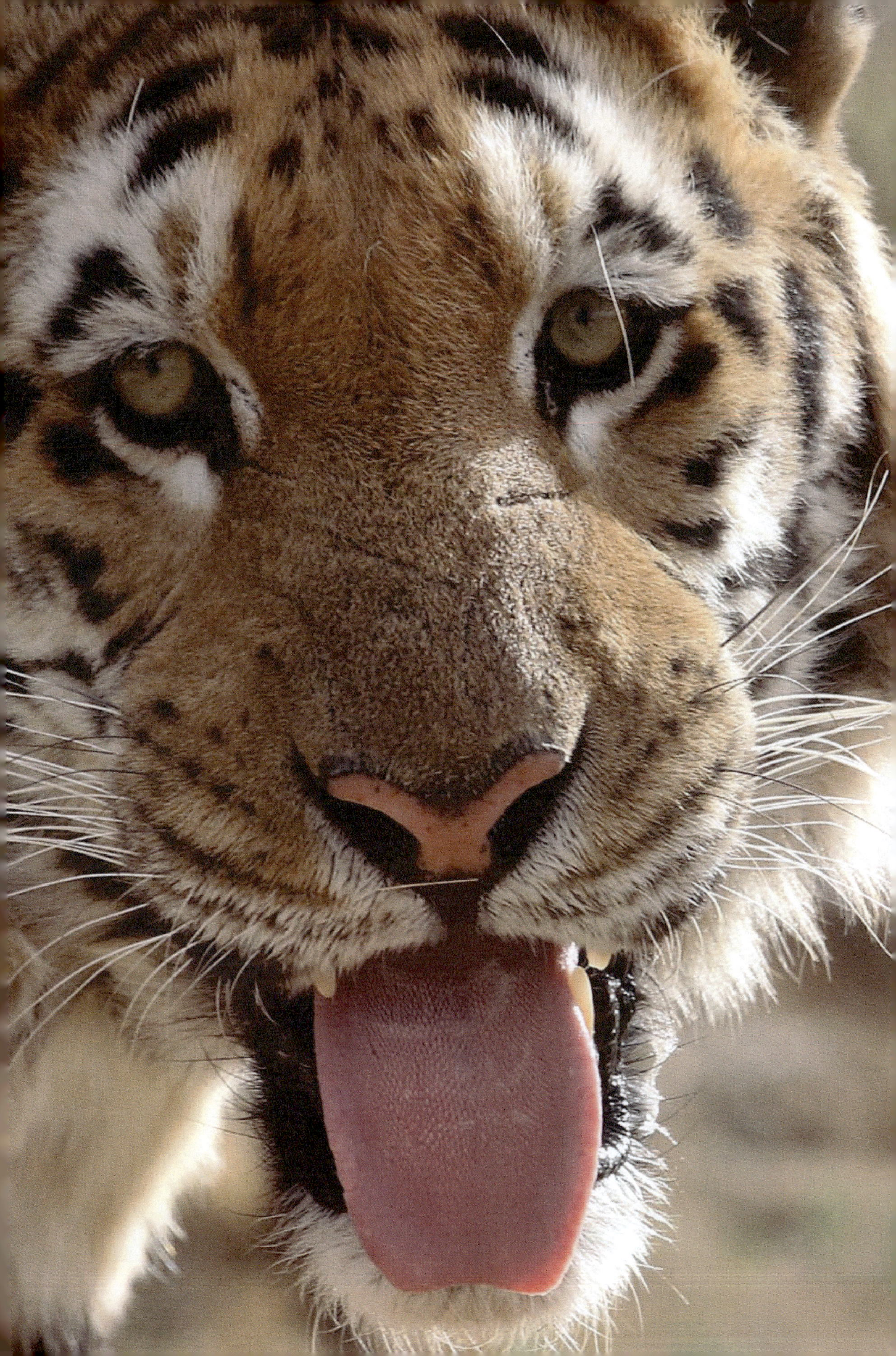

Laziz: the Tiger of Gaza

Even before the war between Hamas and Israel that began in October 2023, people called the Gaza Strip the world's biggest prison camp. Of the 2.1 million people crammed into a hundred square miles, about two thirds of them are defined as refugees by different agencies.

Life in Gaza was lived in almost perpetual state of siege: men under a certain age were not allowed to leave the enclave, and food and power were in short supply.

Perhaps surprisingly, one thing Gaza did have was private zoos: play parks in which animals were incarcerated in tiny pens and cages. The irony was that those who very fairly complained about being confined in cramped spaces appeared unperturbed by the sight of tigers, lions, pelicans, monkeys, tortoises, porcupines, emus and wolves all kept in small enclosures which restricted their movements and which could easily have larger. The animals' plight was made worse because after the 2014 war with Israel, dozens were left to starve to death as supplies ran short.

I had visited Gaza in the 1990s during a previous conflict but it was an invitation from Austrian charity Four Paws that took me back there, accompanied by Allan Hall. The charity was launching a rescue mission called Operation Noah's Ark, aimed at bringing all the animals out of one of these private zoos, in the city of Khan Yunis, so they could be rehoused in sanctuaries elsewhere in the world.

The first challenge for Allan and me was to get into the Strip, hemmed in by Egypt, Israel and the Mediterranean. There are only three entry points, and we were at the Erez crossing—essentially a huge metal box with floor-to-ceiling windows, and filled with rows of immigration counters serving the people who were then allowed to cross the border.

It's a surreal place. Vehicles aren't allowed near the building, which is surrounded by large concrete slabs. You have to dodge these like a slalom skier when walking in with your luggage, while the hot wind blows tumbleweed and stray bits of newspaper across your path.

Getting through is a simple process if you have the right pass. Allan and I didn't. The tight schedule of the zoo rescue meant we hadn't had time to obtain the journalist permits from the Israeli security office several miles away. Lacking this vital piece of laminated plastic meant our progress was held up

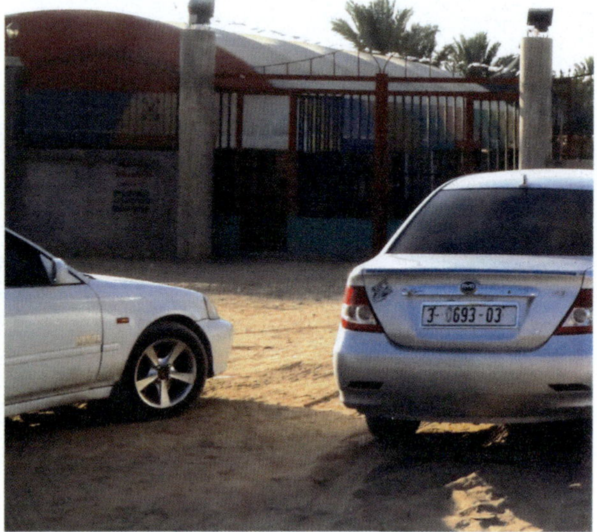

while phone calls were made, questions asked and forms filled in, the clock ticking down all the while.

Finally, the permission to let us out of Israel arrived. We went through the scanners and turnstiles on the Israeli side and through a metal tunnel to the Hamas immigration post. We were subject to more scans and inspection of paperwork by various officials, some in uniform, others not. Whatever else you can say about the place, bureaucracy is alive and well in Gaza.

When we eventually stepped from Israeli onto Gazan territory, a driver was waiting for us and we were soon driving at high speed past bombed-out buildings, homes, factories and warehouses. The citizens did their best to keep the streets clean and tidy, but the whole place inevitably had a run-down and ruined look.

Arriving at our hotel, we were told that our

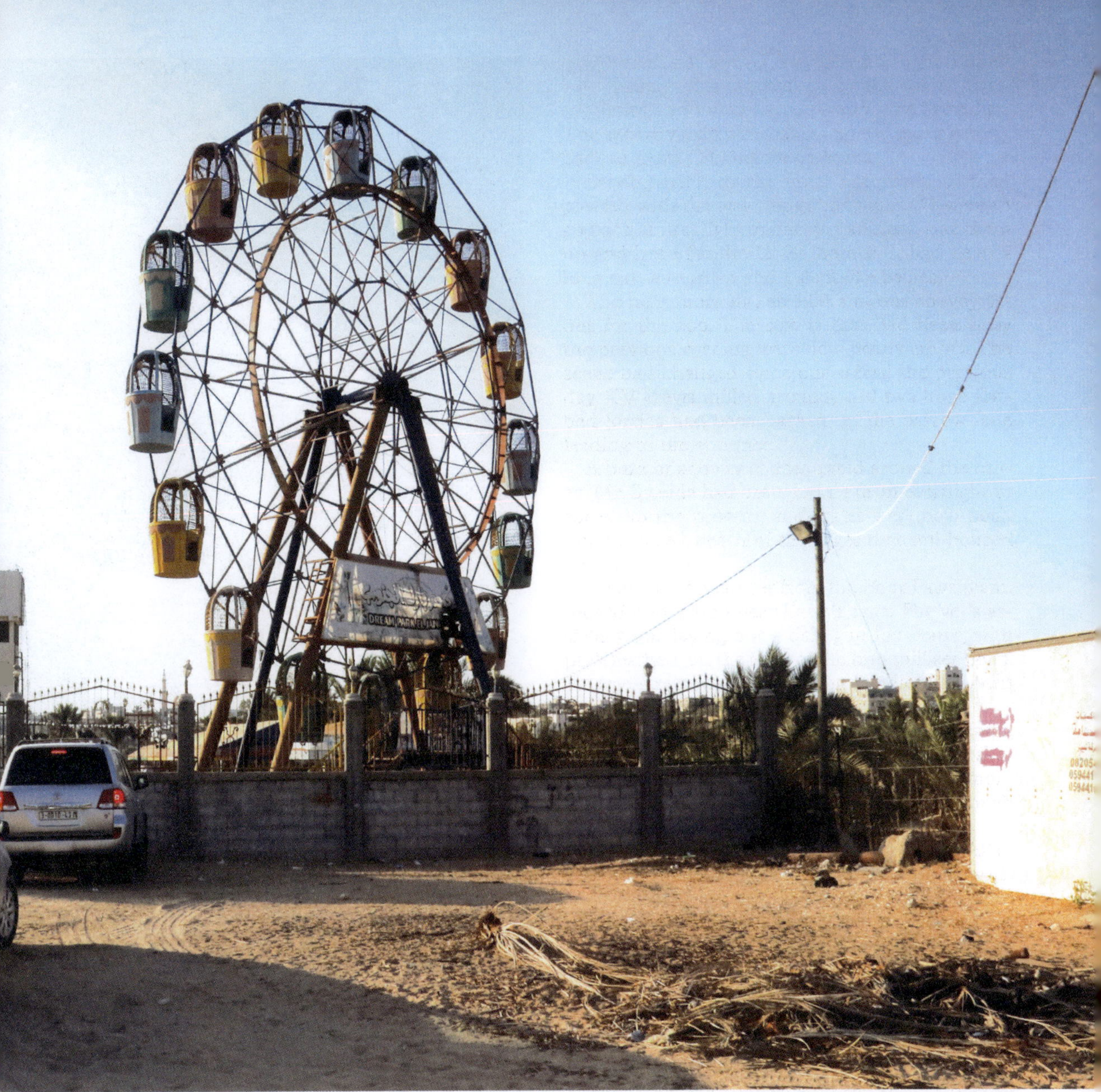

friends from the Four Paws charity were in an open-air restaurant. They were holding a meeting when we walked in: forty people surrounded an Arab-looking man who was outlining the logistics of the rescue.

The team's security officer had heard that the likelihood of Israeli military action had risen. That meant moving within the next half hour to get to the zoo.

While I got my cameras together, a forty-year-old woman introduced herself. She was Ioana Dungler, the director of animals at Four Paws. She said she needed to get to the zoo to build crates and prep the animals for the rescue, and she invited us to join her.

A small convoy of people carriers threaded their way through the traffic. The middle of Gaza City was as chaotic as any other Arab town, with endless streams of cars and flat-bed trucks weaving past randomly parked vehicles, and somehow avoiding running into street sellers offering watches, mobile phone cases, fruit and drinks. One moment we were passing donkeys pulling carts laden with bricks, the next we were being overtaken by top-of-the-range Mercedes with blacked-out windows. We saw battered cars that looked ready for the scrap heap but also a man resplendent on a white stallion. It was a strange mix.

We stopped twice on the way to the zoo: once to buy electric fans to cool the animals on their journey and then for hay. What we found when we arrived was a sad collection of flimsy and rusting enclosures linked by overgrown paths. Faded information boards stood in front of the animal cages. Water ran from a broken tap and pooled outside the monkey house.

Across the road from the zoo was its other half: the fun park, the only such facility for miles around. It had been abandoned after the 2014 war, leaving children with even less than they had before. Its helter-skelter leaned ominously to one side and an octopus ride stood with its arms flopped down among empty kiosks with clowns painted on them.

The zoo owner, Mohammad Oweida, had a menagerie, which he had tried to save but with barely enough provisions for people in the territory, his attempts to feed his animals were in vain and they had died. Not wanting to let the zoo go, though, he had had the dead animals stuffed and placed back in their cages. It was when coverage of this strange twist started being shared worldwide that Four Paws's interest was piqued.

The charity was determined to rescue the zoo's remaining residents, the most prominent of which was Laziz, a magnificent male Bengal tiger. Its thirty-strong team was led by Dr Amir Khalil, an Egyptian vet who had worked with Mr Oweida.

The rescue team had just two days to build wooden crates, line up the rescue lorries and get the paperwork in order, as well as negotiating with Hamas and the Israeli authorities. It was a logistical nightmare.

While the team built the crates, Allan and I wandered round the dilapidated zoo. The cage that Laziz was living in was no bigger than a family living room. It took the poor animal only ten paces to cross this space and it was constantly plodding back and forth. Inside the pen was a metal bucket for water and to one side was a dark, damp area where the tiger slept.

It was pitiful to see such a majestic creature reduced to this level of squalor in the middle of what need never have been a war zone if the combatants on both sides had not thought of the others as animals.

Allan and I continued to explore the area, my camera snapping away at what we found. An emu's head with a quizzical expression poked through a broken fence; a group of fallow deer huddled together looking fearful; a pair of wolves prowled the perimeter of their enclosures, very obviously stressed and on edge.

One side of the zoo was lined with monkey cages. As we walked towards them, the monkeys started throwing themselves at the bars, in a frenzy. It was like something from a Hitchcock film.

At the rear of the complex was a fence about four feet high. Behind it, we found a pelican standing alone in the corner of a shelter. The bird was surrounded by the bones of dead animals. It eyed me warily as I pushed open the broken gate and went in to get a better angle.

The large bird flip-flopped towards me, his webbed feet slapping on the ground. His wings had been clipped to stop him flying off and he looked forlorn, a broken specimen.

Returning to the zoo entrance as the light of day

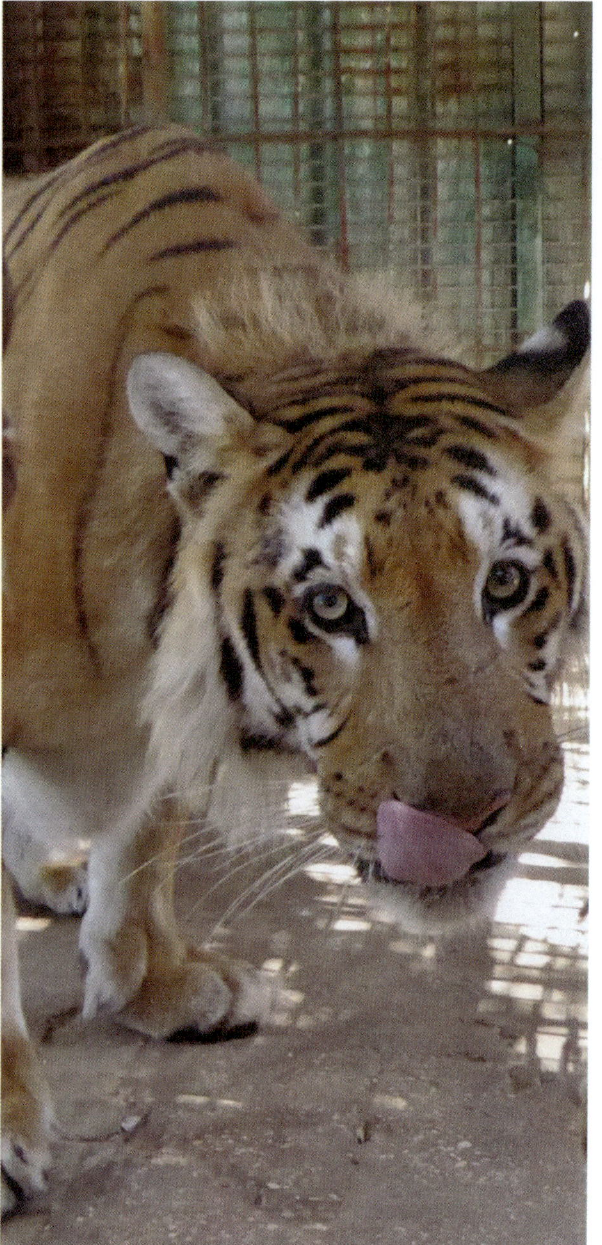

was fading, I decided to concentrate on Laziz and got close to his cage. He was the one inhabitant of this ghastly place who was going to make the story come alive for UK newspaper readers.

The tiger was just inches away from me behind a few metal bars and a bit of chicken wire. He moved slowly along the edge of his space, emaciated, the bones on his haunches sticking out like spikes and a layer of skin hanging down from his body. On his face he had black patches where he'd rubbed his head into the bars.

I got the urge to reach my fingers in to tickle his nose but thought better of it. One more move towards his space would have resulted in me losing my hand. Just because Laziz was in this condition

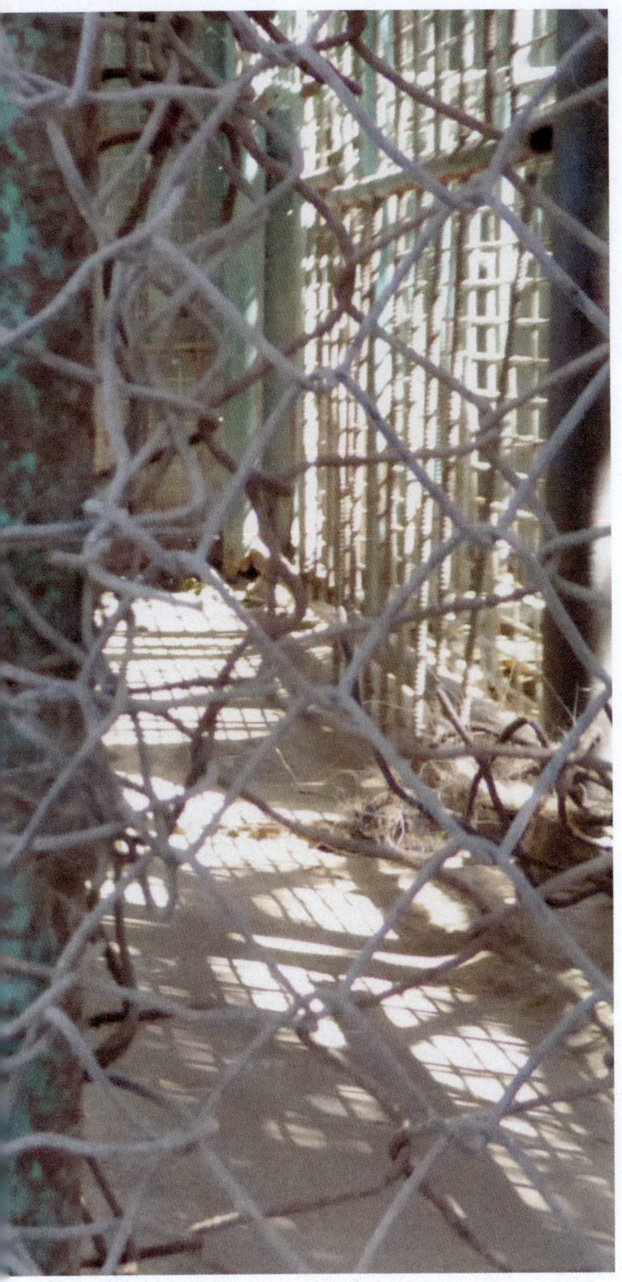

The sun was setting fast, its fading light filtered through dust kicked up by the wind. Swallows and swifts darted around the buildings. The security man was making noises about getting back to Gaza City before darkness.

Driving back to the hotel everybody seemed pleased with the way things had gone. We were to go back at first light to dart the animals, box them up and head for the Israeli border. It had been a long day, and Allan and I slept like babies.

The next morning, at 6:00 am, our convoy set out for the zoo. The streets that had been busy the previous evening were now nearly empty. The scene had changed since our arrival the previous day: TV crews milled around, and two huge flat-bed lorries had been backed up the narrow lane leading to the entrance.

A buzz of activity concentrated around the cages. Mr Oweida had brought in a team overnight to speed up the process, and crates were now positioned close to each of the cages that still housed a living animal.

Frank, a German vet from the Four Paws team, moved into action near Laziz's cage. The vet's assistant was laying out a dart gun for Frank, with pink feathers on the ends of the tranquilliser bolts. A large stretcher with carrying handles had been made ready outside the cage.

The tiger had been locked in his small sleeping den to make it easier for Frank to get a clear shot when it came to knocking him out. I took more pictures of Laziz's sad face looking out through the bars of his cage.

While everything was being made ready, Allan and I went to look at the pelican, which was waddling around his carcass-littered cage. Much to our surprise, Dr Amir arrived and asked us to help capture the bird by herding him towards one of the team, Jamal, who was ready to wrap him in a towel.

You might think a pelican with his wings clipped would be easy to catch in a small enclosure. You'd be wrong. I stood behind the bird while Allan stood to one side, blocking off an exit. The pelican shot between the pair of us with amazing speed, and every time we moved he thought of a way to escape. Jamal tried to close in with the towel but he was far too clever, outmanoeuvring us with great skill.

Our hopeless efforts went on for fifteen minutes until Jamal had had enough. He walked out of the pen, leaving Allan and me standing guard over the bird. We were all gasping. Allan and I puffed and panted in the morning sun, a sheen of sweat on our brows; the pelican opening and closing his large bill, gasping for air. Attempting to capture and avoiding capture are strenuous activities.

Jamal reappeared holding a fish and threw the towel to me. As soon as the pelican spotted the fish, he started walking towards it. Allan and I crept round behind him and just as he was about

didn't mean he could be taken for granted. The speed and power of any tiger is amazing. As their paws come forward they extend their claws, which can cut through flesh like butter.

Even in this sorry state, Laziz was a born killer. I decided just to take his picture.

Allan asked Ioana how the animals, especially a Bengal tiger, had got into Gaza in the first place. It turned out that they had been smuggled in from Egypt through the same illegal tunnels used to smuggle arms. She said that in 2007 the zoo owner had been importing animals from Libya and Sudan. Little care was taken. A baby elephant had been transported on a trolley but died soon afterwards.

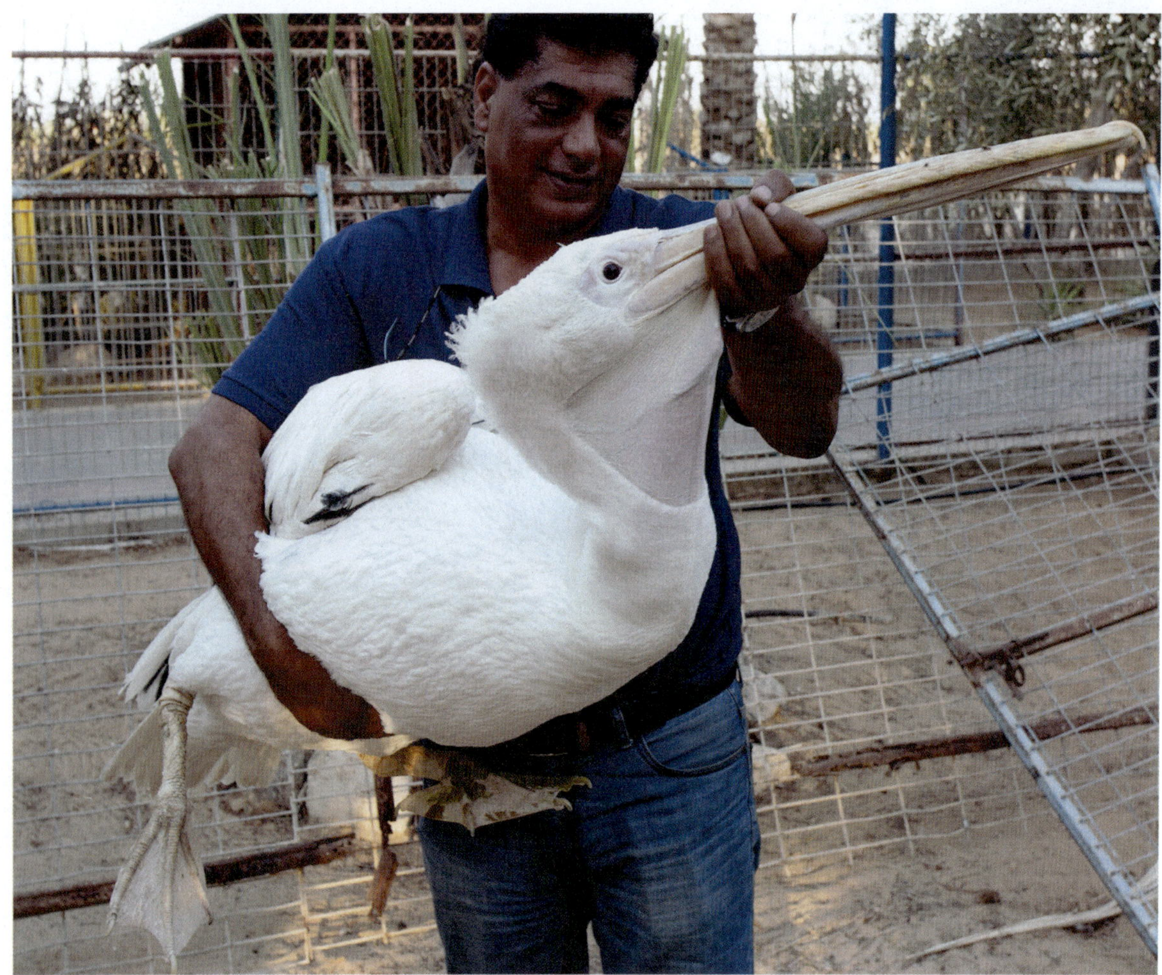

to grab the snack, I smothered him with the towel and Jamal clamped a hand round the pelican's huge bill. I ran to get my camera to photograph the bird being carried away to be packaged up.

After all this commotion, everyone was told to quieten down. Frank was about to dart Laziz.

He put the barrel of the dart gun through the bars of the cage and fired. Laziz flipped round, snarling and spitting at Frank, but fifteen minutes later he was fast asleep.

As we waited for him to be removed from his prison I got into conversation with Yaser Murtaja, a local video journalist and photographer who ran a media company in Gaza City. We chatted about life in the territory and he told me how hard it was to get his work recognised in the outside world. He gave me his card and told me to call him before we left.

Frank poked Laziz with a pole. When an animal has been tranquillised, there is a chance it may wake up suddenly and you don't want to be anywhere near a tiger when this happens. When Frank was sure the animal was still in the land of nod, he ordered someone to unlock the cage.

Frank went in and started checking Laziz's teeth, paws and eyes, while the webbing stretcher was brought in and placed to one side of the tiger. Four men including Frank rolled him over onto it. Even in his shrunken state, it took all their strength to manhandle Laziz out of his cage.

I took some striking shots of the tiger laid out on the floor, with nothing between him and the camera.

The vets continued to work on Laziz. A patch of fur was shaved on his leg, blood samples taken and an intravenous drip inserted. One of the team kept a check on the time, telling the vets how long he'd been out for. His heart rate, blood pressure and vital signs were constantly monitored. It was a very impressive operation.

Dr Amir decided it was time for Laziz to be put in his travel crate, which was then hoisted onto one of the flatbed lorries.

Time had evaporated; it was now 11:00 am. The team had got the headline act onto the lorry, but the convoy could not take off until they had got all the monkeys, emus, deer and wolves into their crates and onto the lorries as well.

Allan and I watched and photographed them at work for a couple of hours until we had enough pictures and information for the story to work. We took a taxi back to Gaza City, but by the time we

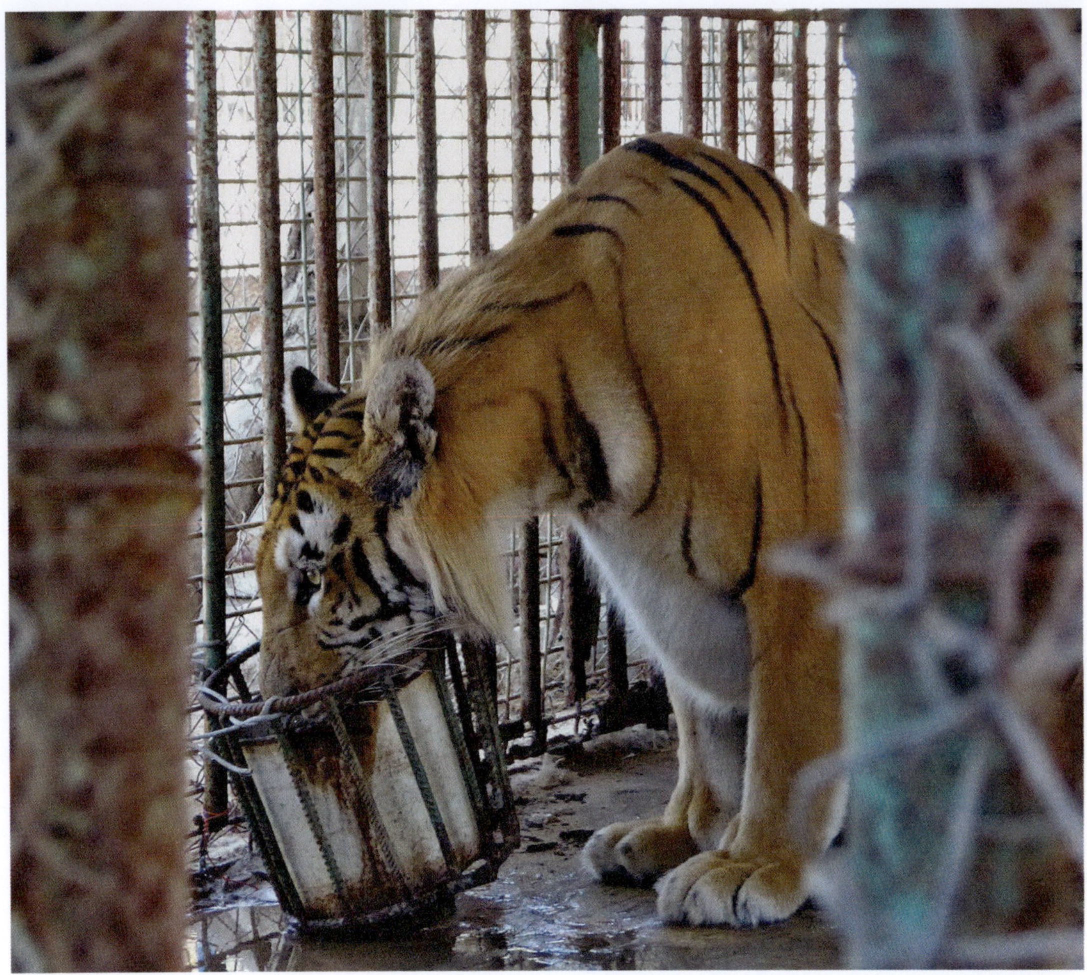

got there it was too late to cross the border, so we spent another night at the hotel.

I called Yaser, the photographer I had met, and he invited us to his office on the fourth floor of a modern block with mirror windows that looked out towards the Mediterranean. He greeted us with mint tea, and over the next hour or so he showed us his setup. It was impressive

Three photographers worked for him shooting video and stills, and he put their work out online, despite the very slow internet service in Gaza. He showed us stunning pictures of daily life in the territory, as well as corporate videos and coverage of clashes with the Israel Defense Forces.

Among other things, he showed us a short film that followed a man who'd been called by the IDF to say that his flat was about to be bombed. The reason they gave was that one member of his family was a member of Hamas and was therefore a legitimate target.

The camera follows the man into the stairwell as he shouts to his neighbours to get out. Convinced the flats have been cleared, he stands at the end of the street waiting for the missile to arrive. With two minutes to go a cry goes up that somebody is still in the building.

The man runs back into the front door screaming, followed by Yaser. With just seconds to spare, a woman is brought out. The film then shows the explosion as the laser-guided bomb obliterates the building.

The aftermath is one of panic and confusion, the fire brigade fighting in vain to put out the blaze. Just as things seem to calm down, another call comes through to say that there will be a second strike.

It is a gripping document of the realities of life in Gaza. The film ran for eighteen minutes and an American TV company used it in full.

We left Yaser and his team editing their pictures of the zoo mission. It was time for Allan and me to get back to Jerusalem. Before we left Gaza, we saw the lorry convoy with lines of wooden boxes containing the animals. Laziz was panting beneath the electric fan on top of his cage.

The next time we saw Laziz was at Lionsrock, the Four Paws sanctuary three hours south of Johannesburg, South Africa. We watched as he was released into a vast area of rocky veldt with a large pool of water, a small wooden shelter, long

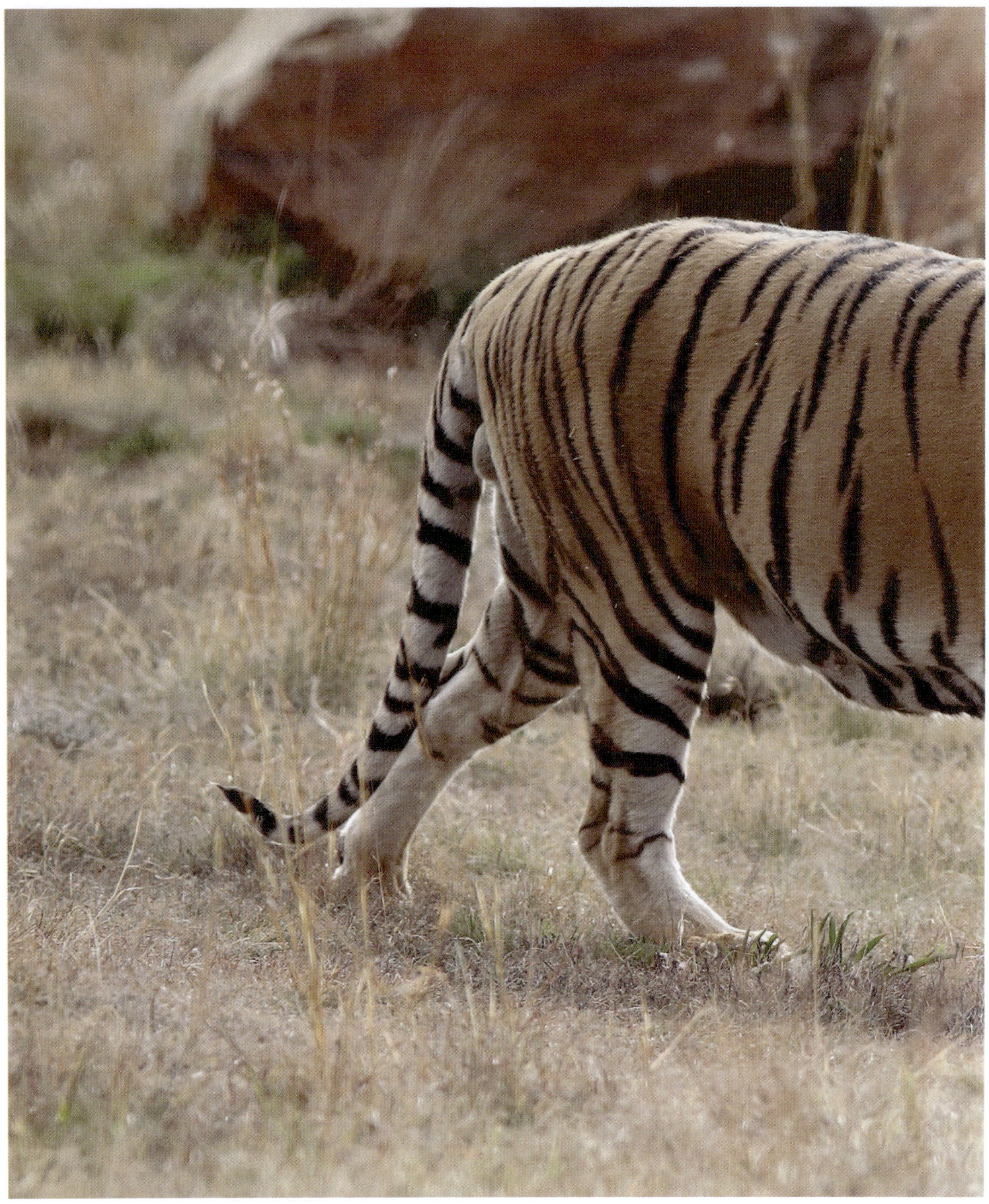

grass to hide in and another tiger in the next enclosure. Allan calculated that Laziz's new home was 10,000 times bigger than the one in Gaza.

Shortly after dawn the next day, I was dropped off outside Laziz's enclosure. Double twenty-foot fences kept Laziz safe. I settled down in the long grass on my side of the wire with my camera trained on Laziz looking out at me from his wooden house.

There was no movement for well over an hour but eventually the tiger emerged. This was the moment I'd waited for. He stretched, yawned, then ran towards the dividing fence housing the other tiger before coming up to the wire to take a closer look at me. I thought of the moment I had wanted to reach into the cage of a damaged and depressed creature back in Gaza.

I spoke softly to him and walked a few paces to my right. Laziz mirrored my steps. I ran a few paces and he did the same. I turned and ran back a bit further; the tiger bounded along on the other side

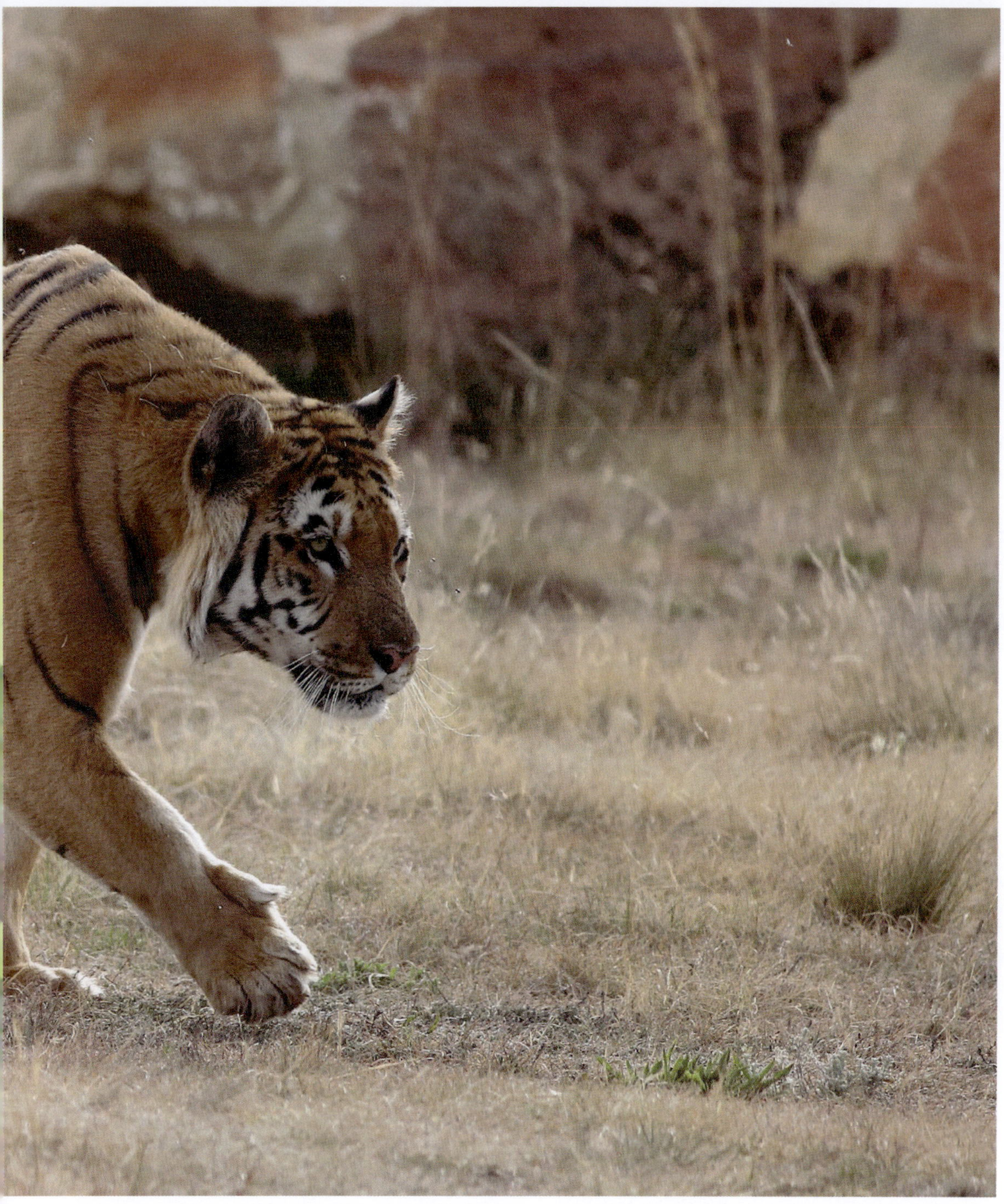

of the fence. This was infinitely better than a tickle on the nose.

Just as abruptly as he had approached me, Laziz returned to his hut, but I was grateful for those special few moments playing with him. *The Daily Mail* used the pictures and *Mail Online* posted over twenty images. It seemed like the perfect end to the story.

But there was to be a sombre postscript. A year later, I watched on the BBC news as a man on a stretcher was shown being taken from the protests at the border fence near Gaza's Erez crossing. The person was wearing a flak jacket with the word PRESS on it.

It was Yaser. He had been shot accidentally by Israeli security forces while filming a border protest for Al Jazeera and had died in hospital an hour later. He was married with a small son. He was also a very brave and skilled photographer with dreams of seeing a wider world. In all his short life he had never left the Gaza Strip.

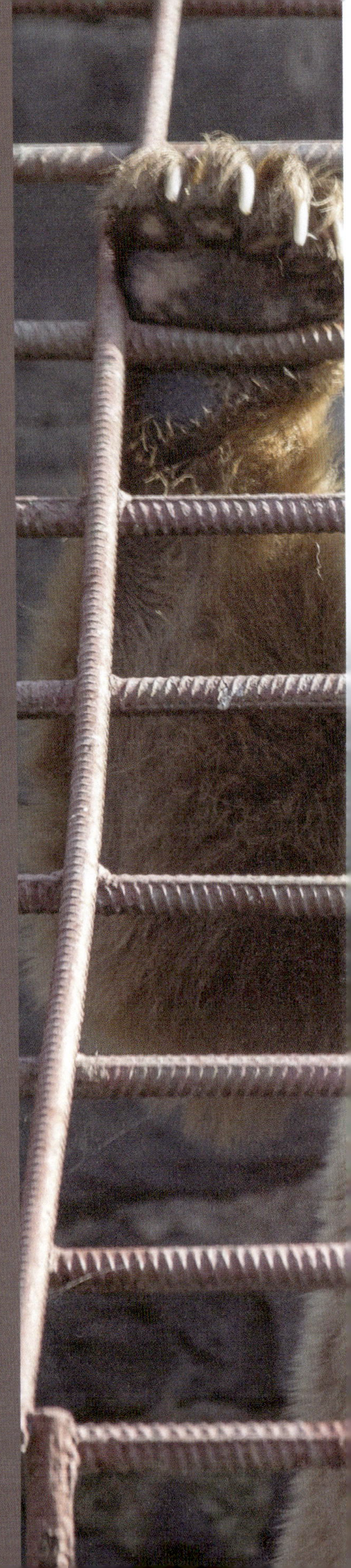

Dasha

The Great Bear Rescue begins

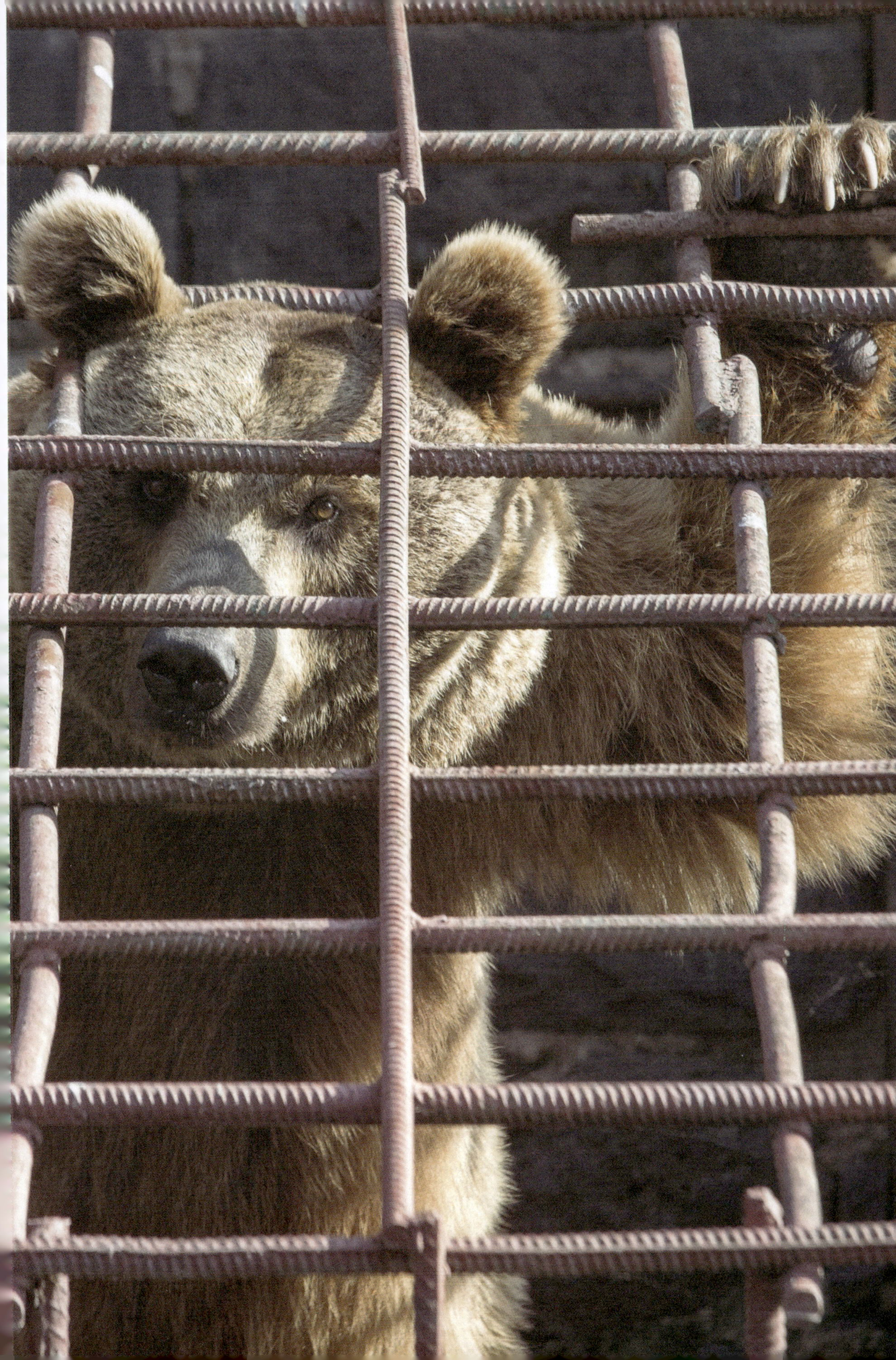

Dasha: The Great Bear Rescue begins

True to his word, Alan Knight invested in a bear rescue operation in Armenia. Following our adventure with the Gyumri lions, he met government officials and put up €30,000 to build a bear rescue centre next to the new lion enclosures.

I flew back to Armenia with Alan for two reasons: to check on the work carried out and to seek out two bears caged in a Yerevan restaurant.

A furnace-like wind met us as we stepped off the plane; the temperature was near forty degrees Celsius.

We drove straight to the eco-lodge where, if anything, it was even hotter, with the wind channelling down a gorge between two mountains and hitting the lodge full blast. Even with mobile air conditioners pumping out cold air night and day, it was stifling.

The work on the bear enclosures was moving along well; high double fencing had been erected outlining the huge area where they'd be able to roam. The vet centre was also going up. Everywhere there was evidence of great industry.

Down in a dip away from the noise and activity was an old shipping container housing two baby brown bears that had been rescued from a garage forecourt. The youngsters would be the first bears to be released back into the wild the following spring under the IAR's Great Bear Rescue project.

I walked gingerly up to one of the holes punched into the side of the container. It was very dark inside but we needed pictures of the pair for a fundraising campaign.

The bears were kept in near isolation for their own good; the more they got used to the sound of people, the more endangered they would become in the wild.

In the darkest corner of their home two wide-eyed bears peered back at me. Without saying a word, I adjusted my camera and took their picture in low light.

Next morning, we met Ruben, the director of the Yerevan Zoo and the boss of the Armenia-based Foundation for the Preservation of Wildlife and Cultural Assets (FPWC), who had arrived to take us on a drive to see possible release sites for the bears.

A compact man of about forty-five with an easy smile, Ruben had a rather theatrical manner, which was no surprise. As well as being the son of a famous filmmaker, he was a filmmaker himself, and a musician, and much else. His talents were seemingly endless.

Heading down the unmade road from the eco-lodge to the road proper, we passed a village of ramshackle buildings that Ruben told us made up one of Stalin's first farming co-ops in the Soviet Union. Livestock milled around the low cowsheds that Ruben said were the original structures.

Once on the main road south, Ruben drove like all former Russians—fast and with scant regard for what was coming towards him. We crested the switchback road that wound to the top of a 10,000-foot pass and then stopped to look back across a vast plain to snow-capped Mount Ararat. It was an impressive landscape.

A short way down the other side of the pass we came to the main highway, along which articulated lorries thundered south to Iran or north towards Georgia. We joined the stream of traffic heading southwards. After about an hour we turned left into a small village, which looked very similar to the one we had seen earlier.

We drove past field after field of wheat, climbing higher all the time. Ruben gunned his Toyota Land Cruiser up a single-track road before turning off onto a rugged track. The further we went, the steeper it got. Twenty minutes of hard driving brought us to a meadow with an amazing show of wildflowers.

Our destination was a brown smudge on the side of the towering hillside up ahead. This was the potential release site in a national park controlled by the FPWC.

The last part of the journey was twisting and steep, which required the Toyota to use every bit of its four-wheel drive capacity. The brown smudge we'd seen from a distance was now just 200 yards away. It looked like an old quarry but was in fact the result of a rock fall which had happened years before.

As we rounded the last of the corners we came across a pen containing more than a hundred sheep. Beyond it on a piece of flat ground stood a yurt and a battered blue lorry. The yurt wasn't one

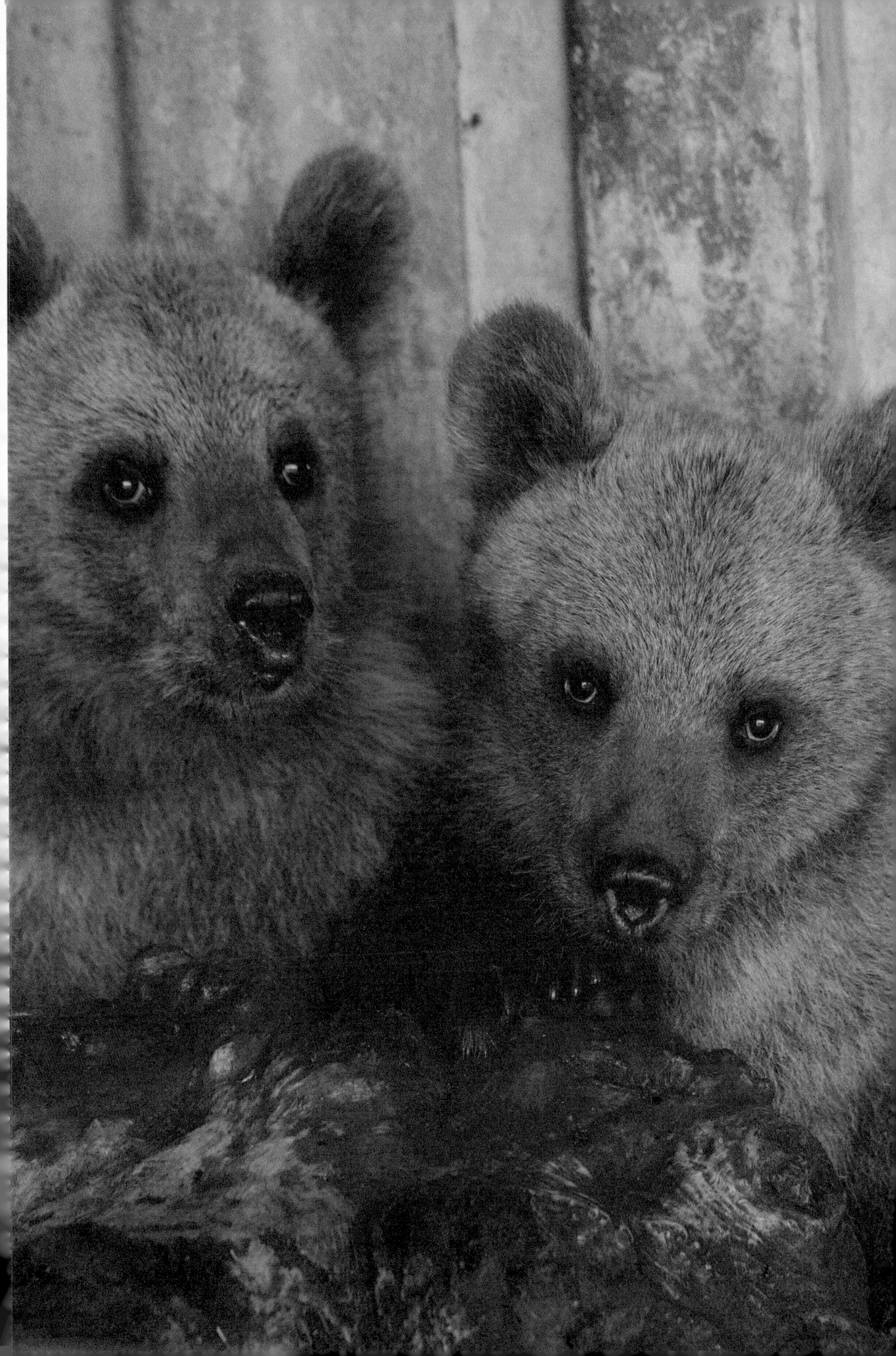

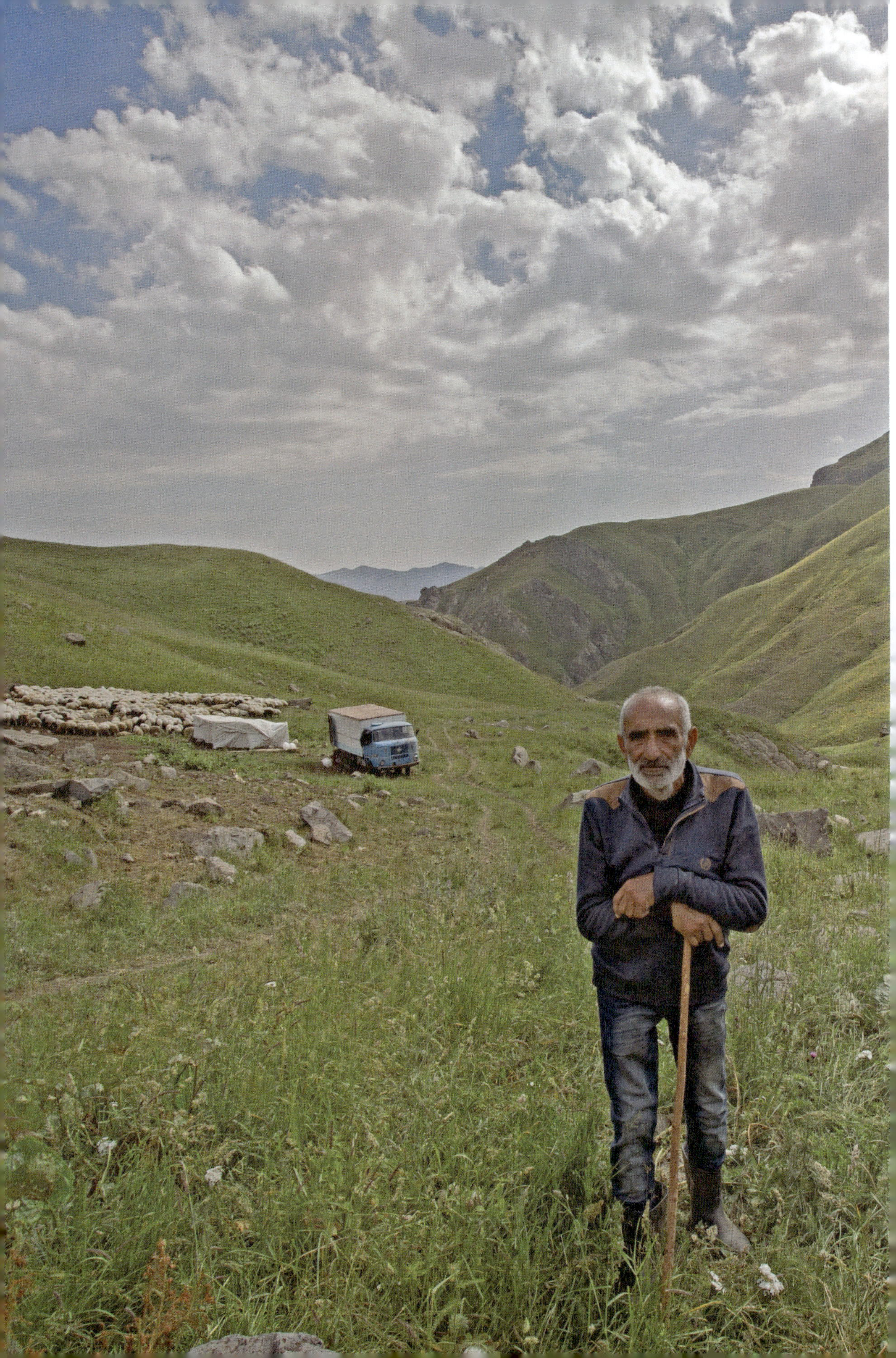

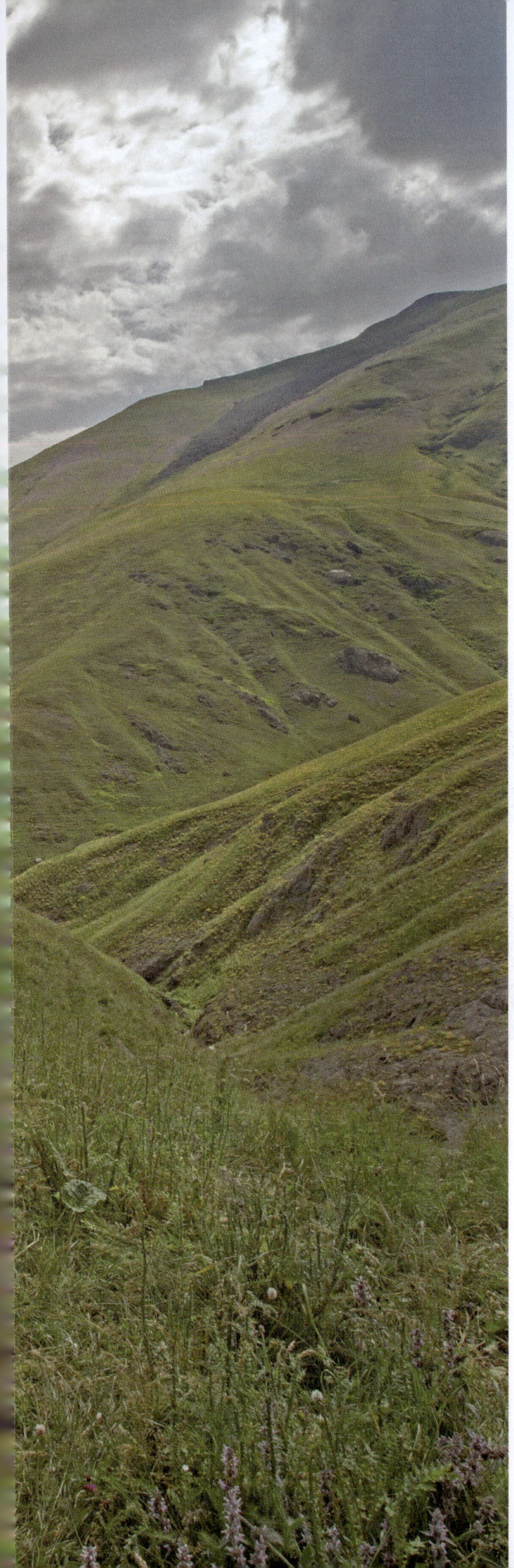

of those expensive structures you see at Glaston-bury but a rough collection of animal skins thrown over a wooden frame.

Ruben explained that this was a shepherds' camp. The herders brought their flocks up here for the whole of the summer.

A man waved us over to join him at a fire outside the yurt. The air at this altitude was fresher than down in the plain. A toothless woman joined us. She looked as if she was sixty years old but was probably only forty. She offered us a glass of tea or coffee but Ruben advised us to refuse.

I popped back to the car and returned with some cans of beer I had bought during our journey. I handed them out and we cracked them open. Another man came out of the yurt and we all sat there drinking. A large white dog greeted each of us in turn, wagging his tail. Enjoying the amazing view with this family of shepherds was a moment to relish.

A call of nature took me off to a patch of nettles close by, where my eyes fell on a massive mound of animal guts. It was three feet high and lined with veins, with what looked like a million flies swarming round it. I couldn't understand what I was looking at

When I came back to the yurt, Ruben explained that the shepherds left out cow offal for the bears, to deter them from eating their sheep.

I photographed the head of the shepherds with his flock and took some shots of the bear release site before we made our way back to Yerevan. It was there that we were to meet our restaurant bears.

Ruben had been told that two bears, a male and a female, were being kept in a cage half-submerged in a river just outside the city. It sounded awful.

Yerevan is divided by the river Hrazdan, which runs along a deep gorge cutting through the middle of the city. Fed with snowmelt from the mountains, the river gives power to the city through large hydroelectric plants.

Apart from the power plants there are riverside restaurants. These are rather good and offer mostly grilled meat with colourful salads, freshly baked bread and cold beer. They're a nice place to go for lunch.

And that is what we did. We arrived at our restaurant at lunchtime, the busiest hour of the day.

Two large wooden verandas stood close to the water with tables laid with colourful tablecloths and sparkling wine glasses. Waitresses darted about, serving couples and families enjoying their lunch.

It looked idyllic—until you looked across the river. On the opposite bank, a tangle of welded bars made up a large cage, one section in the water, the other on a concrete platform. Inside the cage, two bears walked back and forth. Bored brainless, every now and then one of the bears slid into the water and bit on the bars, raising laughter from the diners.

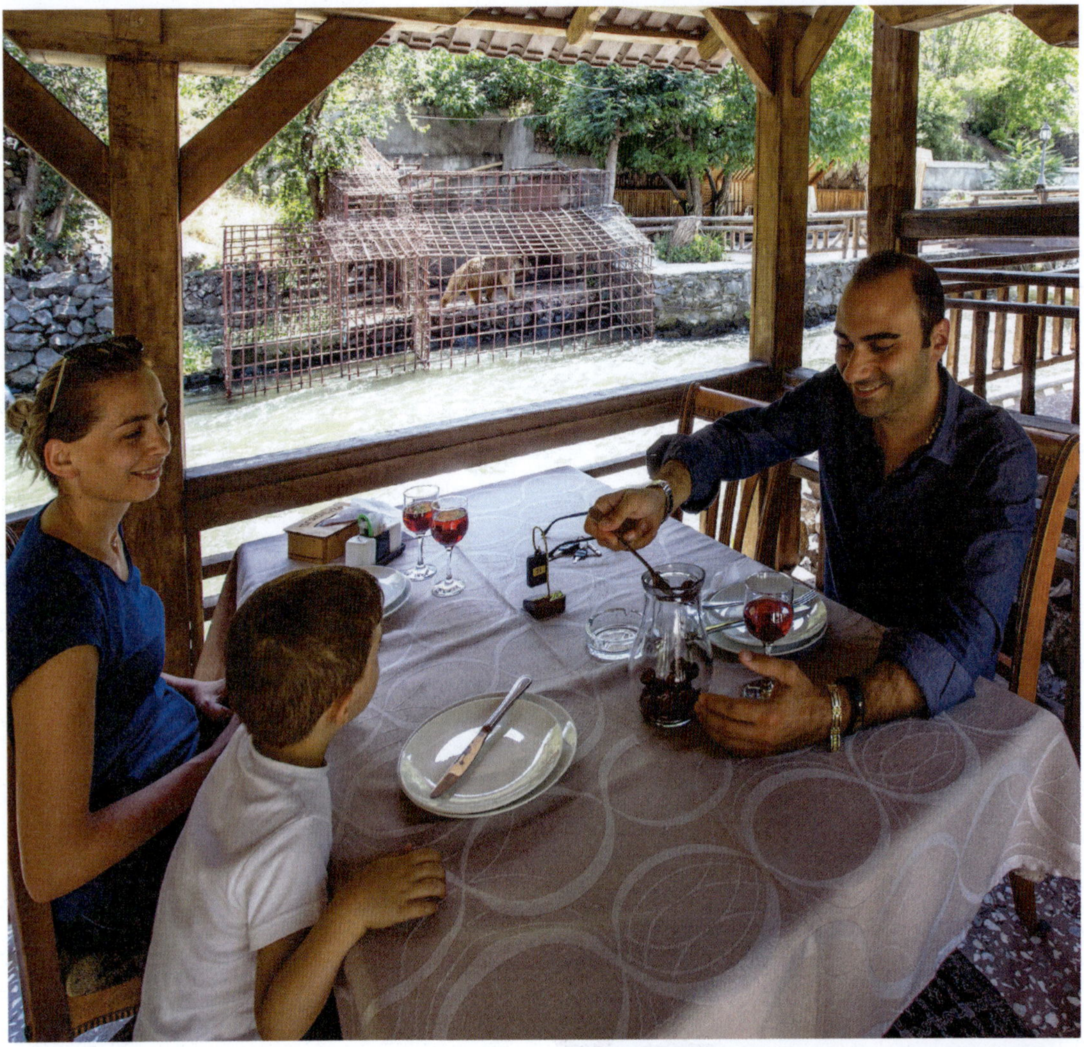

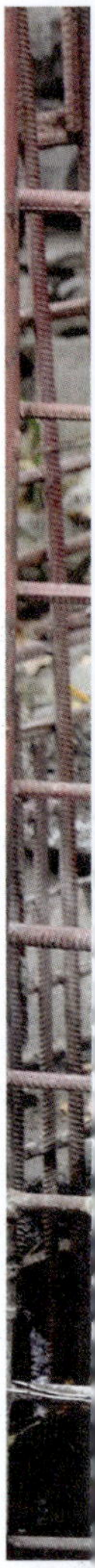

At one table was a perfect couple with a young child. Wine had been poured and they were helping themselves to olives. Ruben asked if we could photograph them. 'Sure,' said the man. And I did. But we had come to photograph the bears, visible in the background.

After a few minutes I wandered across a bridge leading to the bear enclosure. As I approached, one of the bears jumped up and thrust its paws through the broken bars. I'd taken a piece of bread with me and threw it onto the narrow ledge in front of the bear, whom we later learned was called Masha. He grabbed it quickly, giving me the chance to take a picture of his snout poking out of the cage and his paw grabbing the bread.

Alan was enraged by the scene—and thus began a chain of events that would come to a heartwarming conclusion two years later. It began, three months after we found them in the restaurant, with Masha and his female companion Dasha becoming the first bears to be rescued under the Great Bear Rescue campaign.

And Dasha was going to surprise us all.

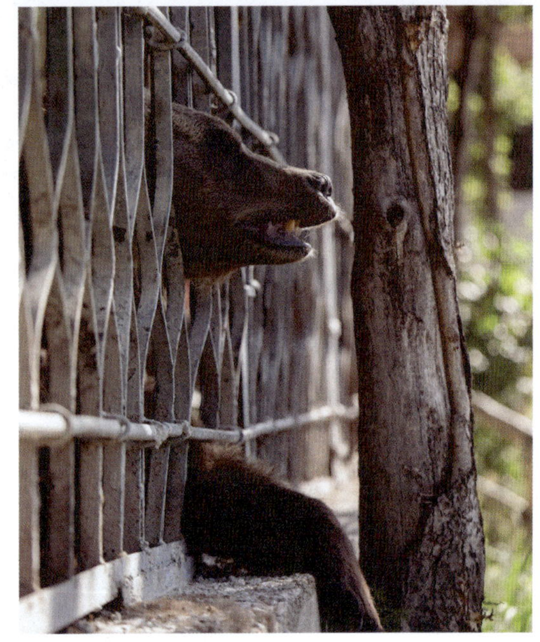

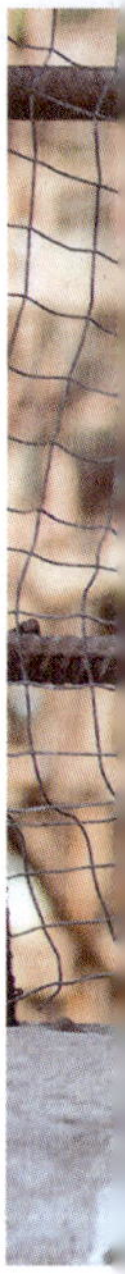

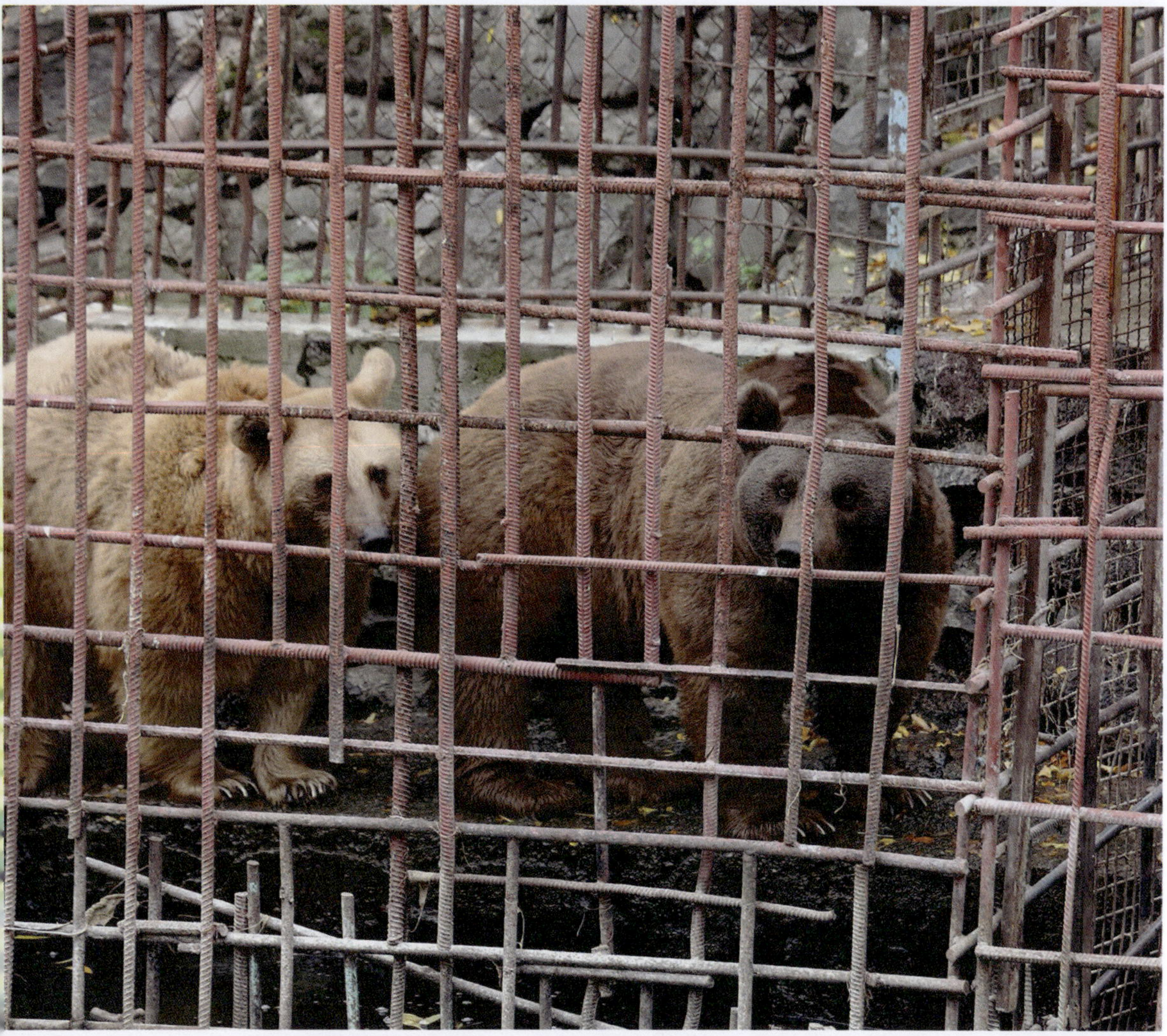

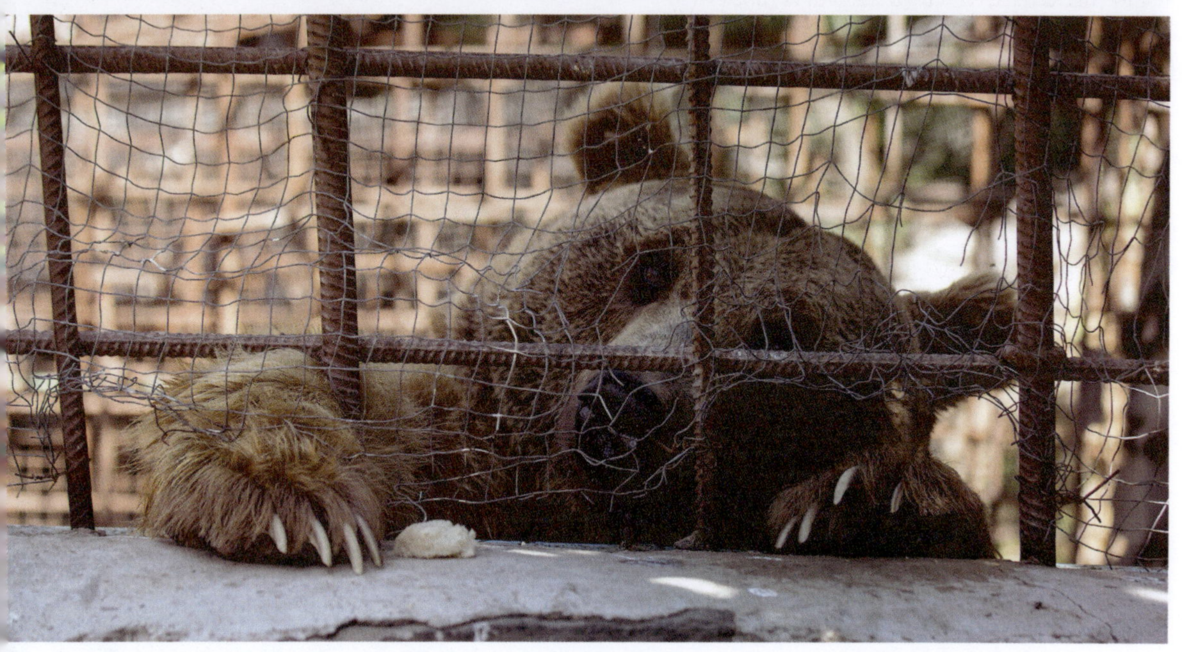

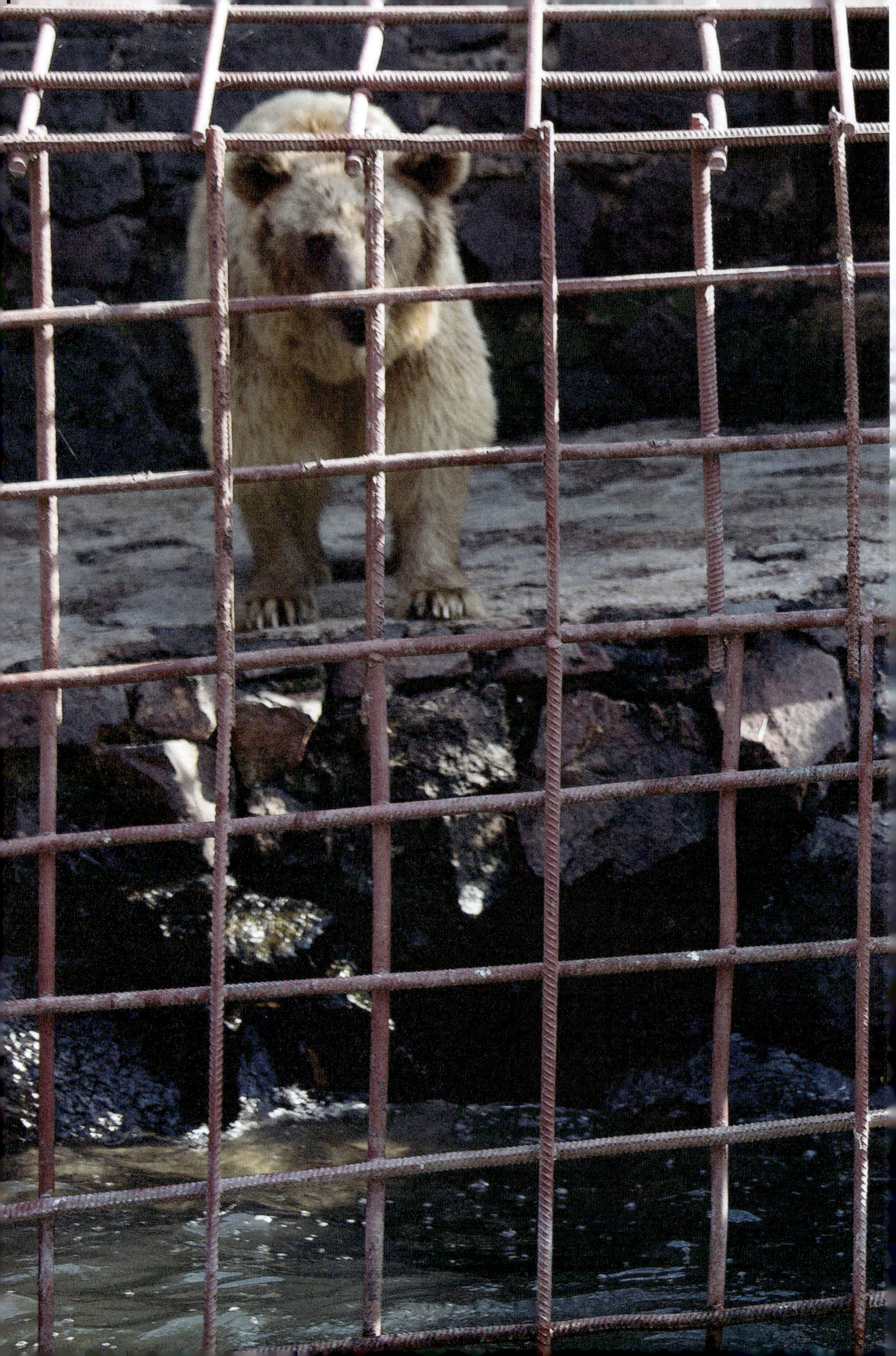

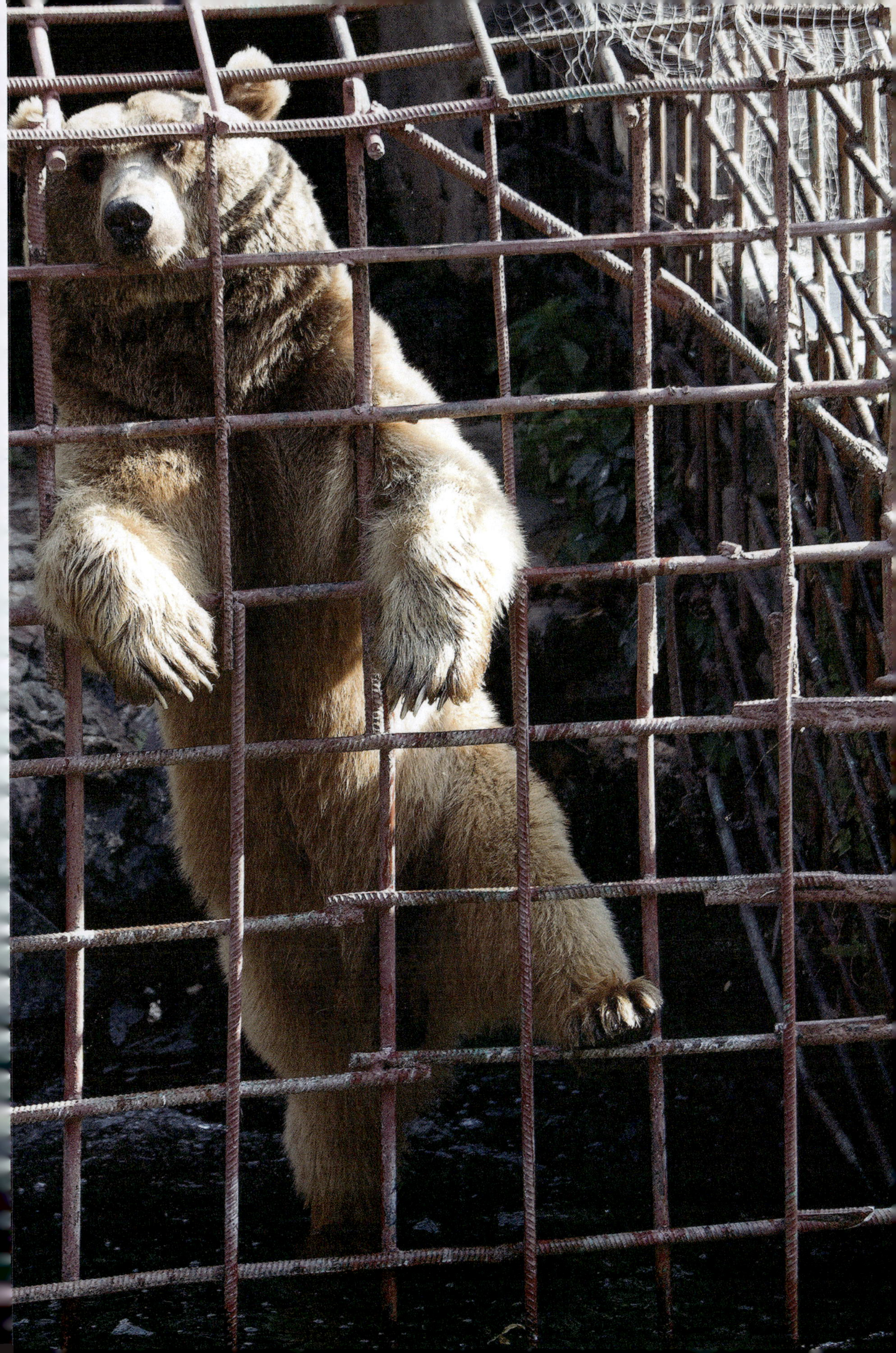

Jumbos in jimjams

plus a rhino and a leopard

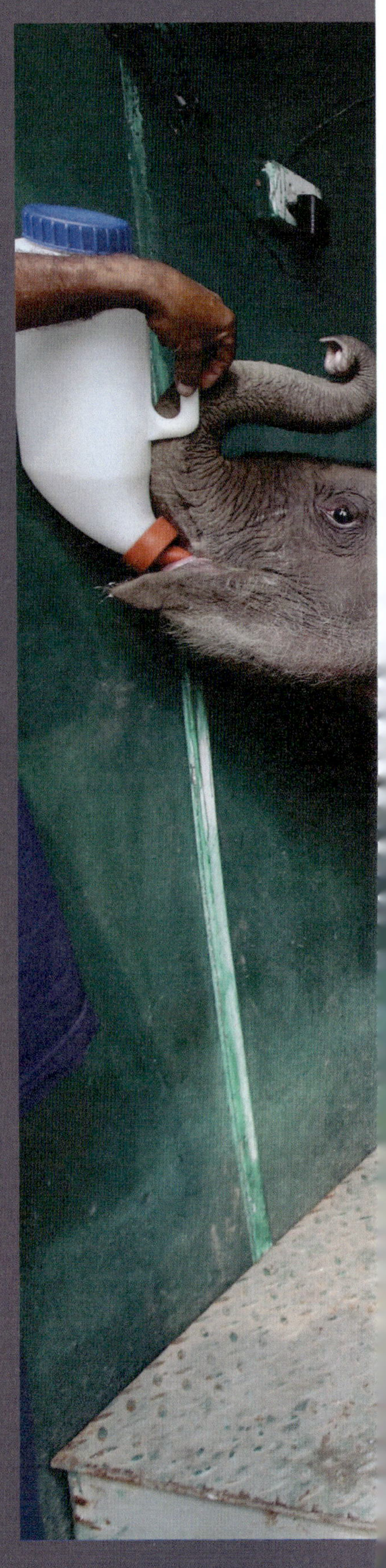

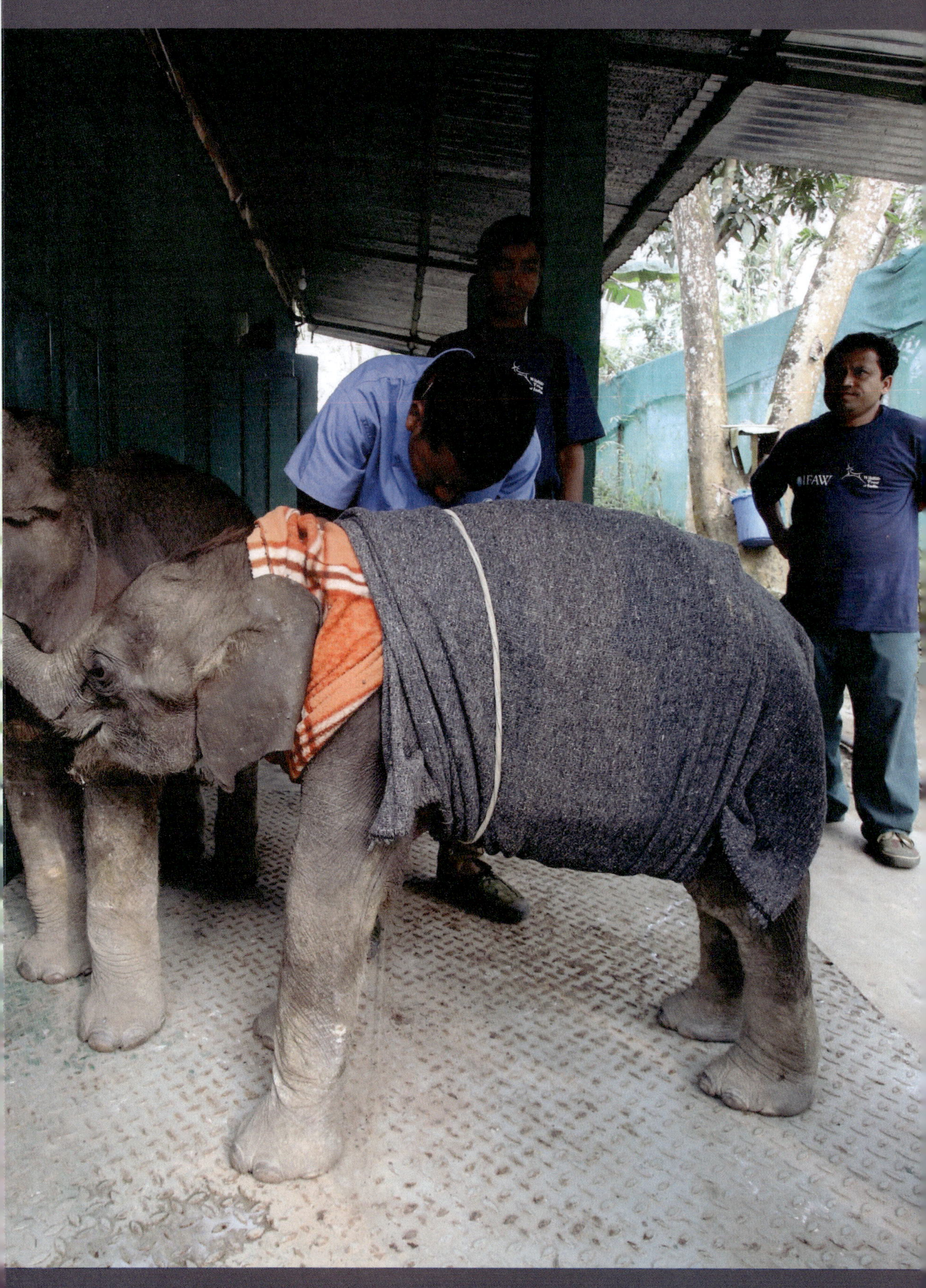

Jumbos in jimjams plus a rhino and a leopard

The Indian rhinoceros, or the greater one-horned rhino, lives in the UNESCO World Heritage site of Manas National Park, at the eastern end of the Himalayan foothills in Assam, northern India. In the 1980s and 1990s the park's wildlife population was devastated by poaching and the rhino was almost completely wiped out.

It was here that Clare Sterling, the press officer of the International Fund for Animal Welfare (IFAW), went to record the delivery of two one-horned rhinos to a new purpose-built enclosure. Clare had worked on regional papers and the *Times*, so she knew the sort of stories I would need for the *Daily Mail*.

Indian rhinos are the ones with large plates of armour, as illustrated in the famous woodcut print of 1515 by the German artist, Albrecht Dürer. The animals are big beasts but very quick on their hooves when they need to be. It was their speed that Clare told me to watch out for as I photographed the new pair, which I found grazing in the park.

The keeper looking after the two was Maheshwar Basumatary, otherwise known as Ontai. His story was a classic poacher-turned-gamekeeper yarn.

He had lived near the park, but the only way to support his family was by poaching and animal tracking. After being caught by the park rangers, he had been offered a job as a gamekeeper working for the Wildlife Trust of India (WTI), a partner organisation to IFAW.

Clare and I did a story on how the former thief had helped the park to develop anti-poaching techniques. Perhaps out of gratitude for the opportunity he'd been given, Ontai insisted on rounding up all the senior staff for the pictures I was taking, so that by the time we had got everyone together and photographed them it was nearly dark.

Next morning Vivek Menon from WTI arrived to pick us in an open-topped Land Rover. We were going to watch the release of one of the world's most elusive animals, the clouded leopard.

Dawn was just breaking as we drove through the gates to the park, birds chattering in the trees and monkeys running along in front of us. A mist hung over the grey landscape and I pulled my fleece round me against the cold.

After bumping along the park's tracks for a long time, we arrived at a river that formed the border between India and Bhutan. By this time the sun was high in the sky and the mist had burned off, allowing the temperature to soar. We found a cooling shade at a ranger's camp of wooden huts.

This remote spot had been chosen for one of the clouded leopard's first 'soft releases'. The animal in question sat in a large cage on the back of another Land Rover. After being returned to the wild it would be closely monitored until the keepers were confident that it could look after itself.

The conservationists were taking special care because the clouded leopard species is on the conservation red list, meaning it is threatened with extinction. The WTI and IFAW work together on rehabilitation programmes for beautiful big cats like this.

The release was an important moment for the WTI, and Assam's environment minister had been driven into the park to watch the operation, accompanied by a retinue of armed bodyguards, drivers and advisers.

All had scrambled over boulders in the riverbed to get a good look at the rare animal, which meant that things had become a bit crowded in the forest and it was thought best to pull back for a while until the leopard settled down. Clare took the opportunity to interview the minister, with Vivek listening to every word, all three perched on white plastic garden chairs while armed guards patrolled the area.

After a while Vivek suggested that Clare and I go 'birdwatching' on the other side of the river. It was his covert way of helping us to find a good spot from which to watch the clouded leopard being released.

Ontai had been put in charge of the cat and he smiled as we approached. He was ten feet up in a tree with a large crate connected to the forest floor by a wooden ramp. The leopard had been transferred into this crate and was snuffling around investigating all its scents and sounds and taking note of sudden movements in its new forest environment down below.

Ontai walked up the ramp and carefully undid the door to the cage before retreating behind it. We sat like a pair of excited schoolchildren on the ground, waiting and watching. With great caution, the clouded leopard slipped through the gate before edging slowly down the ramp, getting its first taste of life on the outside. Suddenly, the big cat leaped off the ramp onto the ground. We all held our breath, waiting to see what it would do.

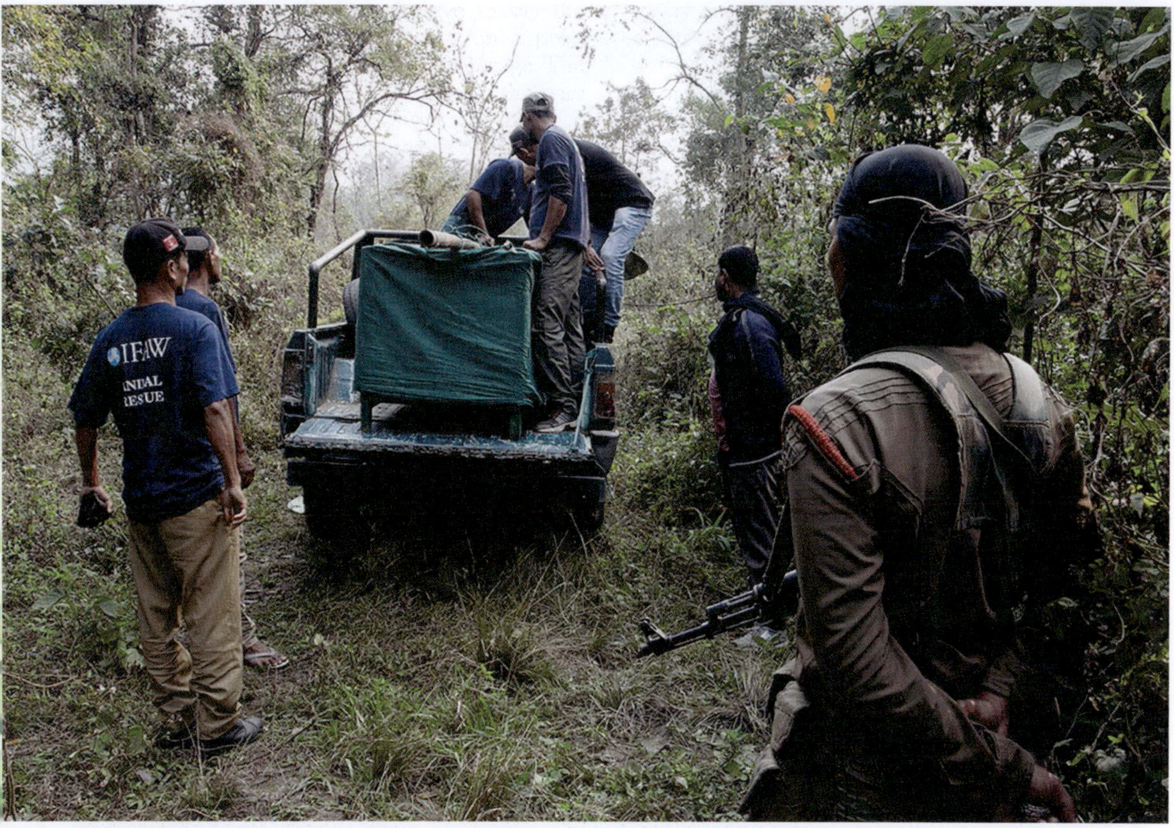

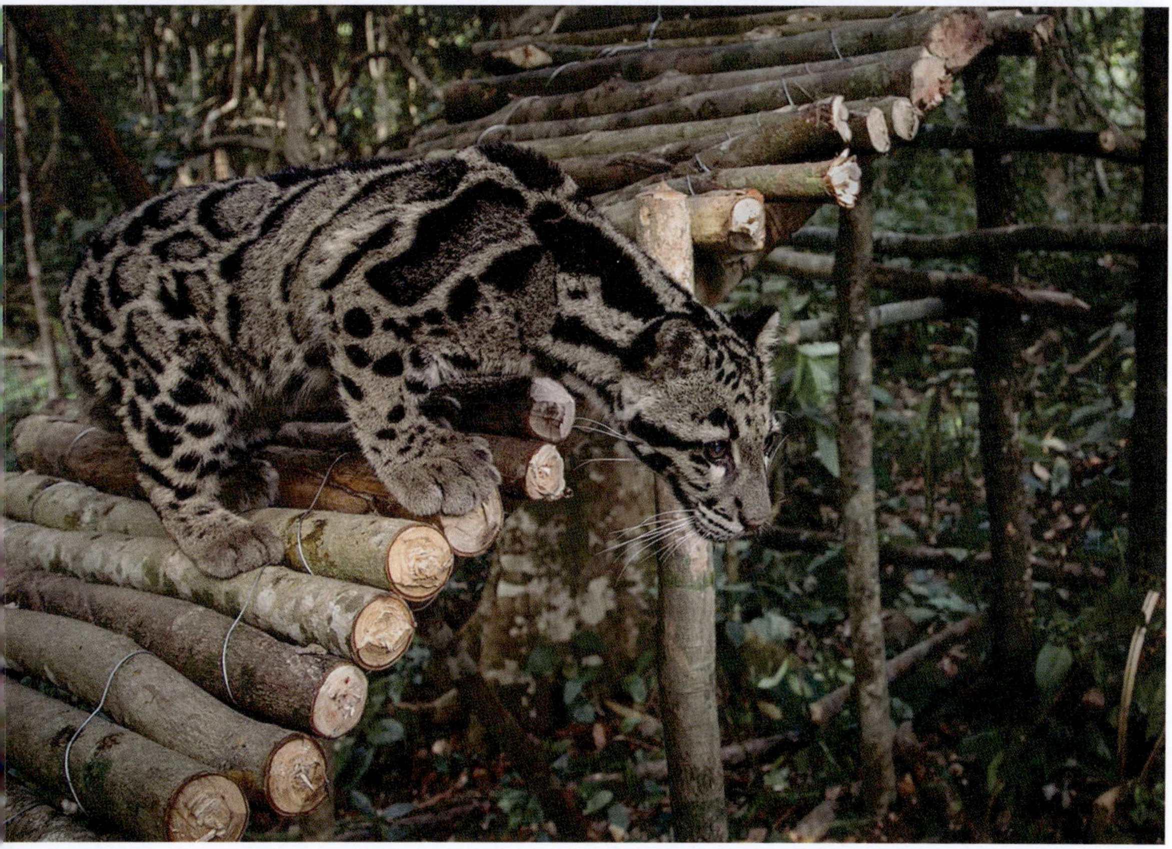

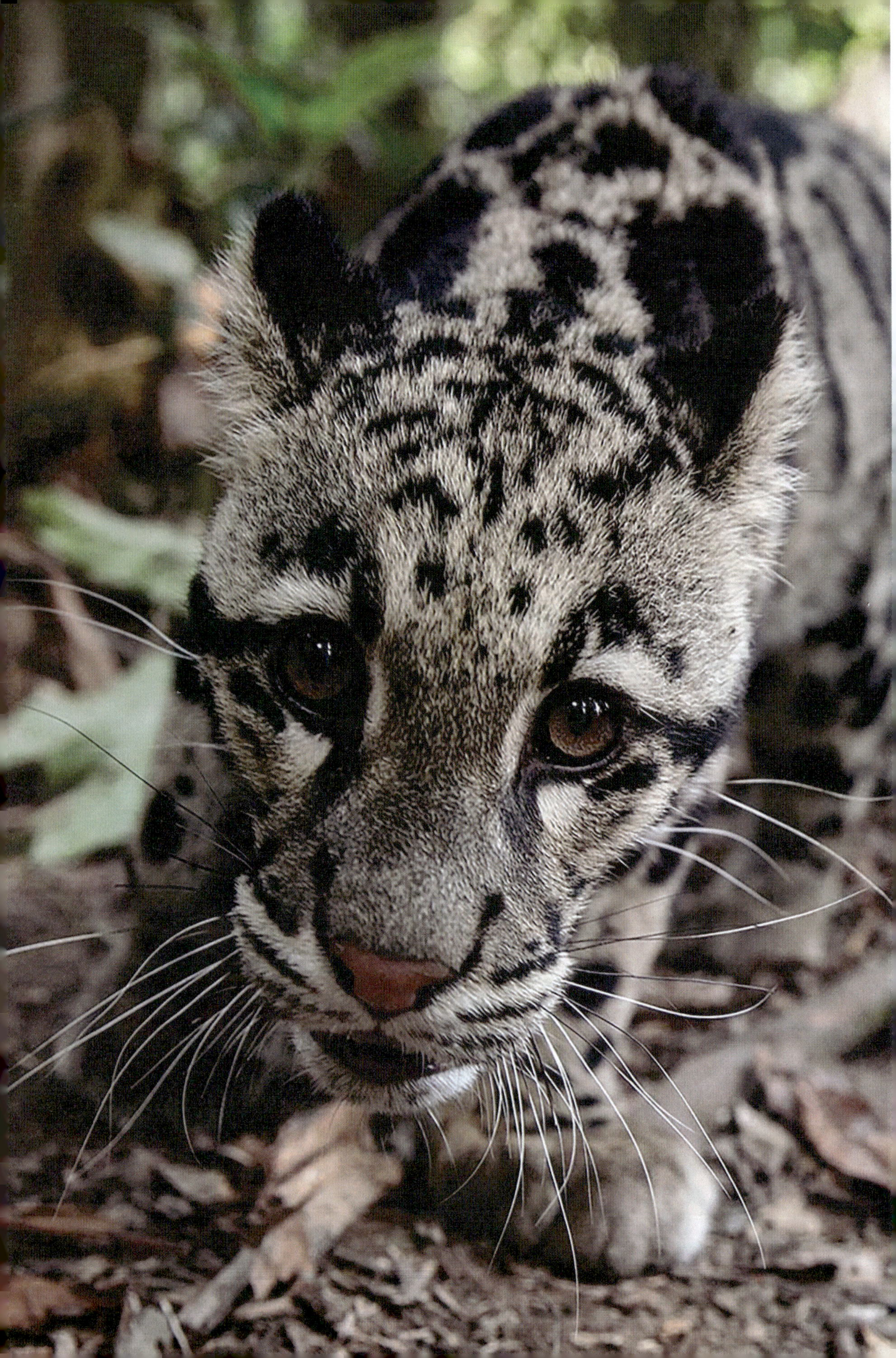

None of us expected what happened next: the leopard did some scent marking around the area, then sauntered over and sat on my lap!

Ontai made a sign not to move. I didn't need to be asked. I had no intention of trying to push away a creature that could remove half of my face with one swipe of its paw. It sniffed me. I must have been calm, not sweating pure fear, because it seemed to like hanging out with me.

I could feel how soft the cat's fur was and got an amazing view of the different shades of brown, grey and black that gave it the perfect camouflage for its habitat. Its tail was as long as its body, to balance its movements when jumping and climbing. It looked at me with intense eyes.

After a while, Ontai moved closer to where we sat. He put his hand out gently and the cat moved off me into the surrounding jungle.

It is an experience I will never forget.

The following morning, the two rhinos were walked through a gate into their new enclosure, and I snapped them. When I had got all the pictures I needed, it was time for Clare and me to move on to another national park, Kaziranga.

The seven-hour drive took us across the mighty Brahmaputra River and past huge roadbuilding projects. As often in my adventures, I found the traffic and the driving wilder than anything one could discover in a wildlife sanctuary.

We visited the Kaziranga IFAW centre, where a herd of elephants and some one-horned rhino were looked after. The British public loves pictures of baby animals, especially baby rhinos and elephants, and the fact that one of the rhino had a metal leg gave us even better photos and a good back story.

But we hadn't stumbled on the real treasure yet. The key to that came in the shape of Panjti Basumatary, one of the park's vets, who suggested we go

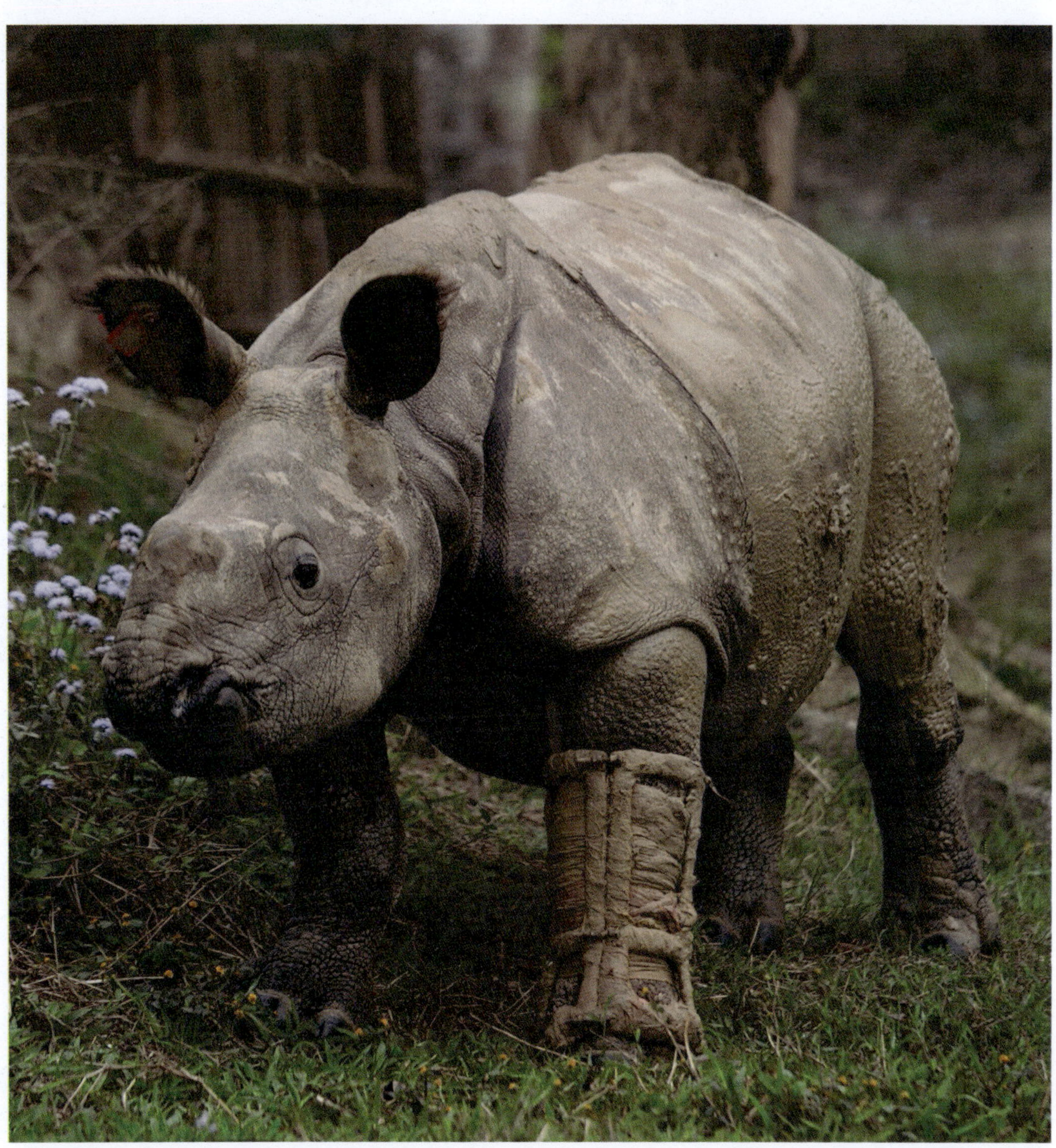

for a forest walk before the elephants went to bed for the night. In the herd were two orphaned baby elephants. Three-month-old Rupa had fallen down a cliff and been left behind by her herd. Aashi, eleven months, had become separated from his mother and discovered wandering alone in a tea plantation.

Now safely at the centre, the two kept each other company while the bigger elephants went about their business. Being so young, they needed a lot of looking after. There was no chance of reuniting them with their mothers, because they had had so much human contact that they were now thoroughly socialised, and would be rejected.

We watched a keeper lead the herd out through a small gate and along a well-worn track into the forest. The two babies stuck close to him, trunk to tail, while the bigger animals slowly but surely plodded on, breaking branches off trees with their trunks and eating the leaves as they went.

The deeper we got into the forest, the more the elephants became distracted by things to eat. The keeper had to keep urging them to keep moving.

An almighty crash sounded above us as two huge hornbills clattered into a tree overhead. I stood fascinated as they set about attacking the branch they stood on, their massive curved bills bashing away at the wood.

After their evening stroll, the herd arrived back at the compound. The two orphans followed the keeper along a separate path towards a brick building. We followed on behind, and Clare asked about the young animals' sleeping arrangements.

Panjti explained the situation. 'I've put two mattresses down so they can sleep together side by side, but it gets so cold at night that they've been waking up at 5:00 am, freezing. So now, I wait until they've had their bedtime milk bottles and then I dress them in booties and blankets to keep them warm.'

Clare and I smiled at each other, knowing that irresistible images of baby elephants in pyjamas would hit the headlines.

As the two youngsters guzzled their milk from bottles held by keepers, Panjti tied blankets round their little bodies with string. Colourful scarves went round their necks and under their ears, before the vet's handmade booties and leggings were added as the finishing touch.

The two young orphans stood side by side like a pair of children, obediently lifting their legs so Panjti could dress them.

The pictures were gorgeous—and were the making of the trip.

Once the babies had been readied for bed, they padded wearily into a small room with Panjti's two blue mattresses on the floor. After downing another bottle of milk they were left alone to go to sleep.

I needed one final picture of the two of them side by side, fast asleep, but with only a faint night light in the elephant's bedroom, getting the image would be a challenge.

We monitored the elephant's activities via a live TV link and saw that they took a long time to settle down to sleep. Aashi lay down and Rupa nudged him, forcing him to get up and allowing her to claim the warm spot on the mattress. Then the routine would be reversed. It was complicated stuff but engrossing to watch.

It took forty-five minutes for the pair to settle down properly for the night. Panjti put his finger to his lips, letting us know not to make a sound as he opened a small observation window into the room.

I'd thought the animals were asleep and, with my camera set at 5000 ASA, I managed to take three frames before Rupa got up to find out what I was up to. The picture was perfect, two baby elephants sleeping soundly side by side, kept warm all night by the ingenious combination of booties, scarves and blankets.

Clare and I were right about the appeal of the story. The *Daily Mail* used six pictures over two pages with the headline 'How to tuck up two baby elephants with jim-jams and bed socks.'

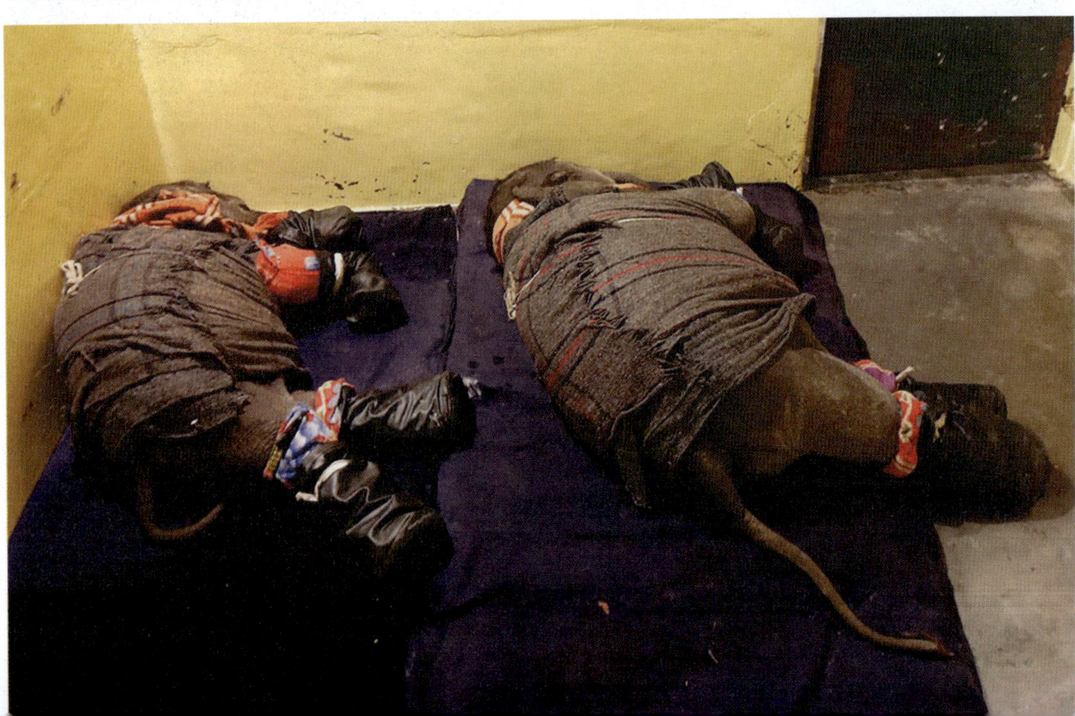

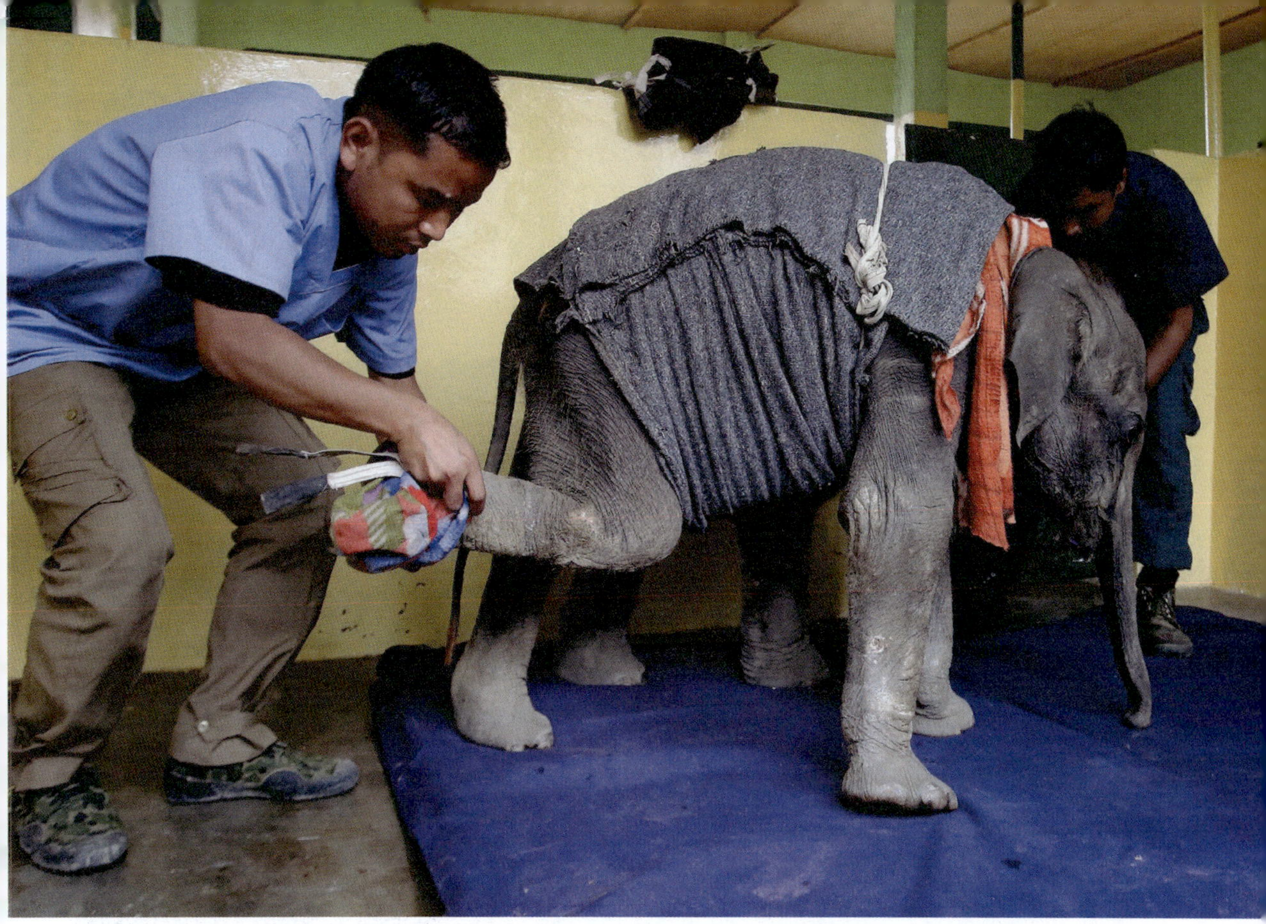

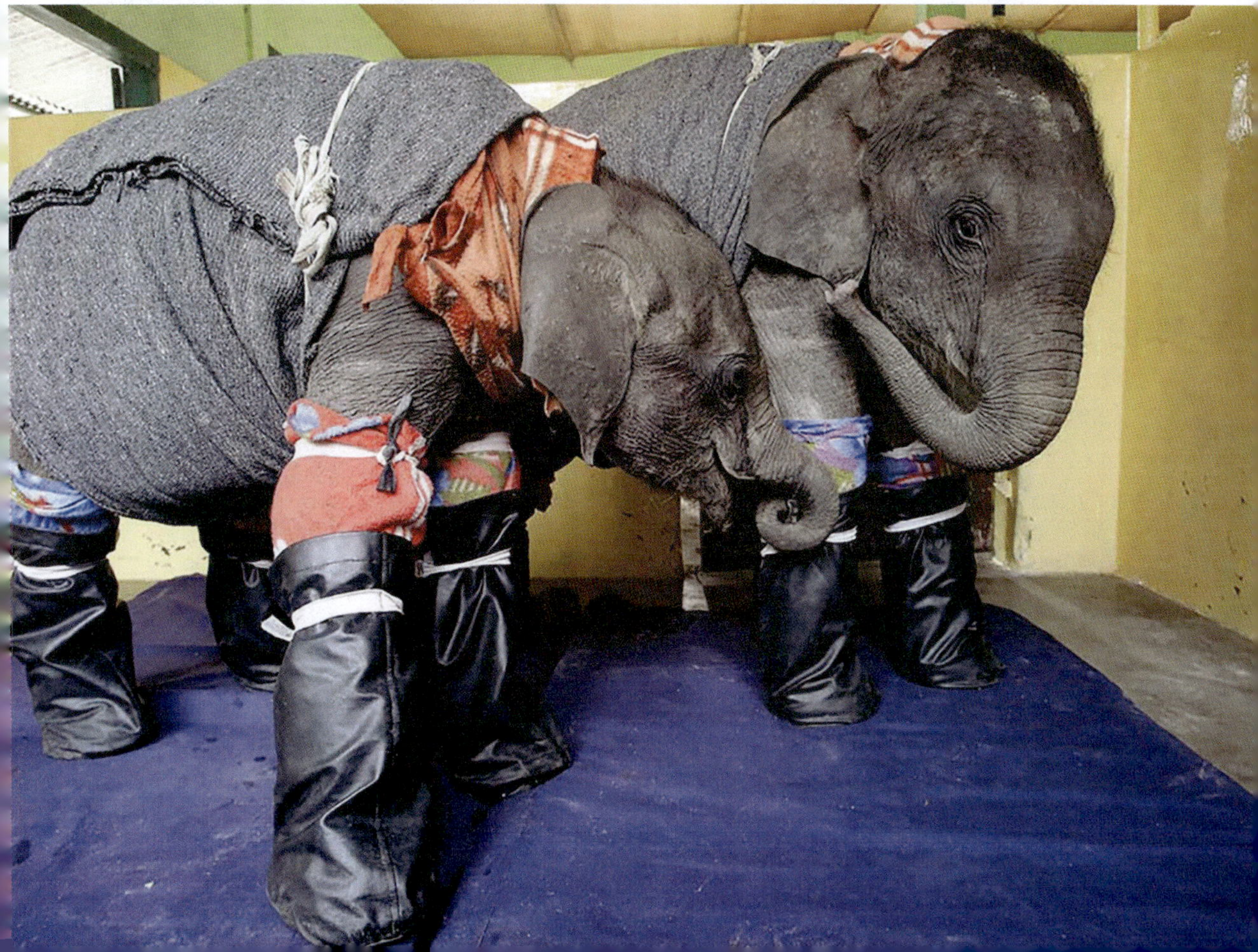

Hunting
the
poachers

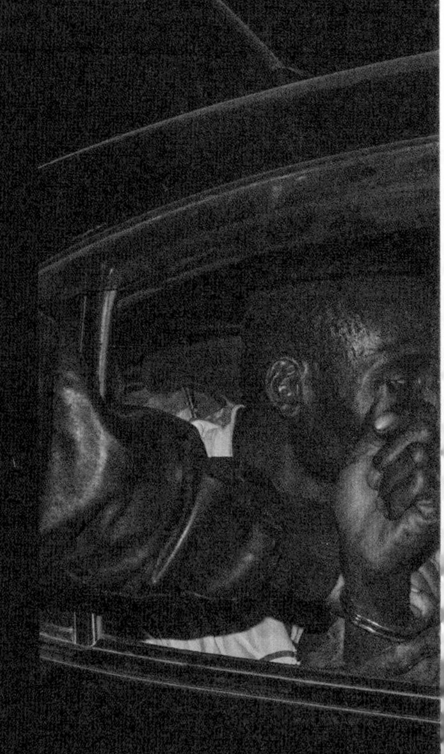

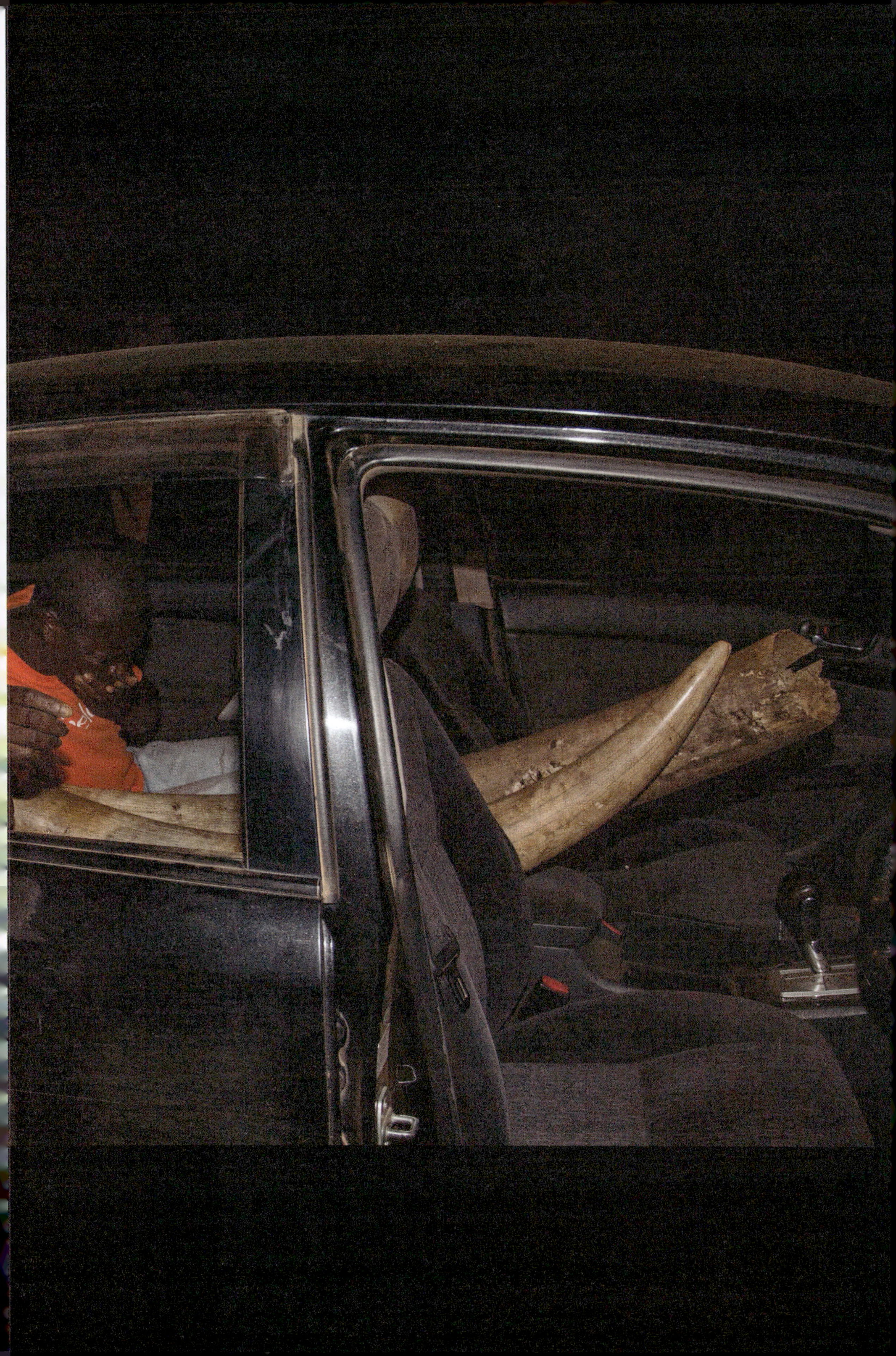

Hunting
the poachers

I have been in the newspaper game for over forty years, covering all kinds of stories, and what I have most enjoyed is working on news, features and undercover work. Of all the things to photograph, news stories are probably the hardest: you have very little control over what is likely to happen, and just when you think you're all set up to take the perfect picture, something happens to spoil the frame. You have to try to anticipate what may happen, devise the best plan, stick to it and hope for the best.

One ambitious plan emerged after I was asked to go to Malawi to join a newly formed commando force. A British charity had put a team together to combat ivory poaching in two national parks straddling the Malawi–Zambia border, where hundreds of animals had been killed over the previous few years.

I sat on a low brick wall outside the shabby terminal building at Lilongwe Airport, waiting for the head of the new unit to pick me up. Before long, a red Toyota Land Cruiser drew up alongside me and out jumped a six-foot-two-inch mountain of a man with a shaved head. He was the only other white man around, and looked very conspicuous. He introduced himself as Mike.

Mike had a reassuring presence and a clipped South African accent. He was my age but had a very different history, having fought as a mercenary in Angola, Mozambique, former Southern Rhode-

sia (now Zimbabwe) and other conflicts. He now lived in Kasungu National Park, north of the Malawian capital.

I was only going to be in the country for a week, and in that time I was due to team up with a police unit and Mike's team as they went after poachers. They would either try to catch them red-handed or lure them into traps when they tried to sell what they had plundered.

On my first night, Mike took me for a *braai*, a South African barbecue, at his house, where I would meet the rest of his squad. When I arrived, a handful of people were sitting around a firepit on a deck, overlooking a lake. Gym equipment stood under a canvas cover nearby. Mike introduced me to Ray, who looked as if he spent a lot of time in the gym; Asi, an Asian tech expert and undercover agent; and Lucy, the youngest of the group, who looked after the logistics.

Ray collected me in the morning to take me to meet the latest commando intake. In a jungle clearing I took pictures of the fresh-faced trainees, all local lads wanting to do some good but also looking for paid work.

In charge of the troop was a Frenchman, an ex-paratrooper in smart battle dress. He put his men through their paces, marching, patrolling in the tall grass and cleaning their weapons, before forming up on the small square outside the accommodation hut.

The following day we visited a small intelligence unit which liaised with the anti-poaching squad. A local man had just come back from Zambia and had heard talk of a shipment of ivory. The details were sketchy but Mike took it seriously enough to make further enquiries and see if his squad could organise a raid.

Mike explained that their modus operandi involved gathering information from people like the man we had met, along with news that the police had picked up from people in the area. They compiled all of this to build up a picture of the poachers' activities. Later that night he confirmed that the latest intelligence was panning out—and that we'd be moving off early in the morning.

Just after dawn Mike's red Toyota pulled up outside my hut with Asi in the back seat. The dark blue night was giving way to an amazing colour show of orange and red streaked with thin white clouds. Birds darted about and mother monkeys ran across the dirt road with small babies on their backs.

We went back to Lilongwe for Mike to visit the head of the anti-poaching team and put together more pieces of the puzzle. A plan was beginning to form, and it had been arranged that we would meet a joint force of Malawian and Zambian police just across the border in the town of Chipata.

The crossing point was a desolate collection of buildings that straddled the frontier. We joined a queue of cars and pick-up trucks while larger trucks formed a second line. We were surrounded by hawkers selling everything from windscreen wiper blades to tourist T-shirts to fishing rods.

We got through the Malawian side and were in the no-man's-land between countries, where people were filling out forms and pleading with officials. Mike had done all our paperwork, so we only had to pass through the barrier into Zambia. An immigration officer approached the car and demanded our passports.

We handed them over. The officer spent a long time studying every page, examining each country stamp with fascination. Just as he was about to hand the passports back, he asked Mike, 'Do you have any weapons in the car?'

I knew that we had two Kalashnikov AK47s under the front seats and a handgun in the glove compartment, but Mike didn't flinch.

'Do we seriously look like the sort of gentlemen who would have weapons in the car?' he asked calmly.

With a flick of his hand the border guard waved us through. We drove past more street vendors, barbecue stands and money changers, and into Chipata, where we went straight to the police compound.

Inside one of the low wooden huts sat a nervous lad of about fourteen, who we were told had information about the poachers. The windows were curtained and a whiteboard had been covered with a sheet. Mike had introduced many strategies to stop intelligence being passed on to the criminals by police staff in exchange for money. It seemed to be working, as the animal kill rates were coming down.

Behind a desk sat a thin man with a chiselled face. He looked about forty and had a hard attitude. He shook my hand firmly and introduced himself as Billy, the head of the anti-poaching unit in Zambia's Eastern province.

Mike turned his attention to the lad and asked him what he knew. The boy looked shyly at Billy, who told him to speak in English.

'I know men who have ivory tusks. They are to bring them to my village in the next few days. I know this because I heard people talking in my village last night,' blurted the boy.

'I want $1,000 to move to another village or they will kill me,' the boy went on. 'I will give you the name of the man who is organising the trade, but I want the money first.'

Mike reassured him that they would help him, but wanted to be sure that the information was reliable. He asked how the boy knew the man who was selling the ivory.

The boy looked up again, but his expression was one of embarrassment. 'He is my grandfather.'

That was a showstopper. The young teenager was selling out his own grandad, gambling everything he had ever known in order to get some cash and start a new life.

Billy summoned two of his team, and told them to take down the details of the village and work out how to arrange a meeting with the grandfather and the men with the ivory. They formed a plan to combine with more men from the anti-poaching squad before either Billy or Asi went undercover to meet the poachers.

One of the longest and best days of my career started at 3:00 am the next morning as we headed out to meet the rest of the force.

The rendezvous point was a rough piece of ground beside the road heading north from Chipata. Two battered cars were pulled over and Mike parked the Toyota beside them as the first rays of the sun were breaking through the low cloud. It was very cold.

Billy introduced us to the crew; they all looked unremarkable, which was perfect for undercover work. After some banter Billy briefed them. The young informant had gone back to village, and would get in touch when his grandfather had made contact with the ivory sellers. We were to drive to a nearby town and wait for news. It all depended on the movements of other people we had no control over. All we could do was hope.

We waited at a hotel that looked like a castle, with round towers at each corner and battlements on the roof. It had been a government rest house in colonial days. Billy arrived about 10:30 to say we might as well drive closer to the village, which was an hour away.

In the car park Mike took out a large wedge of banknotes and divided them into two piles. He placed two 10,000 Zambian kwacha notes on the outside of each stash, disguising the other notes, which consisted of less valuable Malawian denominations. It was Asi who was being sent in, undercover, posing as the buyer, and so he was given the cash.

The AK47s were handed out to Billy's squad but the handgun stayed in the glove box.

The three cars pulled out of the castle car park and drove for forty-five minutes on dusty red earth roads until we pulled up just outside the target village. Asi jumped into the front seat of a beaten-up Mazda saloon, which drove off towards the rendezvous point. From then on, the only communication would be via WhatsApp.

If things went sour, a message would be sent and we would storm in to rescue him. We waited for three hours before we saw the Mazda return.

The deal had fallen through. The villains had found a better option, leaving the grandfather high and dry. I wondered where that left the grandson who had risked everything.

Mike said there was one other possible lead. A ranger at the Luambe National Park had called about three men who were said to have a large haul of ivory. Our only option was to go and check it out, so we set off, making slow progress along potholed roads strewn with rocks. Billy and Asi went ahead in the other car to meet the contact without the complications of having two white men hanging around, as Asi might need to go undercover again.

Mike and I started chatting about our past experiences. He had lived all his life in Southern Africa and had fought with the South African army in vicious regional wars. I told him of the conflicts I had photographed in Bosnia, Kosovo and Afghanistan. Mike was curious about the Balkan wars, admitting he had little knowledge of European geography. He was keen to know whether the British Army was as good as people said it was.

By the time we reached our destination, the sun was low in the sky. It had been five hours since we'd left the failed raid. A WhatsApp message popped up on Mike's phone. Billy had been in touch with the informant and he was fairly confident that a meeting with the ivory sellers was on.

Mike and I were to wait until the sting was due. He told me nothing about what was going to happen as he didn't want to pre-empt anything. We drove with our lights off and parked in long grass close to the only thing that linked us to the outside world—a 150-foot telephone mast with a red light on top.

As we waited in the darkness my phone rang. It was my daughter back in England wanting to chat. The call couldn't have been more inconvenient and I quickly ended it. As soon as I did, another WhatsApp message came in on Mike's phone. We were in business.

Mike jammed the car into gear and raced the car back to the main road before turning off and gunning it through some long grass. We emerged onto the abandoned Chitungulu airstrip, driving fast along the rough runway in the moonlight. As we sped forwards one of Billy's team ran at the Toyota waving an AK47. We slowed down just enough for him to shout that the meet was at the crossroads in the track at the end of the runway.

With the car's lights off and the moon behind a cloud, it was difficult to work out what was happening. We reached the crossroads just as a pick-up truck drew up. Three more of Billy's boys had arrived.

The man with the AK47 came panting up to us and the six of us stood in silence peering along a narrow overgrown path. It was eerie in the darkness but before long a battered car with its headlights on full beam drove towards us.

Mike didn't waste any words: 'It's on.'

Not knowing what to expect, I switched on the flash on my camera. As the car slowed down to meet us, the lights from the pick-up truck suddenly lit up the scene.

Billy, wearing a black leather jacket, was driving the car and beside him was a young man in a red T-shirt. Two other men were in the back seat. As the car rolled to a halt, the man with the AK47 pounced, ripping open the back door of the car.

I fired off a set of frames as Billy grabbed the guy in the front seat and stopped him opening the door. Mike reached in and grabbed the passenger by the scruff of the neck. The young man looked at the camera in shock and horror.

The two men in the back were dragged out by the squad members and handcuffed before being

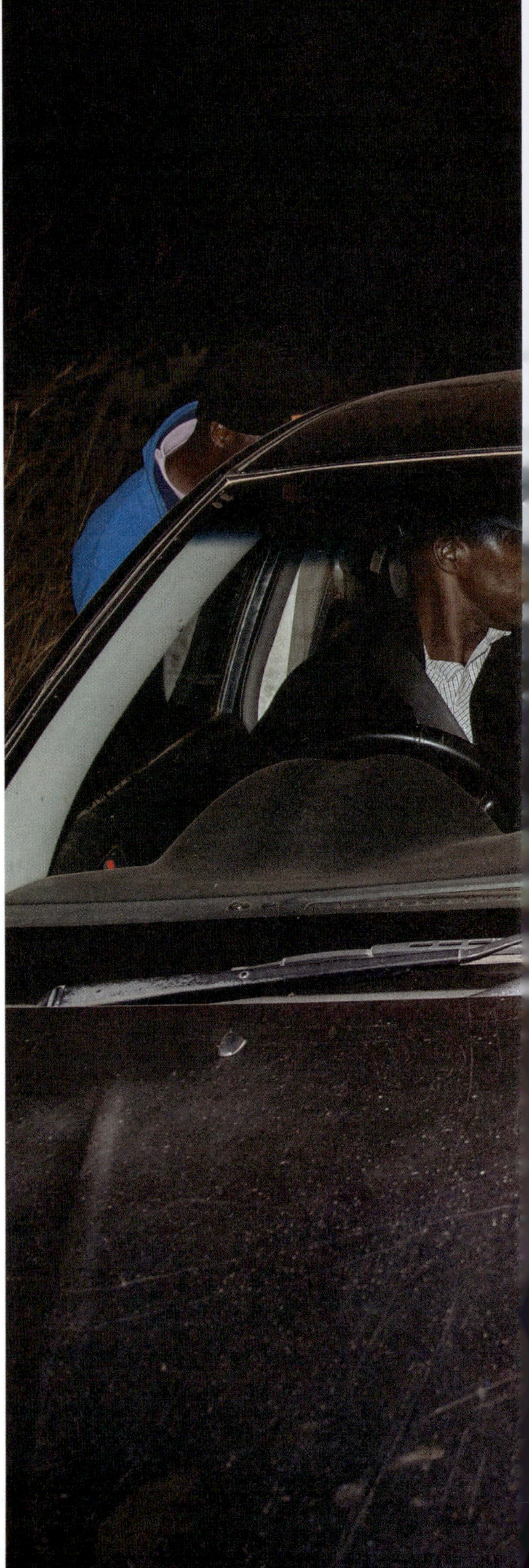

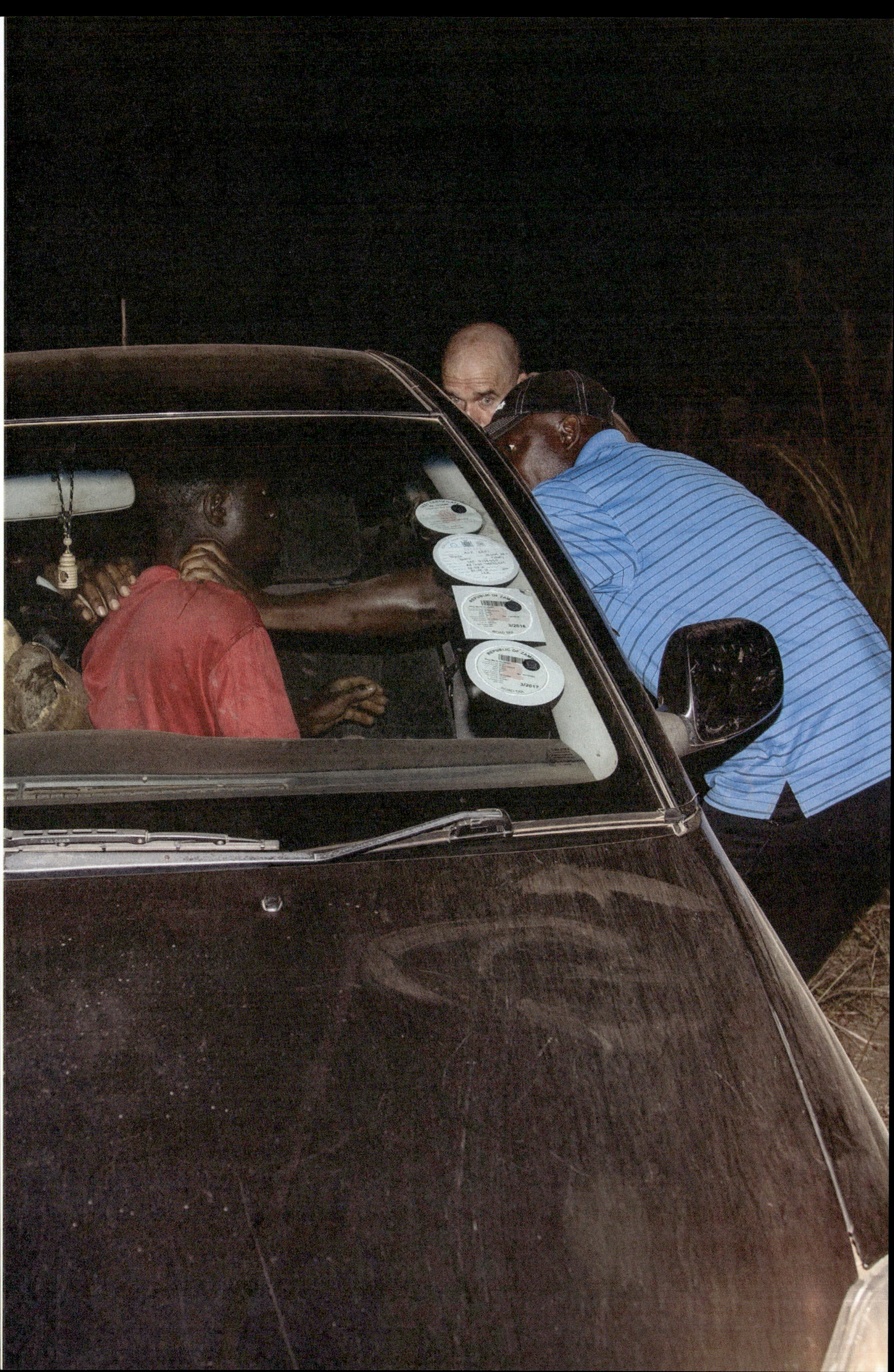

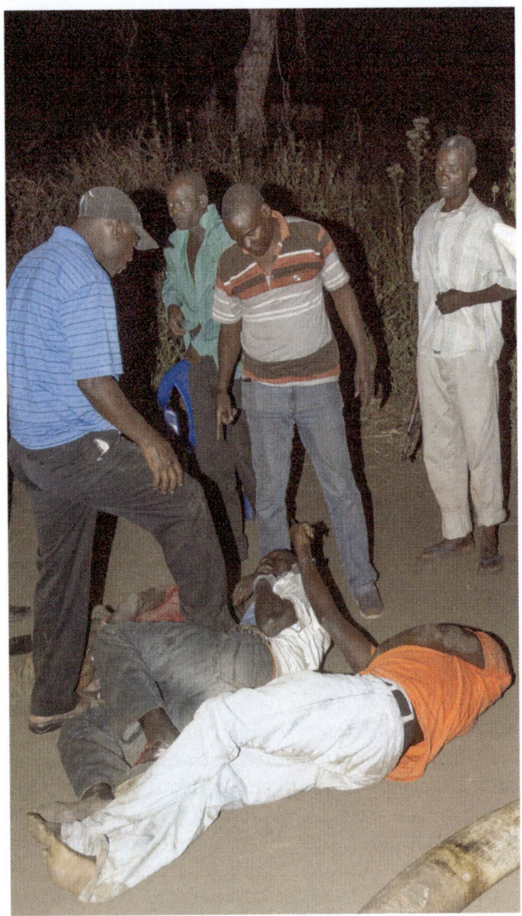

The three poachers were pulled from the pick-up and thrown on the ground along with the tusks. The man who'd tried to fight was shouting. It turned out he was a wanted criminal who had burned down a policeman's home and his car. One of Billy's team walked over to him and kicked him in the ribs.

When we stood one of the tusks upright, it was as tall as Mike. It had come from an old bull elephant. It was heartbreaking to think of his end. After being shot in the lungs he would have had his tusks hacked off with an axe as he lay dying. The anger directed at the men on the ground was boiling up. Mike had to warn the team not to lose control amid a very emotional situation.

The haul was valued at $125,000. Each poacher would have earned $5,000 from the sale, a life-changing sum for them.

The ranger's compound consisted of three round huts and an admin building. Women and children had come outside to see what was going on. Mike and Asi had found two plastic chairs and were sitting watching over the poachers; a third man, not one of Billy's team, sat alongside them with a Kalashnikov. He seemed very pleased to be part of the action and when the two handcuffed men started moaning that they needed a toilet, he seemed happy enough to let them wander off into the bush to relieve themselves.

The situation was only rescued when Mike bellowed 'SIT DOWN' before snatching the gun off the watchman and telling him to go back to his hut.

Billy had been busy establishing who the men were. The man in the red T-shirt was William Ngulube, aged thirty-two. He confessed to shooting the elephant and told Billy where the gun was hidden. Julias Kapomba, forty-two, was the one who had torched the policeman's house, and the other man was a well-known ivory trader, Gabriel Mwale, aged thirty-nine. As far as the cops were concerned, this was a big deal; they'd netted three of the top men operating in eastern Zambia. Billy was confident that further questioning would give him a clearer idea as to who was running things higher up the chain.

Ngulube was taken to retrieve the gun used to kill the elephant and we then returned to Chipata, travelling through the night and arriving at dawn. In the back of the Toyota, I managed to sleep, if fitfully. It wasn't until later that I realised Mike had hidden the young informant in the front seat.

Once back in town, the poachers were hauled off to the police cells and we took rooms at the castle hotel.

After three hours of sleep, followed by a shower, I noticed that one of the hotel screens was showing the BBC World Service. The UK general election had taken place the day before, resulting in a hung parliament. It seemed a world away from the wilds of eastern Zambia, where I had just had one of the longest but most dramatic days of my career. The set of pictures of the poachers' arrest would be splashed across two pages in the *Daily Mail*, *Stern* magazine in Germany and other publications around the world. Victory!

bundled towards the pick-up. One of them had tried to put up a fight and was bleeding from the mouth.

Back at the car the last remaining poacher was kicking off. Mike had no more handcuffs, so he took out his bootlaces and bound them round the passenger's hands. As the man was being carried along to the pick-up, he started shouting, trying to alert villagers to rescue him.

In all the madness of the last five minutes I'd failed to notice the poachers' prize—two huge bull elephant tusks wedged inside the car. I looked at the pictures on the back of my camera; there were the two tusks between Billy and the man in the red T-shirt. I had caught the poacher at the moment of capture along with the valuable haul.

Mike was shouting at me to get into the car; we had to move fast, as men from the village were stirring. They would protect the poachers with guns if necessary, so if we stayed any longer we could end up in a firefight.

The convoy of three vehicles roared out of the bush towards the main road and the safety of a ranger's compound. Driving at speed made it hard to control the Toyota. It was bucking the pair of us about like mad. In the back of the pick-up the three poachers along with their ivory were being held down by two squad members. By the time we arrived at the rangers' house we all looked shattered.

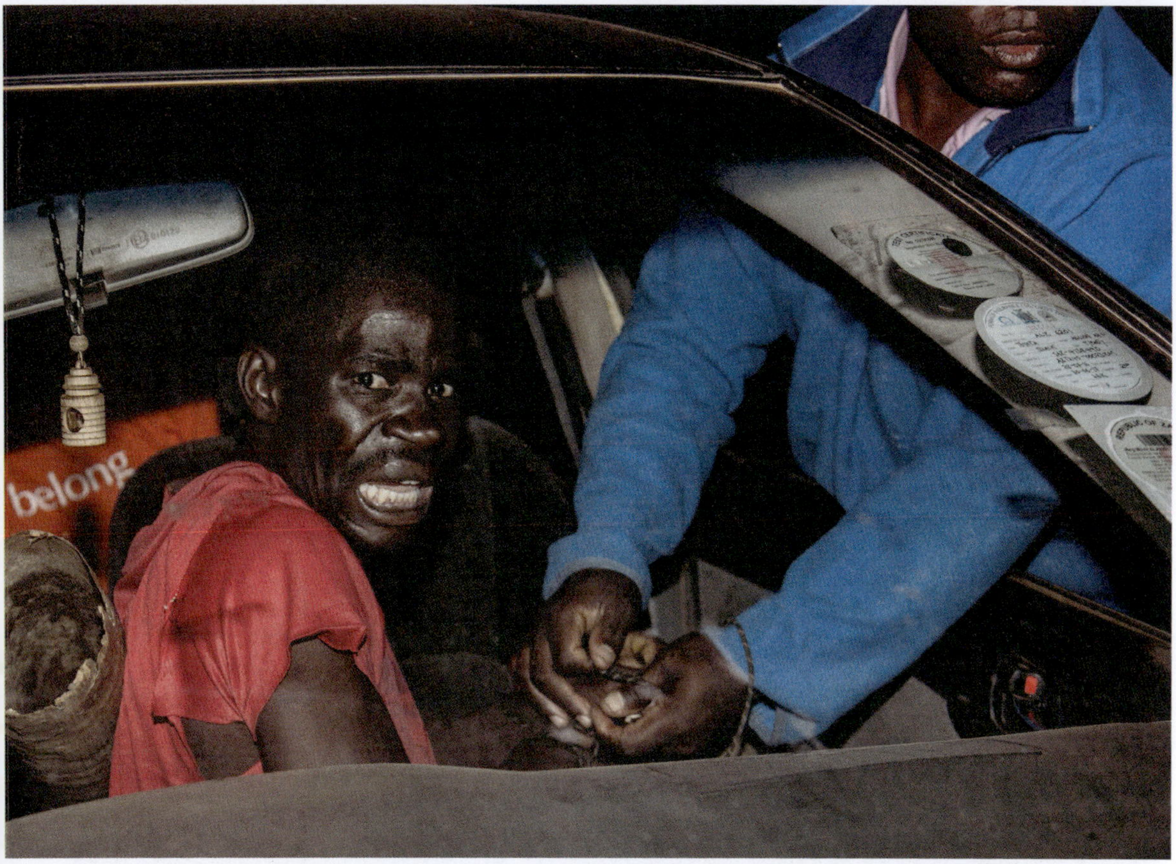

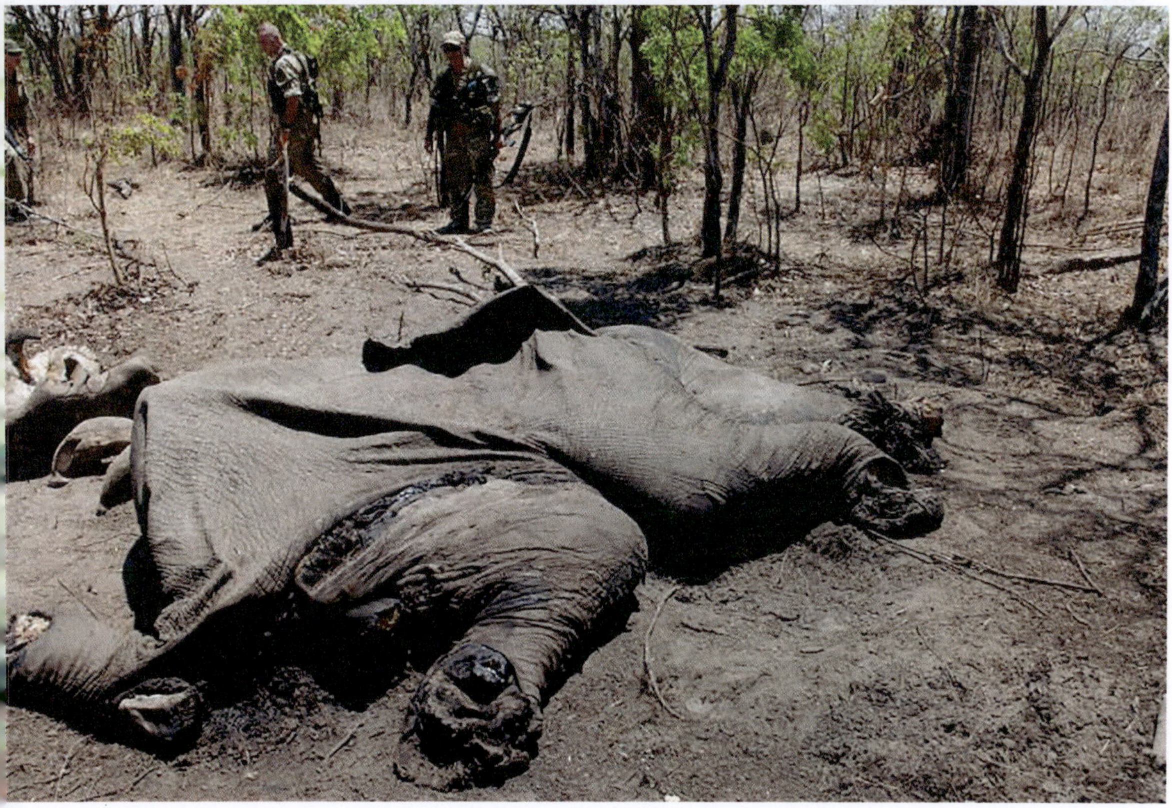

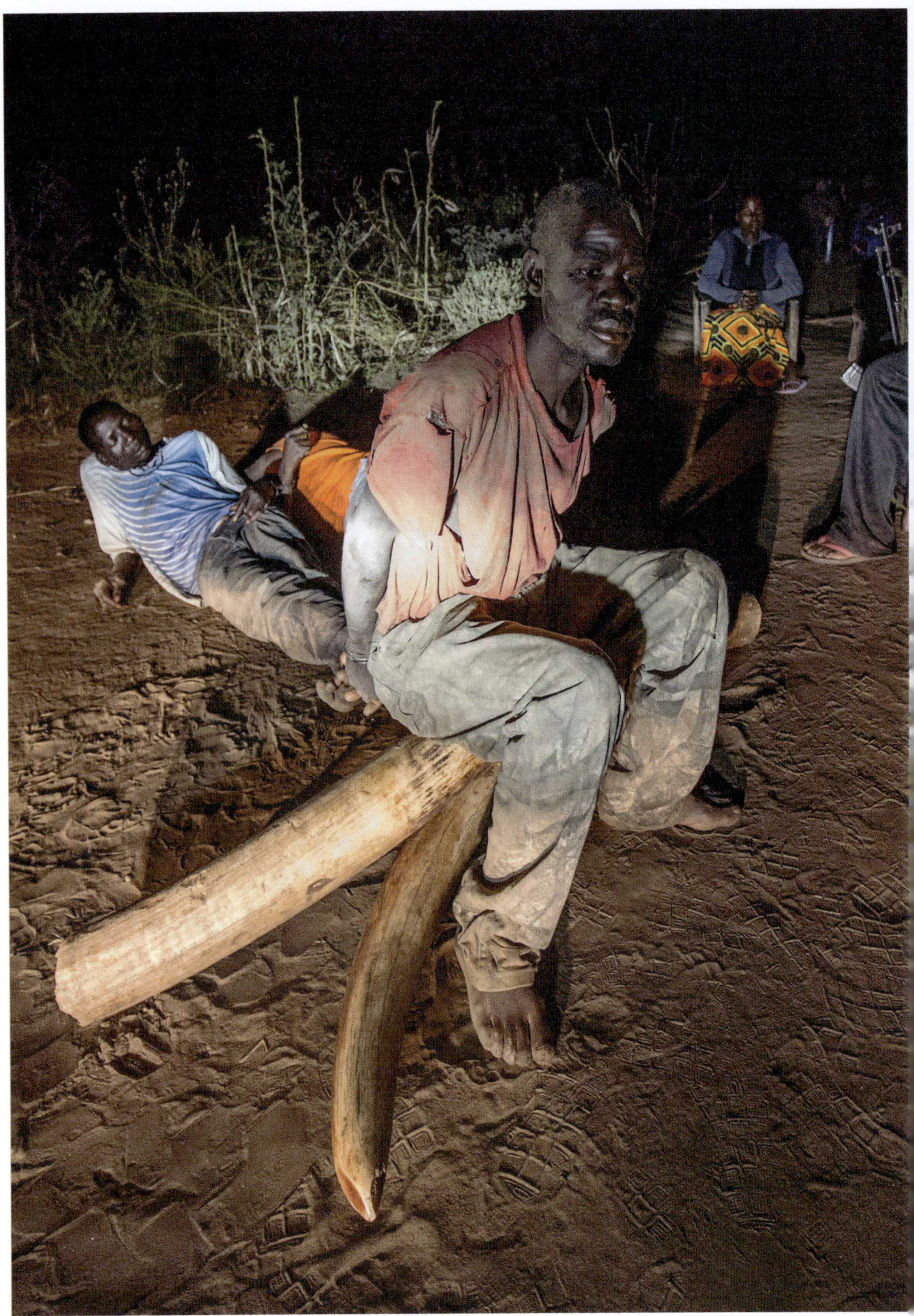

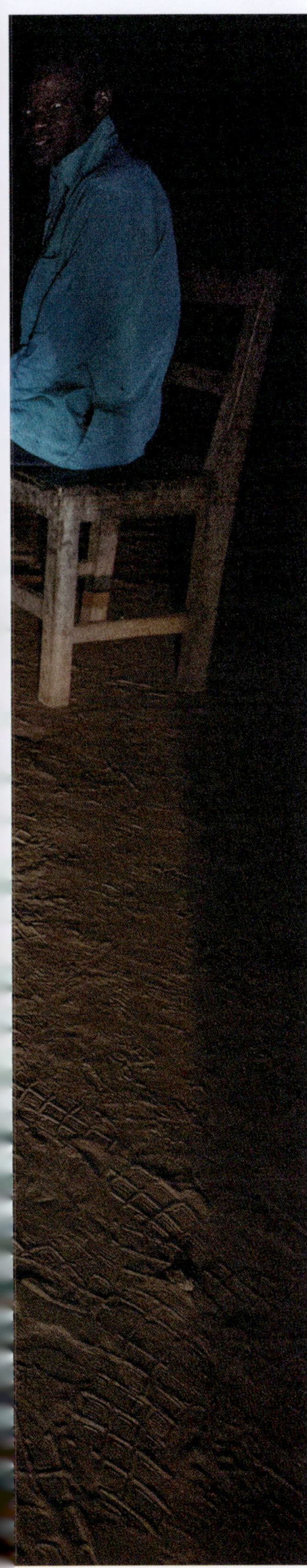

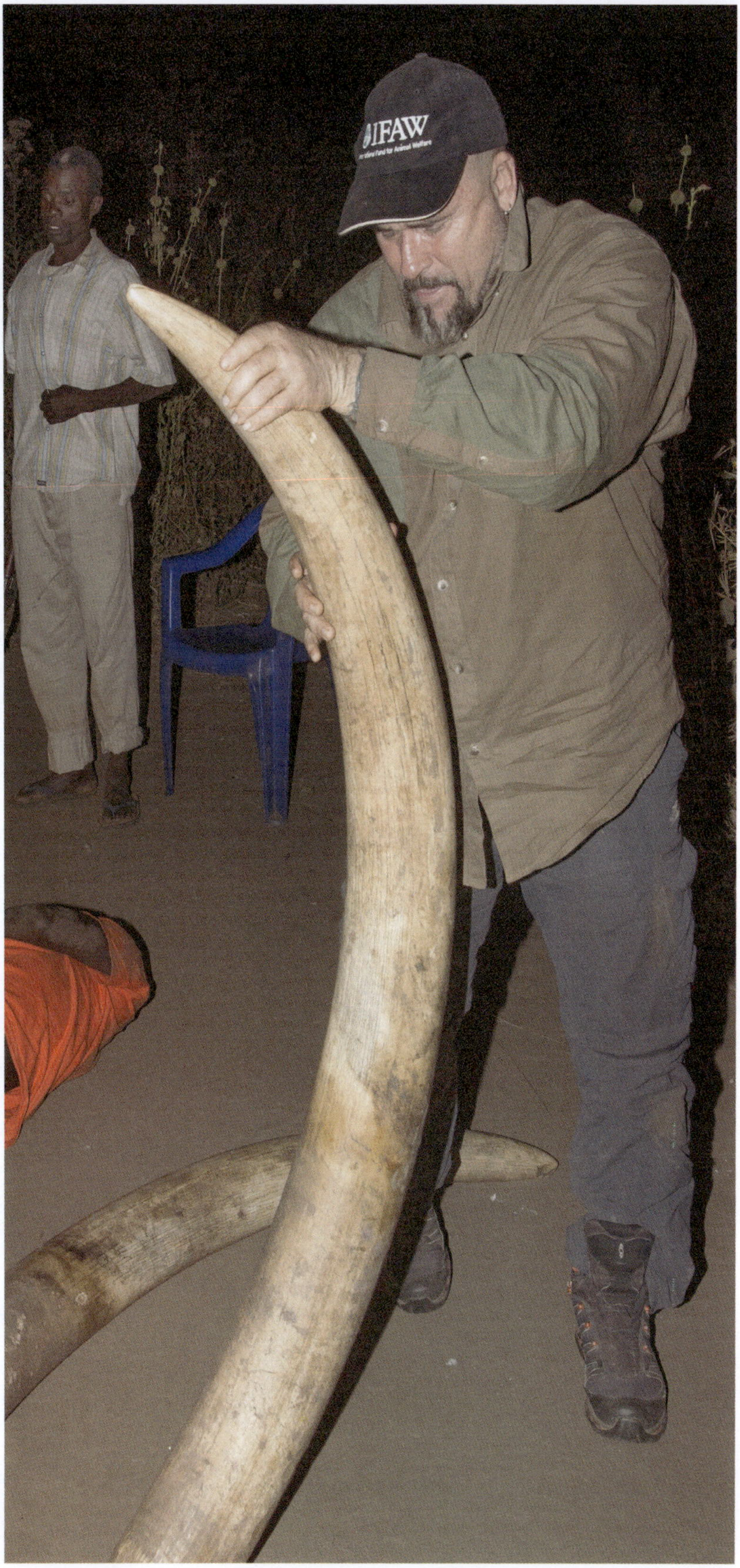

Dasha and her happy news

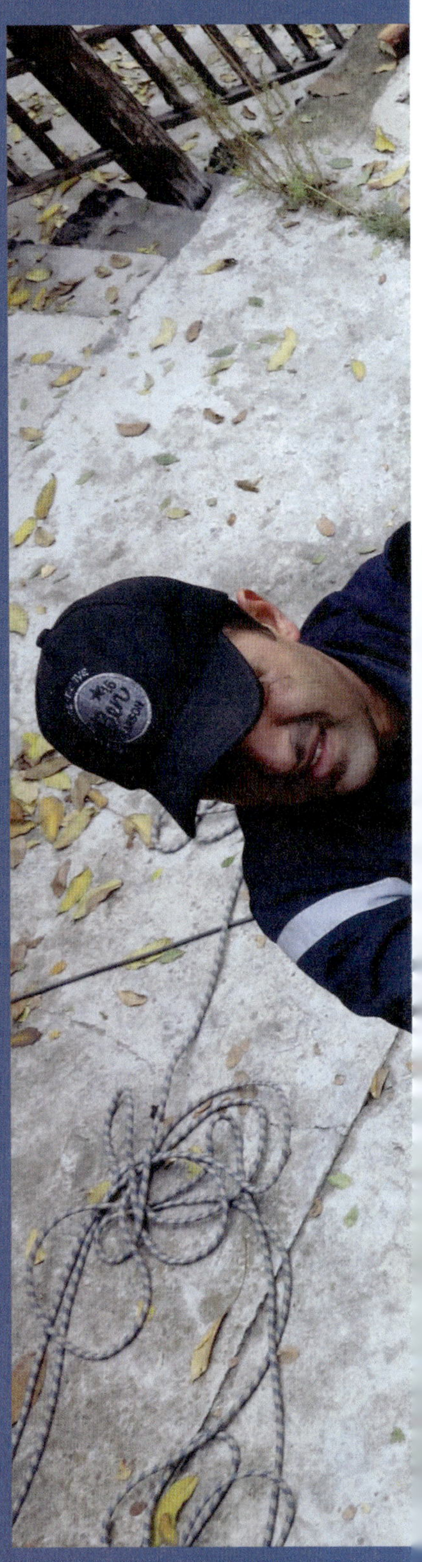

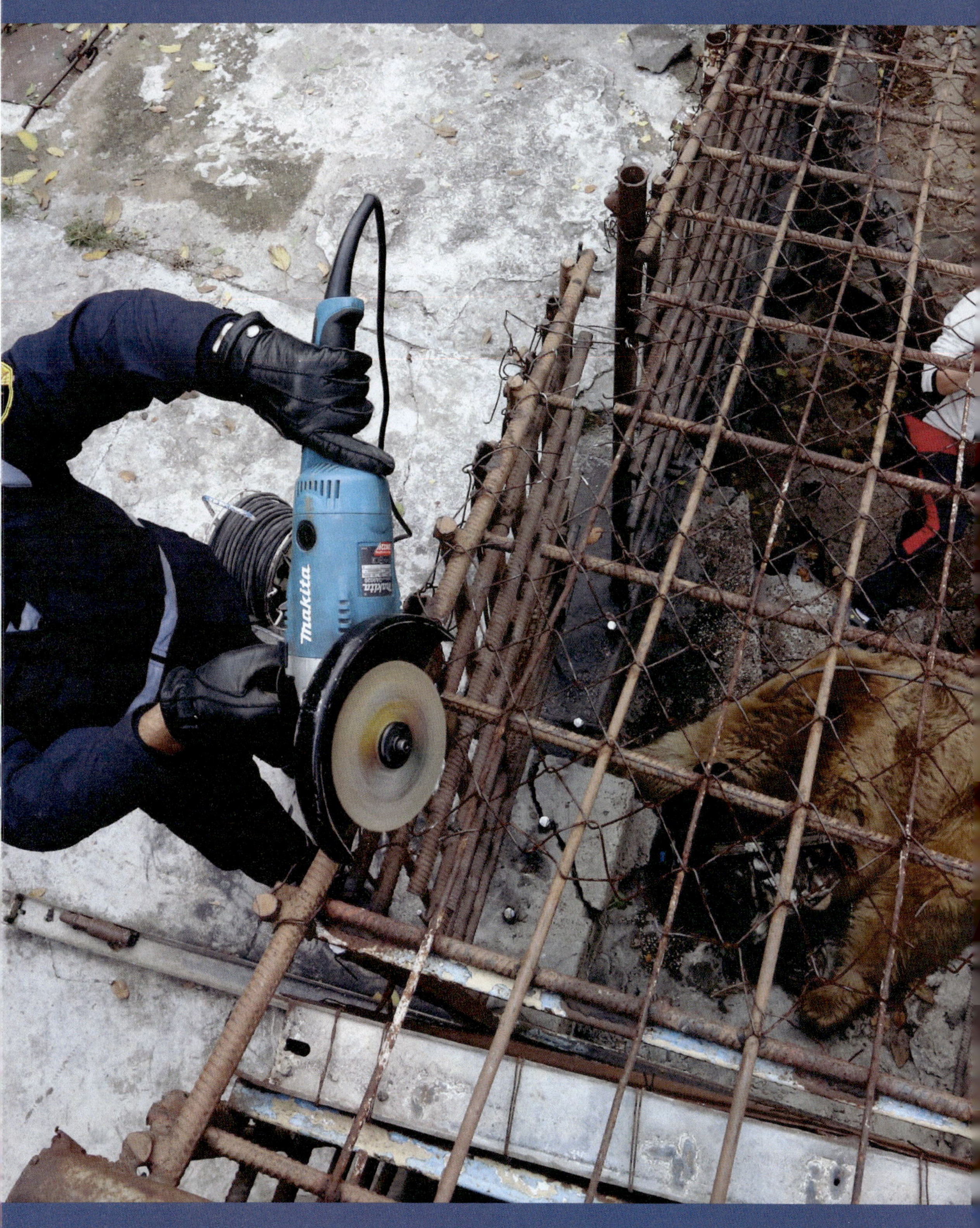

Dasha and her happy news

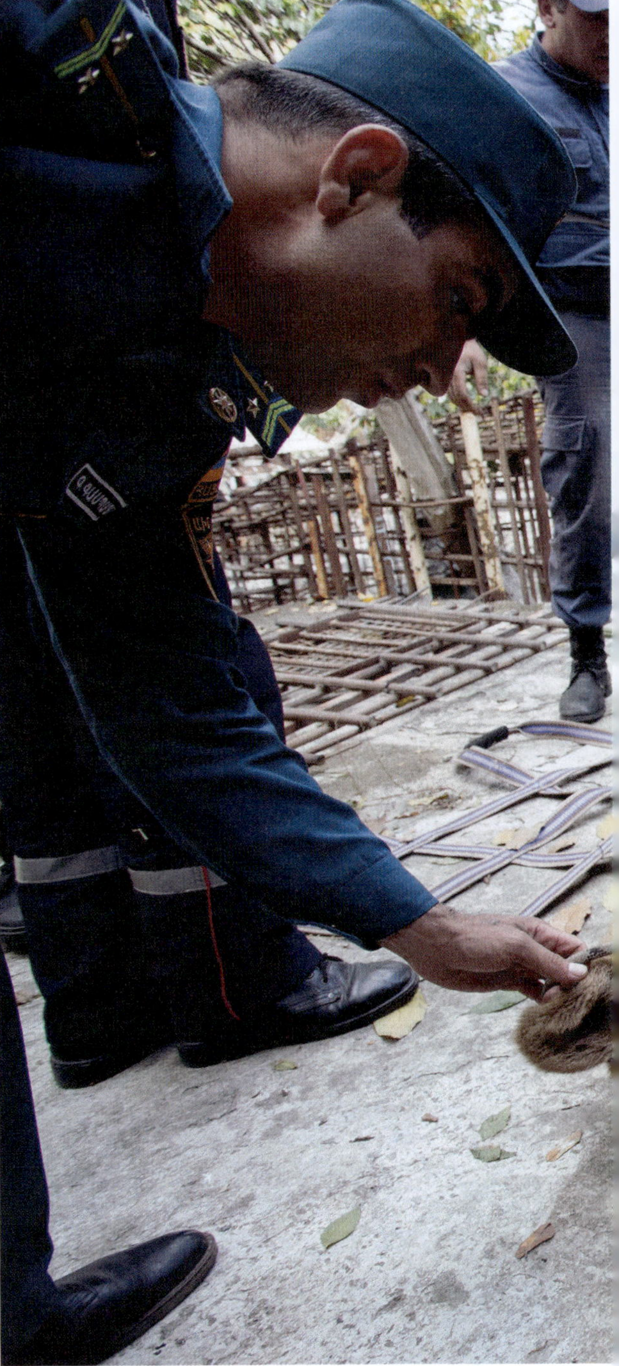

Since first highlighting the plight of the Gyumri lions, I have returned to Armenia eight times. Alan Knight had pushed ahead with his promise to rescue bears from hellholes all over the country and a new centre had been built at the eco-lodge ready to accept the animals.

After the publicity surrounding Masha and Dasha at the river restaurant, authorisation was given for the emergency services to carry out their rescue.

On a chilly October morning two fire engines and twelve firefighters arrived at the restaurant equipped with power tools able to cut through the bars of the bear cages. Armenia's press corps was on hand to record the event, which started to take on a carnival atmosphere. The firefighters posed for pictures with the bears, coffee was handed out and reporters from the Yerevan TV channels gabbled endlessly into their phones for Facebook livestreams.

The vets took out their tranquiliser guns, prepared the pink-feathered darts and laid out the mobile razor for shaving the bears' fur to take blood samples and insert lines for intravenous drips. We reporters were told to stay on the other side of the river while the fireman got to work. That way, it was said, the bears would cope better with the terribly high-pitched shrieking of the cutting and grinding tools.

It wasn't because no one had a key or that the locks had rusted that the cages had to be cut open. The tangle of iron bars had simply been welded around the two bears, with no intention of their ever being set free. The animals had been in there for years.

To get them out, the cage had to be divided into two isolation sections so the bears could be kept separate once they had been tranquillised. Within twenty minutes the grinding tool started to eat its way through the metalwork, throwing up a shower of sparks. Why this couldn't have been done once the bears were sedated wasn't clear, but it must have been massively stressful. The bears looked terrified: Masha moved as far as he could from the noise while Dasha stood in the fast-flowing water on the lower level.

The Norwegian vet supervising the rescue managed to coax Masha onto one side of the dividing line so he could be isolated. They needed Dasha to get out of the water and into her own section.

With all animal rescues, patience is the key; nothing happens quickly and while the animals are still awake they are liable to act unpredictably. Dasha

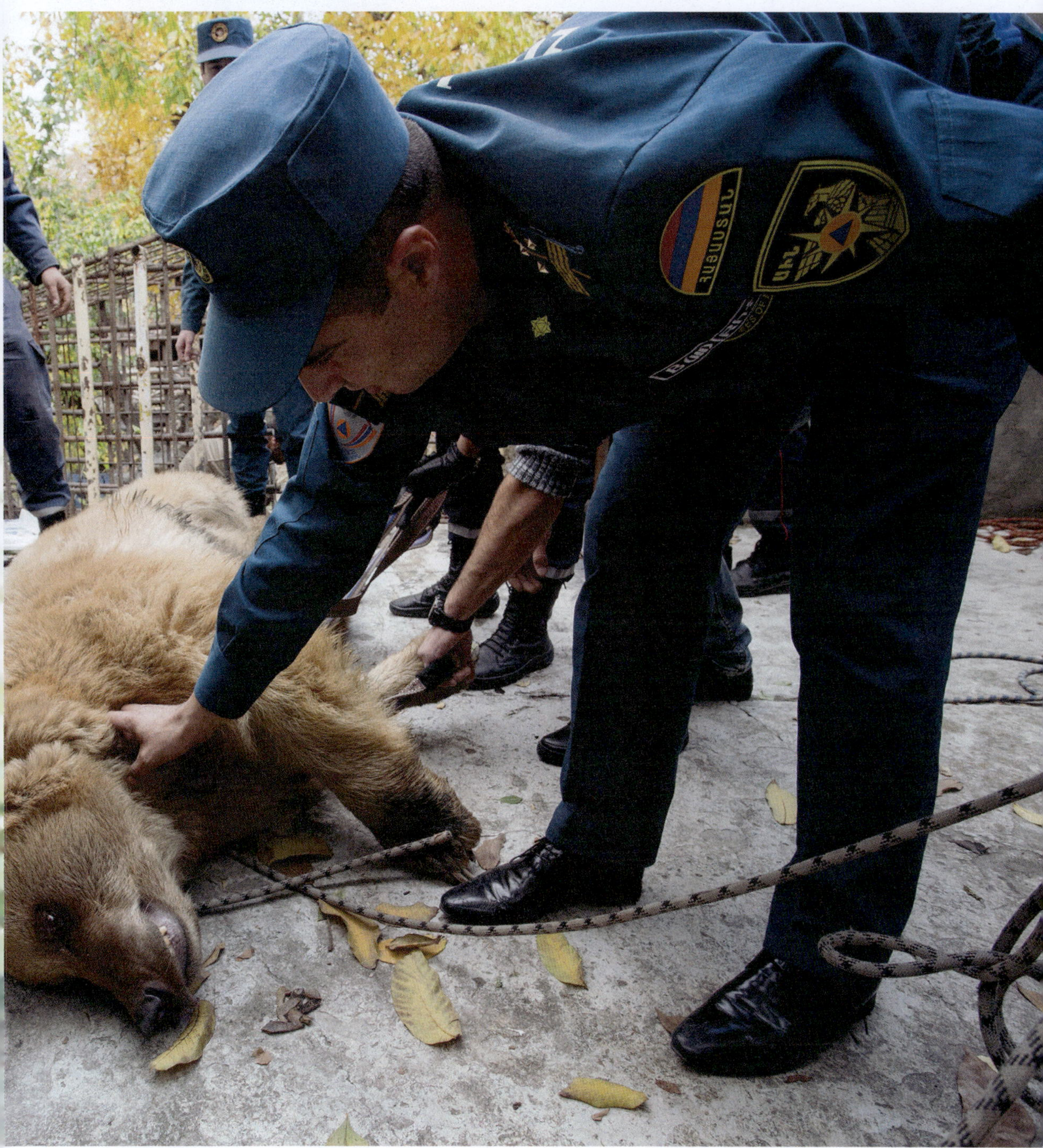

seemed frozen in fear, so it was decided to halt the operation for at least an hour while she regained her confidence.

Almost an hour into the operation Dasha hopped up onto the platform where the sleeping den was. From there, she followed a trail of juicy titbits that had been thrown into the cage, leading her into her own isolation wing, where there was a bigger pile of food. She didn't seem too perturbed when the gate slammed down behind her.

With both animals now in the right place, the delicate operation of darting the two bears could begin. There are considerable challenges in moving unconscious bears so everything had to proceed smoothly.

The vet asked for quiet, aimed the dart gun at Masha and moved closer to the edge of the cage to get a clear shot. The bear gave a roar of pain and shock as the dart lodged in his backside. He swung round, pulled out the dart and worried it in his mouth for a second before spitting it out, but then the tranquilliser started to take effect.

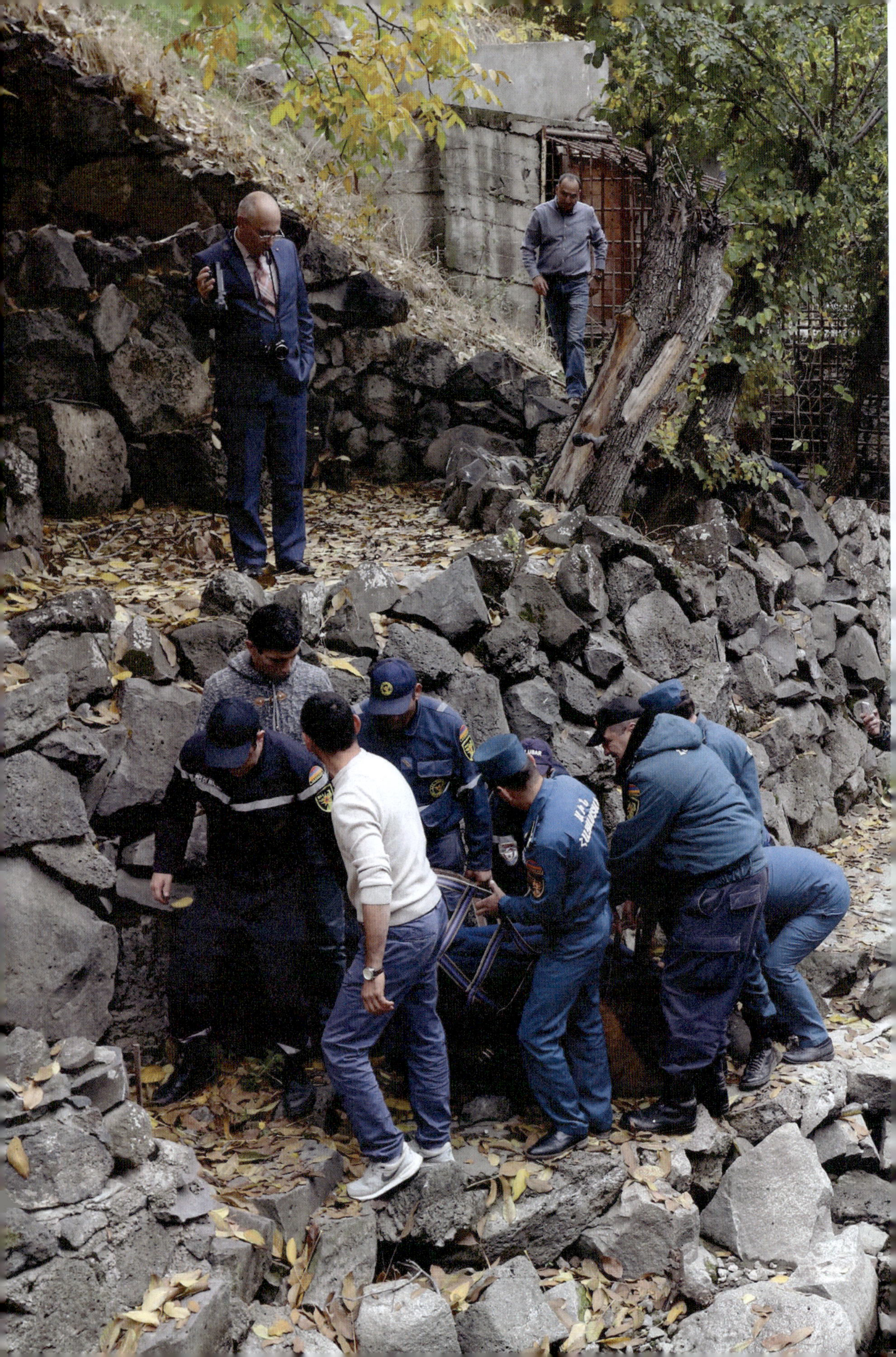

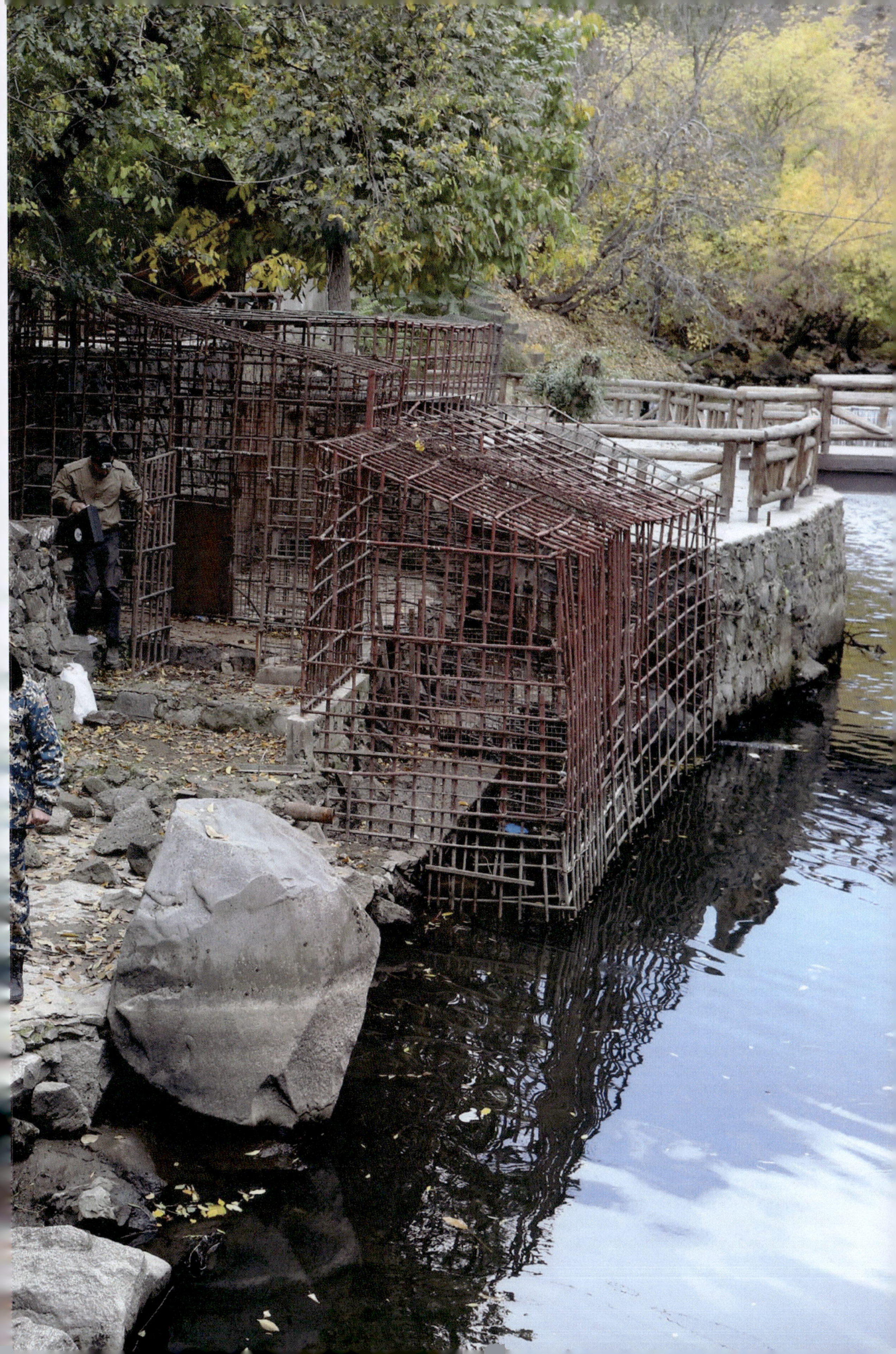

The worry was that Dasha would freak out at the sight of Masha being unconscious, raising her adrenaline levels too high for her to be knocked out. But she remained calm, and the vet decided to wait until Masha was out cold before darting her.

After a lot of prodding at him with a pole, it was deemed safe to assume that Masha would be out for at least forty minutes. Dasha wandered into the right place to be darted and the gun was fired again. She reacted in the same way as her mate: pain followed by anger. Twenty minutes later both bears were sleeping.

Masha was the first to be removed. An opening had been cut close to where he'd fallen asleep. It took a team of ten men to manhandle his heavy frame onto a webbing stretcher and carry him along the riverbank, over a bridge and into a waiting transport crate, to be lifted onto the back of a flatbed lorry. The scene of the men staggering along the river with a huge bear looked great through my lens.

The fire crew then started cutting the other section of the cage while the vet held a coat over Dasha to protect her from the sparks. Speed was of the essence, and the bear's vitals, blood pressure, heart rate and breathing were monitored throughout.

I had climbed on top of the cage to look down on the action. Five burly men stepped forward as soon as the panel of rusty bars had been cut away. Dasha was heaved up and out of her grimy prison. She was free.

She too was carried across the bridge, and laid on a bed of fresh straw in her transport crate, which was in turn hoisted onto the lorry. At last, she and Masha were on their way to the sanctuary in the Caucasus mountains.

I arrived to photograph the pair in their new home the following morning only to be greeted with bad news. Masha had died. It turned out he'd been in bad shape before his release because of the conditions in the cage and the neglect he had suffered. A post-mortem would later discover a whole catalogue of major organ complaints; the poor fellow had survived in pain for years.

On the other hand, Dasha seemed totally at ease as she looked around her new home in a quarantine block. Her diet was now full of goodness with round-the-clock attention from the keepers.

By the time I left the eco-lodge the wind had begun to whip down from the mountains. Snow was falling on the highest peaks and bright-red Boston ivy leaves stood out against the grey drabness of the village. The seasons were moving from autumn into early winter. In one of the dens that had been dug out in her enclosure, Dasha had made a nest for herself. She was preparing to hibernate.

In May the following year, the two cubs I had photographed in the container were deemed fit enough to be released into the wild. Found abandoned in a factory on the outskirts of Yerevan, they were now eighteen months old. This was a big mo-ment for IAR, Alan Knight and everyone at FPWC because these were to be the first releases under the Great Bear Rescue project.

It was a bright crisp morning as we all gathered round to dart and load up the two cubs. A tracking collar was fitted to the male as he lay unconscious so that the team could keep track of the pair after their release.

It had been decided that the release site we had visited the previous year, where we had met the shepherds in the yurt, was too far away from the eco-lodge for the conservationists to respond if anything went wrong. Instead, the convoy of trucks and four-by-four vehicles packed with vets, IAR personnel and a team to carry the crates and bears trundled four hours into the national park next to the eco-lodge

We reached a flat expanse of land filled with bright, tall yellow flowers next to a small lake with three-foot tall reeds ringing with the song of thousands of frogs. It looked heavenly, a perfect spot for two young bears to be set free. Rising up at the far end of the meadow was a large copse and behind that the high mountains of the Caucasus.

The lorry drove to the side of the lake and Ruben's team heaved the two cages onto the ground. The bears were kicking up a storm. They had only ever seen the inside of a shipping container—what would they think of grass, flowers and sky, let alone frogs?

Once we'd all moved a safe distance away, the front panels of the crates were pulled up. Out the cubs came like a pair of greyhounds, the boy first out of the traps and his sister right behind him. At one point she looked back at the cage as if unable to believe she was free.

The pair ran into the middle of the meadow before stopping and standing on their hind legs to take a look around. I took a photograph of them surrounded by the yellow flowers and wondering which way to go. After a few seconds they carried on towards the wooded slope and the trees. When they reached the top of the grassy rise they turned and looked back at us then walked slowly into the woods.

We were all overcome with emotion. These little orphans were now on their own in the big bad world. One of Ruben's men brought out a large tablecloth and laid it on the ground so we could enjoy a picnic, enjoying the lifting of the tension we had felt on the way to the release site. This had been a successful day.

But there was even better to come.

Back at the eco-lodge, a young German volunteer who fed the bears told us that Dasha had come out of her den that day for only the second time since the start of hibernation—with a cub!

What a story, and what a great ending to Dasha's journey. All I needed was a picture of the mother and baby.

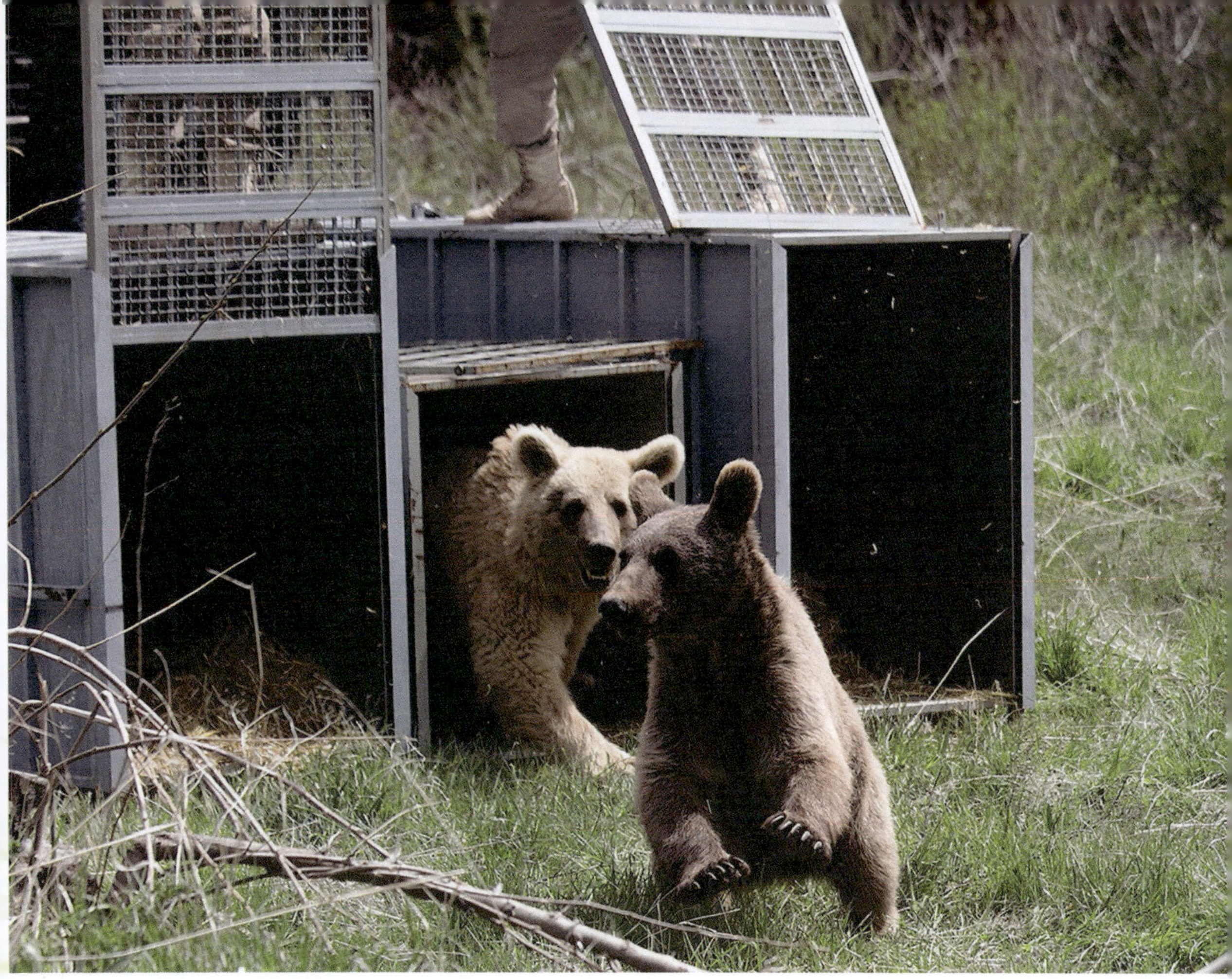

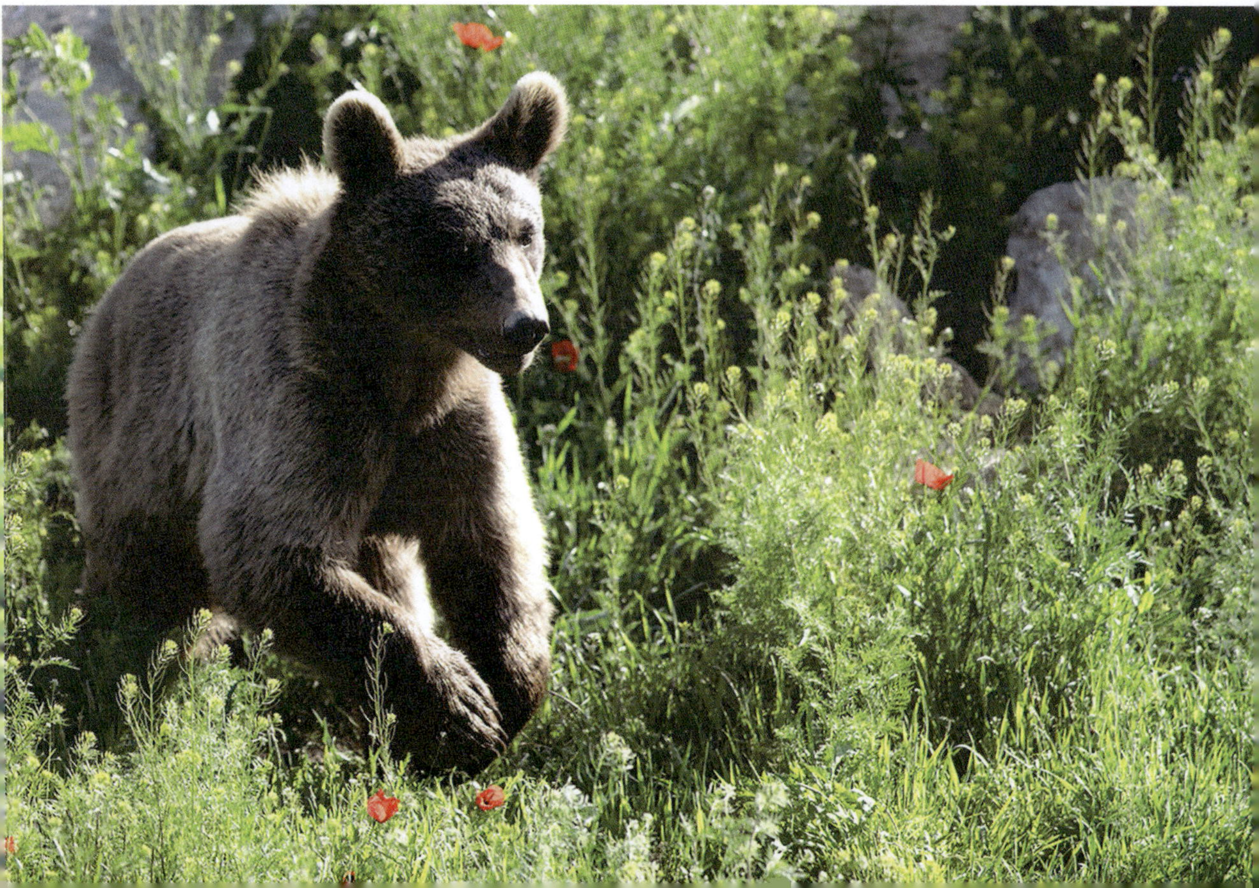

I got myself set up early in the morning to catch a picture of the mother and cub as the sun rose with snow-capped Mount Ararat picked out against the azure sky. The ground was drenched with dew as I settled down to wait for Dasha to emerge. I had a perfect view from an unoccupied enclosure, my long lens trained on Dasha's den.

An hour later the German volunteer arrived with a bucket of apples. She started to throw them over the fence and call for Dasha, saying the bear had come out at this time for the past few days. I tried to communicate that I could have avoided a long wait in the cold if she had told me that the night before, but it was lost in translation.

Ten minutes later, the top of Dasha's head appeared at the bottom of the slope that rose in front of her den. I focused my lens as she slowly emerged and started munching on the apples and looking around in the morning air. As she stood on the lip of her den a small bundle of fur struggled out of the hole. It was my first sight of the cub.

I got pictures of the little one arriving at Dasha's side and the mother looking down at her with real pride. I didn't think it could get any better, but then a second cub tottered out of the den. The two stood together under mum's chin in a truly heart-warming scene.

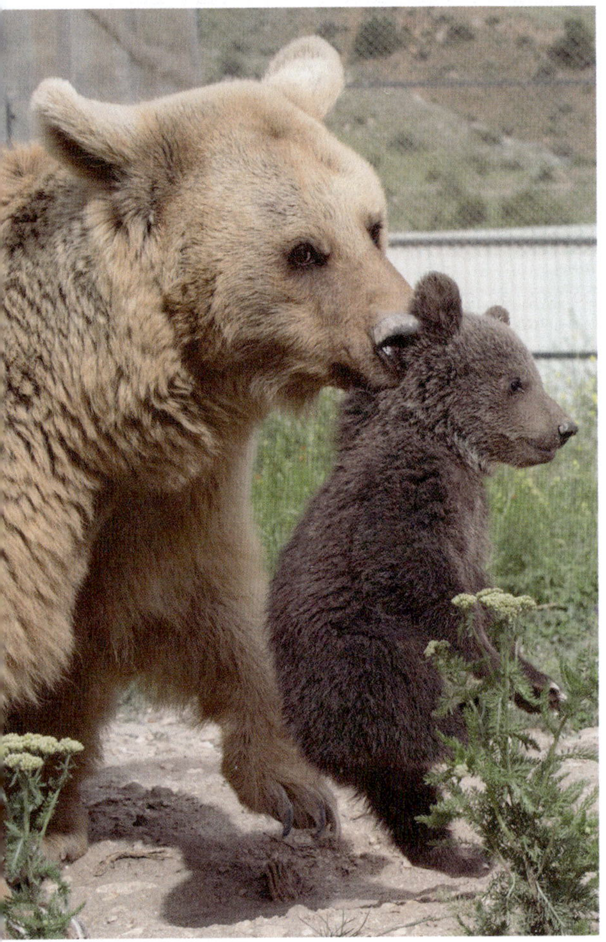

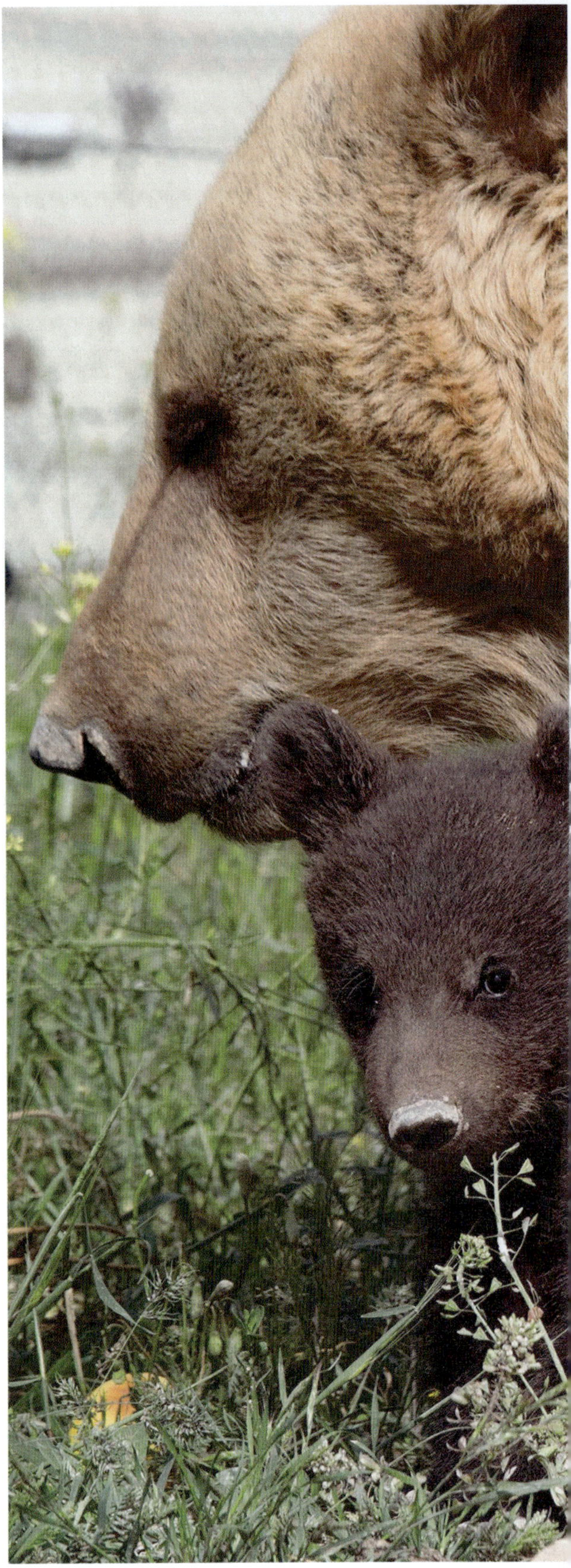

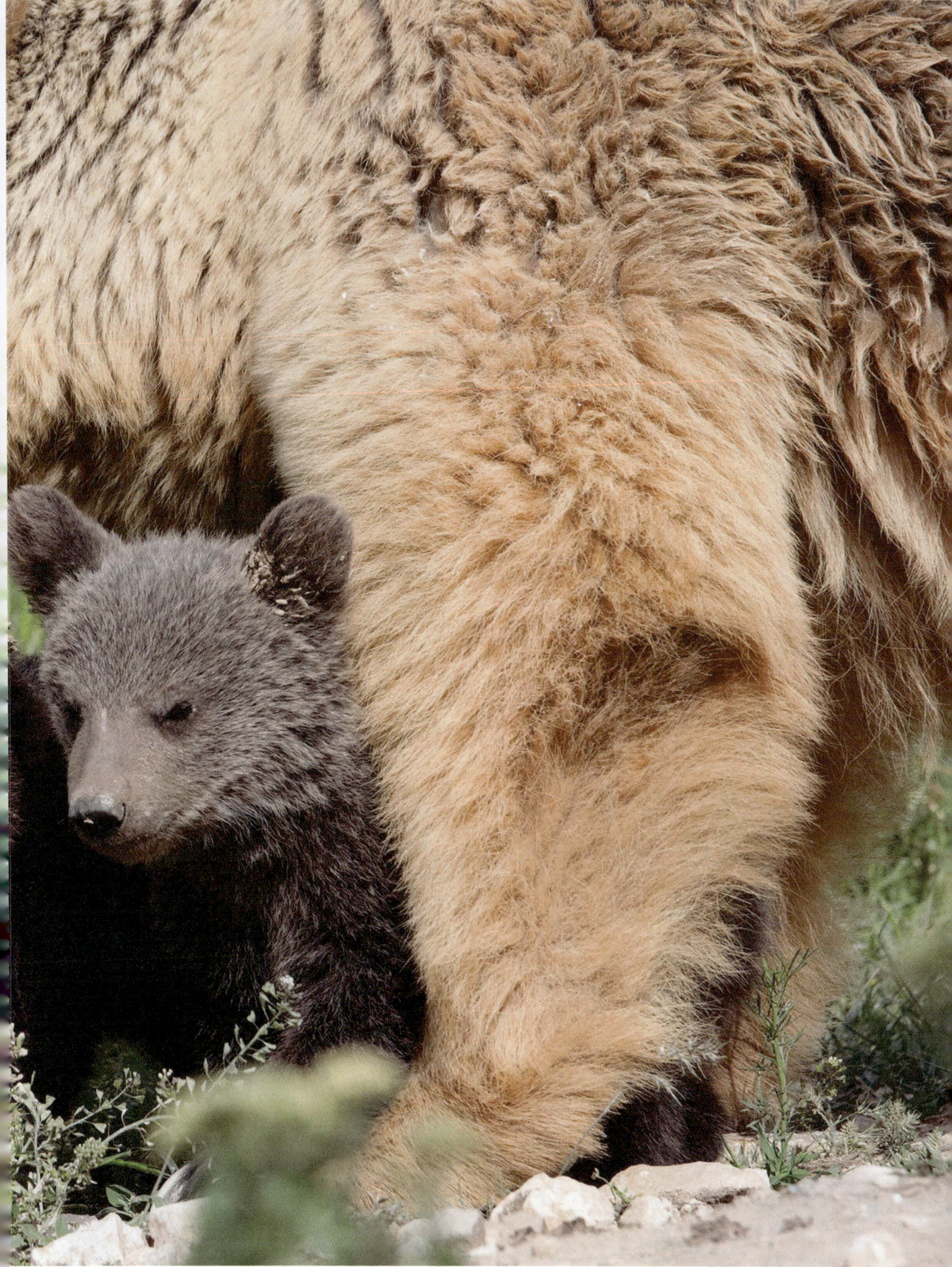

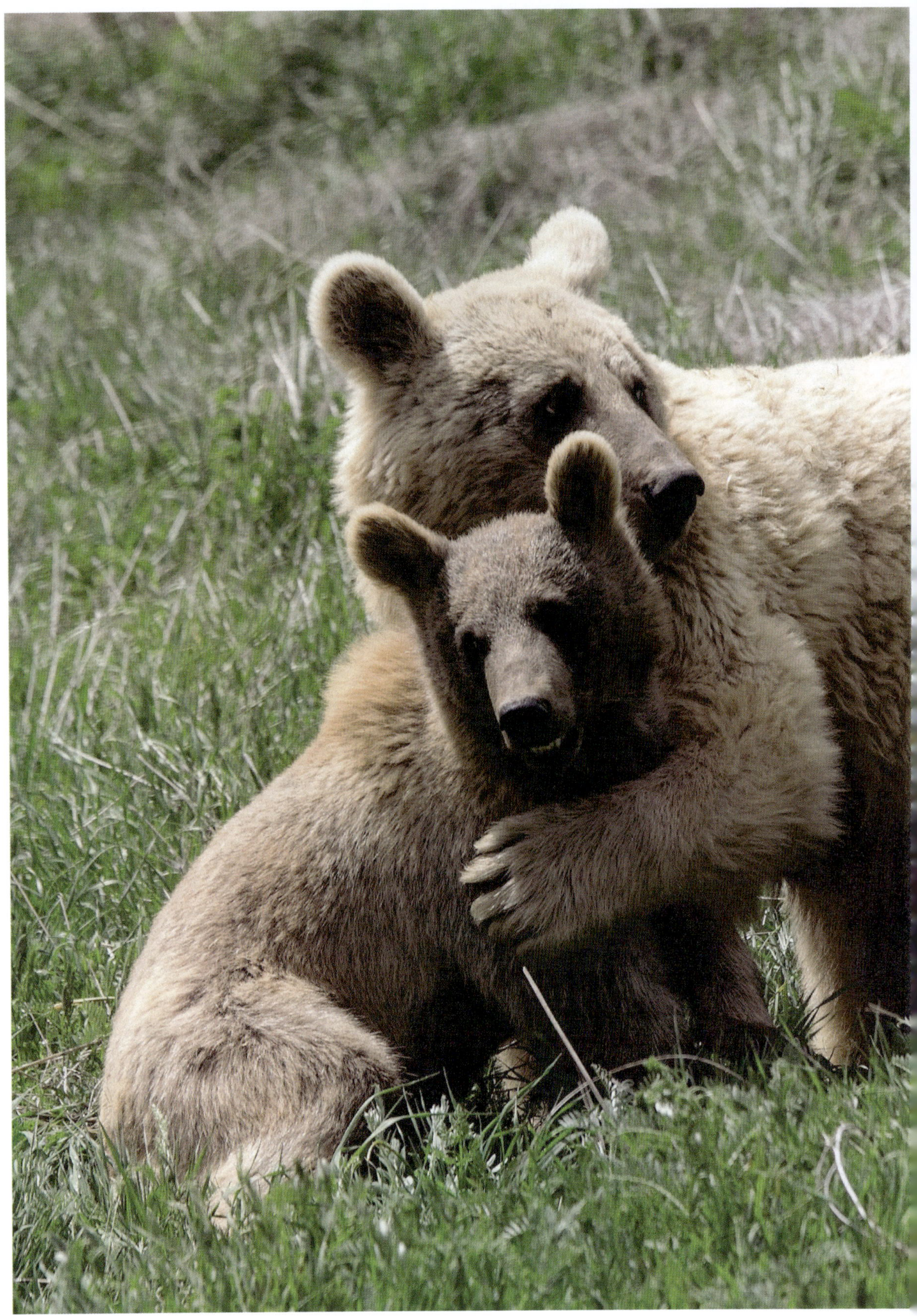

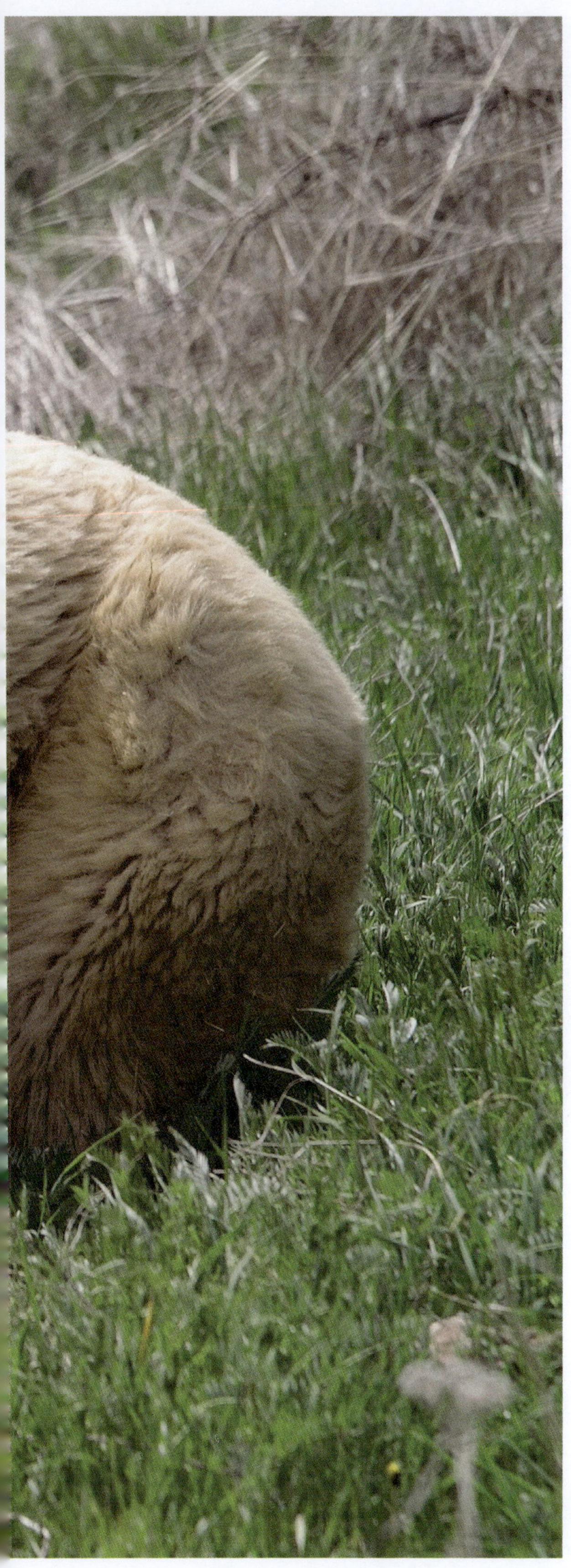

One of the cubs started to wander off and Dasha, a bear who had spent her whole life being laughed at in a cage, instinctively grabbed it by the nape of the neck and took both of her offspring back in the den.

'Wow!', cried the volunteer. 'That was amazing. Two cubs! Did you get a picture?'

I had got some beauties, and Dasha was soon featured in both the *Daily Mail* and the *Mirror*. The *Mirror* did a timeline of her story from cage to cubs.

A year later it was the turn of Dasha and her cubs, Luka and Coco, to be released into the wild. They needed a remote spot with the right amount of tree cover, water and food for them to make a life for themselves. This time, instead of heading north towards the Caucasus, the team took the family south to the shadow of Gnishik Mountain near the Iranian border.

Dasha was fitted with a tracker on the assumption that the cubs would stay with her for up to a year before making their own way in the world. Just the thought of Dasha and her babies out there on their own made us all nervous, but it had to be that way if rescuing bears from misery was to mean anything.

The release site was much like the previous one, with water, trees and meadow. When the gates on the transport crates were lifted, Luka sprang out and ran right past us. Second out was Dasha, who sprinted forward before turning to see where her daughter was. Coco was more hesitant, not knowing what was happening.

For a few seconds we wondered whether Dasha would follow Luka and leave little Coco. But she waited, and when the cub eventually ran up to her mum, Dasha put a protective arm round her and drew her close. The photo I got of that moment was a real tearjerker.

The male cub had quickly run up the slope towards the higher tree line. Dasha and her daughter prowled around for a while checking out the grass, trees and flowers. An orchard of untended apple trees made for a perfect place for her and her daughter to take stock of where they were. In a picture of the pair of them walking close together through the trees, I am sure Dasha has a smile on her face.

The tracking collar told us that within half a day Dasha had roamed two miles into the mountains. She and her cubs were on their way to a truly natural life.

From one twenty-six-second video clip showing abandoned lions and bears in Gyumri, a campaign had begun that had seen more than thirty bears rescued by FPWC and IAR. five released into the wild to live out a natural existence and more being readied for a new life.

There is power for good in the media.

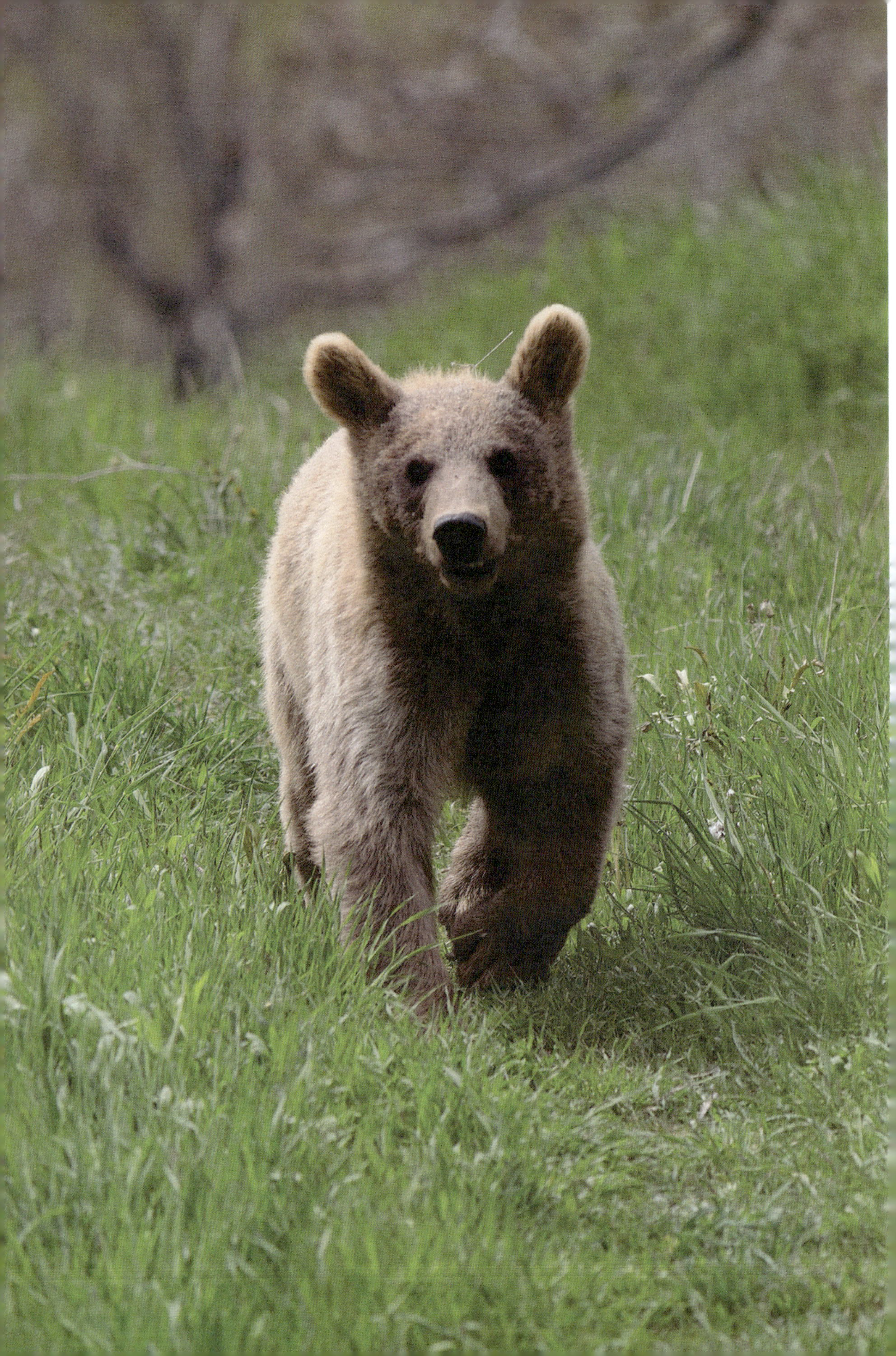

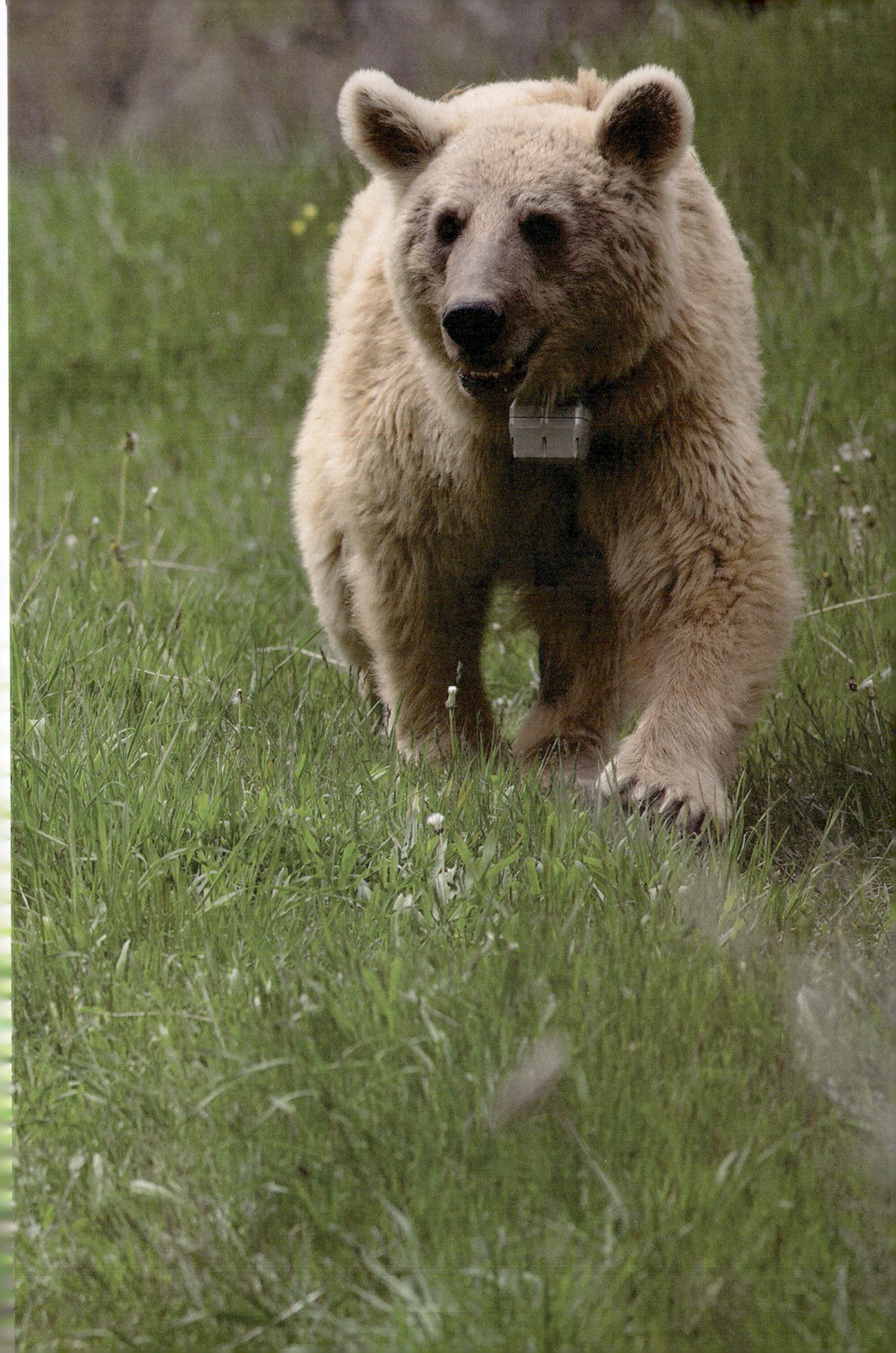

Vera the seal flies first class

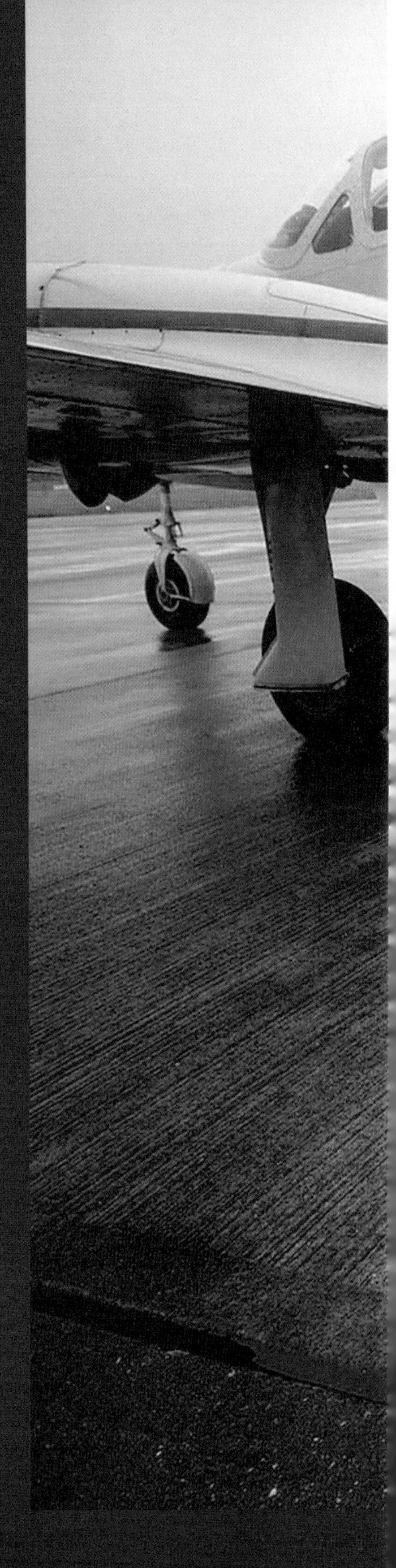

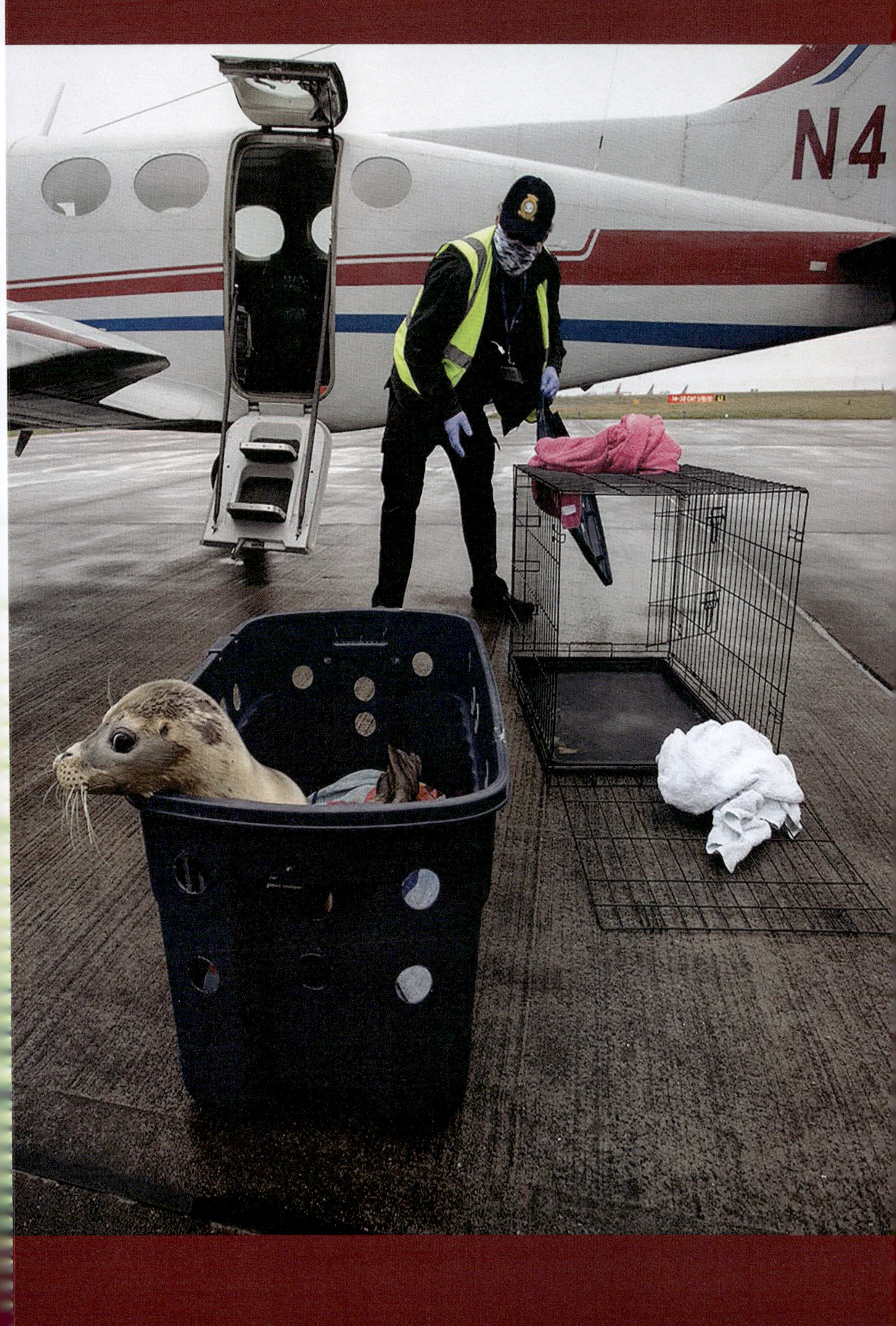

Vera the Seal flies first class

Not many animals get escorted to a private plane by two smartly dressed air stewardesses, but then not many seal cubs get named after a TV detective. It all happened after a dog walker found the furry creature floundering about in distress on Roker Beach in Sunderland, an area used as a film location for the television series *Vera*.

If healthy grey seals see a wounded or helpless pup, they tend to attack it, so with time running out to save the round-eyed youngster, a rescue plan was hatched with British Divers Marine Life Rescue.

The first port of call was Tynemouth Seal Hospital but it was full. The only other place to take her to was hundreds of miles away in Hastings, East Sussex.

The quickest way to collect her was by plane, and I quickly accepted the invitation to join the mercy flight. We took off from an airfield near Silverstone Grand Prix circuit, seventy miles northwest of London, but soon got a message saying that fog at Newcastle made landing there impossible. Instead, we headed to Leeds Bradford airport, just outside

the fog zone, and waited for our special passenger to be brought to us by road, a ninety-five-mile drive. Our twin-engine six-seater Piper had to wait in a remote part of the airfield until a battered green van arrived and we were moved to the private aircraft area. Our little plane was dwarfed by executive jets bound for warm and exotic destinations.

Vera, as she had now been named, looked very poorly as two smartly dressed women in high heels and red scarves crate carried her out of the van. She weighed only twenty-seven pounds, less than half of what she should have weighed at her age. She was fed a few fish and urged to drink some water. Looking for our own refreshment, we nipped into the executive lounge and were offered fresh coffee and snacks.

The executive manager told us we'd be able to load Vera onto the plane as soon as the cabin staff arrived. We tried to explain that Vera wasn't the CEO of a multinational, or even the star of the TV series inspired by Ann Cleeves's novels, but their policy was that any passengers, human or otherwise, had to be handled by cabin crew before boarding an aircraft.

Twenty minutes later the assistants strode into the lounge to escort us to the plane. We all joked about boarding cards and flying first class. Even Vera perked up, trying to open her wire crate with her flippers as she got carried to the aircraft steps. Everyone cheerfully posed for pictures with the rescued seal before waving goodbye.

Vera then needed to be transferred to a special box to keep her warm and hydrated. Manhandling

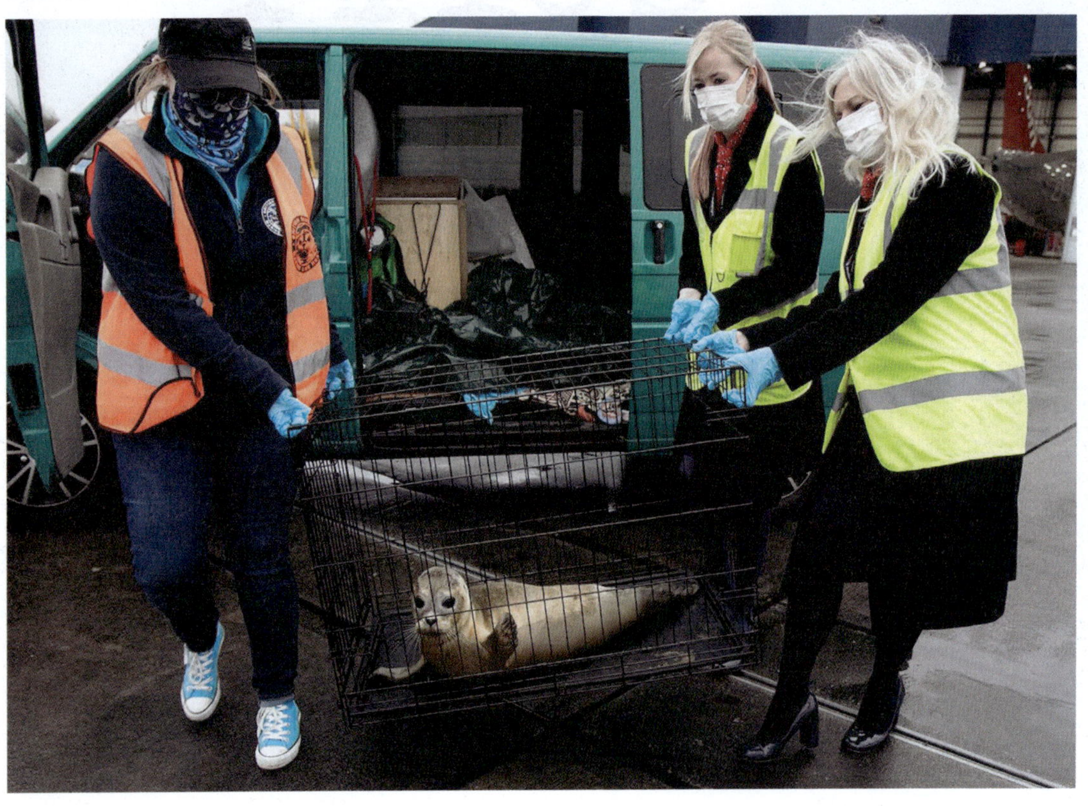

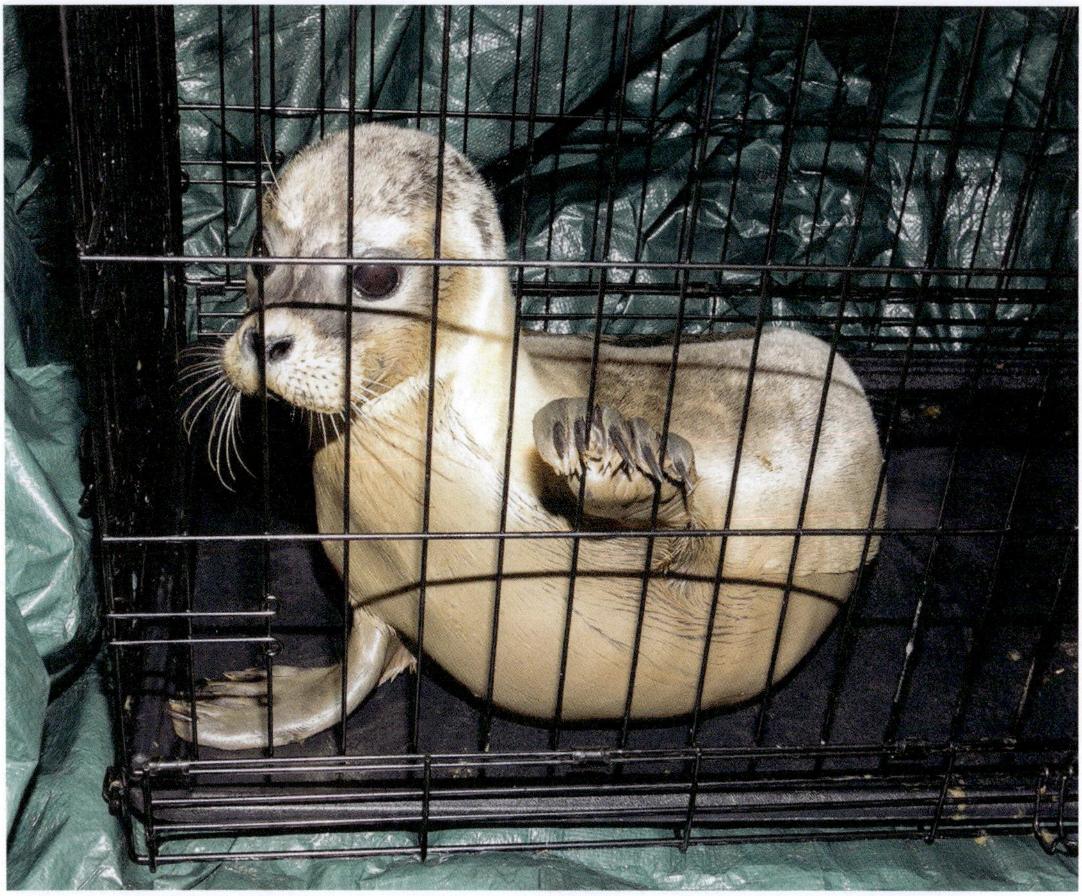

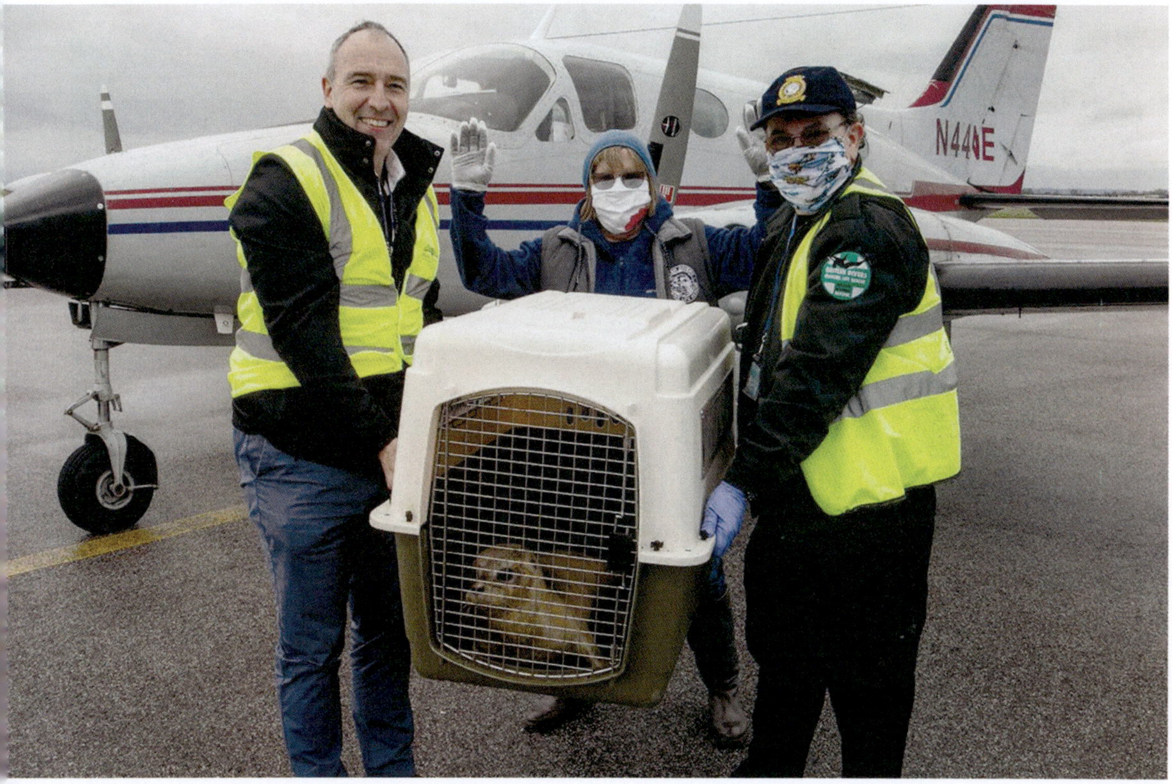

a wild seal can be dangerous: their mouths contain quite a cocktail of bacteria, so one bite would mean a dash to hospital for treatment with penicillin.

The person who was best able to deal with Vera was the veterinary nurse who had escorted her to the airport from the seal hospital in Newcastle. With someone else distracting her, the nurse reached into the crate to cover her with a fluffy white towel. At first, Vera twigged what was about to happen and snapped at the nurse but then the smell of a fresh fish made her forget about the towel and she was soon safely wrapped up.

I snapped away as Vera was carried the few paces to the box. She looked cute and doleful, peering at me from under her white towel.

All the seats had been removed from the aircraft to make way for Vera's large box. The pilots took their seats in the cockpit while I sat with my back to them, facing the live cargo. We were all wearing face masks at the time, because a COVID-19 lockdown was underway, but it soon became apparent that a mask was not enough to protect us from the smell that Vera gave off: an appalling mix of fish and poo. Even with a second mask in place the stink was overpowering.

We rolled onto the strip of runway and before we knew it Vera was on her way to safety.

The pilot warned that the flying conditions would be 'challenging'. Soon afterwards, the aircraft began to pitch and roll. I turned to look at the control panel; our height was still only 4,000 feet and we were flying in thick cloud. On top of that, the reek from Vera's box only got stronger and stronger. I took her white towel and wrapped it around my own head in an attempt to ward off the pong.

Halfway through our bouncy flight, one of the pilots came back to check on the seal. He carefully opened the lid of the box at one end so Vera couldn't slip out into the cabin. As daylight appeared in the box, the seal's head popped out and she took a look at her strange surroundings. I quickly caught the funny picture of her nose, whiskers and two large eyes of this marine mammal travelling high in the sky.

She seemed pleased with the flight, not one bit bothered by her own smell or the turbulence. At least one of us was enjoying it.

Two hours and nearly 300 miles after take-off, the landing lights of Lydd Airport came into view. Outside another executive lounge, a staff member from Mallydams Wood RSPCA centre in Hastings waited to transfer Vera to another van.

The woman grabbed Vera with great confidence to wrap her up in a new towel—pink this time—then deposited her in her new travel crate. We laughed and waved as Vera was driven away.

At Mallydams Wood, a regime of fresh fish, antibiotics and basking under sun lamps would help Vera grow to the fifty-five pounds' weight she needed to reach before she could be released into the English Channel.

Just a month later, she flopped her way down the pebbly beach into the sea to start a new life fishing for herself. First class.

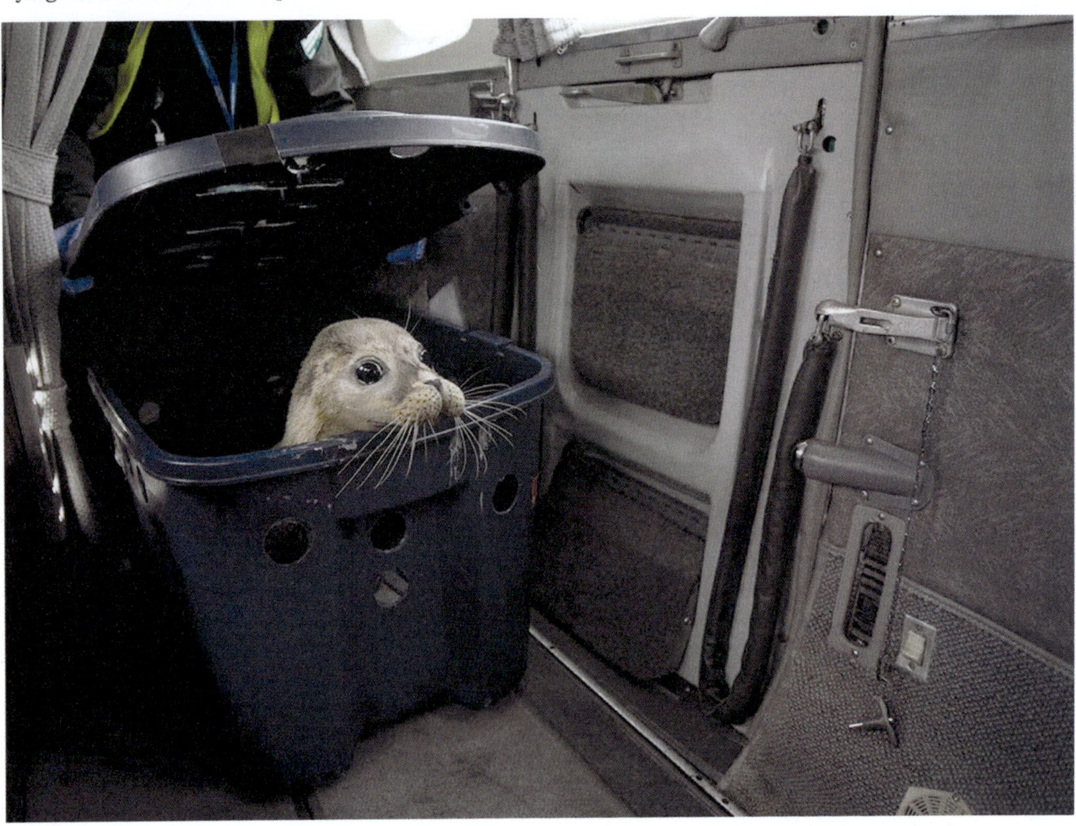

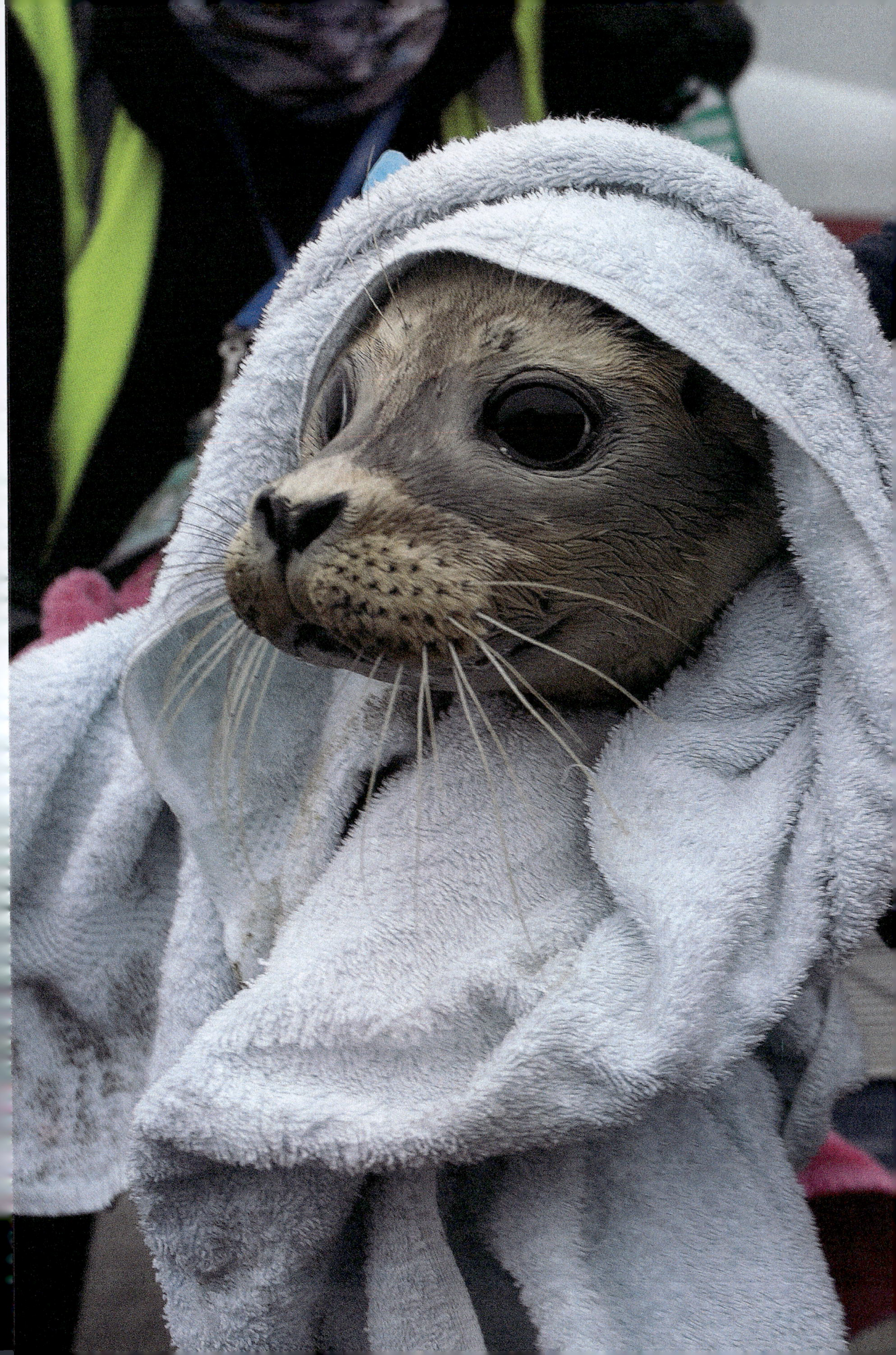

Rhinos

The chase is on

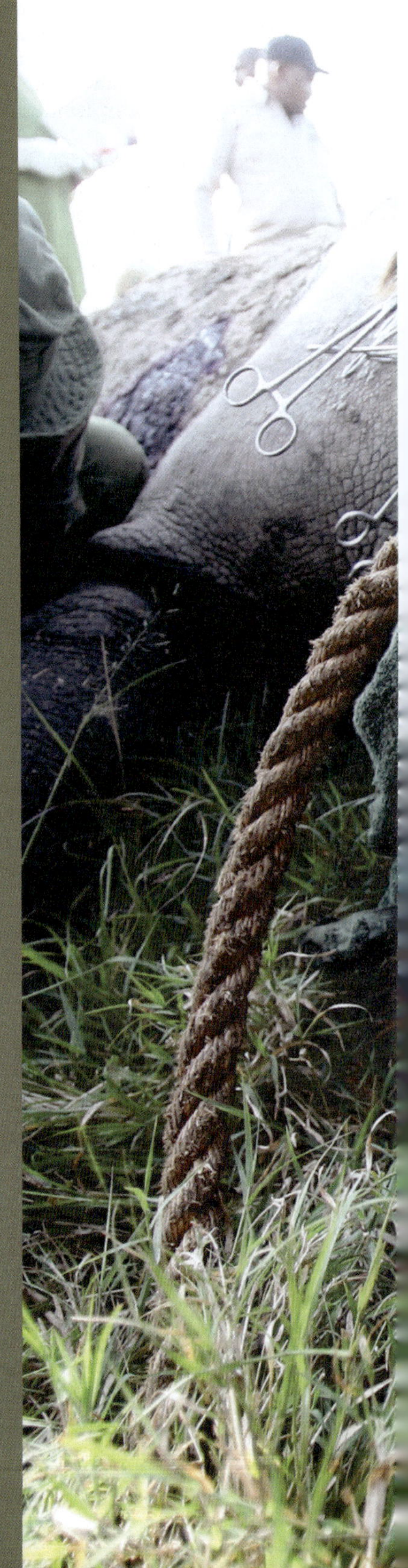

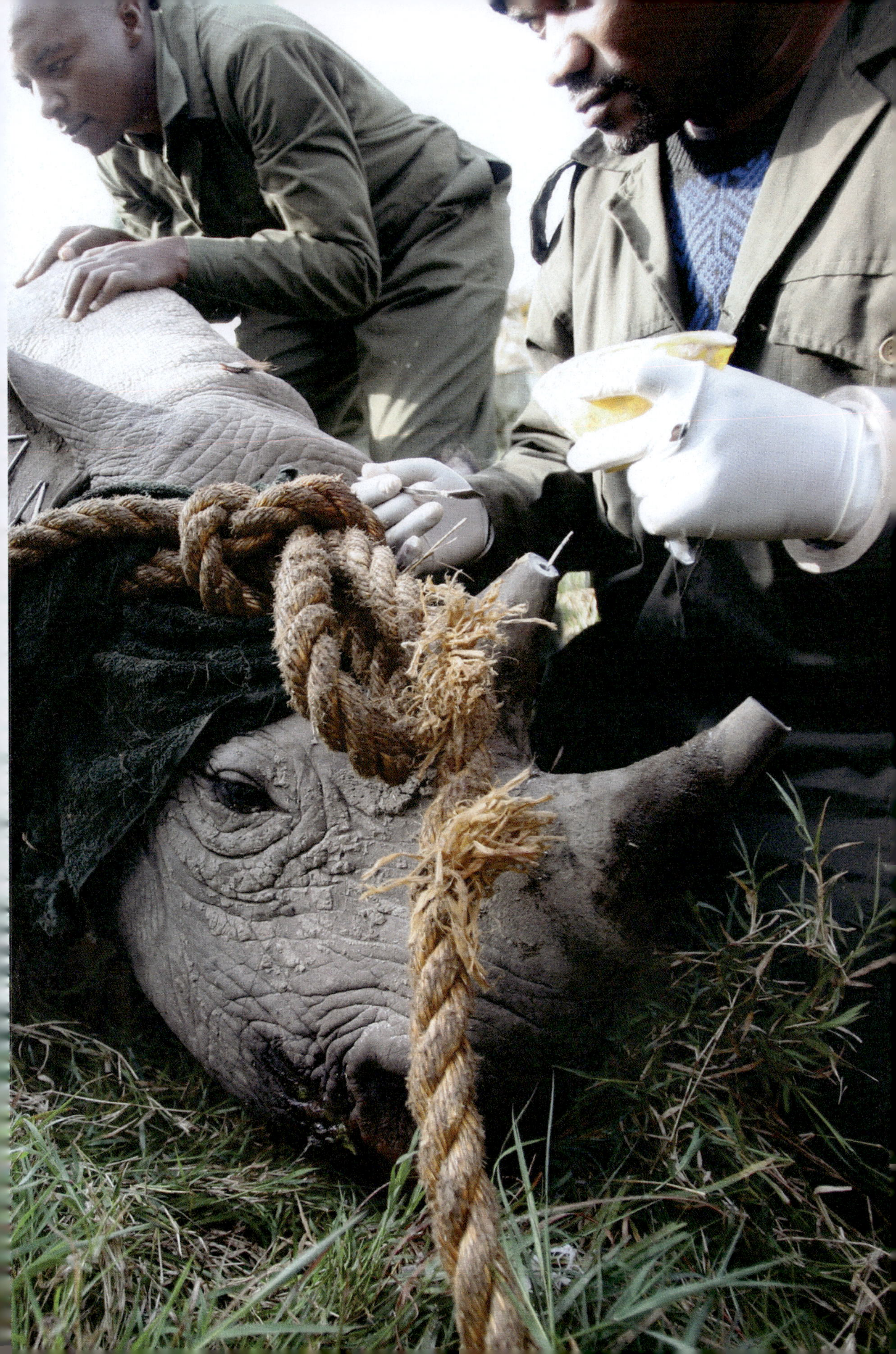

Rhinos: The chase is on

The black rhino can weigh as much as one-and-a-half tons and run at up to thirty-five miles an hour. It is a formidable and dangerous beast when roused.

Any kind of interaction between humans and rhino carries its risks and needs to be handled carefully. When the task is to find and sedate fourteen endangered black rhinos and relocate them from one side of Kenya to the other, it becomes a major exercise in logistics. Every second that each animal is unconscious needs meticulous preparation and teamwork.

I had been sent to Kenya to cover the rhinos' relocation by the World Wildlife Fund. Their breeding programme in the east of the country had worked so well that the group could now be sent to repopulate Tsavo East Nation Park. What had been known as 'Rhino Valley' had become a playground for poachers, who hunted the species to near extinction. Over two decades, the number of rhino dropped by ninety-six per cent from 20,000 to just 300.

At the start of the mission a workforce of forty-four—made up of four vets, two helicopter pilots, various spotters and scientists and fifteen rangers—gathered together one early morning. We stood in a large semi-circle as the team leader said prayers for everybody's safety. By 6:15 am the helicopter had lifted off carrying one of the vets, his rifle armed with the first of many pink-feathered tranquilliser darts.

I stayed on the ground with the spotters and, before long, the clatter of the chopper's rotor blades made one rhino break cover from the dense trees. The helicopter swooped low over the animal and with a precision shot from the vet, a pink tailed dart was soon sticking out of the beast's rump.

The shock of being darted made the animal run towards the trucks waiting on the dirt track. As it picked up speed the team began climbing out of its way onto the large transport crates waiting to be filled with the armoured beasts. At the last minute, fortunately, the animal changed direction and ran into a large open plain.

I had a long lens trained on him, and as he leaped over a small ditch I pressed the shutter. The picture caught the airborne rhino with the breaking dawn light picking out the pink feathers of the tranquiliser dart.

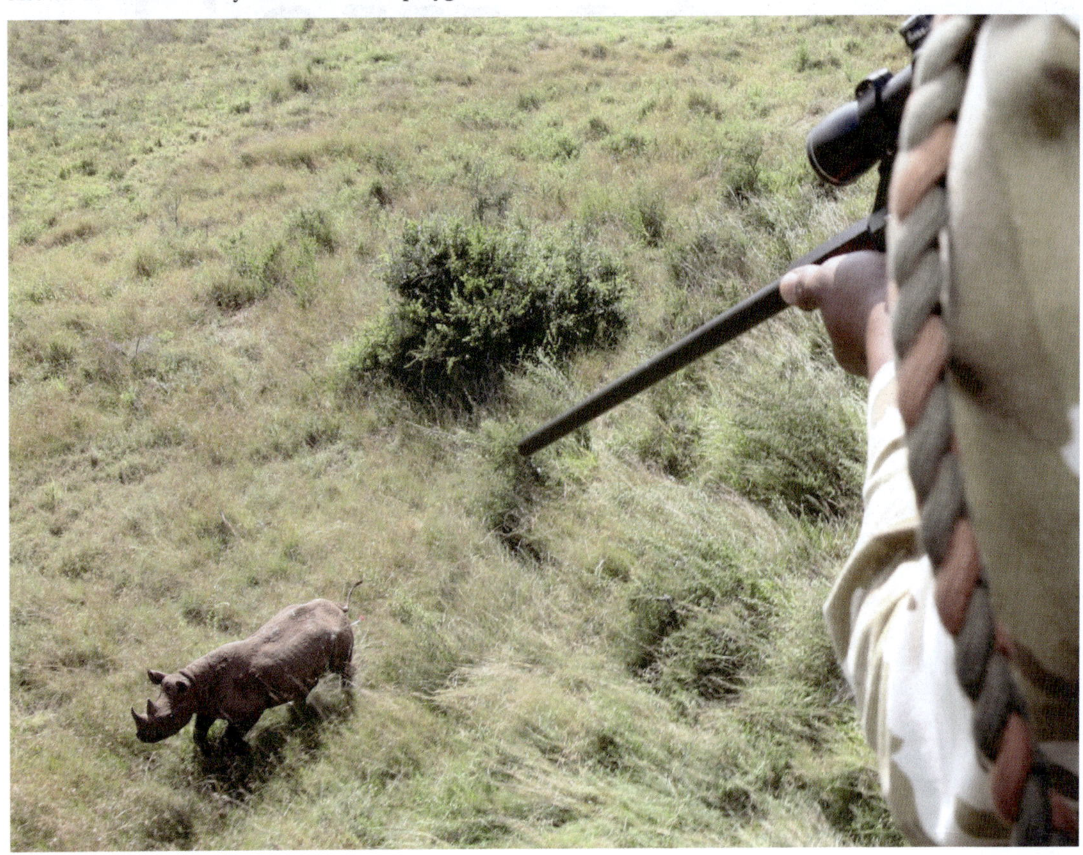

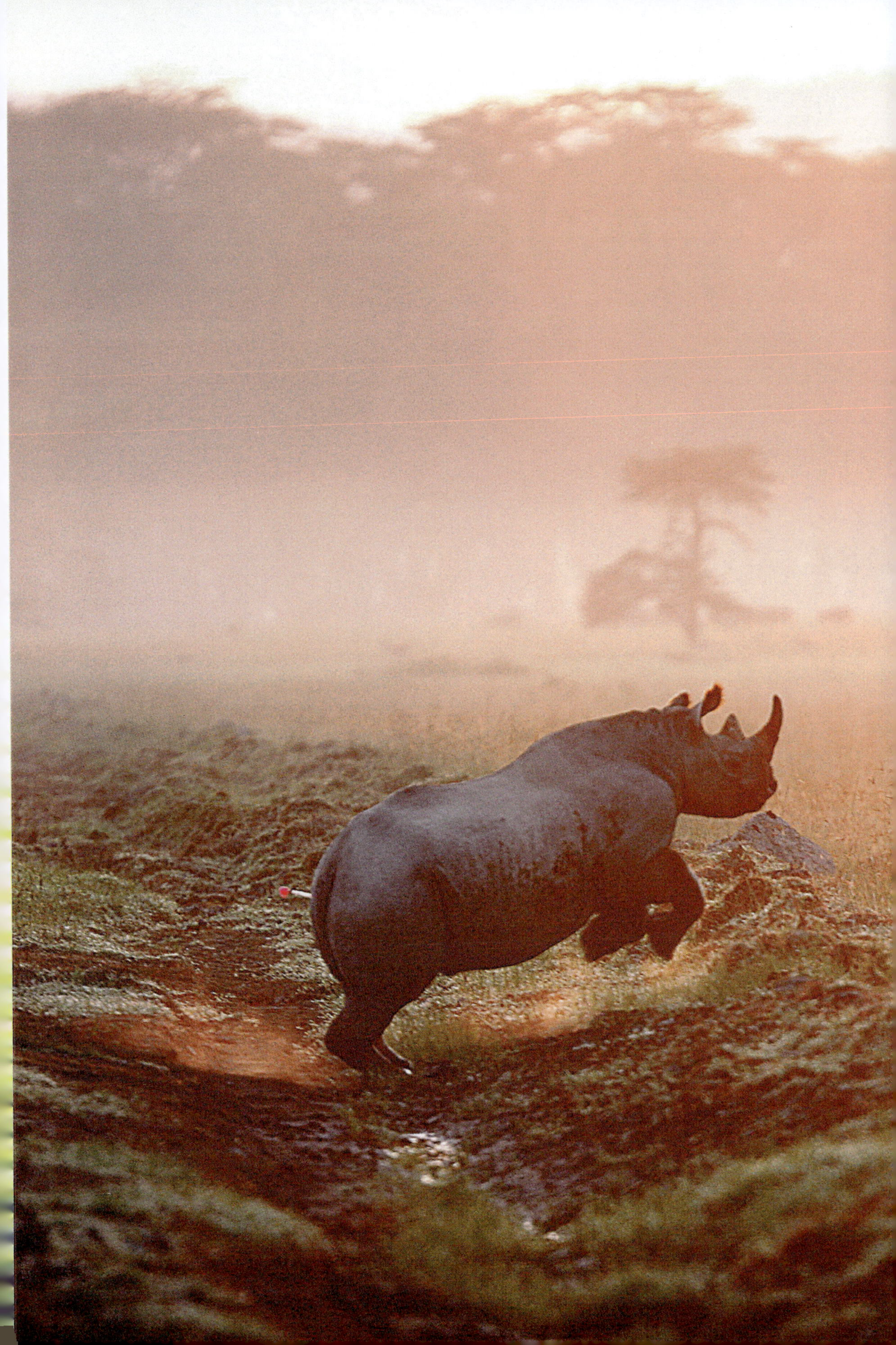

While that moment was frozen in time inside my camera, the frantic chase got under way. Rangers jumped down from the crates and ran to close the gap between them and the charging rhino. Within a few minutes, the startled animal began to slow down as the drug coursing around its body began to take effect.

The rangers sprinted towards the faltering animal but stopped short of approaching it. This was the most dangerous part of the operation as the rhino weaved left and right, fighting against the tranquilliser. It was a matter of waiting for him to drop.

As soon as he was down the team piled in—vets, scientists, lab technicians all getting to work while the rangers looped a rope over the beast's head. One person drilled into the base of the horn to fit a radio transponder and microchip. Another sawed off most of the horn, making the animal worthless

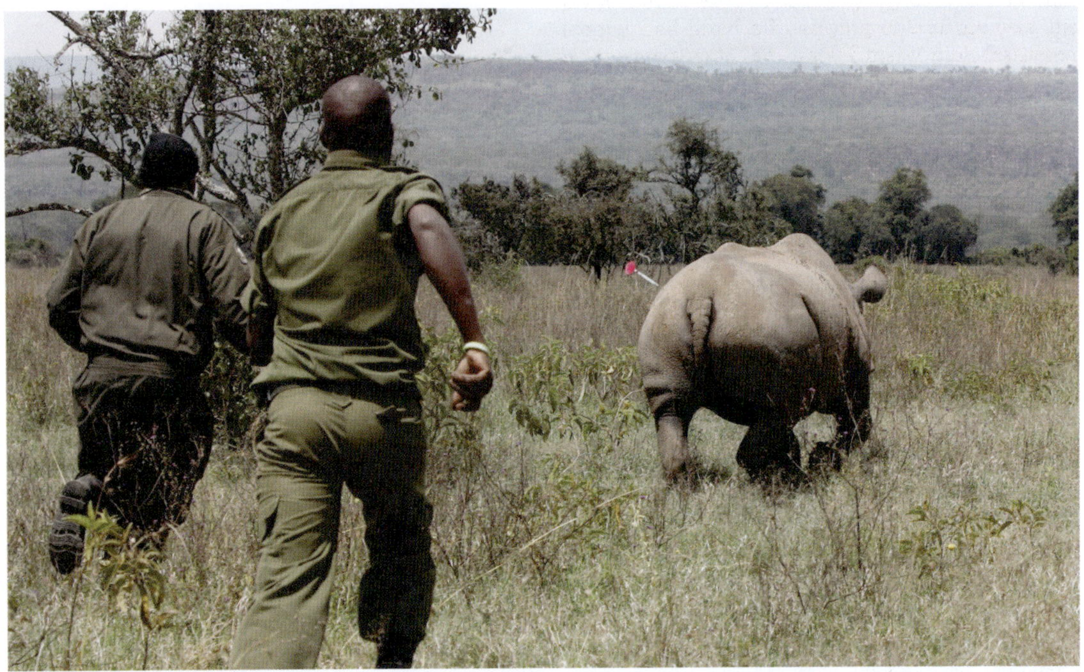

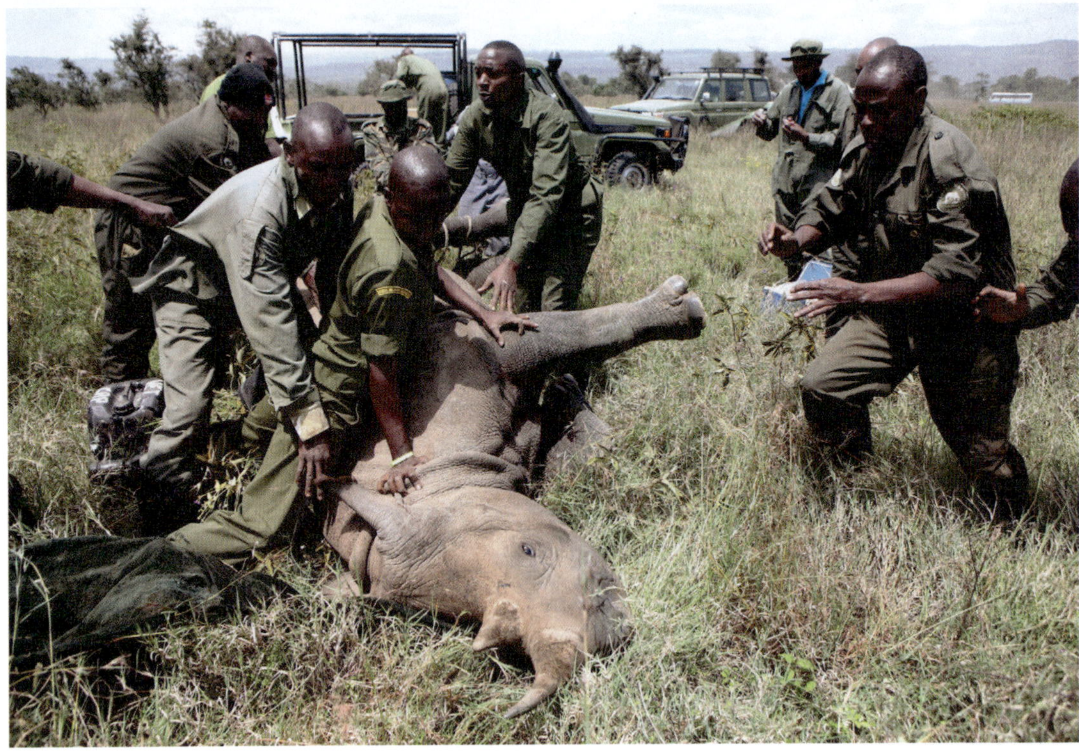

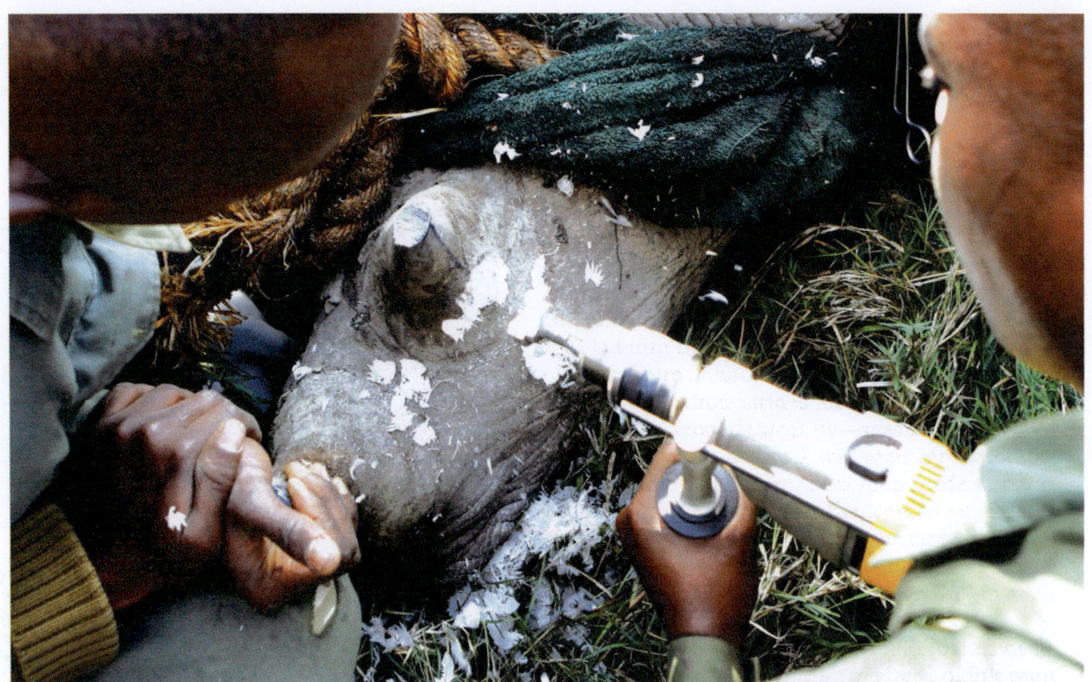

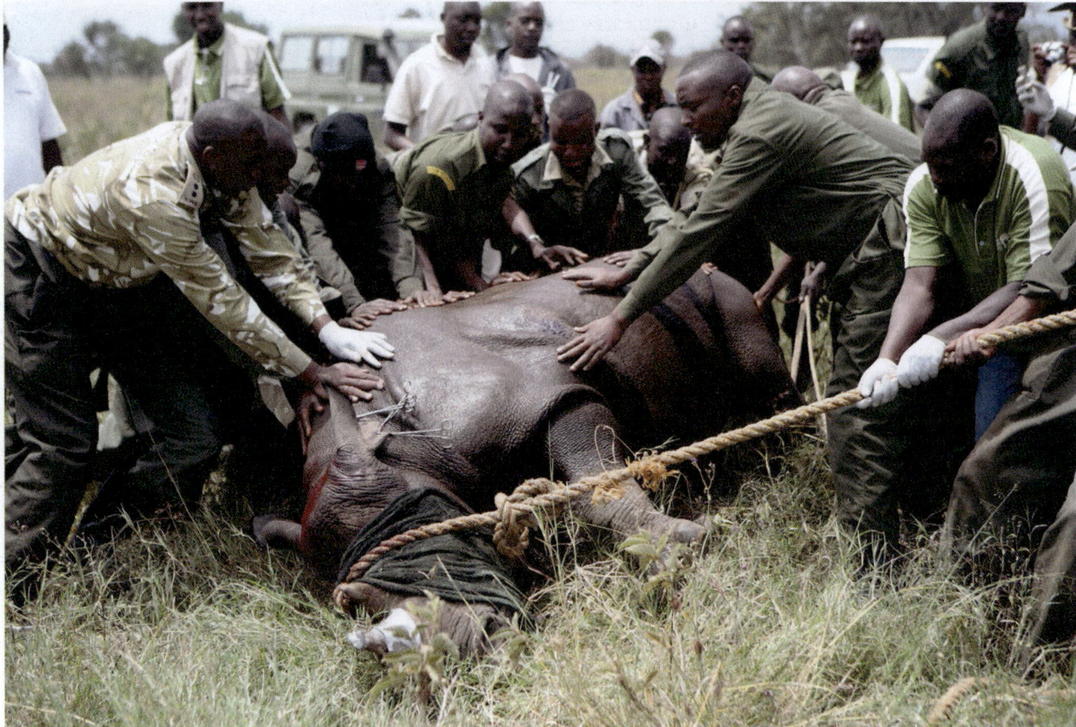

to poachers. A third notched the rhino's ears with a distinctive identification pattern.

For the twenty minutes that the animal was out cold, a vet was checking its breathing and heart rate. Blood samples were taken before its quivering belly and twitching legs indicated he was beginning to come round. It was time for the wake-up drug to be administered.

A truck had been moved close to the stricken animal and a crate unloaded next to him. The more awake he became, the faster the team had to move.

The rope around the rhino's head was fed into the crate and out through an opening at its rear. With the animal becoming more alert every second, three men attached the rope to a tractor that would pull him into the crate.

A tug of war got under way as the rhino began to wake up properly.

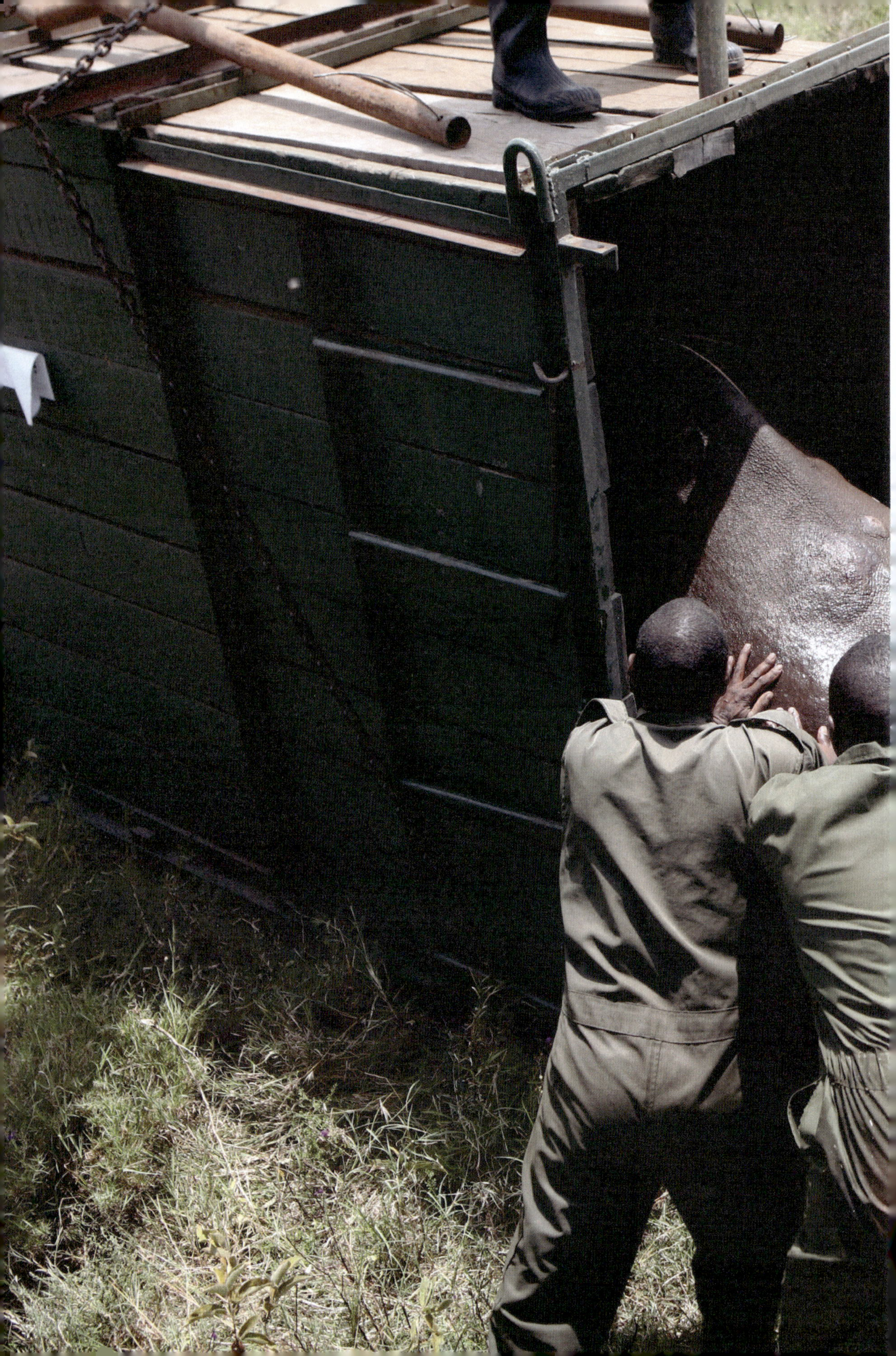

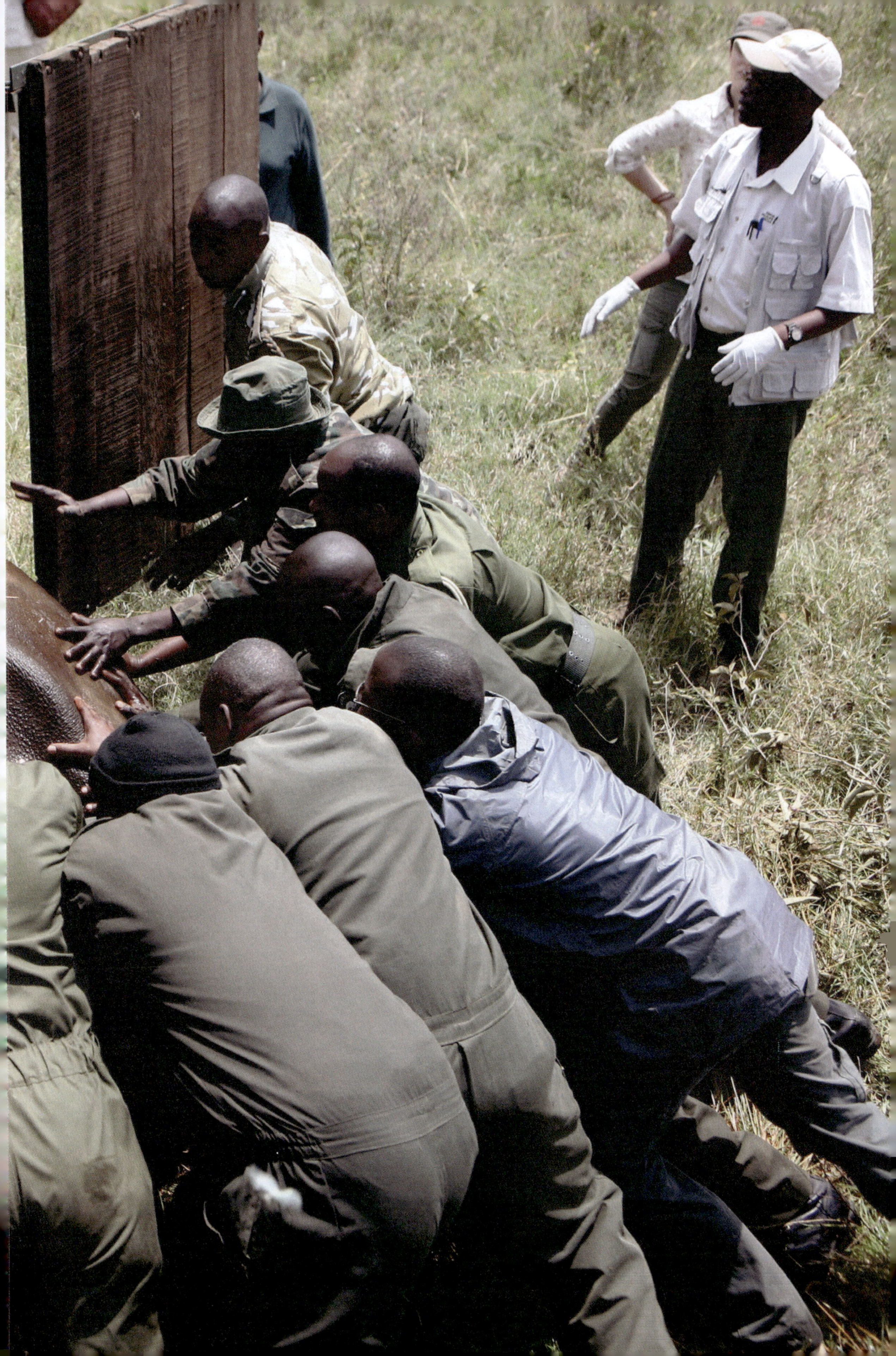

'Hurry up! Push!' shouted one of the vets. 'If he gets on his legs, we're all in trouble.'

The tractor belched out a puff of smoke and pulled harder; eight men pushed against the rhino's backside. Just as the doors of the crate slammed shut the one-and-a-half-ton animal kicked out behind him. The doors bent outwards but held.

One down, thirteen to go.

The next animal had been spotted about half a mile away, This time I jumped into the chopper alongside the vet. As we swooped over the forest waiting for the signal from the spotters, a huge lake appeared. A massive flock of flamingos took flight, some running on the water before lifting off before joining the main body of pink birds.

The radio crackled into life as we tracked back towards the open plain: 'There's a female running on the flat west of the camp.'

The pilot turned the helicopter to follow the running animal and came alongside her, flying at just a hundred feet above the ground. Once again the vet hit the bullseye with his rifle dart.

Bushes and small trees don't mean a thing to a rhino, even after being shot with a tranquilliser. This female ploughed straight through most things in her way, as she headed for a forest, which made it difficult for the rangers running behind her.

The pilot overtook the charging animal and swung the helicopter around to face her. She turned on her heels and thundered towards the rangers, who held their nerve as she got closer and closer.

The lead ranger swung a rope high above his head and lassoed the approaching animal on his first throw, the other seven men grabbing the rope and taking the strain. Between the drag that they offered and the tranquilliser kicking in, the rhino slowed to a halt.

Soon the huge grey beast was on her side and panting, but just as the team moved forward to start the drilling, sawing and testing she sprang back to life. Like a huge jack-in-the-box she popped up onto her four legs and made a break for freedom.

It was a scary moment, but it didn't last. Before long she had given up the ghost and flopped down unconscious. The same procedure as before went into motion and the crated animal was soon lifted onto a lorry for the fourteen-hour journey to the other side of the country.

Two down.

As soon as four animals were ready to hit the road, the first convoy started out on the great trek while the team set about capturing the other ten. It was 2:00 am when the convoy rolled into Tsavo East National Park.

Two of the crates were lowered to the ground and anyone who wasn't a ranger climbed to safety on the empty flatbed truck to wait for the doors of the wooden boxes to be opened and the rhinos to encounter their new home.

There was no charge out of the crates this time. The two animals had become quietly comfortable in their boxes. With hay, food and water laid on, why bother going out into the wild of an unfamiliar place?

One hour became two and everybody was falling asleep waiting for the beasts to take the air. Then, we spotted some movement: the female took a few small steps out of her crate, soon followed by the male. Before long both animals had emerged into the night and stood horn to horn, sizing each other up.

Happy that the pair would find their own way into the forest, we headed to bed for some much-needed sleep.

Later in the morning I returned to the release site with the tracking team. Equipped with a rotating aerial we tried to pick up the radio signals from the transponders. After we had walked into the bush for a few minutes, the beeping noise became louder.

'This is the signal for the female,' whispered one of the rangers. 'She is very close. Please be careful—if she smells us, she could charge. Be very quiet'

Just as he spoke a flock of yellow-billed oxpeckers rose up. These birds sit on the backs of rhinos removing ticks, clearing parasites from any open wounds and raising the alarm if danger is close by.

The ranger hissed at us to be still: 'She is right there, straight in front of us. Don't make any sudden movements.'

Just fifteen yards away, behind two large bushes, was the rhino I had watched being pushed into her transport crate. We inched forward. A rhino's eyesight is very poor, but her nose was telling her we were there. To her, we were a potential threat, and that made her a danger to us.

She edged past the bushes towards us. It was as if she knew I needed a clear shot of her, and I raised my camera slowly to get the image.

Moments later, the ranger was warning us to retreat. The rhino had worked out that the people who'd put her through Hell the day before were now right in front of her.

We made it back to the truck just as she burst out of the bush and stood snorting on the dirt track, wondering where we'd fled to.

It took a few days to transport all fourteen rhinos to Rhino Valley. I photographed the chief ranger as we stood overlooking the vast plain. He pointed out a rail track on the valley floor and told me that the British and Germans had done battle there during the First World War. 'Now we have a different war,' he added, 'stopping the poachers taking away our precious animals'.

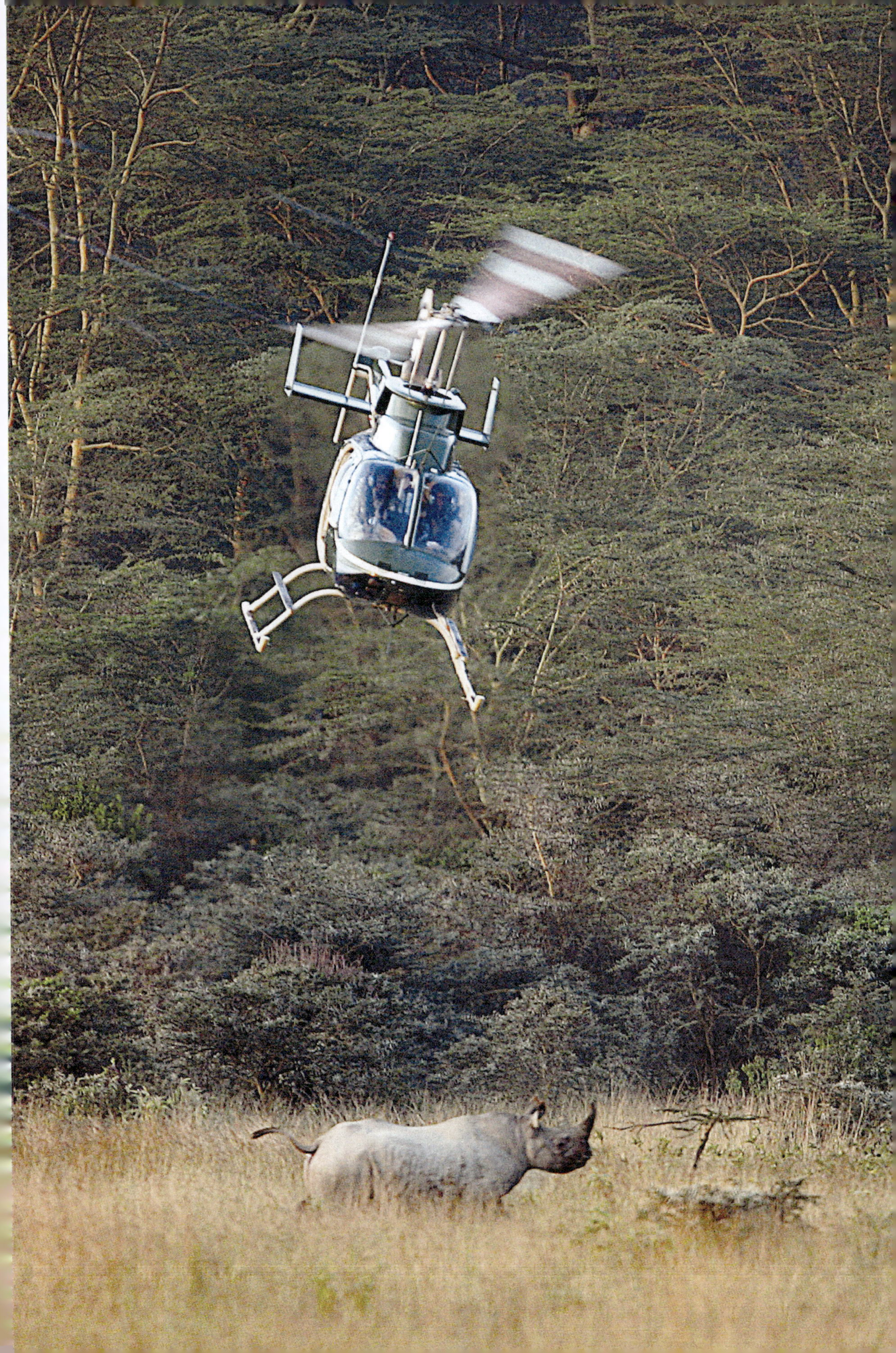

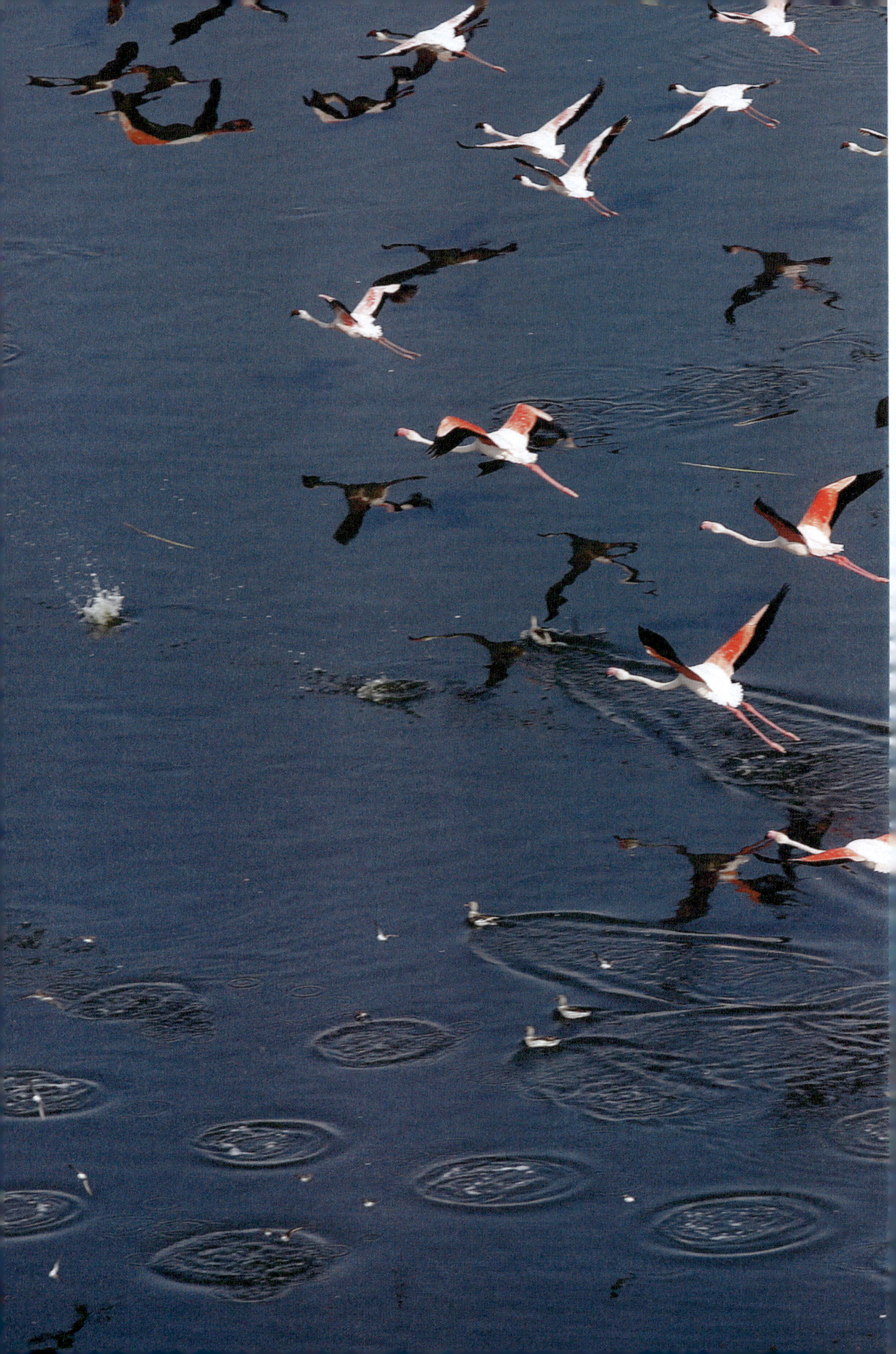

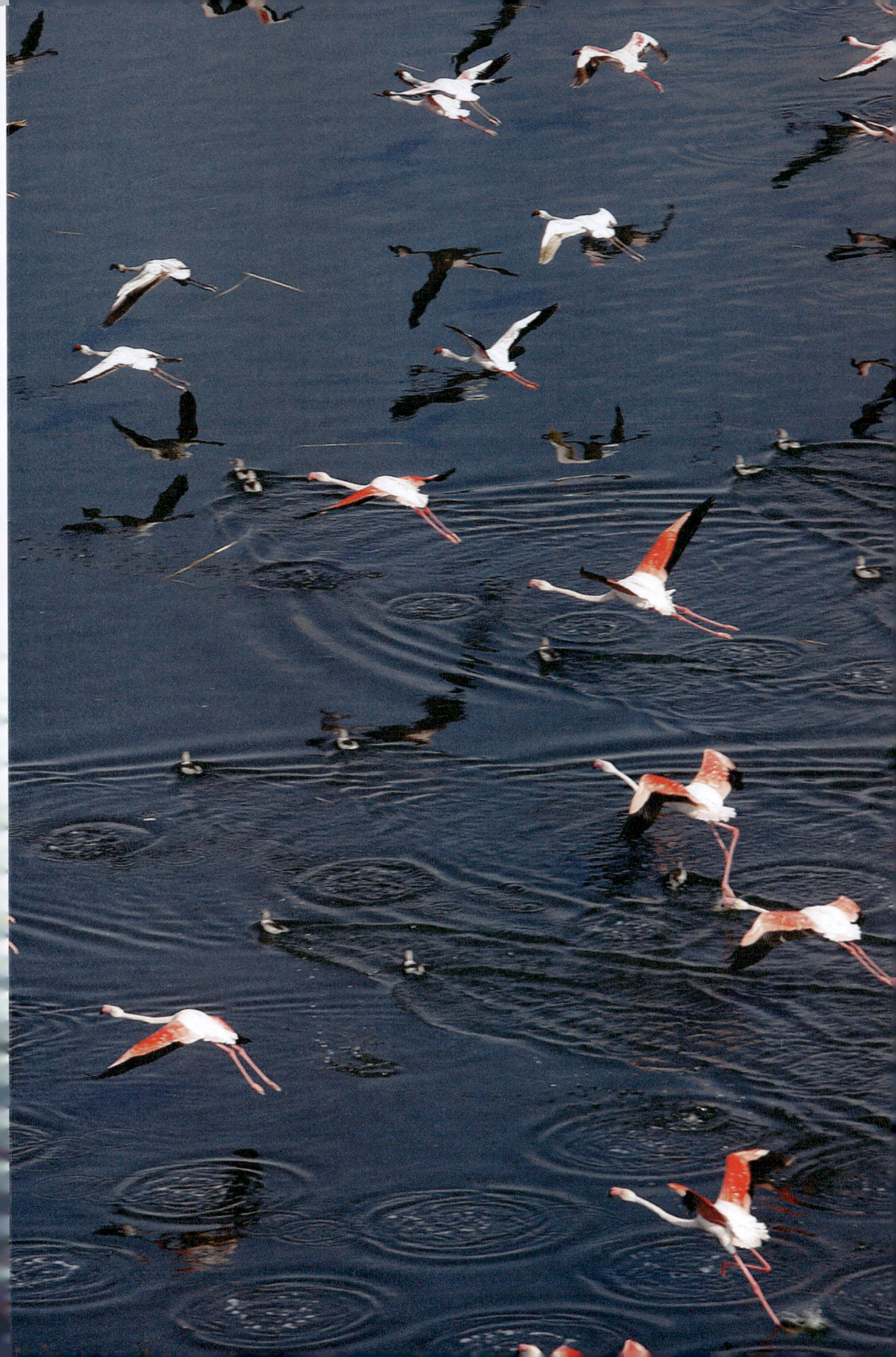

Don't
go
past
the
fence

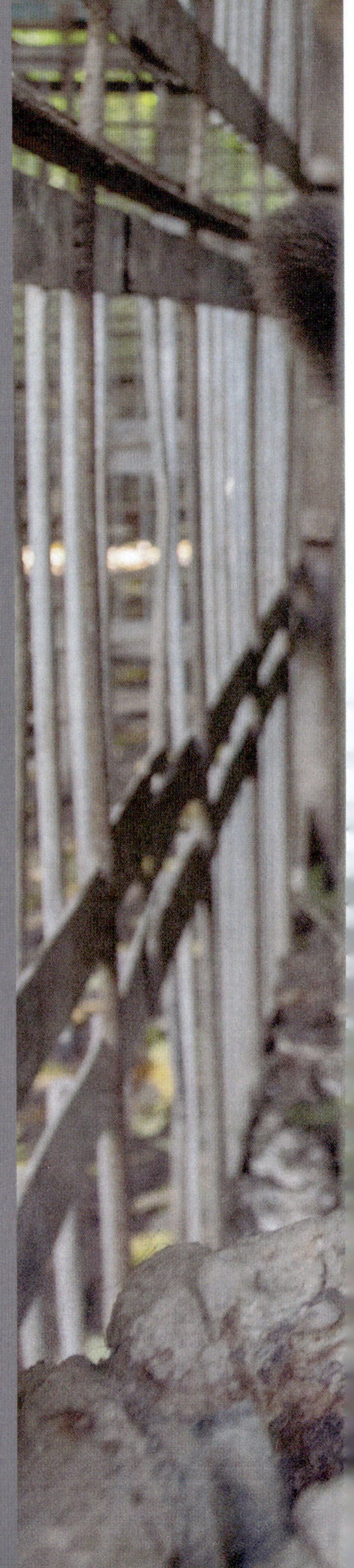

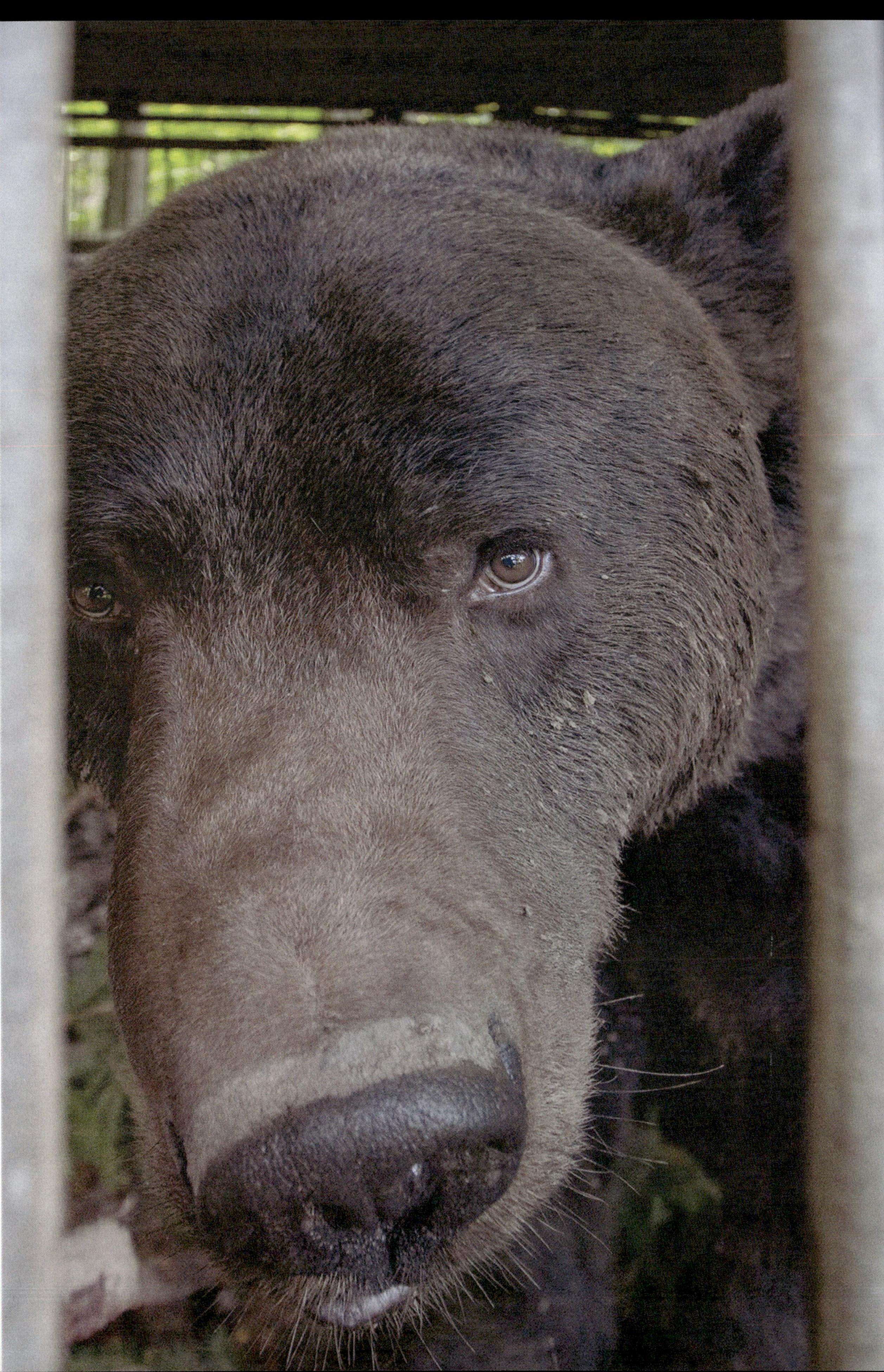

За огорожу
не заходити!

(Don't go past
the fence)

From the twelfth century, tying a brown bear to a pole and releasing a pack of dogs to torment it was seen as good entertainment in England until it was banned in the nineteenth. Especially in the sixteenth and seventeenth centuries, purpose-built 'bear gardens', like those in Southwark, were popular public attractions; even Queen Elizabeth I was known to attend. Interest began to fade in the eighteenth century, as public attitudes shifted, but it wasn't until 1835 that new legislation made bear baiting and other blood sports illegal.

Until then, bear pits could be found in or behind the gardens of inns and taverns across the country, where drunken men would bet on which dog would inflict the most damage on the captive animal. Pubs had names like The Bear and Ragged Staff, the Dog and Bear, and The Bear Inn, their painted signs often showing a bear standing next to a pole, a gold chain around its neck.

Bear baiting has continued into modern times in Ukraine, and the Four Paws charity made rescuing bears from baiting the main focus of its operations in Eastern Europe from 2018 onwards.

After arriving in Kyiv on a freezing night in November, Allan Hall and I found ourselves driving through a snowstorm to Ivano-Frankivsk, a city in western Ukraine, at the foothills of the Carpathian Mountains, near the borders with Poland, Romania and Hungary. There we met a twenty-strong Four Paws team.

Bleary-eyed early the next morning, Allan and I attended a team briefing. The bear that had been targeted for rescue was being held in a remote village outside the city. The poor animal, named Tyson, had been held by a group of soldiers, many of them battle-hardened veterans from the ongoing conflict in the east of the country.

Dr Frank Goeritz, a vet from Berlin's Leibniz Institute for Zoo and Wildlife Research, addressed the meeting. He explained that the bear had been held for sixteen years in a squalid cage no bigger than twenty feet by sixteen, in a wooded glade, far from prying eyes. The cruelty inflicted on him ranged from having dogs brought in to attack it to being inadequately fed.

'Tyson weighs 500 pounds, which is huge,' Frank explained. 'We need to be quick and on our game. The cage is not only small but very low, so getting him out is going to be difficult. Everybody must know what they are going to do and stick to it. Once he's out of the cage, it's all go for heart monitoring, bloods, teeth and paws; any major problems we can look after when he's safe at the sanctuary. So let's go and rescue Tyson!'

Everybody in the room cheered. It was like a commander rallying the troops on the eve of a battle.

Background talks had been going on with Tyson's captors. Two days before the rescue was mounted they had agreed to hand him over, but on the morning of our arrival they had changed their minds.

We were met by a group of ten men in paramilitary uniforms.

Allan and I kept our distance. We had been told not to mention that we were from the British press. Frank and Carsten, a Four Paws director, opened negotiations. At first, it appeared that the men were ready to fight to keep possession of their bear. Owning such a large animal was a status symbol and a matter of pride for them, and their response to us was aggressive.

Apart from wanting to protect their own machismo, they were concerned about being portrayed as guilty of animal cruelty. They also feared losing the respect of the community because their service on the frontlines had made them heroes in the eyes of many. Behind that, though, they just wanted to continue coming to this hidden spot to drink and grill meat on the barbecue while Tyson was taken from his stinking cage and abused. They would laugh as the dogs came at him, and they cheered both when he was bitten or when he managed to injure one of his attackers. They also made money out of him.

Somehow, a deal was struck: Tyson could go free if his owner's children could travel for free to see him in his new home. The Four Paws people agreed to this. They went further: they promised to explore the possibility of opening another bear sanctuary at the site of Tyson's captivity.

As soon as everything was settled, we entered the wooded area. Tyson was standing on his hind legs and sniffing the air. Next to his home was the men's drinking den, littered with discarded food, vodka bottles and a battered old barbecue.

Fifteen minutes later Tyson had been darted. Four men from the medical team stooped and entered the low cage to fit a saline drip, take blood samples and monitor the bear's vital signs before getting him out of his prison for the last time.

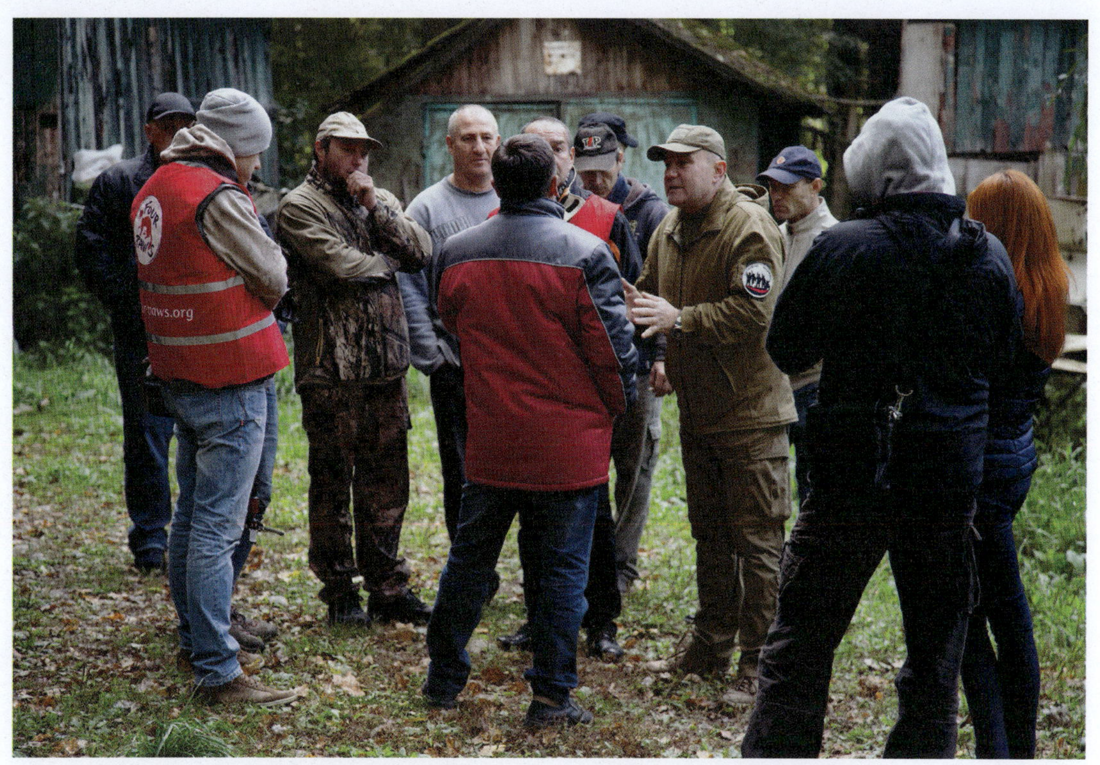

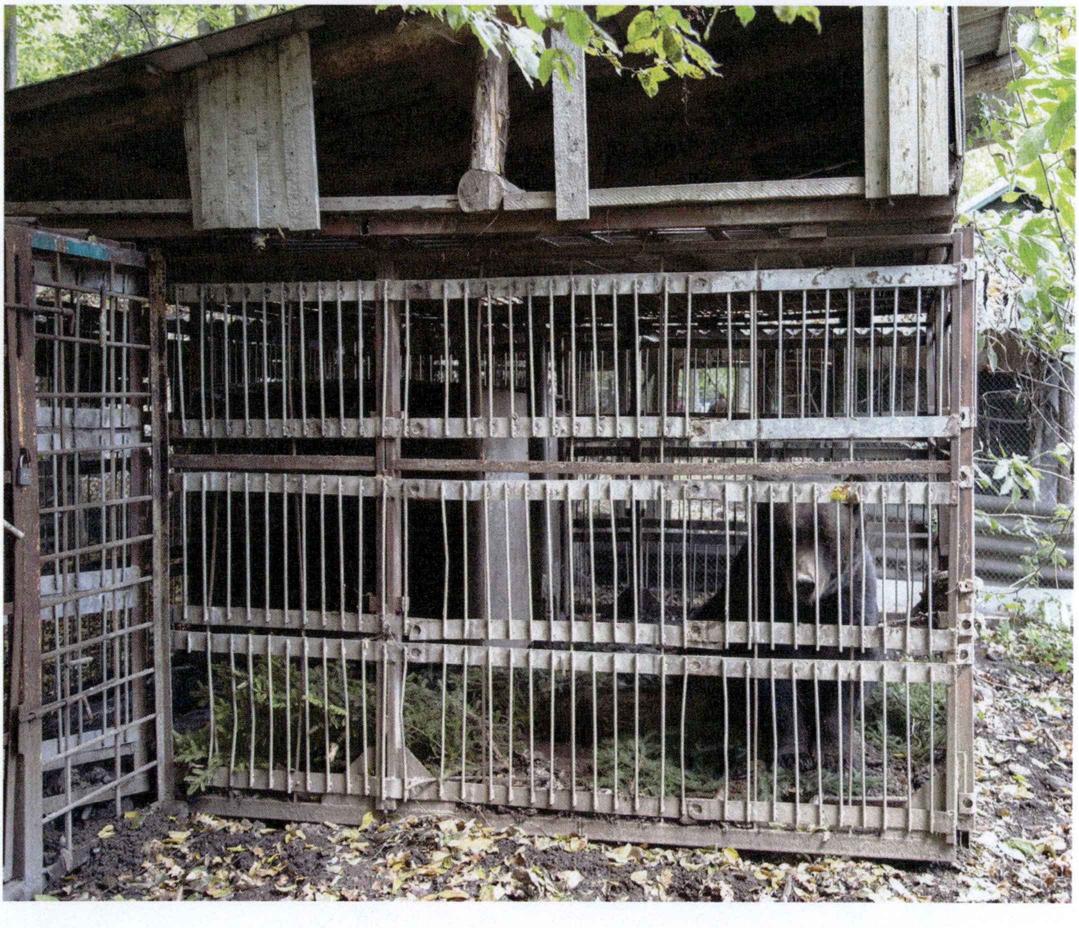

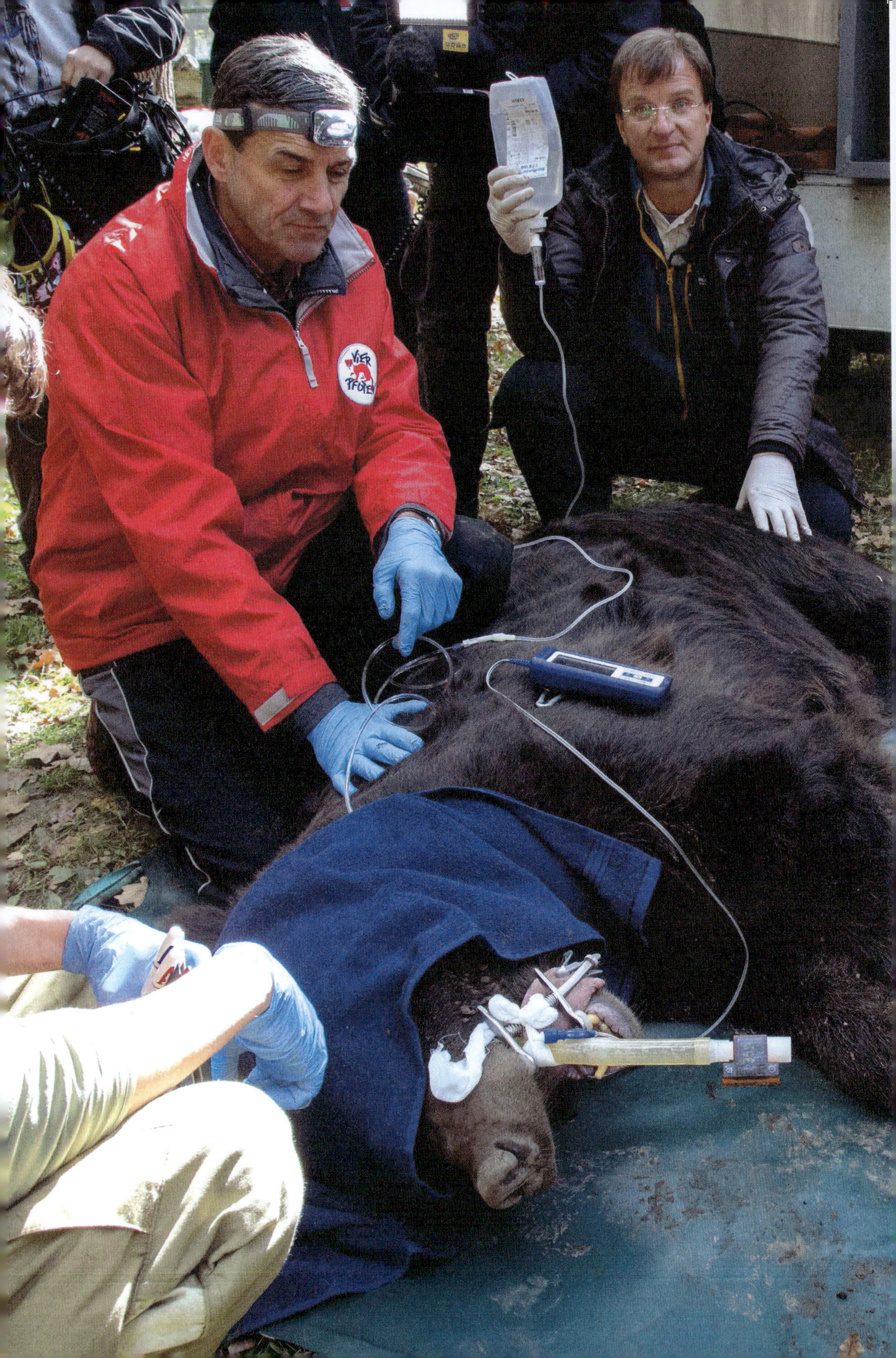

It took five men to pull Tyson through the hatch and onto a rubber stretcher. They heaved him fifty paces from the cage, where the vets were able to examine him more fully.

Frank pointed out that the bear's teeth were worn down as a result of him biting the cage bars over the years. He had tried to get away but never could. Despite being a little underweight because of his insufficient diet of bread and corn, Tyson's internal organs and eyes were in good condition. To everyone's relief, he was essentially a healthy animal.

Tyson was manoeuvred into a cage in the back of a small Four Paws truck and driven to a sanctuary near the city of Lyiv. There he'd able to meet other bears for the first time and live out his days roaming the sanctuary's huge forest.

But Tyson was just one of many bears that needed to be rescued. The team's next destination was an isolated hunting station near the town of Terebovlya, 190 miles west of Kyiv.

Kvitka, a female, had been subjected to a living Hell for eight years, pacing to and fro in a cage measuring just forty square feet. The only time she was released was to be tormented by dogs when her rich owner and his pals arrived for a weekend's entertainment.

Her misery was compounded by being kept within earshot of the packs of huskies that were bred to attack her. Every time the dogs barked, she froze, fearful that she'd be bitten again.

Again the site was hidden in a heavily wooded area. The team drove along a dirt track through the forest to arrive at an open field. Large wooden sheds stood on the field, and from inside we could hear the high-pitched barking of the huskies.

We couldn't see where the bear was housed.

A man dressed in filthy clothes emerged from a corrugated-iron hut. He was angry that his morning had been disturbed by our arrival and shouted in Ukrainian for us to leave.

Carsten handed the man a government document saying we had the right to seize the bear. The man looked bemused by the words, and I had a strong suspicion he couldn't read.

The watchman was becoming more agitated and threatened to call reinforcements, so I needed to get some pictures of the poor bear before the heavy mob arrived. I looked around for the cage and spotted a rusting green structure beside the dog sheds. It was made from the bars used to reinforce concrete. From inside this iron prison the desperate face of a large brown bear stared out at me. Her eyes were dead; she had nothing to live for.

I started shooting pictures before anybody could stop me. This animal needed all the help she could get, and the best thing I could do was to show the world her horrid life, her fear, her helplessness.

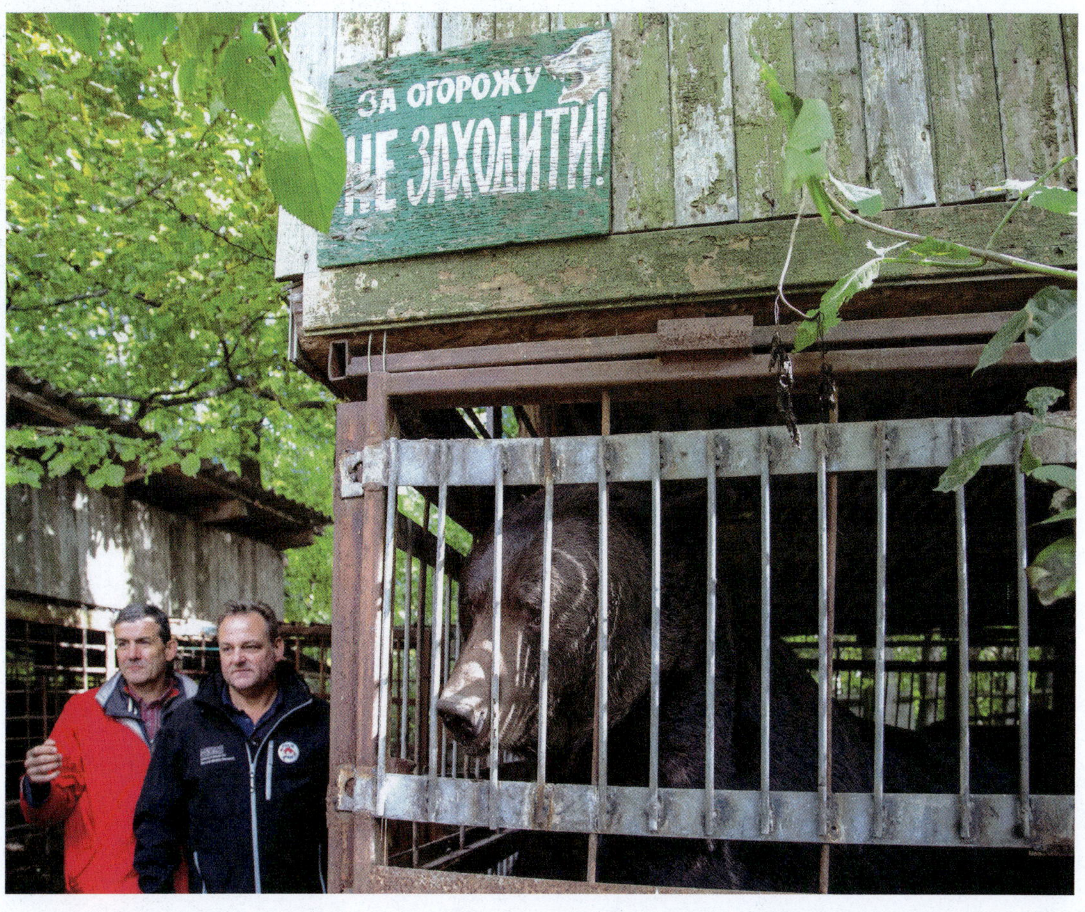

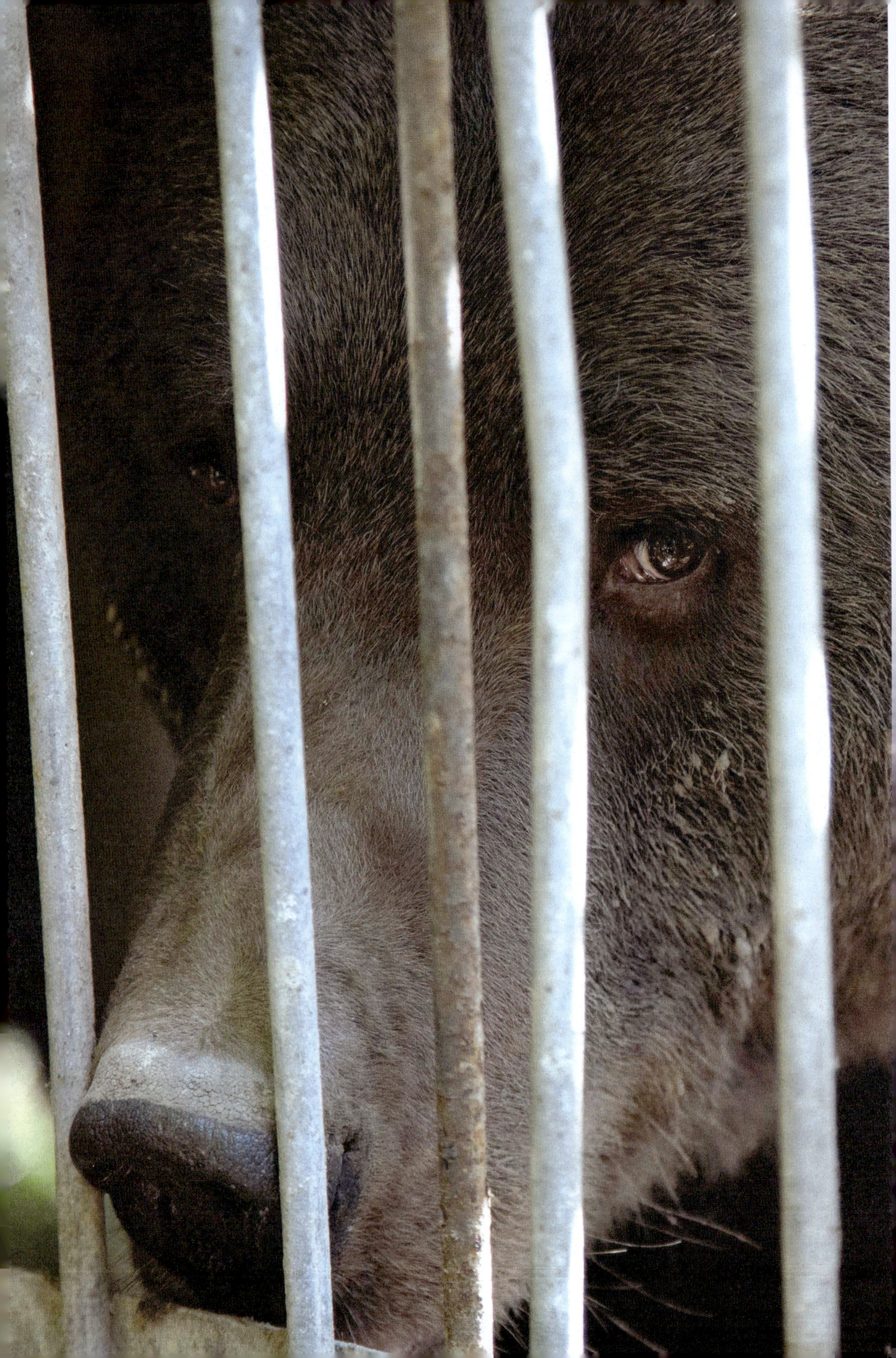

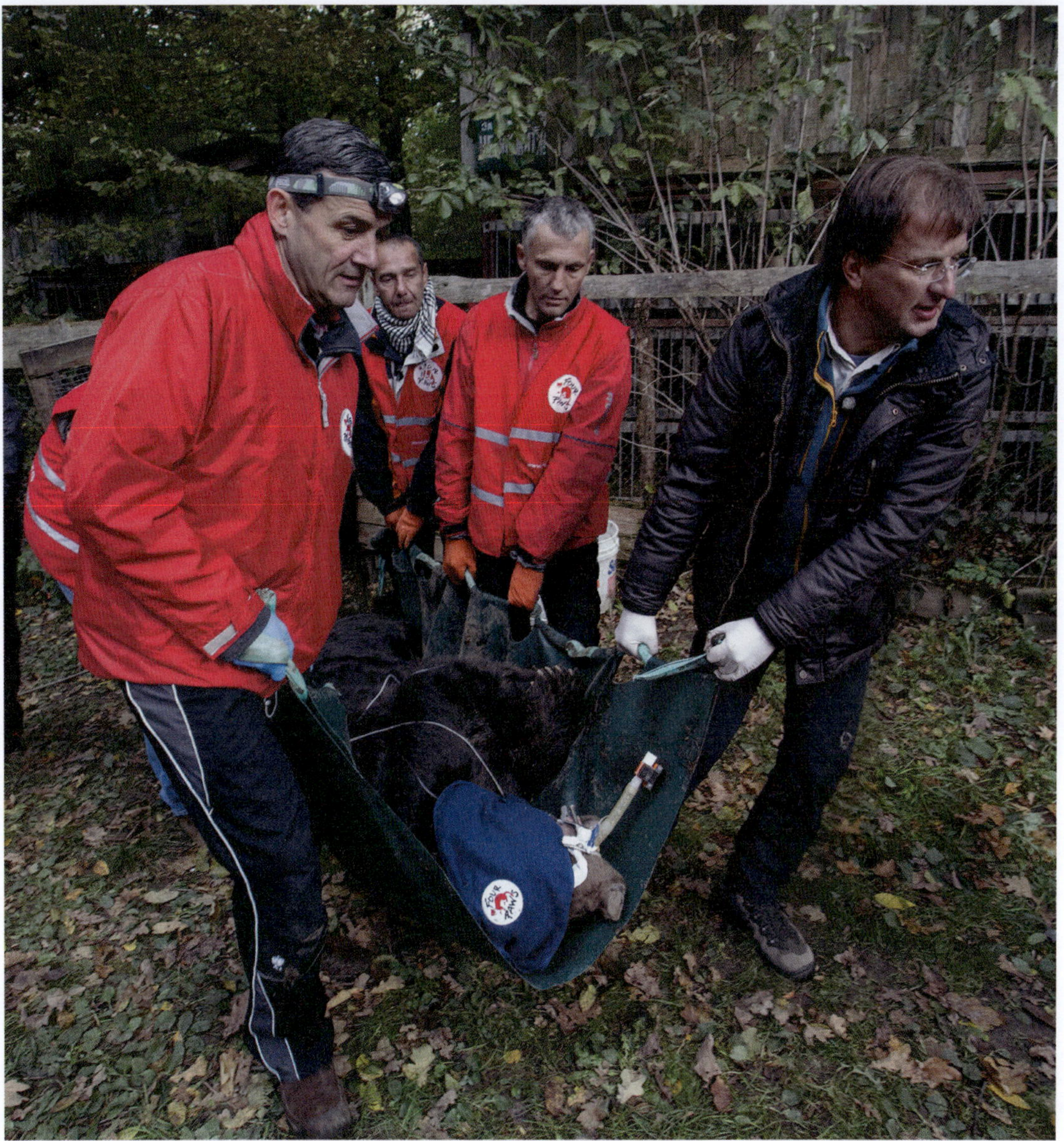

I heard shouting behind me and turned to see three men heading my way. I'd been caught red-handed. I tried to return to the Four Paws group but the men barred my path, telling me to stop taking photos.

I tried to reassure them that the pictures were just for the charity, to show whether the bear needed any medical treatment. It seemed to be enough to defuse the situation.

But having shots of the bear herself, I wanted to get some of the dogs and the bear pit. It looked impossible: both gates to the shed were shut and there was no view in at all.

Meanwhile, the Four Paws team had begun unloading their rescue kit. Frank was priming his dart gun and the rubber stretcher was laid out ready to carry Kvitka away. Frank wanted to move fast. If the bear's rich owner did turn up, he probably wouldn't come alone. He would most likely have a heavy mob in tow— or the local police chief.

After the bear was darted and the team began their work, the watchman and the other men just watched, perhaps waiting for the owner to arrive and make us stop so they could keep their plaything.

I moved my car along the dirt track and parked on the verge facing out of the woods. I didn't want to be hemmed in when the time came to leave.

Kvitka was now laid out and about to be moved into the van. The vets had seen that she needed emergency treatment for exposed nerves in her mouth. Her teeth were badly broken from repeated biting on her metal cage and from duelling with the snarling dogs.

I still wanted a picture inside the huts.

Frank had persuaded the group of men to help with the bear lift. While their attention was on the task, one of the Four Paws team, Janice, came with me to the nearest and largest hut. The dogs, sensing

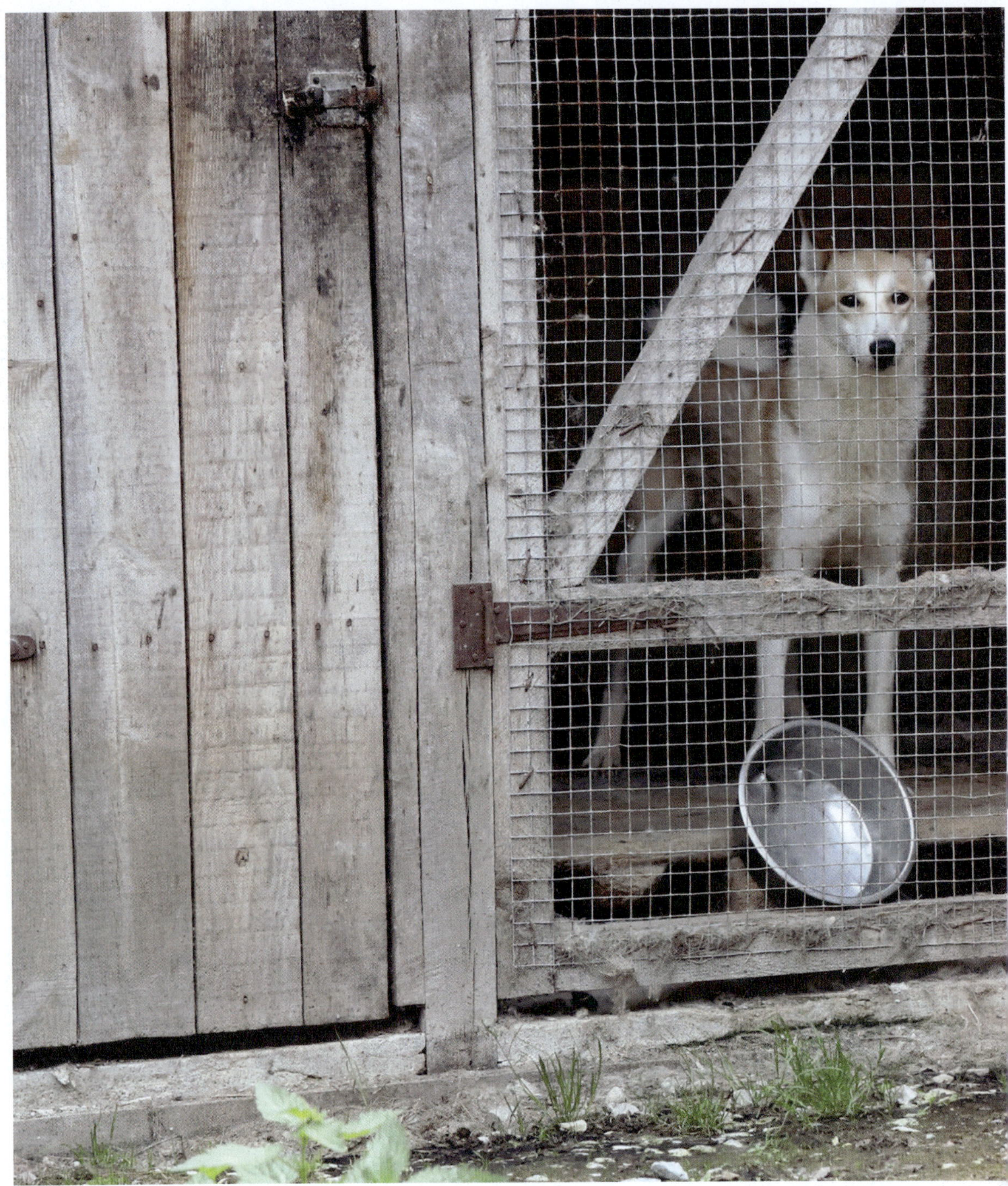

our presence, began to bark and howl. It was now or never to get a picture.

Janice slid back the bolt on the wooden door to the hut and I slipped into the kennels, finding myself in an open area with a courtyard of mud and tufts of grass. Behind wire doors, dogs with their ears pinned back jumped up and barked at me.

Within seconds I had fired off twenty frames of five different dogs, and spun round to see if I'd missed anything before signalling to Janice to let me out. In the middle of the open area I saw a met-al pole fixed into the ground. Just what I wanted, but as as I raised my camera, the door to the shed swung open.

It was one of the three men who had stopped me taking pictures of Kvitka. He was angry and shouted loudly at me. I had visions of becoming the dogs' next victim, but Carsten heard the commotion and came to calm things down.

I told Carsten that I'd see him back at the sanctuary and headed straight for my car. As I drove down the track to freedom a black Mercedes G

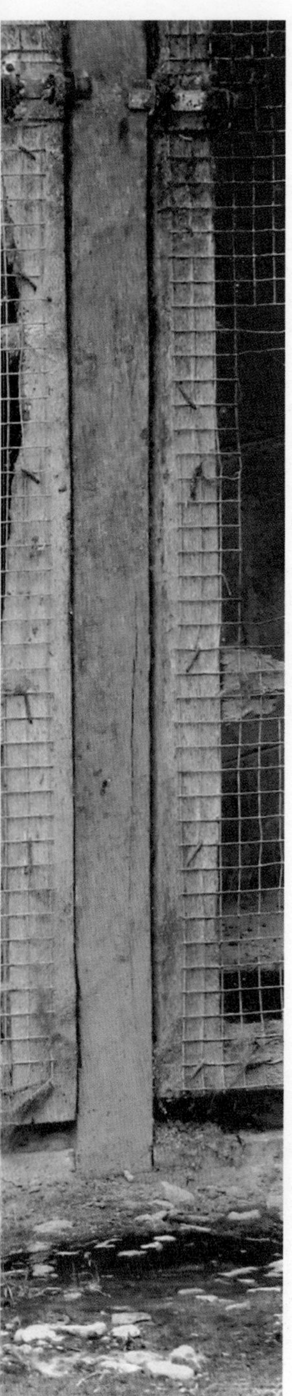

wagon followed by another black SUV barrelled towards me. I had to swing off the dirt road to let them flash past, and I didn't hang around to find out who was in them.

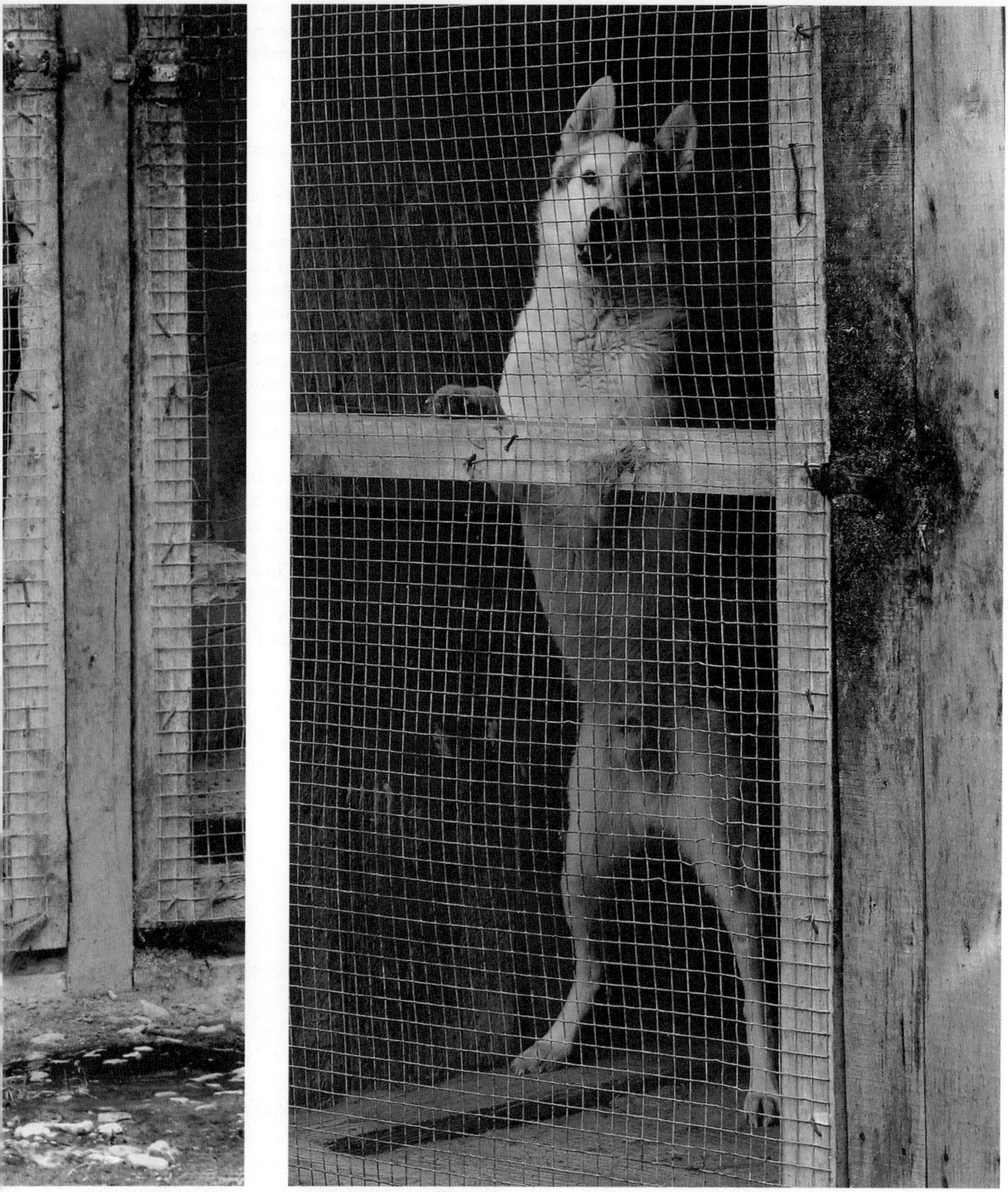

Whoever they were, Carsten must have done his magic again, because Kvita arrived at the sanctuary late that night.

By the time she was released into the large grassy paddock outside the veterinary centre the next day, she already looked like a different bear: her coat was shinier and her previously dead eyes now looked alert, darting around to check out her new surroundings. It rounded off my set of pictures, from Kvita's prison to the rescue efforts to her hunting for apples that had been dotted about the paddock for her.

Everything was looking good for the bears of Ukraine. Four Paws was working through its list of bears to rescue. Then the Russian army invaded and everything changed. Once again human conflict would not only cause destruction and the deaths of many people but endanger the wildlife and captive animals caught up in the fighting.

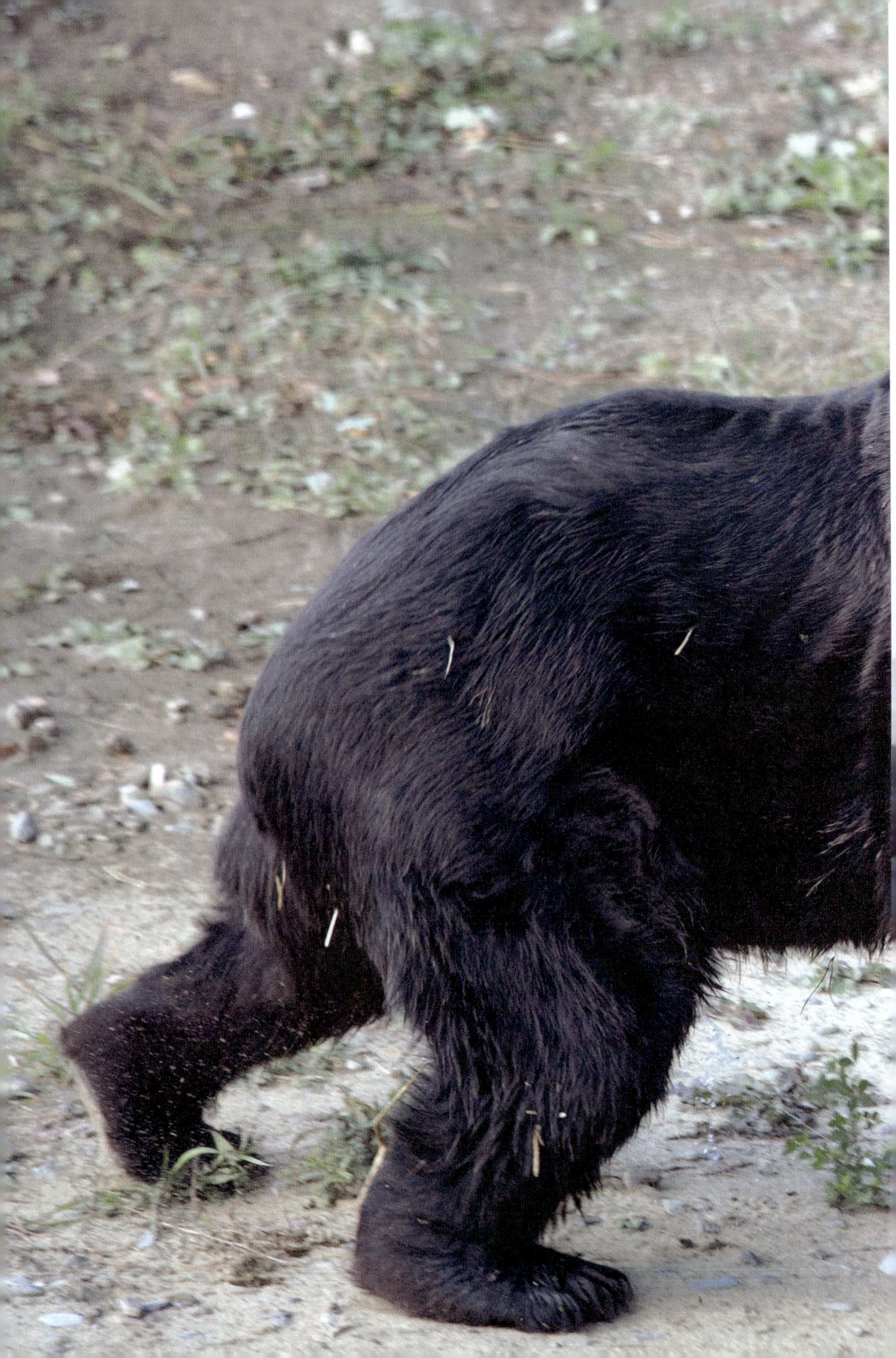

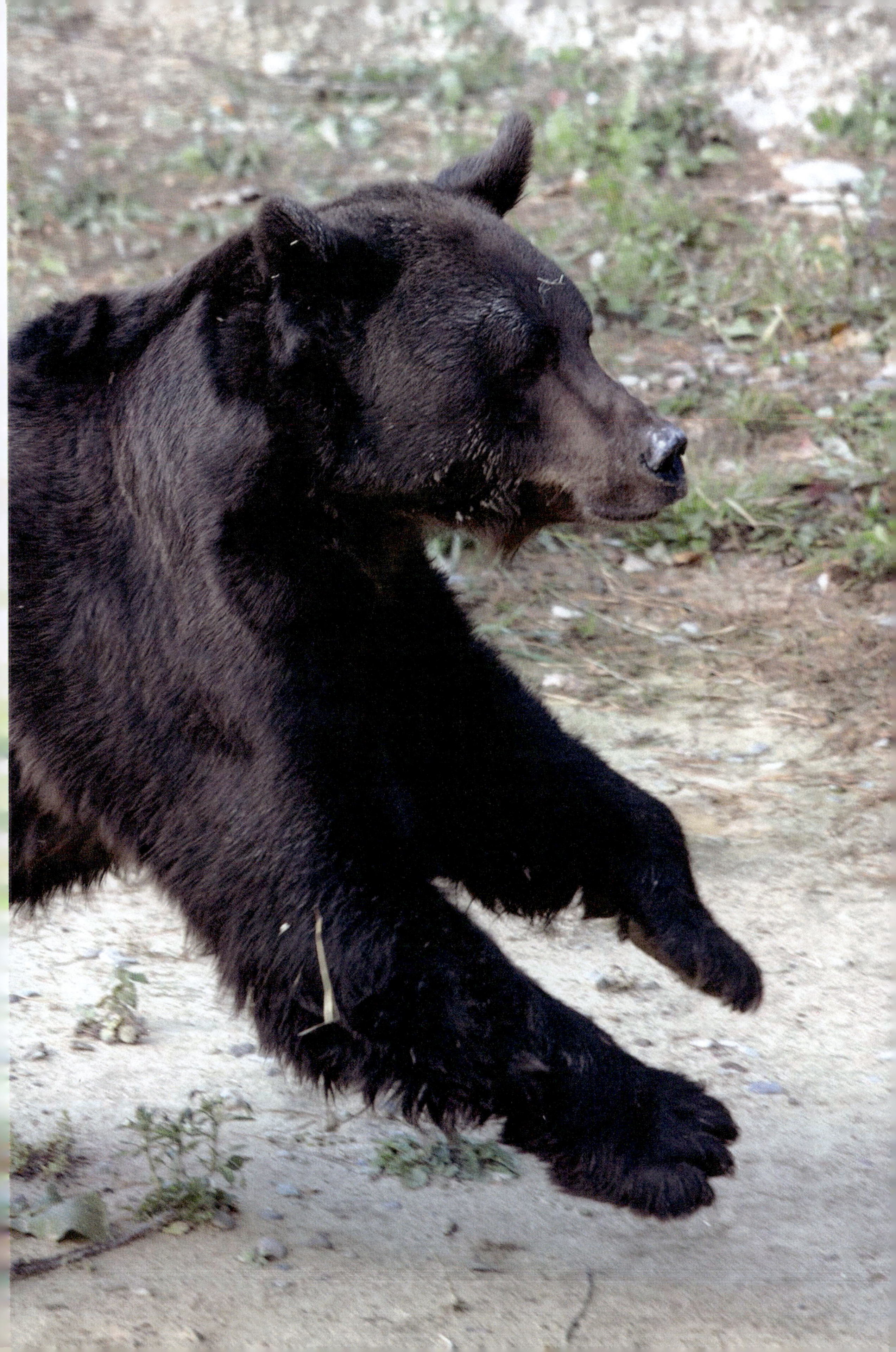

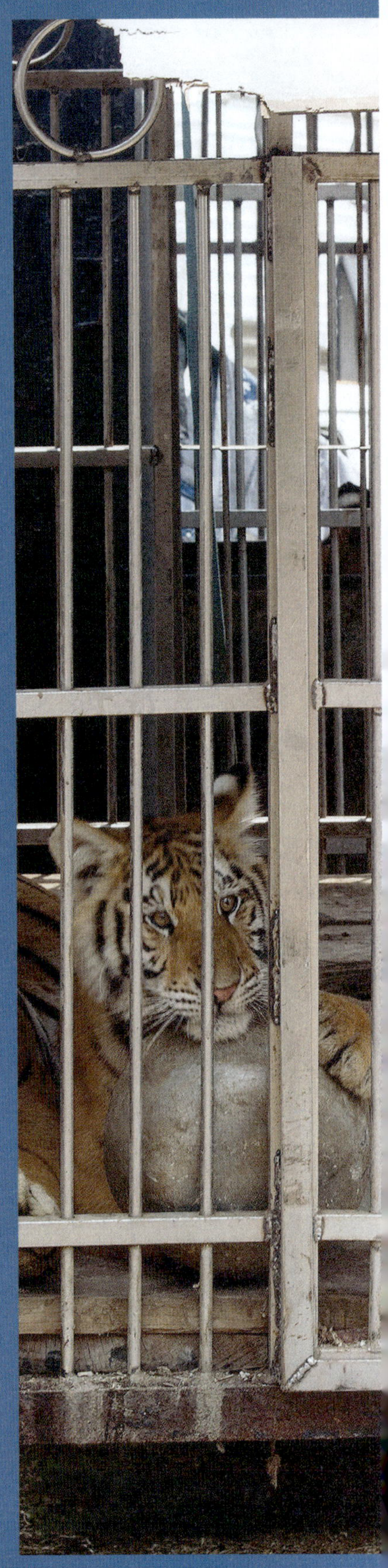

All the fun of the unfair

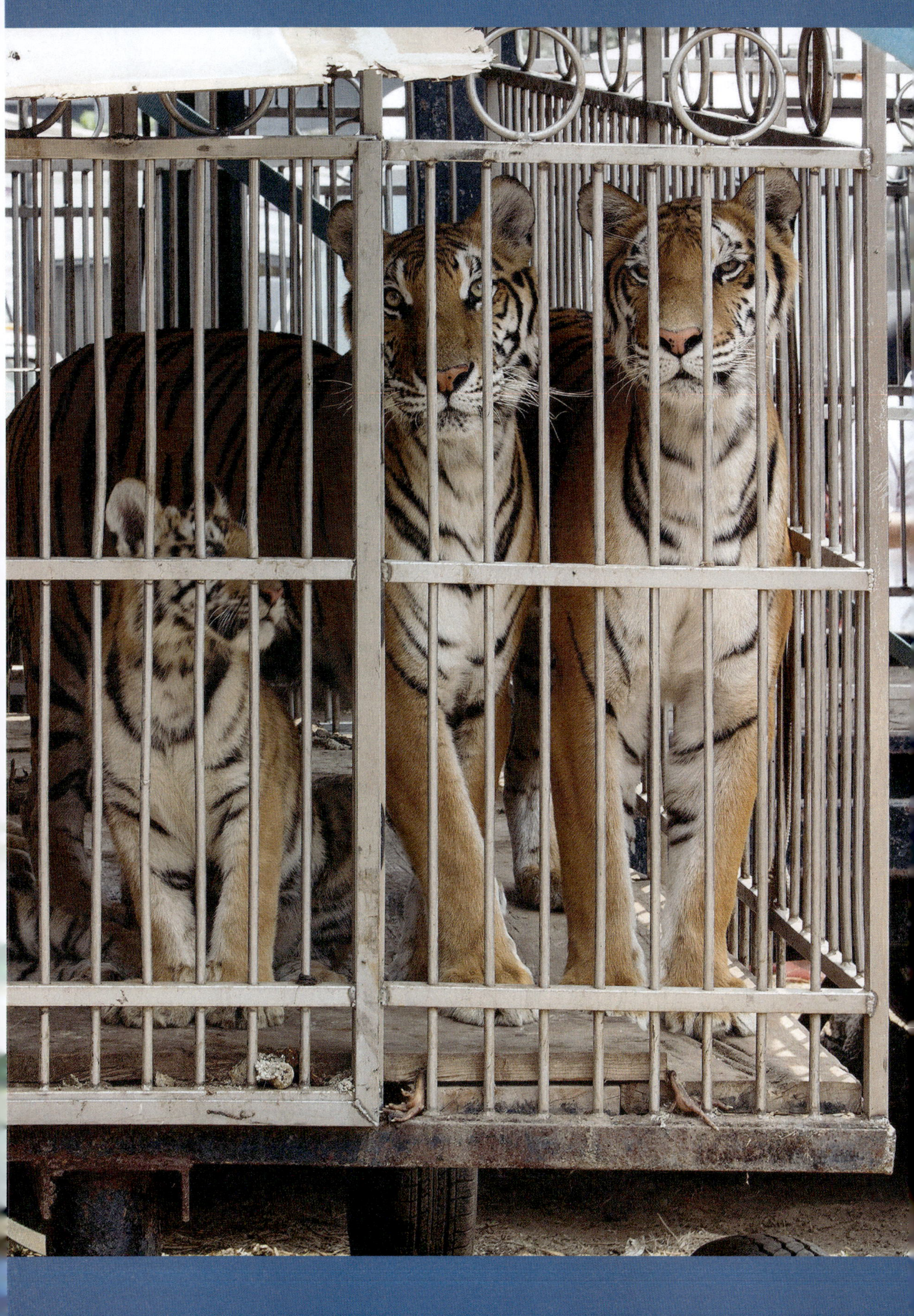

All the fun of the unfair

The intention was good but the outcome was terrible. The Guatemalan government had just announced that zoos and circuses would no longer be allowed to showcase performing animals.

Good call. But it meant that forty-three tigers, twelve lions and a pair of pumas no longer had any purpose or value, as far as their owners were concerned, and so remained locked in transport cages, unable to exercise or carry out any other activity that would keep their muscles in shape.

The news of this came to my attention from Animal Defenders International (ADI), a very active British charity that had worked in Central America over many years, rescuing lions and tigers.

Tim Phillips, one of the directors of ADI, called and asked if I could help raise the plight of the affected animals in the UK papers. The situation was dire because, in addition to their newly enforced inactivity, the heat in the cages was intense and there was nothing the animal could do to escape it.

After a call to the *Daily Mail*, I found myself on a flight with reporter Danny Buckland to try and save the big cats before time ran out.

If the circuses couldn't send these large and beautiful animals animals out each night to stand on their hind legs or take up choreographed posi-

tions on platforms or play dead on command, there would be no money to feed them and they would starve.

As for re-homing them, the local government said there wasn't any money. The poor creatures were on death row.

The first circus that Danny and I drove to when we got off the plane was the Circo Ponce, positioned on rough ground with a badly potholed parking area. The circus sits on the edge of a deep ravine, at the foot of which flows the Rio Las Vacas, a river which carries away Guatemala City's raw sewage and is so badly polluted that its waters contain little aquatic life and in turn pollutes the Motagua River, into which it flows, and the entire marine ecosystem of the Gulf of Honduras.

The big top was huge and surrounded by caravans and large generator lorries; high fencing prevented us from walking directly onto the site. At the ticket office—a tatty caravan showing pictures of tigers jumping through hoops of fire and being made to perform degrading stunts—we asked to see the boss.

After a fifteen-minute wait, a burly man dressed in shorts and dirty vest approached us.

With his smattering of Spanish, Danny told the man that we wanted to see the tigers that were being held in cages. He explained that we wanted to help the animals and show the world how cruel the government was to prevent them from performing.

While they talked, I started casting about for a gap in the fencing where I could nip onto the site and take some photographs. It would be risky but I knew it would be worth it. I couldn't break in, though.

As I wandered back, I heard the man in the vest say he would call the circus owner.

We went back to the hire car and waited. An hour later the man returned. He didn't look happy but agreed to grant us entry to the circus ground for a short while.

Walking past the big top through a tangle of ropes and cables, we came to the area where the animal cages were stored. It was a shocking sight. A wheeled cage the size of a family car was home to two fully grown tigers and their large cubs. There was no room for them to turn round, and if they wanted to lie down, they had to flop down in a heap on top of each other.

Knowing that time was lacking I started taking pictures of the captives. As I did so, the mother of the cubs put her face right up against the bars, as if pleading with me to do something. She looked tired.

Beyond the first cage was a trailer slightly larger than the first crate, and with bars down one side. Inside it were two huge male tigers, prowling up and down.

In a surreal aside to this scene of horror, I saw a lama tied one of the tent posts. He was the only animal who looked happy.

These pictures alone provided me with the story

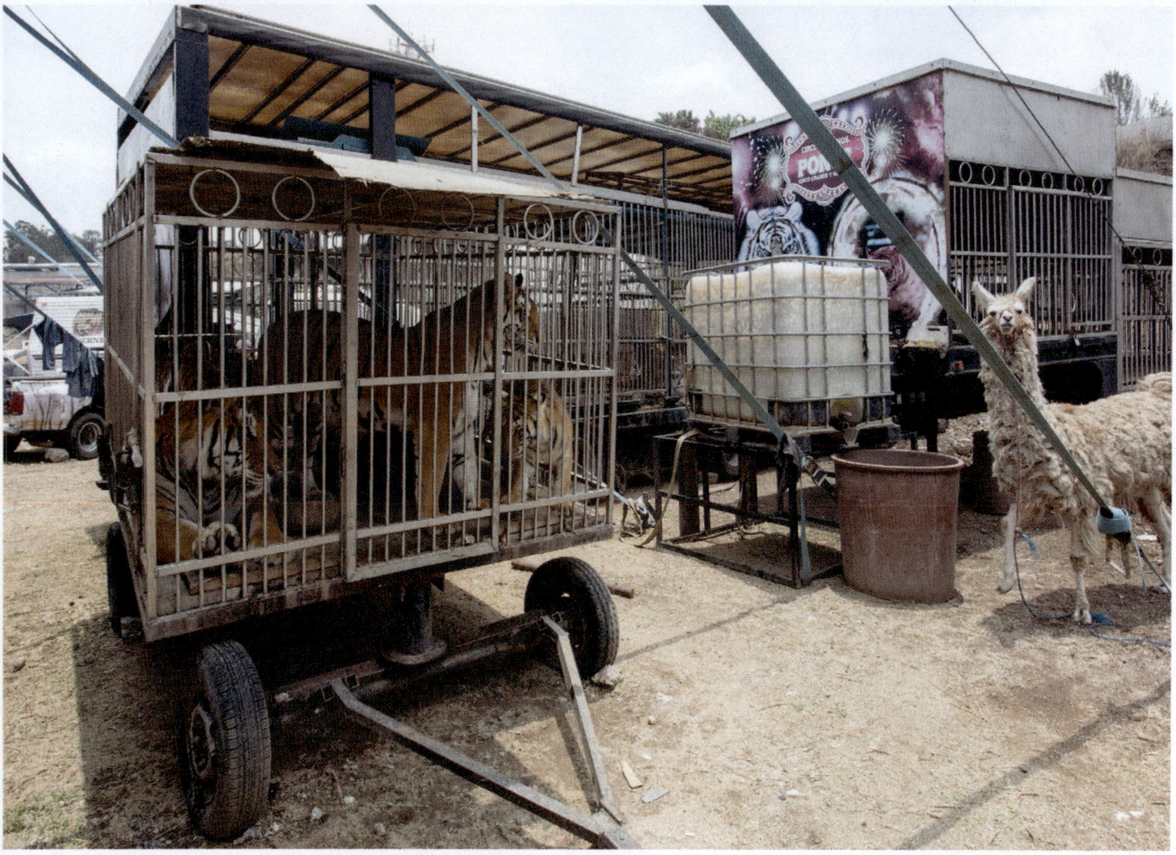

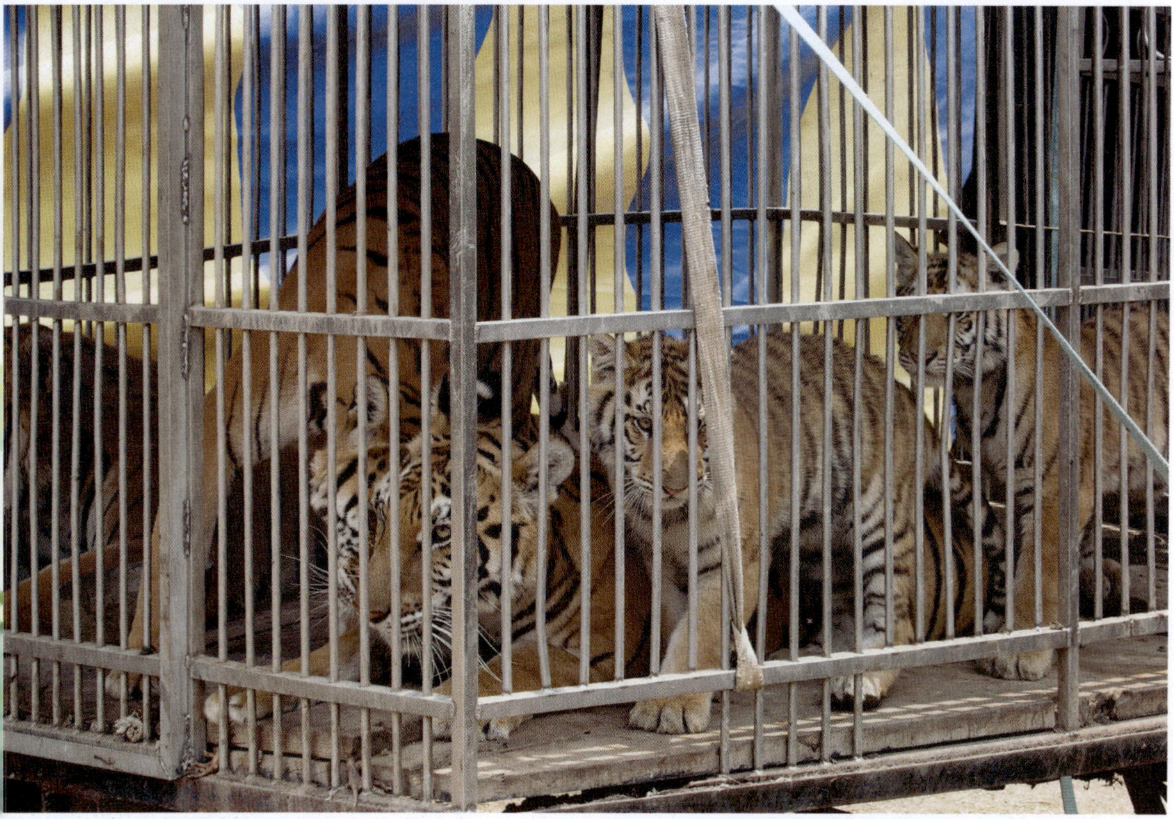

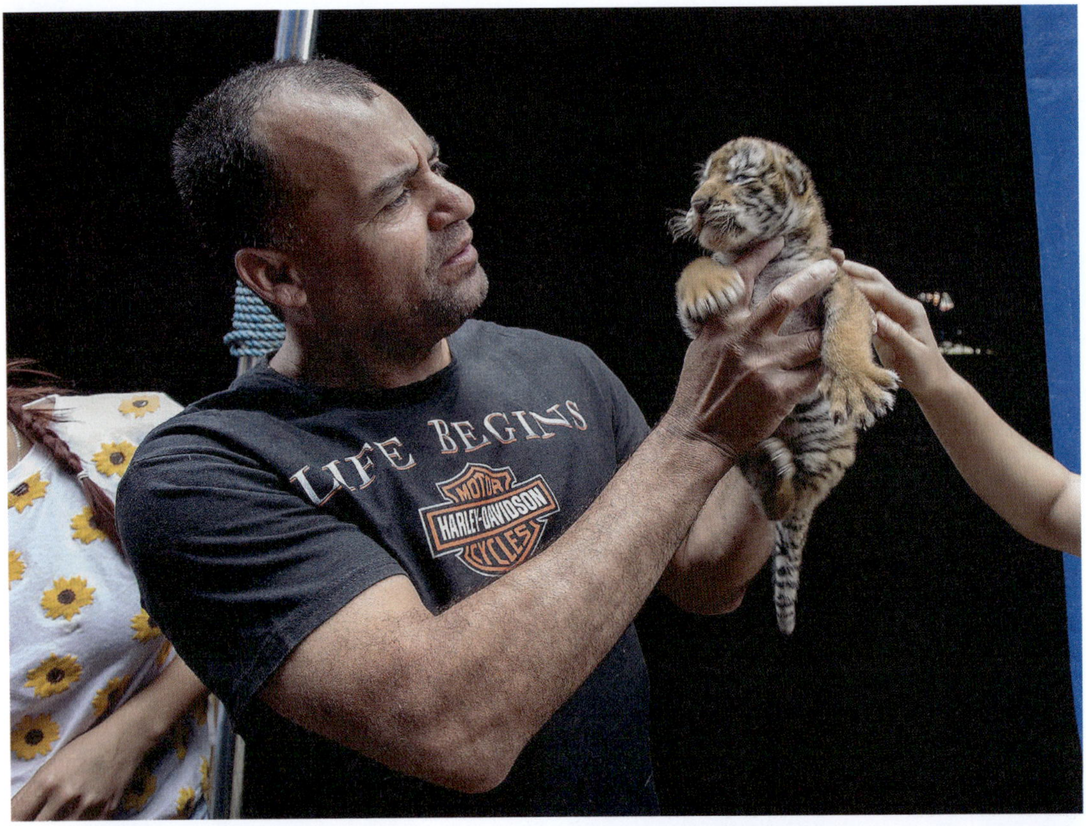
LIFE BEGINS
MOTOR
HARLEY-DAVIDSON
CYCLES

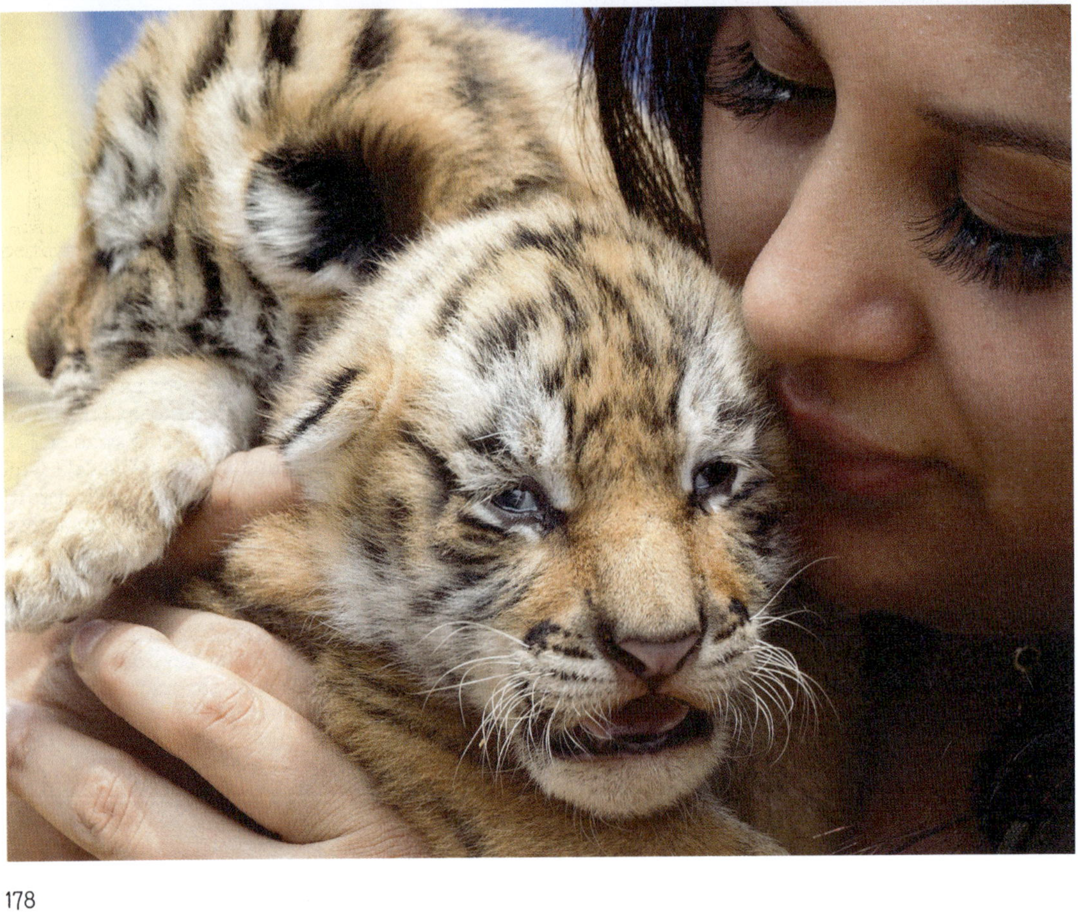

I wanted, and we were about to leave when the man in the vest told us to follow him to the big top. As we approached the entrance to the tent, the flap flew open and man appeared holding three young tiger cubs, just a few days old. It was bad enough that the circus could not adequately accommodate a whole group of fully grown tigers and their year-old cubs; now another three babies had arrived to add to the pressure.

No one seemed especially troubled. The man who had brought out the babies held them up proudly for me to photograph. Then his daughter arrived, carrying more. This was crazy. For a country that tigers aren't native to, Circo Ponce had an awful lot of them. If they were being bred for profit, that was very disturbing, given that they could not be housed humanely; what was more disturbing was to learn from the circus boss that if he couldn't afford to feed the animals because visitor numbers were down now that performances had been banned, the animals would have to be killed.

Circo Navarro, the second circus on the list, was just outside Guatemala City. It was situated in a large open field, and the set-up looked very much like that of Circo Ponce with huge lorries and generator trucks and the big top in the centre. We found Tim Phillips and his fellow ADI director, Jan Creamer, in talks with the circus owner.

After thirty minutes Jan Creamer walked over to tell us that this owner at least could see that there was no point in fighting the ban and had agreed to send the animals to a better place. They were, in any case, in a bad way. One was suffering from an infection on his hind quarters; the other, a female, had become neurotic.

Jan started measuring the trailer. As she did so, I took pictures of the animals. The big male with the infection had his head pressed into the bars, not moving. The female was biting at one of her paws. In the corner of the cage was a solitary bowl of water for the two of them. It was pitiful to see.

The next morning Danny and I headed out to Antigua, the former capital of Guatemala and now UNESCO world heritage site. The city was founded in 1543 as the capital of the Kingdom of Guatemala, which covered most of Central America, and was so badly damaged by earthquakes in 1773 that the capital was moved to present-day Guatemala City in 1776.

The pretty, colourful streets were laid out in a grid system at the foot of an active volcano, two miles away, which puffs out smoke, rumbles, spurts lava and glows at night. (And there are another two volcanoes just ten miles away, to the west and southwest. It's a very unstable area geologically.)

We had come in search of Circo Rey Gitano,

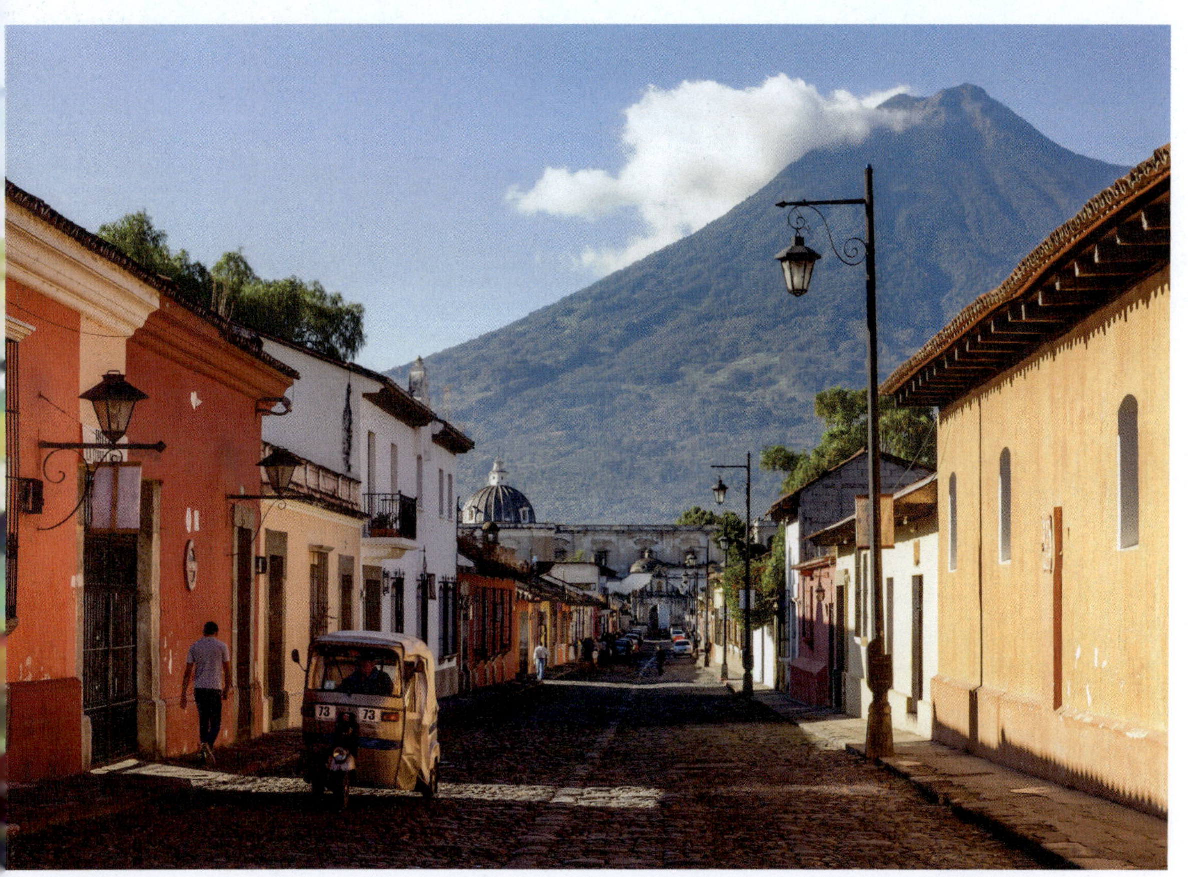

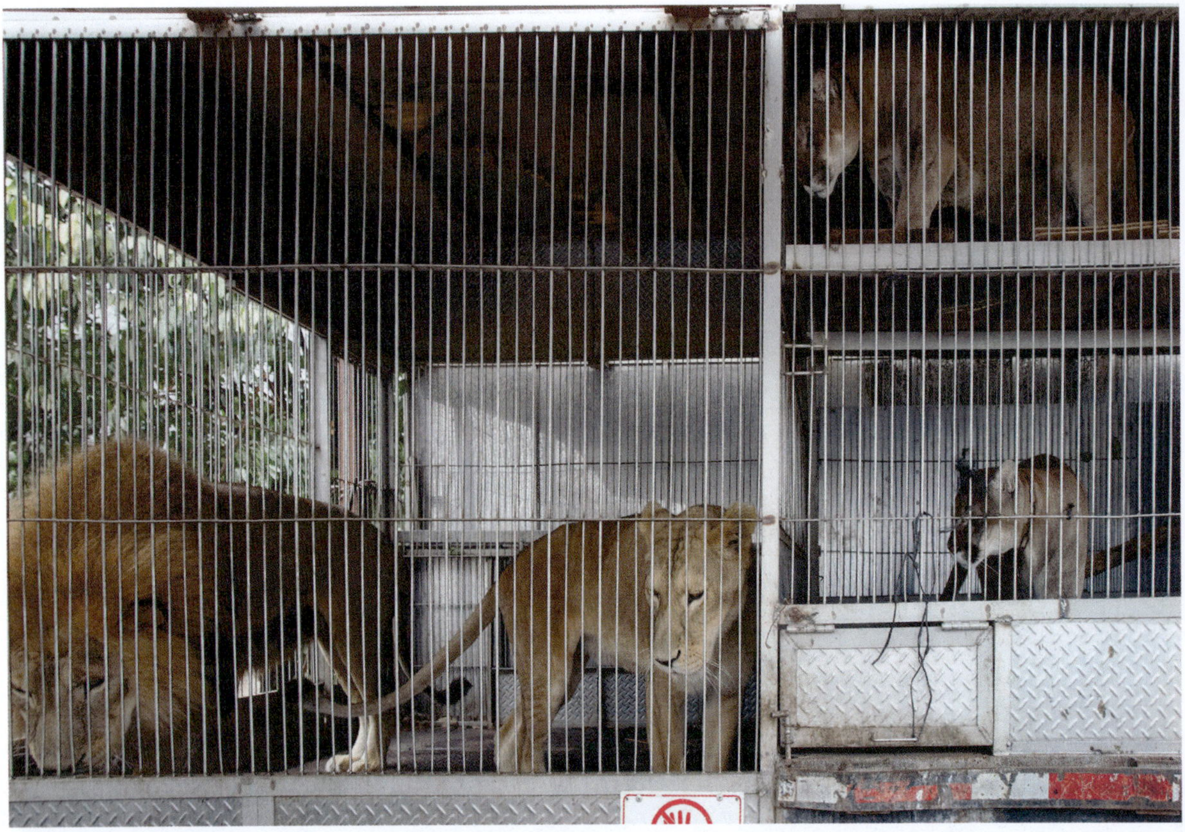

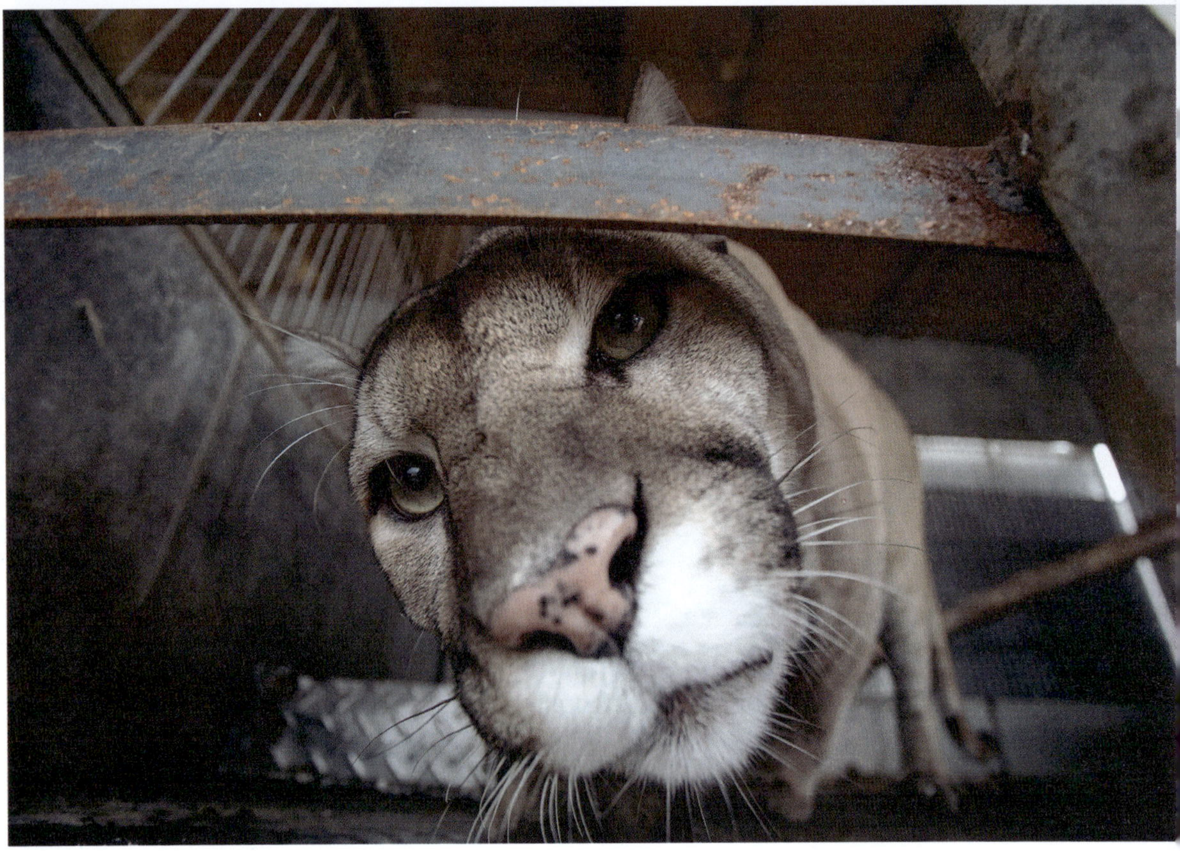

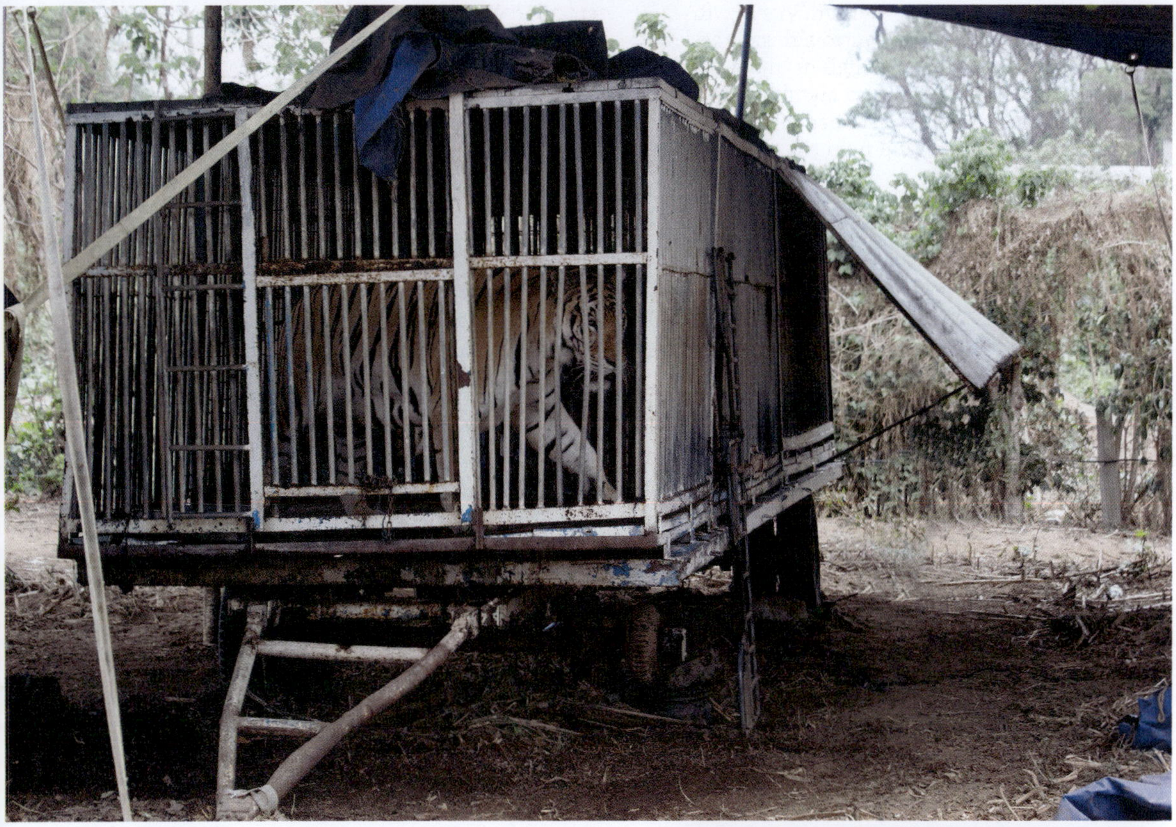

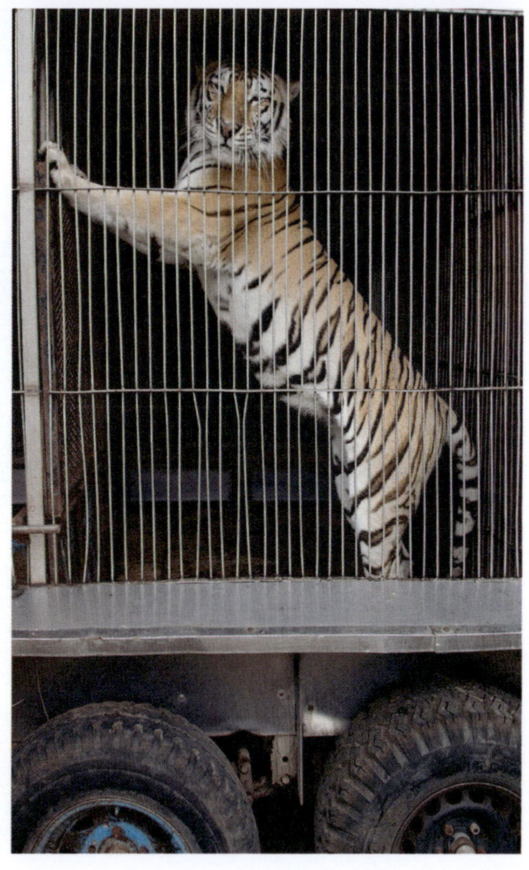

which we'd been told housed a range of different animals including lions, tigers, pumas and monkeys. After getting a coffee and asking directions, we drove to a big roundabout on the edge of the city and found the circus, on another patch of waste ground, with its lorries and caravans and generators. (Do all circuses look the same?)

As we approached the entrance, a small blond-haired woman asked, in English, what we wanted and then led us through to the rear. There, out of sight of public view, was a jumble of rusting flat-bed trailers with cages on their backs. One of them, thirty-foot-long, had been sectioned into five cages. In one part, lethargic lions flopped around lethargically in their prison. Another section contained five tigers. In a third, a huge tiger stood on his hind legs against the bars.

The heat was not exceptional—86 Fahrenheit—but above average for the elevated location and, to their credit, the owners had tried to offer some protection from the sun by hoisting a tarpaulin over two of the trailers, one housing two lions, the other with two pumas. It was another scene from Hell.

As I started taking pictures, a man dragged a blue hose pipe through the dust and began hosing one of the tigers' cages down. The trapped animals opened their mouths to try and catch as much water as possible.

Two men walked over to where I was working and told me they were going to take one the tigers through its paces, and did we want to watch. For

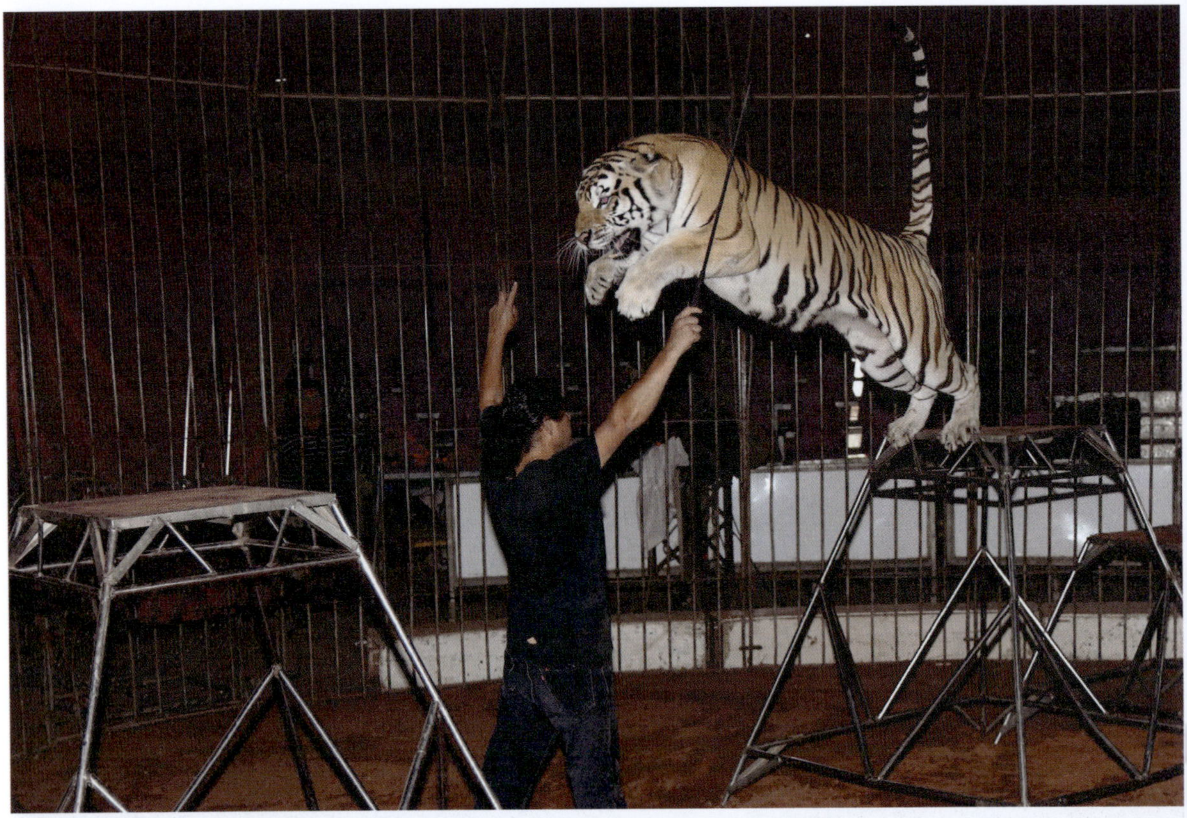

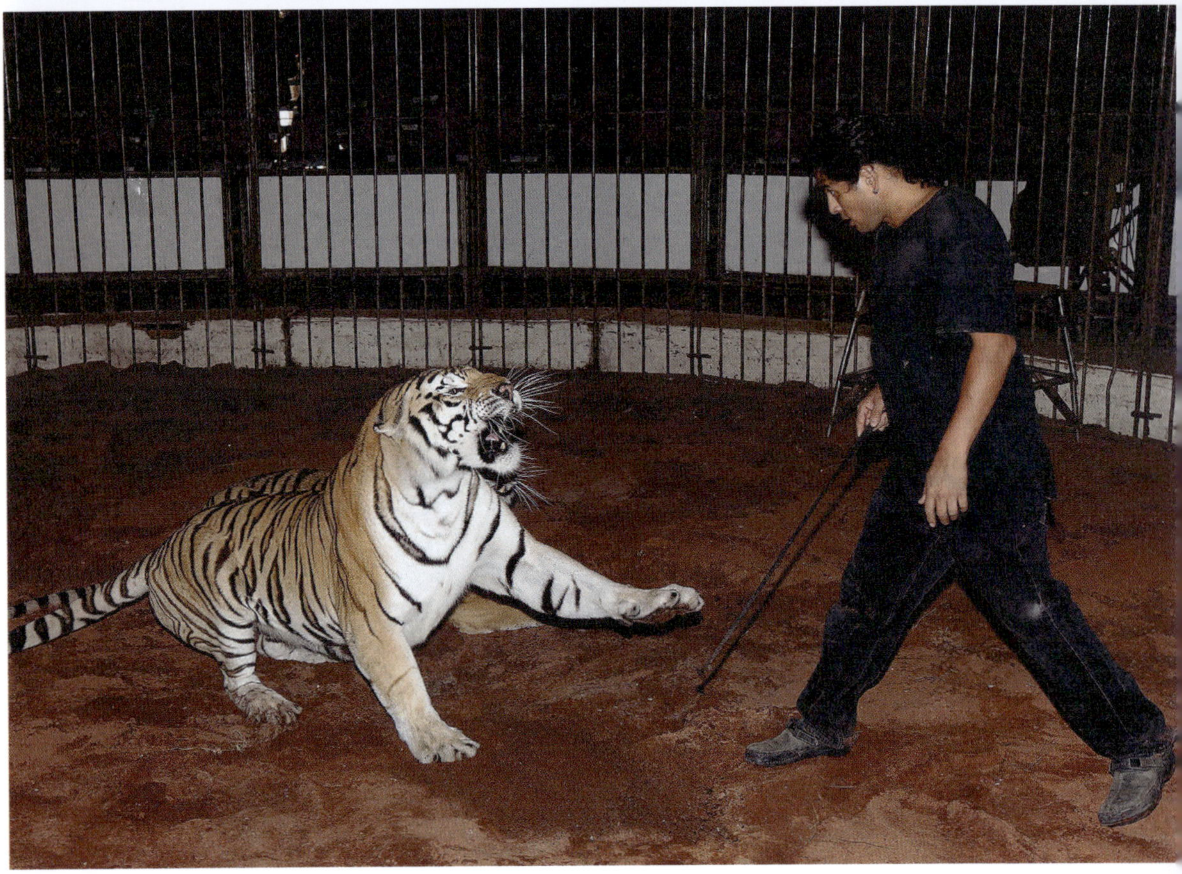

the sake of the story we were covering, we said yes. Rightly or wrongly, we wanted to see exactly what the government had rightly chosen to put a stop to.

Looking back, I regret that we agreed. It gave me the opportunity to take some pictures I wouldn't otherwise have got—those on this pair of pages—but it was horribly exploitative: the very thing I had spent my life campaigning against. I now feel rather ashamed—but journalism can sometimes requires that one compromises oneself in order to bring a message to the world.

The interior of a circus tent with its lights on and glitter ball turning but no crowd makes for a sad picture, but to see a huge tiger leaping over a ringmaster's head or fearfully anticipating being lashed with a long horse whip or beaten with an iron rod is an outrage, and we quickly felt that we'd seen enough.

As we turned to leave, an overweight white tiger, very evidently arthritic, appeared in the ring and was made to do some tricks but after a few minutes the boss, Christian Lopez, herded him back out of the ring through a chain link tunnel.

It was time to go. After hearing from three different circus bosses how they loved their animals like sons and daughters, and how it wasn't their fault but the government's if their animals were now at risk, both Danny and I felt we had got the measure of the place.

It was now up to ADI and Guatemalan officials to get the paperwork done and arrange import licences so the animals could be sent to South Africa and the USA.

Four years later I stood watching two fully grown tigers playing in the South African sun. Tim stood next to me.

'Those two are from Guatemala,' he told me. 'The last time you saw them, they were just a few days old.'

Without charities like ADI, these animals would have remained trapped in cages no bigger than a double bed, abused and mistreated in every aspect of their lives, going crazy and dying a slow death.

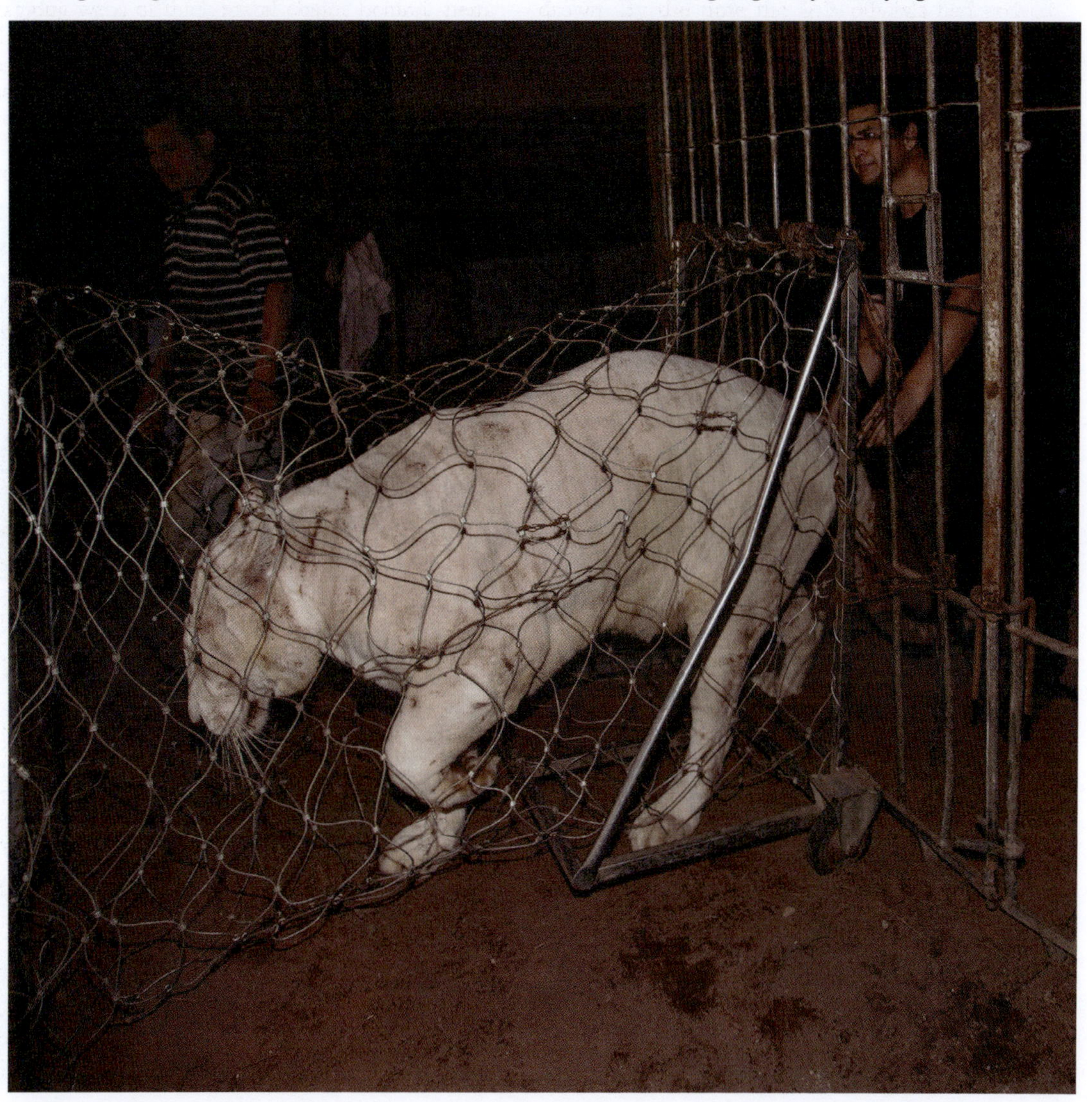

Escape from Kuwait

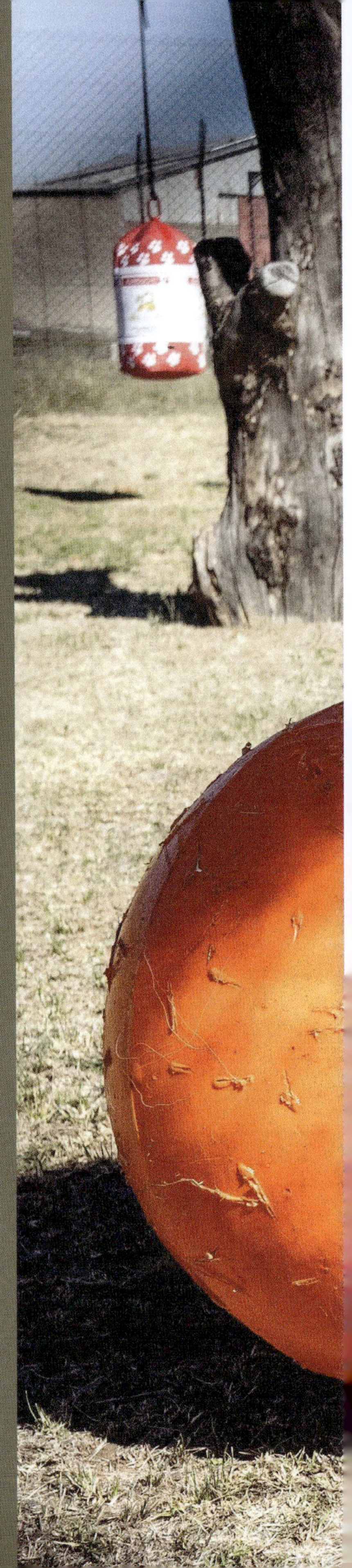

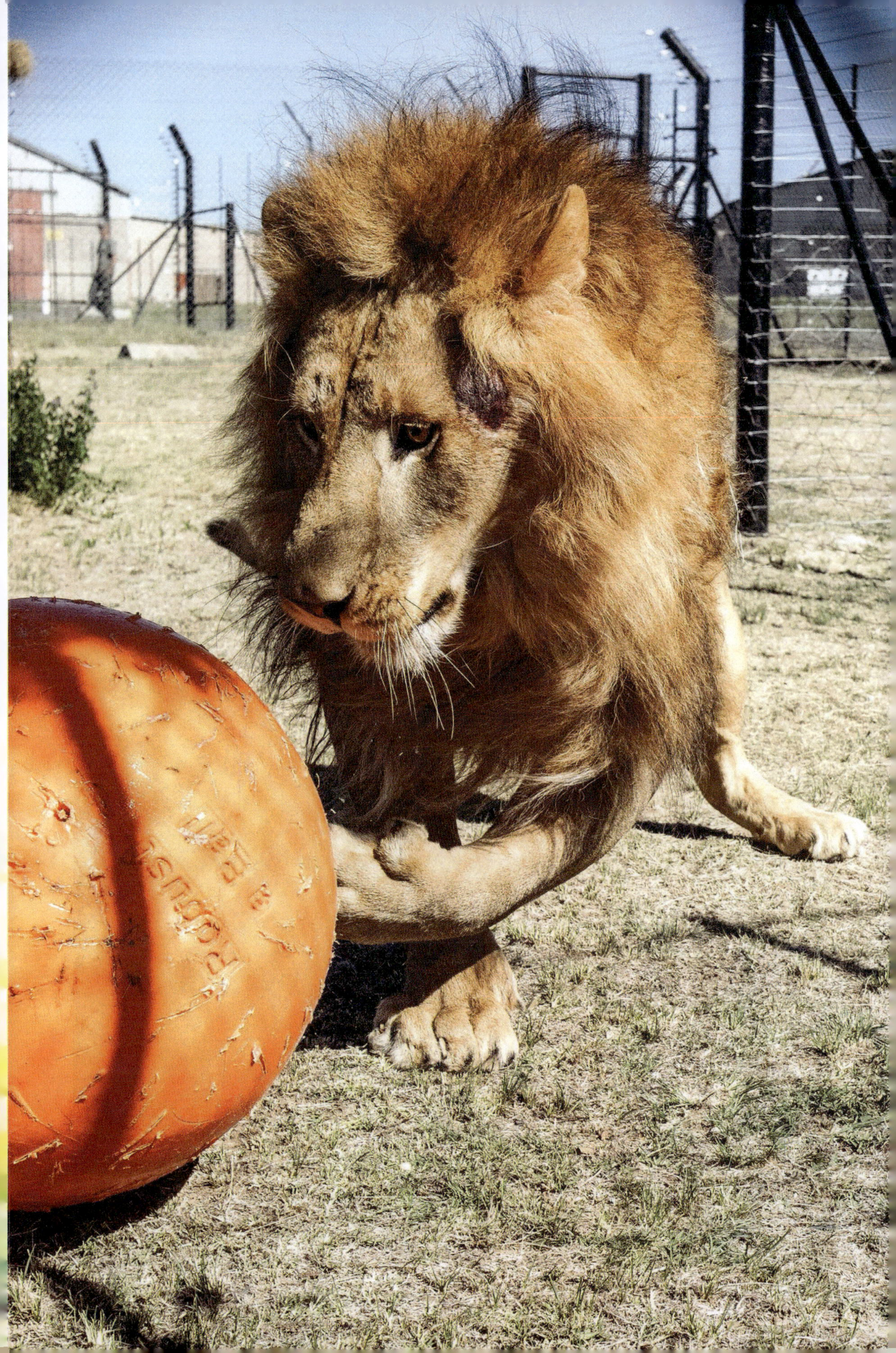
ROBUST
a BAM

Escape
from Kuwait

Alion cub left to die in the heat of a Kuwaiti wasteland. Two others abandoned on the streets of Kuwait City. Two more left outside the zoo in Omariya.

All five had been part of the illegal pet trade in exotic animals, which allows rich owners to buy wild animals for the entertainment of their friends and children and wives. And as the cubs had grown, it had become too hard to keep them at home—of course. So they got thrown out, with the rubbish. It makes one weep.

The five young lions were lucky, though. Kuwait Zoo stepped up to the challenge and housed them temporarily. That was no small effort. The zoo had been closed to the public in March 2020 as a precautionary measure during the COVID-19 pandemic, and had remained shut ever since, while the administrators took the opportunity to carry out a programme of renovations.

By the time I reached the Gulf State to photograph them, the five lions had already been at the zoo for two years. By then they were young adults, feisty but sad-looking, trapped behind their green iron bars, constrained in their movements and under-stimulated, though no worse off than the zoo's other animals.

In fact, although the zoo was closed, reports show that its animals continued to be as well cared for as zoo animals can be. And although taking in five extra animals had been an unwanted burden, these lucky lions would soon be leaving for a better life. The charity Animal Defenders International had agreed to put together a plan to airlift them away from the desert heat and concrete pens and fly them to a spacious grassy sanctuary in the Free State province of South Africa.

Getting five lions onto an aircraft involves more than issuing them with a boarding card and shepherding them up the steps. It involves mountains of paperwork, teams of people, armies of vets and the ministerial cooperation of the countries involved. In this case, that meant talking in two different languages and writing in two different scripts.

I found that visiting Kuwait Zoo was a very strange experience. Among its roster of roughly 1,800 animals, it has large mammals (lions, tigers,

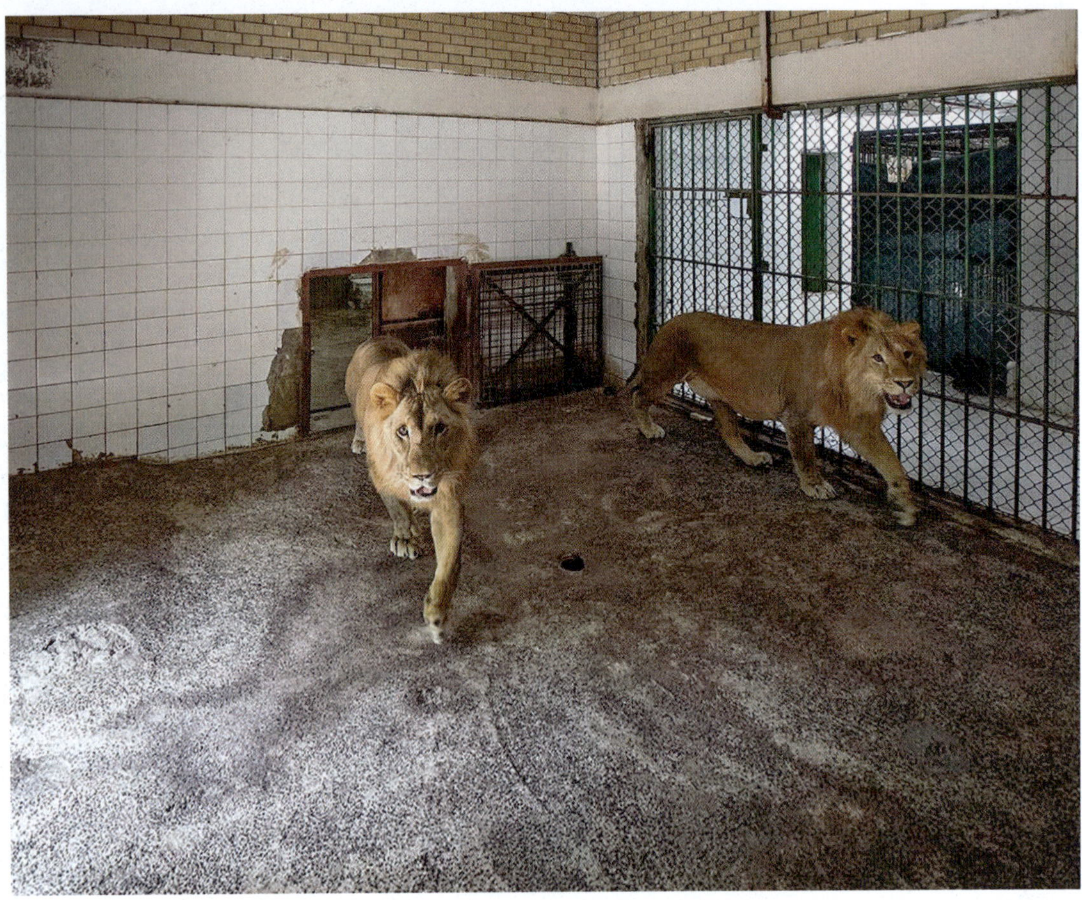

bears, elephants and hippopotamuses), primates (chimpanzees, monkeys and lemurs), reptiles (crocodiles and snakes) and numerous birds (parrots, vultures and white peacocks), but there was no one to see them. Perhaps they like it better that way.

Or perhaps not. I photographed all the lions, who appeared overheated and dejected as they endlessly paced back and forth beside the bars of their cages—a behaviour typically associated with stress. The biggest cage was occupied by two brothers, Shujaa and Saham, and they gave me some powerful pictures, but I had to spend a long time waiting for them to emerge, cramped and desperate, into their white-tiled prison.

While I concentrated on photographing the two brothers, Tim Phillips and Jan Creamer of ADI were overseeing the building of five huge transport crates for the lions. The crates needed to be assembled in a particular way, with all the right bolts in the right order and the floor of the cage flat and level. If anything were to be built wrongly, a cargo manager at Kuwait airport might deem it unsafe and the evacuation would be off.

After a few false starts, a crew of zoo keepers got the hang of assembling the crates, with their large metal sides, roofs and floors. One problem was the simple one of miscommunication. Relying on a zoo manager to translate from English into Arabic (and back again) was not ideal but it was the sort of problem we had encountered before. Less familiar was the crew's need to break off to pray five times a day, which cut into the work schedule and left the rest of us kicking our heels.

Sitting in the hangar where the crates were being built sat Jan, behind a picnic table, watching and instructing, jumping up to point out any problem that came up, and simultaneously wading through pages of veterinary reports on the animals' weight, ages, and vaccination certificates, all translated into English for our benefit and that of the South Africans. One wrong number or a slight wording mistake could also derail the whole trip.

Her ring binders filled with paperwork, Jan checked and double-checked the data. Hammering and drilling continued all the while until the transport crates were ready for two huge male lions, two young brothers and a very scared lioness.

After two days of documents being ferried backwards and forwards between the zoo and the environment and agriculture ministries, it was time to work out a timetable. A truck big enough to take all six crates to the airport was needed and a decision had to be taken on when to sedate the animals. Space had been allotted on a huge Qatar Airways cargo plane, and if all the loose ends didn't marry up, that would be another factor that might cause the lions to remain stuck in the heat of the Kuwait. Yes, I worried about it all going wrong.

Peter Caldwell, Africa's top expert on lions and other big cats, flew in on the final day to make sure that all the animals had received the right amount of sedation and to check that the identifying chip in each lion matched its number on the paperwork.

Peter was a tall quiet man in his fifties and ran a veterinary clinic in Pretoria, just north Johannesburg. He was jolly and fit, having once played football for South Africa, but a serious man when it came to animal welfare. The difference between his expert eye and a more casual approach to caring for animals would be tested later, in the early hours of the following morning.

The two vets at the zoo didn't appreciate Peter's presence and his need to oversee what their operations, and chose to ignore him, a discourtesy that was evident to all. Confident of his own expertise, he took it in his stride.

A timetable had been agreed. The animals would start being sedated at 5:00 AM, with all the crates having been loaded on the lorry an hour-and-a-half later. The journey to the airport should take less than half an hour, and the animals would be processed like any other piece of heavy cargo at 7:00 AM. It was tight but not impossible.

Tim, Jan, Peter and I all agreed to head back to the hotel to get a bite to eat and five hours of sleep before returning to the zoo in the early morning. Perfect.

At midnight fifteen, the phone rang on my bedside table. It was Tim. The plan had changed. The cargo agent had decided that the animals needed to be at the terminal two hours earlier. That meant that the darting of the animals now had to start at 2:00 AM, to allow for other imponderables. We had to be downstairs and ready to move in thirty minutes.

Arriving back at the deserted zoo for 1.30 in the morning was rather unnerving. As we walked along the empty paths towards the lion enclosure, birds began squawking. This set off consternation among the zoo's residents. Llamas spat, tigers roared, and the moon bears loomed up on the rocks in their enclosure. Just as we walked into the entrance of the lions' den, the hippo emerged from the his watery home, his red eyes glowing in the darkness.

Arc lights had been set up around the enclosure, making it look like a film set. The four of us walked into the lion house, which consisted of a corridor with four separate pens, one with the two brothers, another with a male and a female, a third with a female on her own and the fourth with big boy Muheeb, who had a full main and stuck his tongue out all the time, which could look cute but was caused by a brain injury.

The zoo staff were standing around in a group, with drivers, vets and staff to lift and carry the animals to the waiting cages and onto the lorry that would transport them to the cargo terminal. Nobody spoke to Peter but the vets looked at him with suspicion.

The first animal was darted, walked around in circles for a few minutes and then lay down and fell asleep. The team of lifters poked him to make sure he was out cold before grabbing him by his legs and

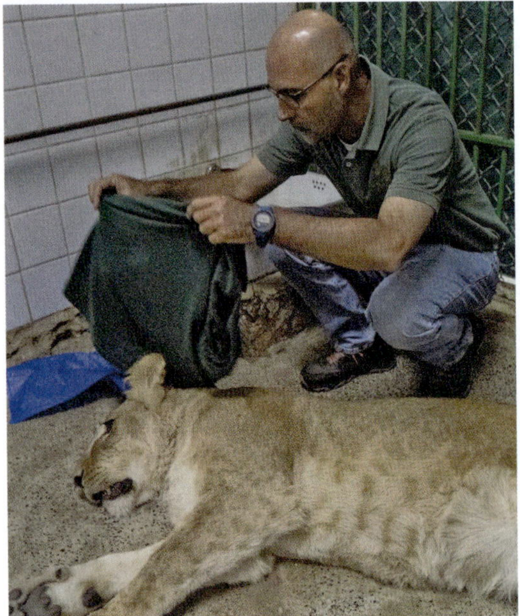

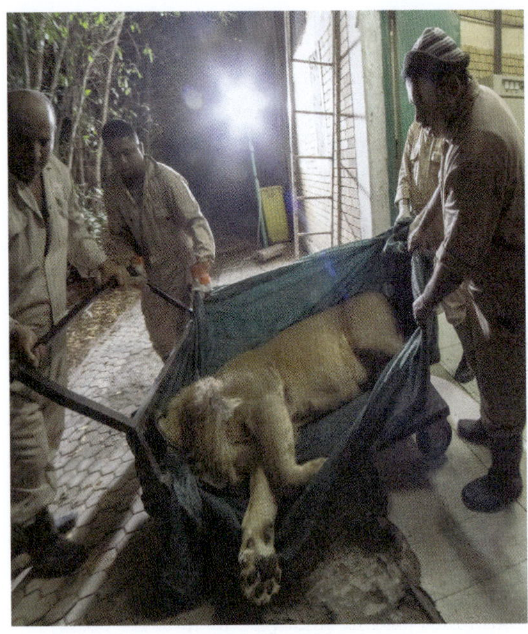

pulling him towards a tarpaulin. This was too much for Peter and he leapt into the enclosure, ordering the men to stop.

'You don't pull an animal across the ground,' he told them. 'You roll it onto a sheet, as you would a person.' He knelt down beside the beast, checking him over.

'Where is the hood to cover his eyes?'

'Hood? Hood? Why hood?'

'So he doesn't panic if he wakes up. Give me a t-shirt quickly.'

One of the men handed over his own sweaty shirt and Peter wrapped it around the face of the lion, blocking out the light. Problem Number One dealt with.

Problem Number Two followed when, after carrying the sleeping lion from the lion house to the create, the men loaded him in head first.

'You never put an animal in head first,' Peter had

to explain again. 'The head has to face the door. Get him out and turn him round, so if there's a problem we can deal with it.'

Seeing that Peter knew his stuff, the vets started acknowledging him for the first time and asked his advice on what dosage to give the other animals. The second lion, a very nervous female, had been given too much ketamine and was twitching and trying to get up.

The vet entered the lion's enclosure and very calmly put his hands on her head. She flinched and tried raising her paw to attack him but didn't have enough coordination. Peter had judged it right.

After administering a second dose of anaesthetic, the loading of the animals went smoothly and soon they were all on their way to the airport and freedom.

Qatar Airways had made space available on a cargo flight to Johannesburg, along with four seats

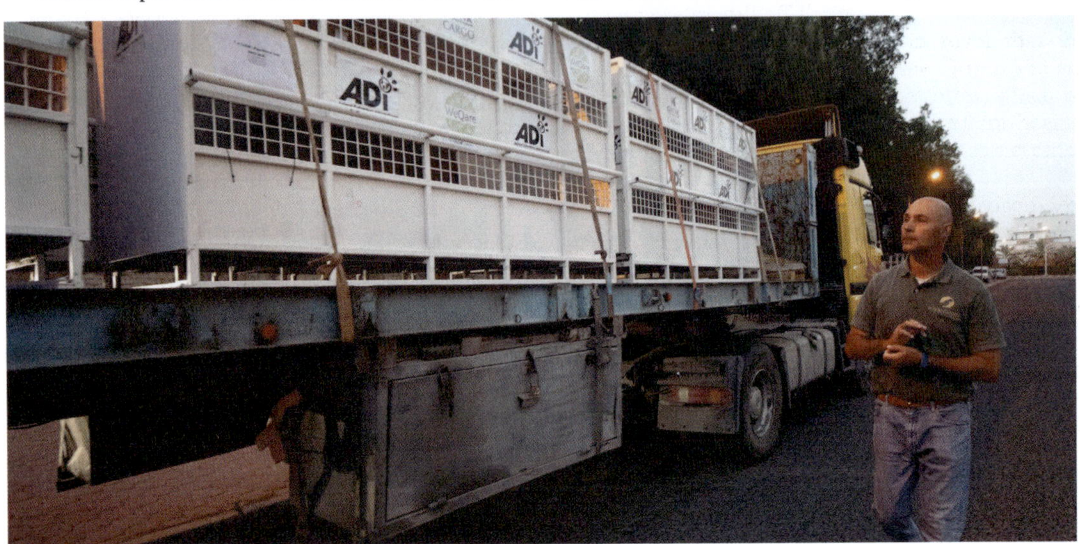

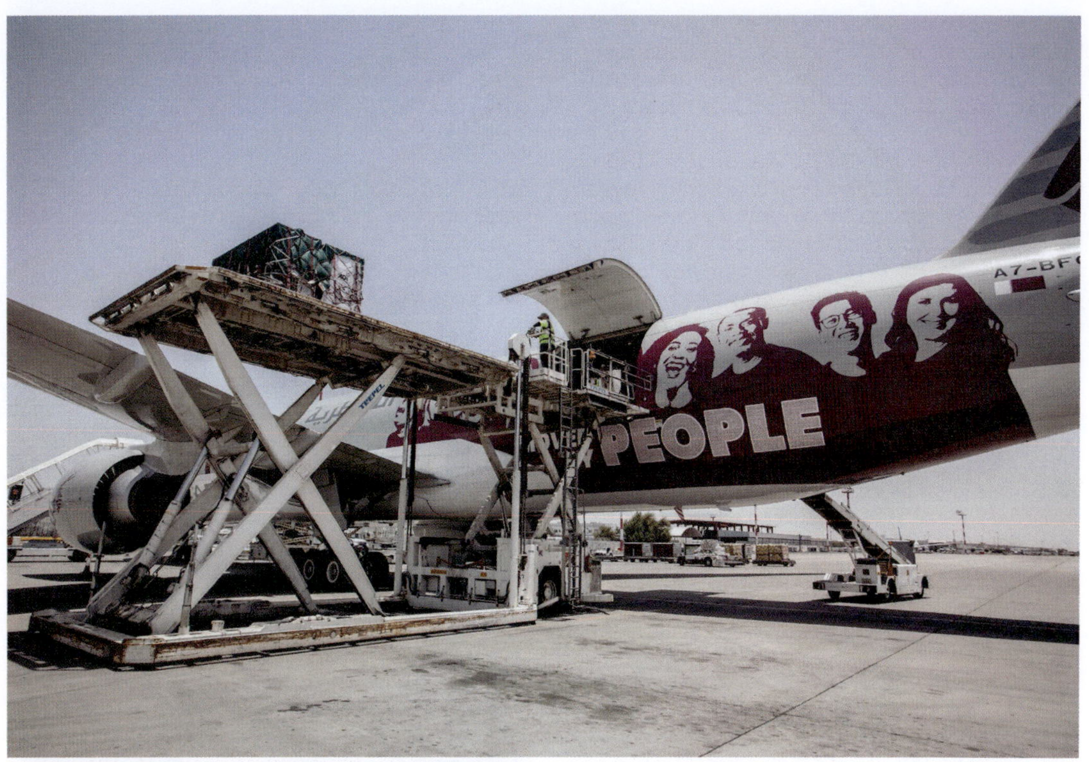

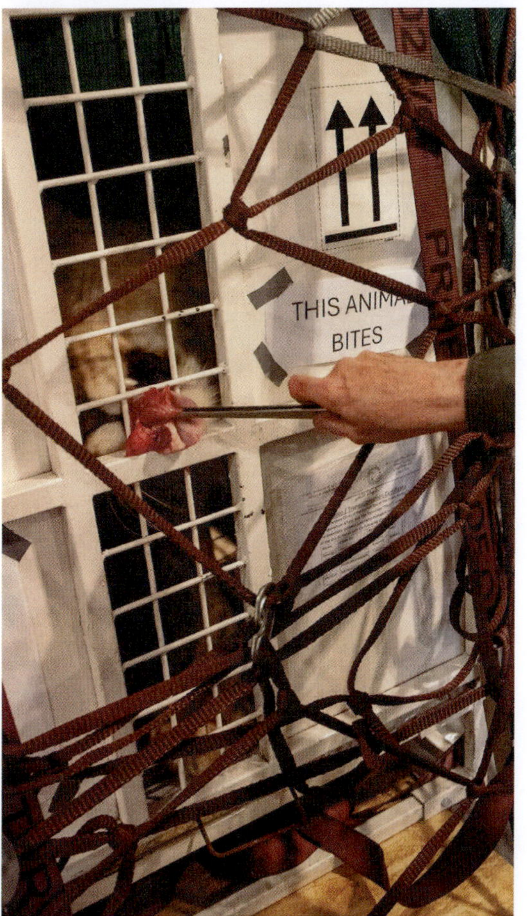

in a small cabin behind the cockpit. Our only other stopover was in Doha to pick up more freight.

An hour into the nine-hour flight, Tim and Jan went back through the small door into the hold, now loaded with 106 tons of shipments. Among them were barbecue tongs and watering cans, which we had bought before leaving Kuwait, along with some buffalo meat. Jan used the tongs to feed chunks of the meat to the lions, and used the watering can to fill their drinking bowls. So we all had in-flight service.

Arriving at 1:00 in the morning, Johannesburg time, meant the government vet was not yet on hand to give the all-clear to the new arrivals, so we all settled down and waited. When she finally turned up, she found a discrepancy in the paperwork.

Jan tried to persuade her that the discrepancy was an unintended error in the translation but the sanctimonious official wasn't having it. The error went up the food chain within the veterinary department, and a message came back saying that the animals had failed the import criteria. We could either return the animals to Kuwait or they would be put down.

The news was absolutely devastating and it hit us in the pits of our stomachs. We were in despair. It had been eight hours since we landed, and the poor lions were still confined to their crates on the tarmac. The sun was climbing higher and the heat was intensifying. Something had to be done.

Lawyers from Johannesburg had arrived to wade through the paperwork, and Jan had commandeered a desk in the dispatch office and was

189

refusing to move until the situation was resolved. Meanwhile Tim got to work with the airside officials, insisting that the lions, which had started to become agitated, be moved out of the sun and into the shade, and that they be fed. Jan and the lawyers did battle inside the cargo office, but it took another hour before the animals were moved.

In defiance of the officials and their red tape, Tim also took to Facebook to highlight the lions' plight. As airline staff began arriving at the various cargo offices above the dispatch area, word quickly spread online.

While Tim's followers flooded social media with their outraged reactions, Jan was busy trying to track down the government vet at the centre of the problem—but she had conveniently vanished. Formal complaints were lodged with the head of the veterinary department. The hours dragged on. By now, the lions had been trapped in their crates for nearly thirty hours.

Women from the Air Canada offices arrived at our makeshift camp in the car park, bringing tea and coffee. Then the head of Qatar Cargo stepped out of a meeting to invite us up to his air-conditioned office, which was a relief. He expressed his dismay at the way we had been treated and took immediate action, helping Tim gain access to the airside area so the lions could finally be given some food.

It wasn't until 2:00 in the afternoon that the chief vet got to read the paperwork and agreed that the mistake in the paperwork was an innocent mistake and that the lions were free to continue on their journey—once they had been given another dose of anti-parasite treatment. That should not have been necessary because the correct injections had been administered in Kuwait but the chief vet insisted on their being done again, and on calling Peter back to the airport to do the dosing. They weren't making it easy.

At long last the flatbed and support vehicles pulled away from the airport to start the four-hour drive to the lions' new homes.

It was midnight before the small convoy drove onto the ADI sanctuary near the town of Winburg in Free State, wood smoke from the nearby township hanging in the cold night air.

The lions were restless, letting out low growls and the occasional muffled roar. They could tell that other lions were in the area: even after having spent all their lives in captivity, they could still sense the unseen presence of their own kind.

All six lions were carefully unloaded into their sleeping quarters, each of which was set within its own grassy enclosure. After a lot of half-hearted growling and snarling, the weary cats collapsed onto their straw bedding and drifted into a deep, much-needed sleep.

The next morning, a cold wind swept across the sanctuary. As the sun rose into a clear blue sky, the lions caught their first-ever glimpse of grass. The two brother lions were eager to leave the night shelter and explore their new surroundings. Muheeb was no different. The big, powerful older male paced in front of the gate, ready to be let out, and was rewarded with being the first to be offered freedom.

But as the men hauled on the lever that raised the gate, Muheeb faltered. He stood wide-eyed, trying to take in this unfamiliar world. With one paw on the grass and the other three firmly planted inside the safety of the sleeping quarters, he lifted his massive head and sniffed the air, trying to absorb the strange new scents of a different world.

A full ten minutes passed before he felt secure enough to step completely into the bright morning light. After forty-five hours confined in a crate over the previous two days, he stretched his powerful body to its full length and gave his magnificent mane a vigorous shake.

One of the keepers tossed a huge orange ball into Muheeb's enclosure. The moment he saw it roll across the grass, something instinctual kicked in and he snapped into hunter mode. He lunged at the ball, swatting it left and right with his massive paws, nudging it along with his nose as he chased it down. Within minutes, he had come into his own: no longer a captive cat, but a true lion of the wild.

Next up were the two brothers, Shujaa and Saham, whose new enclosure was set slightly apart from the others. As we approached their shelter, we could see them pacing eagerly, anxious to be released. The keeper raised the gate and I stood ready, camera in hand, to capture their first run to freedom. But like Muheeb, caution held them back. They sniffed the air, ears twitching at the distant roars and movements of other animals nearby.

Eventually, Saham stepped out, his eyes scanning left and right, alert to any danger but clearly awestruck by the wide open space stretching beyond his patch of grass. Before him lay new possibilities: a climbing frame, a water pool and the reassuring shelter of the warm sleeping house behind him.

Saham completed a slow patrol of the enclosure, pausing to investigate every new scent along the way. Then the younger Shujaa stepped out. He, too, explored the space with quiet curiosity before the two of them settled side by side in the doorway of the shelter. It was a perfect picture of contentment—the contrast in their coats and manes, the newfound sparkle in their eyes. Just one night of proper rest and a sense of safety had already begun to transform them.

By the end of the day, all the rescued lions had been settled into their first enclosures. The vast expanses that would eventually become their permanent homes were still weeks away, but each day would bring them closer to that freedom, one discovery at a time. Their former lives, confined and dusty, was hardly even a memory. Now, under the South African sun, they were where they always should have been—roaming the open spaces, free at last.

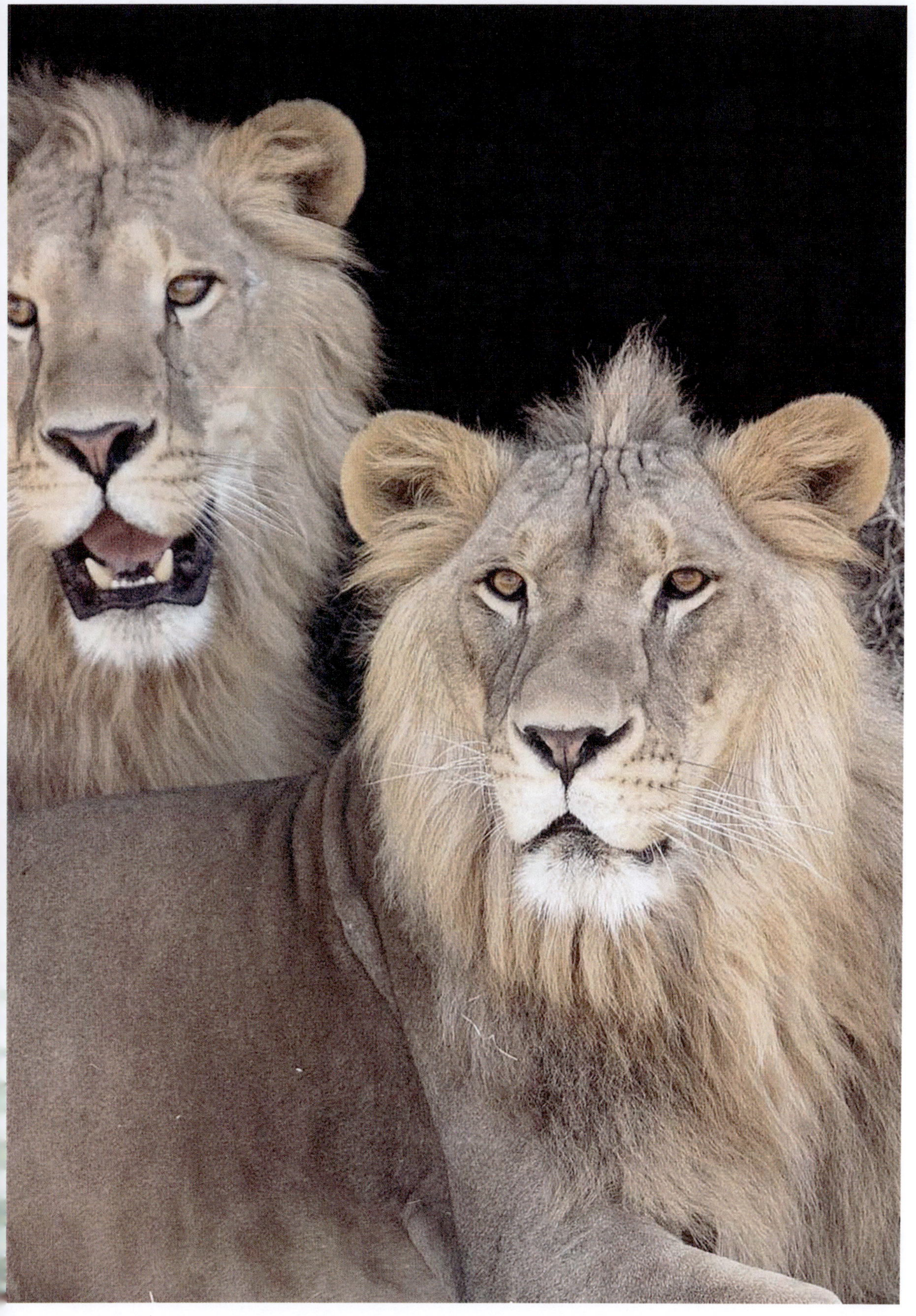

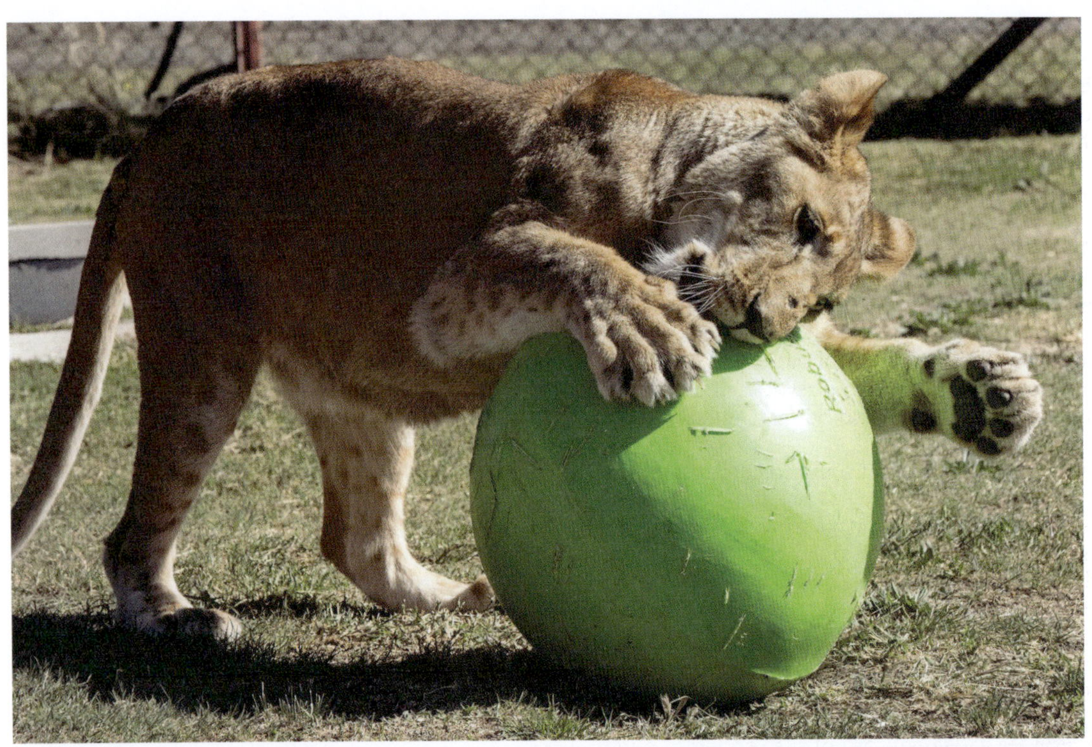
KUNDUCHI
Pet Products
THE SIGN OF CATNIP QUALITY
CATS ALREADY KNOW
THE DIFFERENCE

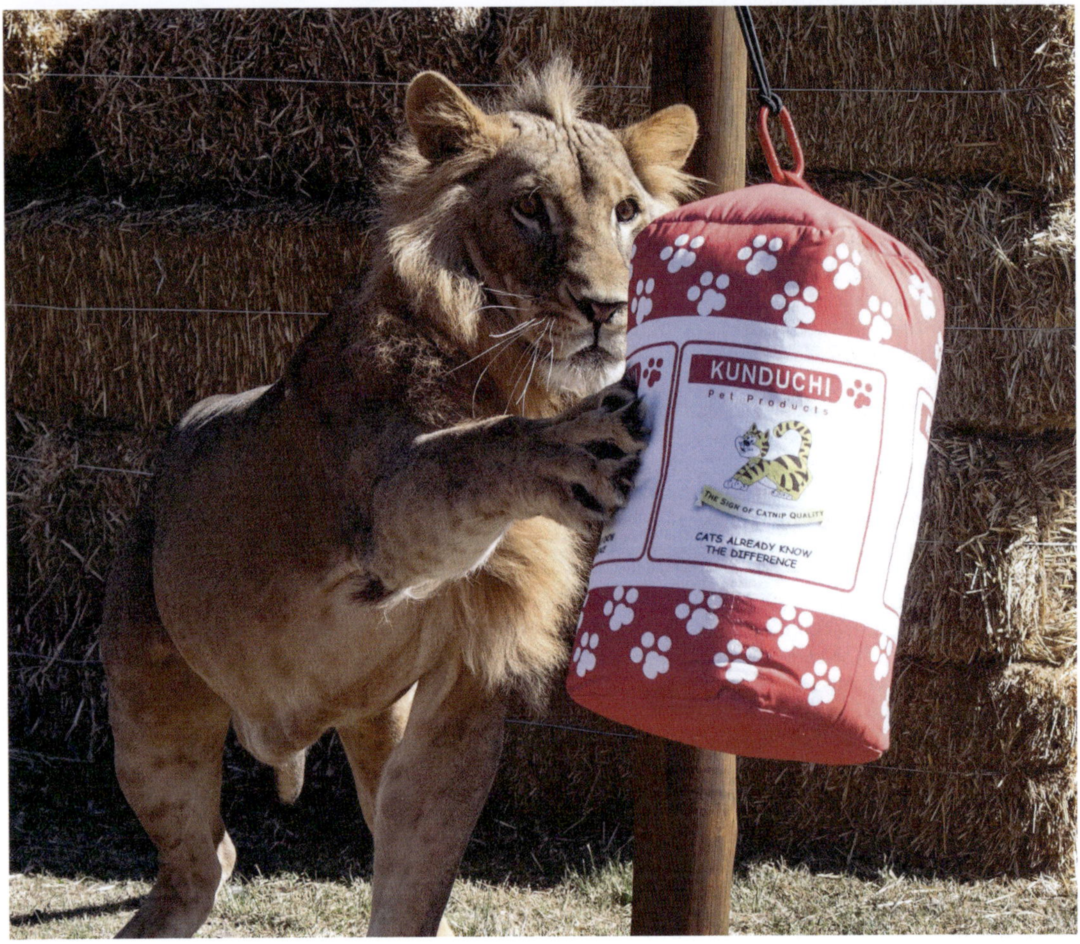

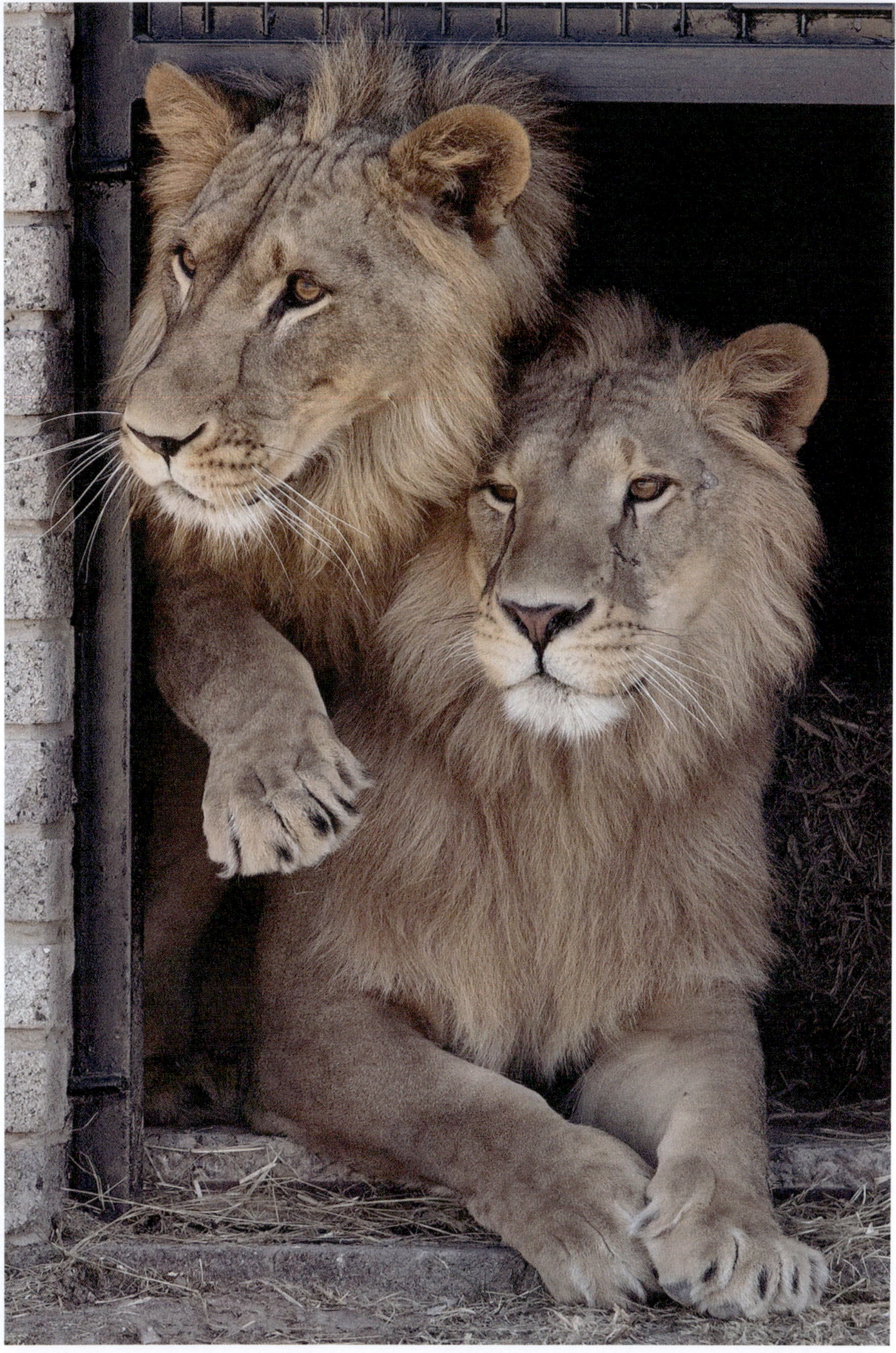

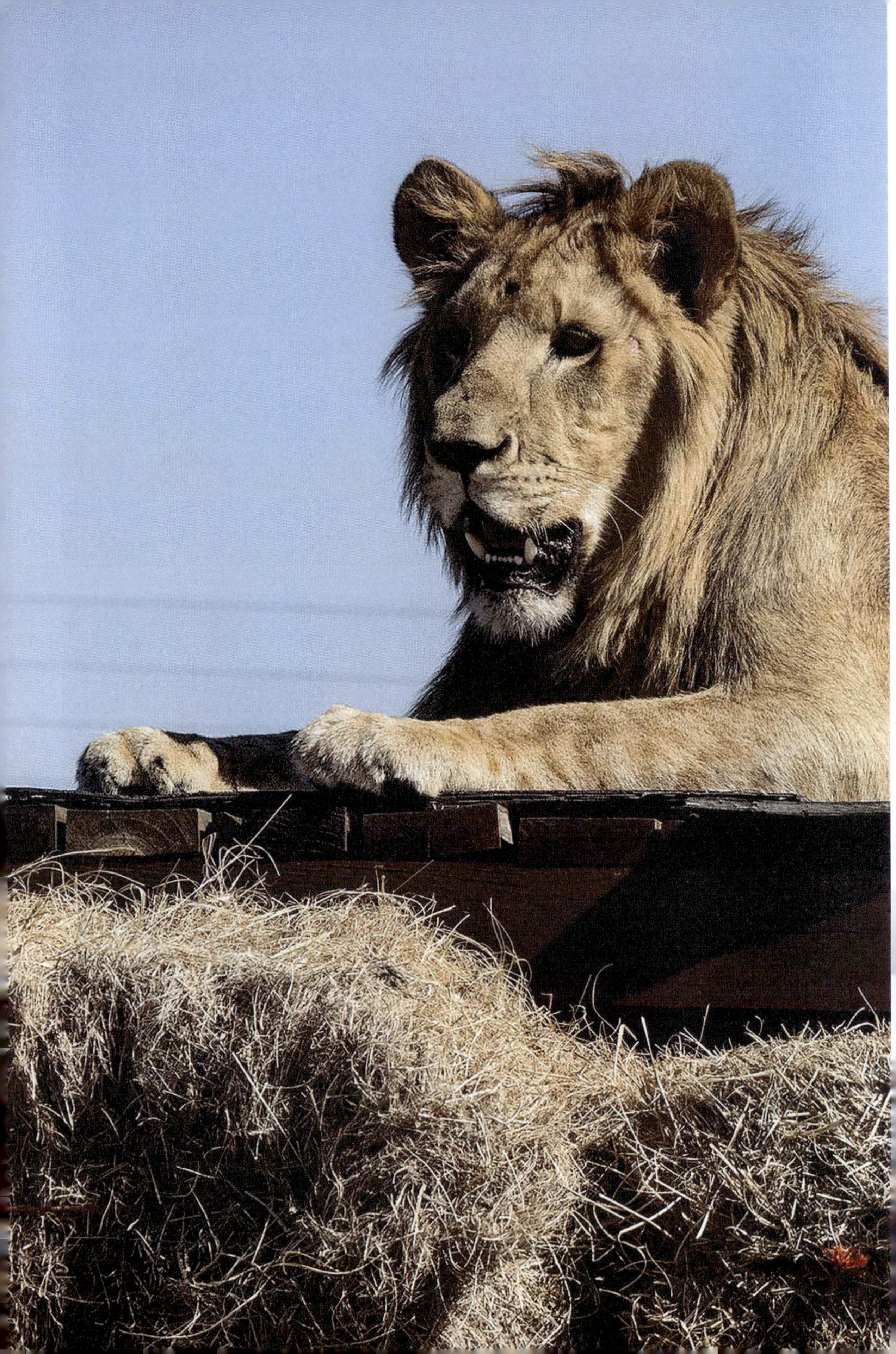

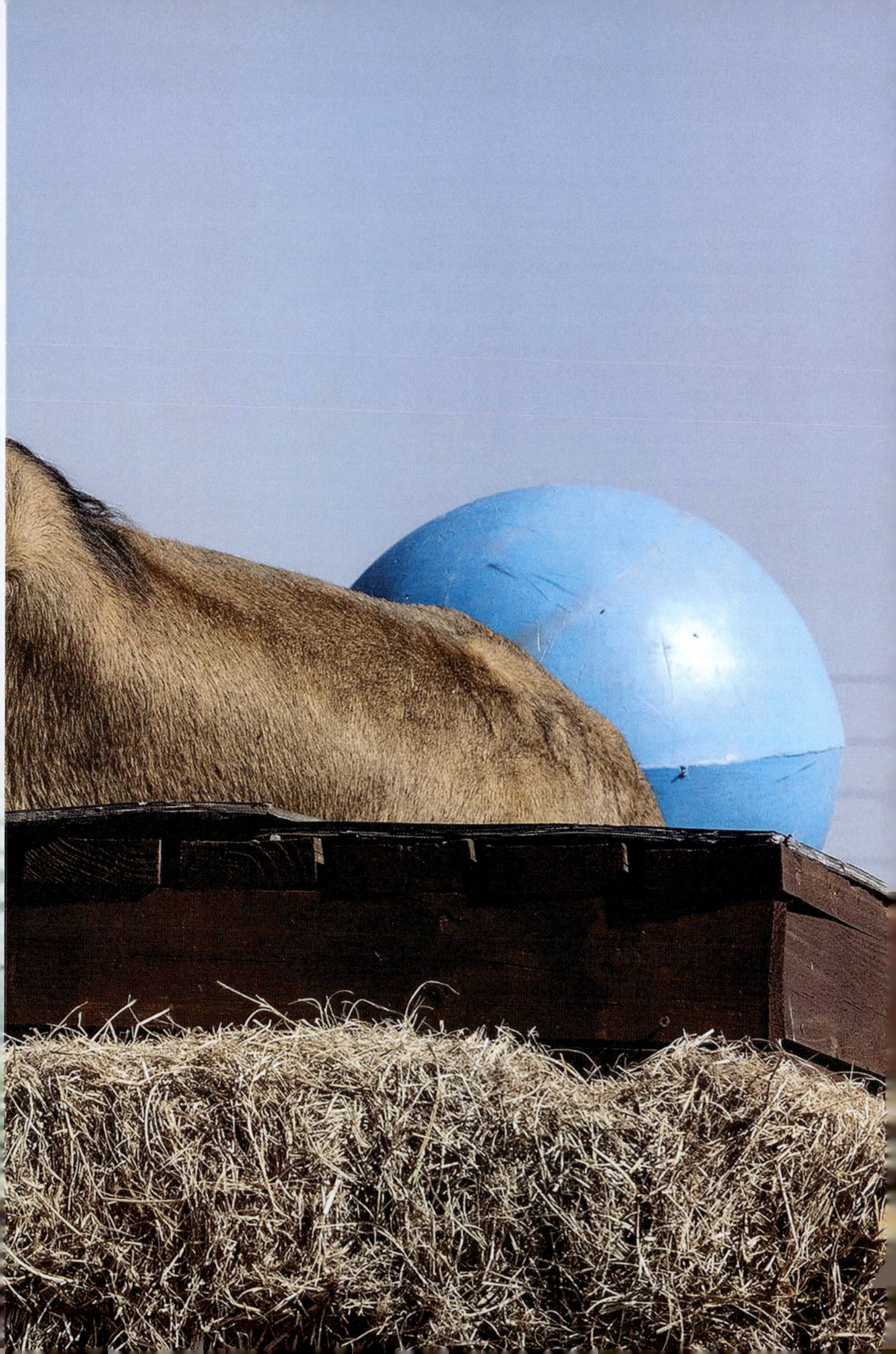

Published by

EnvelopeBooks

www.envelopebooks.co.uk

Printed in Great Britain
by Amazon

b363bd93-07bf-40e3-bf8a-1192620ca86bR01